DIDCOT LIBRARY
THE BROADWAY
DIDC

G
R
p
o ... States h.

T...*e Romans for Dummies*, and is a Fel... of the Society of Antiqu....
London.

Further praise for *Praetorian*:

'De la Bédoyère, a British historian and broadcaster, has quite properly set
this very detailed account, backed with excellent appendices and extensive
notes, in the full context of contemporary history … Any future researcher
into the subject will certainly begin here.' Peter Jones, *The Times*

'A definitive and highly readable account of a key institution of the Roman
Empire.' Tom Holland, author of *Rubicon: The Last Years of the Roman
Republic*

'An unusual and useful account of [the praetorians'] roles.' Peter Stothard,
Times Literary Supplement

'Lively and full of insight, de la Bédoyère traces the history of the praetorians and the emperors they served, murdered and made, through three
hundred years of intrigue and drama.' Adrian Goldsworthy, author of *Caesar*

'Conveying complexity, without subjecting the reader to the dozens of
triple-barrelled Roman names that make up the finer grain of imperial
politics, has long been de la Bédoyère's metier, as has been the easy charm
with which good popular history distinguishes itself.' Michael
Kulikowski, *London Review of Books*

'Filled with eng٤   storical
record with adm   tudent
of the tribulatio   *Review*

3303397143

PRAETORIAN

THE RISE AND FALL OF
ROME'S IMPERIAL BODYGUARD

GUY DE LA BÉDOYÈRE

YALE UNIVERSITY PRESS
NEW HAVEN AND LONDON

OXFORDSHIRE
LIBRARY SERVICE

3303397143	
Askews & Holts	23-Apr-2018
355.0093709015	£10.99

Copyright © 2017 Guy de la Bédoyère

First printed in paperback in 2018

All rights reserved. This book may not be reproduced in whole or in part, in any form (beyond that copying permitted by Sections 107 and 108 of the U.S. Copyright Law and except by reviewers for the public press) without written permission from the publishers.

For information about this and other Yale University Press publications, please contact:

U.S. Office: sales.press@yale.edu   yalebooks.com
Europe Office: sales@yaleup.co.uk   yalebooks.co.uk

Typeset in Adobe Garamond Pro by IDSUK (DataConnection) Ltd
Printed in Great Britain by Hobbs the Printers Ltd, Totton, Hampshire

Library of Congress Control Number: 2016958591

ISBN 978-0-300-21895-4 (cloth)
ISBN 978-0-300-23438-1 (pbk)

A catalogue record for this book is available from the British Library.

10 9 8 7 6 5 4 3 2 1

Gaius Plinius Secundus (AD 23–79), known to us as Pliny the Elder, author of the Natural History, *has been a personal inspiration for years. His belief that to be alive is to be awake, and that everything is of interest and everything worth exploring, combined with a relentless and unassailable curiosity, made his life the model for open-mindedness and enquiry without any sense of boundaries. Today's world of education could learn a great deal from him.*

I would also like to dedicate this book to my first grandchild, Eleanor ('Nell') Rose de la Bédoyère, born at exactly the time it was finished in the early summer of 2016, and to my mother, Irene de la Bédoyère, whose love of history was always an inspiration and who died in July 2016 at the time this book was delivered to the publisher.

CONTENTS

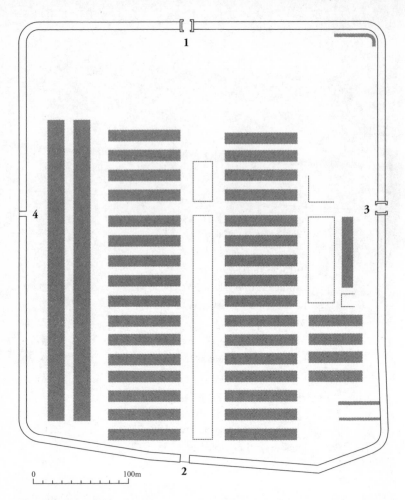

Plan of the Castra Praetoria

The area of the praetorian camp was 41.2 acres (16.72 hectares). The west and south walls were demolished by Constantine along with the west and south gates. Their exact positions are now only hypothetical. The main road through the camp, the Via Principalis, ran between the north and south gates. The kink in the south wall is explained by the need to conform to existing road alignments. Only fragmentary traces of barracks have been identified, so the blocks shown here are largely hypothetical, too. Even this incomplete plan shows the marked difference from a conventional fort because of the apparent lack of major buildings such a headquarters premises (*principia*) and commandant's house (*praetorium*). Blank areas are only zones where nothing has yet been found due to lack of exploration; they are not indicative of open areas in antiquity.

1. Porta Principalis Dextra (north)
2. Porta Principalis Sinistra (south)
3. Porta Decumana (east)
4. Porta Praetoria (west)

INTRODUCTION

O N 28 MARCH AD 193 the emperor Pertinax was murdered after a reign of just eighty-seven days. His efforts to rule Rome with integrity and order had been generally welcomed. The Praetorian Guard, Rome's spoilt, privileged and elite imperial bodyguard, was the most conspicuous exception. Pertinax had tried to instil meaningful discipline amongst the swaggering praetorians, who had become accustomed during the reign of Commodus to behaving as badly as they pleased, including hitting passers-by. To soften the impact of the new rules, Pertinax had promised the Guard 12,000 sestertii each, claiming he was matching what Marcus Aurelius and Lucius Verus had paid them on their accession in 160. Pertinax even sold off Commodus' property to raise the cash, since the treasury had been reduced to its last million sestertii by his profligate expenditure and wild living. The praetorians, however, took exception to the idea they might return the favour by improving their behaviour. After all, they were aware that Marcus Aurelius and Lucius Verus had actually paid 20,000 sestertii to their predecessors and that Pertinax had possibly only ever paid half of what he had offered. The praetorians killed Pertinax but, terrified of the consequences of what they had done, they dashed back to their camp, the Castra Praetoria, and locked the gates (Plate 1).[1]

Strangely, everything quietened down and the praetorians realized no one had come after them. Fully aware now that they were the ones who

1

were really in charge, they posted a notice at the Castra Praetoria offering the Roman Empire for sale.[2] Most of the senators were suitably disgusted, though the story as written by Dio may owe at least part of its inspiration to the events of the civil war year of 69 and the short rule of Otho.[3] But one of them, a greedy and ambitious senator called Marcus Didius Julianus, drunk and egged on by his equally greedy and ambitious wife and daughter, Manlia Scantilla and Didia Clara, and two praetorian tribunes called Publius Florianus and Vectius Aper, raced round to the praetorian camp having spotted an opportunity. So did Titus Flavius Sulpicianus, who was the prefect of Rome as well as being Pertinax's father-in-law. When Didius Julianus arrived he found that Sulpicianus was already there, busily securing his position and ensuring that Julianus was locked out.[4] Only with the use of placards advertising his promises, and the transfer of a Sulpician supporter called Maurentius, was Julianus able to attract the praetorians' attention.

What followed was rightly called a 'disgraceful business' by Dio, though the sheer theatricality of the description needs to be read with some caution. The praetorians capitalized on the fact that no one could hope to be emperor without their backing. Didius Julianus and Flavius Sulpicianus, each desperate for supreme power, started making rival cash offers to the Guard. The soldiers enthusiastically threw themselves into the auction, running across the camp between the candidates to tell each how much he would have to raise his bid by. Sulpicianus was about to win with an offer of 20,000 sestertii per praetorian when Julianus seized the day with a reckless counter bid of 25,000. Julianus added for good measure the warning that Sulpicianus might seek revenge for the death of Pertinax and also that he, Julianus, would restore all the freedoms the praetorians had enjoyed under Commodus. So delighted were the praetorians by the new offer they promptly declared Julianus to be the new emperor.

This event was so extraordinary, tawdry and demeaning that even now it seems barely credible that the Roman Empire could have stooped so low. Herodian described it as a decisive turning point, the moment when soldiers lost any respect for the emperors and which contributed to so much of the disorder that was to follow in the years to come.[5] The

Praetorian Guard had brazenly created an emperor purely on the promise of a huge cash handout, consummately and nakedly abusing their position and power. Julianus lasted even less time than Pertinax, having injudiciously offered far more money than he could afford. He was executed on the orders of the senate just sixty-six days after he was made emperor. By then Julianus already faced a rebellion in the east in the form of the Roman army in Illyricum under Septimius Severus, and failed to make any use of his praetorians; the civil war that convulsed the Roman Empire from 193 to 197 would be decided by Roman provincial forces, not the praetorians.[6] Severus cashiered the Guard and recreated it with trusted legionaries from his own forces. Even that did not solve the problem. In the decades to come the Guard and its prefects played a decisive role in toppling and making one emperor after another.

How could it have come to this? The praetorians were the most privileged of all Roman soldiers. They were paid the most, served the least time, and enjoyed the best conditions.[7] Their status exceeded that of all the other armed forces; but, in the two centuries or more since their formal foundation as a permanent institution by Augustus, circumstances had conspired to make them the supreme authority. In 193 it was a power they misused in so reprehensible a way it is hard to imagine how they could ever have recovered any of the prestige they had once enjoyed.

Edward Gibbon's description of the Guard's relationship with the emperor is unmatched for the clarity with which he identified the paradox inherent in the system:

Such formidable servants are always necessary, but often fatal to the throne of despotism. By thus introducing the Praetorian guards, as it were, into the palace and the senate, the emperors taught them to perceive their own strength, and the weakness of the civil government; to view the vices of their masters with familiar contempt, and to lay aside that reverential awe, which distance only, and mystery, can preserve towards an imaginary power. In the luxurious idleness of an opulent city, their pride was nourished by the sense of their irresistible weight; nor was it possible to conceal from them, that the person of the sovereign, the authority of the senate, the public treasure, and the seat of Empire, were all in their hands. To divert the Praetorian bands from these dangerous reflections, the firmest and best established princes were obliged to mix blandishments with commands, rewards with punishments, to flatter their pride, indulge their pleasures, connive at their irregularities, and to purchase their precarious faith by a liberal donative; which, since the elevation of Claudius, was exacted as a legal claim, on the accession of every new emperor.[8]

The Guard's ambitions, and those of its prefects, expanded to fill the voids left by inadequate or vulnerable rulers. Thus, Tiberius' self-imposed exile to Capri made it possible for the praetorian prefect Sejanus to try and become emperor himself. The disastrous reign of Caligula in 37–41 led to his assassination and to the Guard appointing its own emperor in the form of Claudius. The loss of the Guard's support played a key part in Nero giving up and committing suicide in 68. During the civil war of 68–9 the Guard played crucial roles in the fight between the rivals for the Empire. In the second century AD the succession of strong and effective rulers meant that from 98 until 180 the Guard rarely appears in ancient sources. The dereliction of the reign of Commodus (180–92) brought the Guard back to the fore once more and it was the behaviour of the praetorians that led to the murder of Pertinax and the brief and tawdry reign of Didius Julianus. In volatile and unsettled times the Guard acted as catalysts and opportunists, and their prefects as major players, for good or ill.

The events of 193 were therefore more or less inevitable, and the seeds had been sown the moment Augustus created the Guard more than two centuries earlier. The precarious balance was bound to be upset sooner or later, though as an institution the Guard survived this venal episode. Finally, in 312 Constantine I disbanded the Guard altogether after its ill-judged support for his rival Maxentius. The praetorians were individually dispersed to the frontier garrisons of the Empire.[9] It was an ignominious end for an institution that had enjoyed a formal and permanent existence for 340 years and an ad hoc role before that as the personal bodyguard of Roman generals in the Republic.

This book does not focus on the details of the praetorians' armour and equipment, a subject amply and excellently covered by Rankov (1994) and Cowan (2014).[10] Instead, this book is a history of the Praetorian Guard from its beginnings right through to its final disbandment. The focus is on the Guard and its role, its formation, structure, conditions, deployment, leadership and its experiences within the narrative context of Roman imperial history. The evidence is complex and incomplete because the Praetorian Guard makes only erratic appearances in ancient sources. There is a great deal that is unknown, and which will probably remain so.

The term 'Praetorian Guard' is a modern one. The Romans knew the imperial bodyguard collectively as the *cohortes praetoriae*, 'the praetorian cohorts', and their fort as the *Castra Praetoria*, or *Praetoriana*, 'the praetorian barracks', or the *Castra Praetorianorum*, 'barracks of the praetorians', rather than conferring on either the Guard or its headquarters a singular title.[11] This makes no difference to the fact that the Guard's evolution into the highest-paid, most esteemed and most influential part of the Roman military machine has always made it a source of some fascination. Praetorians regarded themselves as a cut above the rest of the Roman military machine, as indeed they were. A praetorian centurion called Manlius Valerianus had his views memorialized on his tombstone at Aquileia. He had, he said, 'commanded a century in a praetorian cohort, not a barbarian legion'.[12]

The organization of the Guard, like so much else in the Roman Empire, was a good deal less precise and regimented than is often assumed today. Precedent, circumstances and expediency all played a part in the Guard's history, with the result that there are numerous inconsistencies, such as the number and size of the cohorts, the pay, and even the duties praetorians performed, both individually and collectively. Nevertheless, the Guard emerges as an organization that played a vitally significant and continuous part in Roman history, and which helped define the image of the Roman state both then and now.

Recruitment into the Praetorian Guard at the start of a military career, or as a later promotion for a legionary, meant belonging to the most prestigious part of the most powerful organization in antiquity. It continued to give the men involved considerable standing in the communities where they lived in retirement as civilians. Then, as now, Roman soldiers typified a popular image of Roman power and society. The Roman state evolved with a tradition of compulsory military service for its citizens and with an ideology founded on a destiny of divinely backed victory and conquest. In Virgil's epic poem the *Aeneid*, Jupiter set out the future for the Roman people. Aeneas, the mythical progenitor of the Julian line and ancestor of Augustus, would crush Italy's fierce tribes and his descendant Romulus would found Rome, a city whose people would have no limits of time or space, and an empire that would never end.[13] Rome's wars did indeed expand Roman power, absorbing other states and communities, which would earn affiliated status instead of annihilation if their own soldiers were contributed to service on behalf of Rome. The men of the Roman senatorial elite customarily served as military officers as part of their career path, known as the *cursus honorum*. A huge proportion of male Roman citizens, of whatever class, had some military experience. They had either served as soldiers or as officers and many would have participated in military campaigns. From all this they acquired enormously important skills, not just in fighting but also in practical techniques such as building and administration.

The Roman army, made up of the Praetorian Guard, legions, auxiliary forces and navy, did not exist as a permanent organization under a centralized command. During the Republic, legions were raised from the citizenry when required and placed under the command of a senator of consular rank who was temporarily awarded the power of *imperium* (military command), which he could only hold outside Italy, unless exceptional circumstances necessitated otherwise. This legalized but limited his control of a military force. It also facilitated the development of loyalty to the person of that general (*imperator*); in the first century BC this became a particularly dangerous facet of the Roman world. During this age of the *imperatores*, some of these generals saw an opportunity to use their armies for personal glory and advancement. The origins of the Praetorian Guard lay in the bodyguard units men such as Antony and Octavian created to amplify their status.

Part of displaying military prestige for an *imperator* involved having a body of selected soldiers to act as his personal bodyguard. These soldiers, the 'praetorians', were named after the term for a general's tent or residence on campaign, the *praetorium*. The word was derived from the word *praetor*, which meant literally 'the man who goes before others'. In a general sense the word meant 'leader' or 'chief' and was applied to a specific level of senatorial magistracy, the praetorship, with certain duties.[14] A *propraetor* was a man who had served as a *praetor* and could be sent to govern a province. *Praetorium* could then be literally translated as 'the place of the man who goes before others'. His bodyguard soldiers were organized into cohorts (*cohortes*), a standard Roman military term for a body of around 480 men and normally applied to subdivisions of legions. The word also means 'courtyard' or 'enclosure', and the military application therefore derives from this by meaning literally 'a courtyard's-worth of men'.

The Praetorian Guard also served as a vital bulwark for the emperor against the power and influence of the senate. The Guard's mere existence was a constant reminder to the senate of the emperor's ability to use force to assert his position. As Gibbon so memorably observed, the praetorians represented 'the emperor's power and status and gave him the ability to coerce the Roman aristocracy'.[15] It was a precarious balance. The emperor was dependent on a force that he needed to have absolute authority over. The proximity of the Praetorian Guard to the emperor, both in a metaphorical and physical sense, meant that the emperor's prestige and influence had always to be greater than that of the praetorians if he was to maintain control.

It was the idea of men who would protect their general in a military context that Octavian as Augustus would later turn into a permanent institution as part of the greater Roman army (also made permanent under his rule). It was also the component of the army that enjoyed special status by virtue of being closest to him as emperor. By being continuously stationed in Rome from the reign of Tiberius on, the Praetorian Guard became the most visible embodiment both of the emperor's power and of the change in government since the Republic. It is hardly surprising then that the overwhelming popular impression of the Roman Empire is of a highly militarized society. The ubiquitous nature of the Roman army and its dominance of so much of the record have reinforced this.

As a new institution the Praetorian Guard and its command had to be incorporated into the Roman hierarchy and positioned in a way that maximized prestige while minimizing the risk to the emperor. The wealthiest and most powerful members of Roman society were the senatorial families. Their male members served in a number of prestigious magistracies, proceeding along a fairly standardized career path that climaxed with service as one of the praetors, and then as one of the two consuls serving at any one time. Senators who had served as praetors were eligible to be appointed to command legions or govern provinces. Giving command of the Guard to a senator would have been far too risky. The position of 'emperor' as we understand it did not officially exist. Augustus held certain Republican senatorial offices but his real power was vested in his special personal authority and prestige. This involved considerable guile and tact because of the technical equality between him and other senators, any one of whom might challenge his power. A senator with command of the Praetorian Guard might have that potential.

Augustus therefore used for command of the Guard men of equestrian rank, a more numerous body of second-grade aristocrats whose property qualification for eligibility was much lower.[16] These men could serve as procurators, the financial administrators of provinces, as well as in a host of other positions. These ranged from minor procuratorial posts or the prefecture of an auxiliary military unit such as a cavalry wing right up, under the Empire, to commanding the Praetorian Guard, governing Egypt, controlling the grain supply or serving as prefect of Rome. All these latter prefectures were of such importance that an emperor could not afford to give them to senators who might then emerge as his rivals. Equestrians were a far less risky prospect because they lacked the rank equivalence a senator enjoyed with the emperor. The whole system relied on a complex web of patronage, loyalties, interest groups and factions trickling down from the emperor from the time of Augustus on.

The Roman world by the time of Augustus was not only enormous by the standards of the ancient world, but also by our own. It already stretched from Gaul (modern France) to Syria and Egypt in the east and included much of western, central and southern Europe as well as North Africa and Turkey. New conquests ensured its expansion until the reign of Trajan (98–117). The Roman army was widely distributed throughout these territories, with the largest garrisons in key and frontier provinces such as Syria and along the Rhine. Larger and more complex than any other western ancient civilization, the Roman world challenged the logistical and administrative powers of what was still a relatively primitive era. In this context all Roman soldiers, not just the praetorians, were the everyday manifestation of the state. Soldiers took on all sorts of minor administrative and supervisory duties. These ranged from acting as police (an especially vital role that involved centurions bringing 'the power of the central administration to the level of the villages'), overseeing amongst many other duties construction projects, raising taxes, to operating the mint and supervising the movement of grain.[17] Roman soldiers, including veterans, were thus the principal means through which the state acted and enforced its measures.

Not surprisingly, Roman soldiers, especially the Praetorian Guard, were sometimes depicted in the popular culture of the time as privileged bullies who enjoyed a favoured status above the law. Juvenal's incomplete Sixteenth Satire itemizes the various advantages the military benefited from, such as the freedom to thrash a civilian without fear of redress and the knowledge that a soldier pursuing a court case could be sure to have it heard immediately, unlike everyone else.[18] Juvenal was probably writing about the way praetorians, the most privileged of all Roman soldiers, behaved. The state that depended so much on military cooperation and support could not afford to have a disaffected army.

Today the Rome Metro's Linea B includes a stop called Castro Pretorio. Visitors emerge from there on to the extremely busy Viale Castro Pretorio. A short walk leads to the well-preserved original north and east walls of the Castra Praetoria, the Guard's fort and headquarters. Created by the praetorian prefect Lucius Aelius Sejanus in or around 23 during the reign of Tiberius (14–37), the fort based the whole Guard on the outskirts of Rome where it remained until its disbandment in 312. The location, in the north-eastern part of the settled area, was thinly populated and had hitherto mainly been used for burials.[19] It was a tactful setting which conveniently obfuscated the fact that the emperors' power was ultimately vested in their ability to harness military force. Nevertheless, it was close enough to Rome for the praetorians to be on hand in the centre of the city in minutes, reinforcing their fellows in the cohorts serving at any given moment as the emperor's guard. This much is apparent from some of the dynamic episodes when praetorians proved themselves to be the most decisive force in Rome.

The decision to relocate the whole Guard to Rome in AD 23 was one of the most significant moments in the history of the Guard and the Roman world. It was a logical progression from Augustus' decision to make the Guard a permanent institution, itself a revolutionary move, and place it under commanders appointed by him. Now that it was based in Rome the Guard could influence political events directly. The only obstacles in its way were emperors with the power and prestige to control the Guard and harness its power. The moment an emperor fell short of what was expected of him, it was all too often the praetorians who determined what happened next.

The Praetorian Guard, whether in its barracks, performing any one of a multiplicity of practical duties or being with the emperor on campaign, was fundamental to the exercise and retention of imperial power. The challenge for any emperor was to keep the Guard and its prefects under control. As Gibbon pointed out, that was extremely difficult to do. The Roman Empire has always had much to teach us about the consequences and dangers of absolute power in a state where so much could depend on the abilities and circumstances of a single person. The Praetorian Guard was one of the most potent ingredients in the story of the Roman emperors and it is hoped that this book goes some way to telling its story.

* * *

I am very grateful to Heather McCallum at Yale University Press for her interest in the idea of this book and the part she played in helping shape it. Tom Holland kindly read an early draft of the final text, making some invaluable comments on detail and other infelicities, but his endorsement of the idea of the book was also enormously valuable. Roger Tomlin helped out with the cryptic legal fragment referring to Marcus Aurelius' modification of privileges afforded the praetorians' fathers-in-law in 168. I am also extremely grateful to the Roman military expert and historian Adrian Goldsworthy for scrutinizing the text in considerable detail and making specialist comments on it, as well as some excellent suggestions that broadened out the scope of some important points. Kym Ramadge also identified some infelicities of style and other errors. It would also be appropriate to pay credit to the vast amount of work performed by scholars over many decades without which this book would have been impossible to write. I hope that the Bibliography is an appropriate acknowledgement to that. I would also like to thank Rachael Lonsdale and Melissa Bond at Yale who saw the book through production efficiently and offered useful advice, and Charlotte Chapman for her meticulous editing work on the final version of the text. Inevitably, a book about a subject drawn from so many different and disparate sources has been very complicated to assemble. Every effort has been taken to ensure its accuracy, but any errors and omissions that remain are the author's and his alone.

Guy de la Bédoyère
Welby, Lincolnshire, 2016

CHAPTER 1

EVOLUTION

(44–31 BC)

By the mid-first century BC it had become established practice for a Roman general to protect himself and demonstrate his prestige by appointing a bodyguard of troops. In the aftermath of Caesar's assassination in 44 BC Octavian and Antony followed this trend. These ad hoc praetorian units lacked any formal designation, organization or terms of service, reflecting the unsettled conditions of the time. Their loyalty was far from guaranteed but they could save a general's life at crucial moments. Octavian's victory at Actium left him in control of not just a vast army but also a huge collection of praetorian cohorts, gathered from his own forces and also those of Antony.

IN SPITE OF AUGUSTUS' claim that he had 'set free the state' and 'restored many traditions of the ancestors', it was plain to most, if not all, that these words were no more than part of an elaborate spin. As Octavian he had risen to power precisely and unequivocally as a result of military force; indeed, Augustus acknowledged this when he said that he raised an army on his own initiative and at his own expense to do this.[1] He was operating in a tradition that had been evolving for decades in the Roman world as Roman armies became increasingly likely to owe their fealty to an individual general rather than the state. In 83 BC Gnaeus Pompeius ('Pompey'), then aged about twenty-three, raised an army so that he could support the former consul Lucius Cornelius Sulla Felix ('Sulla') in his bid to seize

Rome. Pompey had stood in the forum at the city of Auximum (Osimo, Italy), recruited the troops and appointed their officers, as well as fully equipping his force.[2] That relationship would play a crucial part in the development of the Praetorian Guard and its relationship with the emperor.

Octavian's opportunity for power came with the murder in 44 BC of his great-uncle, Julius Caesar and his inheritance of Caesar's name by virtue of having been adopted in Caesar's will as his son. From then till 31 BC Octavian focused all his energy on using military power to defeat first the tyrannicides Marcus Junius Brutus and Gaius Cassius Longinus, and then to eliminate his erstwhile allies, amongst whom the most prominent was Mark Antony. The use of military power, under the circumstances, was hardly unreasonable. Since Brutus and Cassius had their own army, and later Antony had his, Octavian had no other conceivable means of realizing his ambitions. Antony's self-destructive focus on the east, and bigamous relationship with Cleopatra, made him easily depicted as an enemy of the Roman state and as a decadent asocial, especially as his legal wife was Octavian's sister, Octavia. This left Octavian free to pose as the sole defender of both the Roman world and Roman morals. With Antony destroyed at Actium in 31 BC, Octavian then concentrated on creating a template of pseudo-constitutional power in which military power went almost unmentioned. In some respects he had never been more exposed, even if his principal enemies were now dead. Mindful of the need to ensure his own personal security, for the moment Octavian kept his praetorians under his personal control, converting them into a permanent institution soon after Actium.

There was nothing especially innovatory about creating the Praetorian Guard. Bodies of troops attached to a general as his personal escort had been around for a long time. The term *cohors praetoria* ('praetorian cohort') first appears in a reference to the general Scipio Africanus in the late third century BC, though our source, Sextus Pompeius Festus, actually wrote in the late second century AD when he produced an epitome of the works of Verrius Flaccus who lived under Augustus. The reference is merely a definition of the term *cohors praetoria*, which in this case amounted to soldiers who had been selected from the bravest. They were exempt from soldiers' normal duties and received one and a half-time pay, but were not distinguished from the others in battle.[3] Festus uses the term *cohors praetoria* but it is not certain whether it was a term that Scipio Africanus himself used at the time. What is evident is that such soldiers were being rewarded for their performance to date with special privileges; the implication is that they were expected to protect their commanding officer in return. Writing in the second century BC, Polybius provides a description of early praetorian troops on campaign. The consular general's tent, the *praetorium*, was flanked by the tribunes' tents next to which were the quarters of cavalry chosen from the *extraordinarii*, made up of cavalry and infantry. The *extraordinarii* were already the pick of the auxiliary cavalry wings, so the further process of selection made sure that the general's escort was made up of the best of the best. Along with these selected cavalrymen were *evocati*, retired soldiers who had re-enlisted out of personal loyalty to the general. These men all accompanied the general on the march and in battle and at other times remained 'constantly in attendance' on the consul and his second-in-command, the quaestor.[4]

Nonetheless, there seems to have been something inherently fluid about the existence of bodyguard units at this date. It was possible for a general to find himself championed by supporters who effectively acted as self-declared bodyguards, such as the Iberian soldiers who fought for the Roman general Quintus Sertorius during the conquest of Hispania (Spain) in the late 80s BC and nicknamed him Hannibal out of admiration. His choice of Iberians for a bodyguard provoked particular resentment amongst his Roman troops, indicative of an element of *noblesse oblige* in Roman military culture prevailing by then. Creation of, and appointment to, a praetorian force was evolving into an expectation on the part of Roman troops and therefore an essential device by which these men could expect to receive their just rewards.[5] Disappointing them could be injudicious.

The first description of a praetorian unit in action was in 62 BC when the general Marcus Petreius led senatorial forces against the rebel Lucius Sergius Catilina at Pistoria in Tuscany. Catilina initially did far better in the battle than Petreius had expected. Petreius therefore decided to order his *cohors praetoria* to follow him in a direct attack on Catilina's centre. This proved to be decisive, routing Catilina's forces, and leaving Catilina dead on the battlefield. It was therefore already apparent at this early date that the praetorians were not part of the original battle plan. The use of the term is so matter of fact that it reflects the existence of praetorian units well before then, though since we have relatively few references to them we cannot assume praetorians were routinely appointed and deployed.[6]

The term *cohors praetoria* was still only a descriptive one, a generic reference to ad hoc bodies of troops detailed to take care of their commanding officer as with Caesar's use of cavalry detached from the X legion in 58 BC. This was an expression of his trust in the legion and clearly a privilege. In order to do this Caesar took horses from an auxiliary cavalry wing of Gauls and handed them over to soldiers from the X legion to ride as his escort. This was clearly a spontaneous arrangement. There is no evidence to suggest that any of the principal *imperatores* of the late Roman Republic ever organized praetorian units on a temporary or permanent basis, even if they were aware that other generals had them. Even so, during the Gallic Wars, Caesar employed a body of 400 German cavalry, which he apparently kept with him on a habitual basis. In 44 BC he dismissed a bodyguard made up of Spaniards, a moment of arrogant confidence that contributed to his assassination shortly afterwards. Neither of these is described as a praetorian unit and there is no suggestion that Caesar ever created one on a formal and permanent basis.[7]

During the civil war against Pompey in 49 BC, Caesar recorded that Marcus Petreius, now fighting for Pompey, was supported by a 'praetorian cohort of *caetrati*', specialist lightly armed Spanish infantry.[8] This is a useful reference because Caesar was a contemporary source. The term was clearly something he was familiar with and expected his readership to be.

The term 'praetorian' seems to have had varied application at this date. It could be used to refer either to soldiers serving a governor on his staff or as specialist crack troops. The orator Cicero wrote to his brother Quintus in 52 BC and made a direct reference to the use of the term 'praetorian cohort' as an analogous way of describing the governor's personal staff. Obviously, as an analogy, it would have had no currency unless the term was widely understood. In January 50 BC Cicero, then serving as governor of Cilicia, wrote to Marcus Cato and made reference to a praetorian cohort serving as the garrison of Epiphanea in Cilicia. On 26 November 50 BC

Cicero wrote to his friend Atticus and included the fact that he had carried home the will of one Marcus Curius, which had been sealed by three members of Cicero's family and also the seal 'of the praetorian cohort'.[9]

The term 'praetorian cohort' was therefore clearly well established by 44 BC but evidently had a number of different possible applications. From a practical point of view, Octavian was only too aware that Caesar, being convinced that possession of a bodyguard was the sign of a man who lived constantly in fear of death, had spurned his friends' advice to go about with one and paid the price when he was assassinated in 44 BC.[10] Caesar had preferred to rely on what he regarded as the greater security of popular goodwill. When he finally secured supreme power in 31 BC, Octavian took the precaution of relying on both popular goodwill and a bodyguard.

During the period 44–31 BC Octavian and Mark Antony took care to appoint their own *cohortes praetoriae*, principally to protect each from the other but at the time the arrangements were typically vague. Antony raised a praetorian force of six thousand men, divided up into cohorts commanded by tribunes, but he seems to have accumulated it in piecemeal fashion until that total was reached. According to Appian it was made up entirely of centurions. Since that was impossible, it might mean that the soldiers, who were all selected for their experience, were given the rank or at least the pay and conditions of centurions.[11] The creation of this force caused considerable disquiet amongst the senators, who instructed Antony to reduce the numbers; he said he would only do so once popular disorder amongst the plebeians had been calmed down. This seems to have happened because by 43 BC, just before the Battle of Forum Gallorum, he was raising another praetorian force.

Octavian's spies informed him that the army at Brundisium was outraged that Antony had not avenged Caesar. These troops were now prepared to rally to Octavian's side. Antony went off to settle the situation. Worried that Antony might return with the army and take advantage of him if he had no protection, Octavian raised a considerably larger bodyguard of what Appian describes as 'about ten thousand men', each of whom was offered 500 drachmae to join up. Octavian took care to choose men likely to feel some loyalty to him and selected them from Caesar's veterans who had been settled in Campania. At this stage he made no effort to organize the force or even equip it properly; according to Appian, instead of being divided into cohorts, this incompletely armed force was treated as a single unit under one standard.[12] This seems unwise for obvious practical reasons of organization and discipline but since Appian makes a specific point of mentioning this arrangement we must recognize it as a possibility, albeit a temporary one.

While it is possible also that the number of ten thousand was an exaggeration, there is no need to assume this as a matter of course.[13] At this early stage in his career Octavian was still finding his way. The flattering prospect of an unnecessarily large and ostentatious number of Caesar's veterans following him, thereby adding much needed prestige as well as practical support, can hardly have been unattractive. It is possible that Appian was at least partially accurate, even if the number was rounded, rather than that he was simply transposing a figure for the Praetorian Guard in the early second century AD, the time that he wrote.

The existence of these armies created an enormous amount of tension in Rome. With Caesar's assassination so recently in everyone's minds, the prospect of rival forces now lining up presented Octavian with a problem: he could not afford to allow himself to appear as an enemy of the people or in any way to present a threat to them. Octavian addressed the people of Rome in the forum and tried to justify his need to confront Antony. This was exactly what his bodyguard of ten thousand had not wanted to hear. They were prepared to be Octavian's bodyguard but not to support him in a war against Antony, who was not only consul but had also formerly been their general.

Octavian had dangerously miscalculated and it was an important sign that the future Praetorian Guard's loyalty was a commodity that had to be purchased. Octavian had to back off and do so fast. His solution was to reassure the men that he only needed their services for emergencies, again anticipating the purpose of the imperial Praetorian Guard, and promised them more money. In the event he managed to persuade no more than three thousand to stay initially, releasing the remainder to go home. It seems though that this remainder soon decided that they were likely to be better off if they returned to military service. So impressed had they been by Octavian's words, that they collected arms at home so that they could fight properly and returned to him.[14] This story, which is described by Appian, showed that Octavian had learned some extremely important lessons about a bodyguard unit of troops. They could be bought, but only under certain conditions, that their vanity needed flattering, and that they needed organizing. It may well have been this experience that taught him that a praetorian bodyguard on such a scale needed dividing into smaller units. He could not risk an entire force fragmenting and absconding.

The possession by Octavian and Antony of praetorian units in their armed forces was undoubtedly a matter of prestige and a badge of their status as Roman generals. In this respect they were simply operating within a well-established tradition even if the number of praetorians had probably increased. At any rate, it would have been unthinkable for any one of them to be seen not to have had a praetorian unit if the others had them; more-over, they were not the only ones. Antony, who had had to reduce his praetorians in number, had simply raised a new praetorian cohort in time for the Battle of Forum Gallorum in 43 BC when he fought against an army led by the consuls Gaius Vibius Pansa Caetronianus and Aulus Hirtius, and Octavian who also had his own praetorian forces. Antony had raised his new praetorian unit, supplemented during the battle by those of Marcus Aemilius Lepidus, by choosing the best and most reliable men from his army. Cicero, addressing the senate, used this against Antony by calling his praetorian guard a 'royal cohort' made up of 'private guards' drawn from the soldiery. In the Roman world any whiff that a powerful man had monarchical ambitions could be fatally damaging, as Caesar had discovered.[15]

The situation was very complicated. Decimus Junius Brutus Albinus, not to be confused with Marcus Junius Brutus, another, better known, assassin of Caesar, was allegedly the last conspirator to stab Caesar to death. After this he fled to Cisalpine Gaul, a province of which he was the propraetorian governor. Here he raised his own army in anticipation of the war to come but the senate ordered him to hand over the province to Mark Antony. Decimus Brutus refused and took over the city of Mutina, so Antony laid siege to him there. At this point the two consuls for the year, Pansa and Hirtius, arrived with an army, intent on raising the siege because Antony was now earmarked as a dangerous force.

The events that followed illustrate perfectly the monumental chaos and confusion of the era. To begin with, on 14 April 43 BC Antony fought off the part of the army under Pansa and Octavian. The Battle of Forum Gallorum was initially disastrous for the inexperienced Octavian. His praetorians and those of Antony hived off to fight their own battle, possibly due to no more than a chance feature of the local terrain and an elevated road which meant the praetorians and legionaries could not see each other. Octavian's praetorians were completely wiped out by Antony's, while the rival legionary forces fought their own battle.[16] It is interesting that the armies separated themselves out, as if the praetorians regarded the prospect of fighting mere legionaries as demeaning. If so, it seems they had already started to nurse the idea that they were a cut above other troops, as indeed they were supposed to be. Pansa later died from his wounds, but when Hirtius arrived shortly afterwards, Antony was defeated. Antony was defeated again a week later in the Battle of Mutina by Hirtius' forces, Hirtius being killed in the fighting. Nonetheless, Antony withdrew, much to Decimus Brutus' relief, fearing that he might be surrounded by Octavian. Octavian, despite the loss of his praetorians, realized he had the upper hand. Brutus apprehensively thanked Octavian for his efforts but was roundly rebuked by the young man who said he had come to fight Antony, not help Brutus. Shortly afterwards, a delighted Cicero asked the senate to vote for fifty days of thanksgiving for the defeat of Antony. The senate also transferred the consular army to Decimus Brutus' control and put him in sole charge of the campaign against Antony, completely marginalizing Octavian.[17] It was an important moment. This would eventually throw Antony and Octavian together. Moreover, many of the legionaries in the consular army deserted and went over to Octavian.

A decisive moment came when Antony and Octavian settled their differences on a small island in the River Lavinius near Mutina in association with Marcus Aemilius Lepidus. Lepidus had originally been charged with an army to help Decimus Brutus and had been told by the senate after the Battle of Mutina that he was no longer needed. Instead, he threw in his lot with Antony. They divided the Roman world between them and made their plans to destroy their enemies' legalizing the arrangement in the Lex Titia of 27 November 43 BC. They became *triumviri rei publicae constituendae*, 'the body of three men for restoring the constitution', though in reality the very existence of the triumvirate marked the end of the Republic in its original sense. From here the triumvirs advanced into Rome, arranging in the first instance for the execution of senators who were dangerously powerful, their personal enemies, or whose estates could thus be confiscated and the money used to fund the war against Brutus and Cassius.[18]

Octavian, Mark Antony and Lepidus, as legally appointed triumvirs and in this capacity supposed to protect the Roman world, had a mandate that to all intents and purposes entitled them to carve up the Empire between them and legitimized the destruction of their enemies. Lepidus was always the junior partner and was soon marginalized. Octavian's propulsion to centre stage brought with it enormous potential problems such as the fact that he was, in any conventional legal sense, far too young to hold high office. He was barely nineteen. Nevertheless, the times were extraordinary and the nature of the circumstances meant legal niceties were brushed aside. He was made a consul, the highest magistracy any man of senatorial rank could hold, and awarded *imperium*, the legal right to command an army and charged, so he claimed, with the responsibility of taking care of anything that might threaten the state.[19]

In late 43 BC, over a period of three days, the triumvirs swaggered into Rome, each allocated a day of his own to arrive with one legion and his praetorian cohort. Evidently, Octavian had replaced the praetorians he had lost at Forum Gallorum and so too presumably had Antony. It was clearly unimaginable that they would enter Rome without a prestigious escort. This was only a fraction of their forces – Antony and Octavian had had five legions each on the island in the Lavinius – so it is interesting that the praetorian cohorts now constituted a large proportion of the forces they brought into the city as part of the ostentatious display of their power. The reality of the situation was publicly advertised by military standards being displayed in locations around Rome where they would be most widely noticed. The occasion was of supreme significance in Roman history and established a precedent Octavian would follow once he had supreme power and established the Praetorian Guard as a permanent institution, since at the time it was illegal to bring military forces into the city. Another 280 executions of their enemies were ordered, demonstrating that the soldiers brought into Rome were not simply a display of potential force.[20]

What we do not know is how the population of Rome reacted when this happened. But the people had been confronted with military forces in the city and must have realized that even more waited outside Rome. Appian alludes to the horrors of the killing that went on but ruminated on the paradox that one of the triumvirs turned out to be the man who would establish government on a 'firm foundation' and left a lineage and supreme name.[21] He was, on this occasion, obviously speaking with hindsight; at the time, the benefits of the future Augustan era were hardly likely to be obvious to anyone. Far more important would have been the fear engendered by yet more mayhem and the presence of troops on Rome's streets.

The Battle of Philippi in 42 BC, which really consisted of two separate confrontations in October, terminated the ambitions of Caesar's assassins, Brutus and Cassius. The battles were a monumental turning point in Roman history. It is inconceivable that the praetorian cohorts of each of the triumvirs and their associates were not present. There is no reference in any of the extant accounts that would confirm this apart from the fact that, on the same day as the second Battle of Philippi (23 October), a naval battle destroyed a force of Octavian's loyalists in the Adriatic. Domitius Calvinus was bringing two legions, four cavalry regiments and other troops to Octavian. According to Appian, the force also included Calvinus' praetorian cohort of about two thousand men.[22] The force was wiped out by Murcus and Ahenobarbus, supporters of the tyrannicides. The two thousand praetorians cannot have been all of Octavian's praetorian force but were presumably supposed to supplement those already with him.

Conversely, the existence of Roman provincial coins that appear to refer to praetorians at Philippi might also suggest their presence at the battle, but this is a very tenuous argument. The coins are local products, issued as base metal small change as was common across the eastern half of the Roman Empire during the imperial period as part of local autonomy.

The legends make no reference to any of the triumvirs or to any specific later emperor. The coins depict a figure of Victory on one side with the abbreviated legend 'the Victory of Augustus' (a generic term applicable to any emperor from 27 BC), and on the other three standards with the abbreviated legend COHOR PRAE PHIL, 'Praetorian Cohorts of Philippi'.[23] Had Octavian wished personally to commemorate his units at Philippi he would not have restricted the issue to a miserable small change denomination with no reference to himself; nor would he have anticipated the award of the name Augustus fifteen years prior to that event. Had he issued coins in honour of the units present, they would have included other units as well as praetorians and also been struck in silver or gold so that they could be used as donatives to the soldiers concerned (Plate 2).

It is far more likely that the coins were struck at Philippi to commemorate the battle from any time during the reign of Augustus on, but probably no later than the reign of Nero. Philippi was made into a Roman colony by Antony and Octavian after the battle. They named it *Colonia Victrix Philippensis* and settled some of their veterans there. After Philippi, Antony and Octavian released their soldiers who had served their full terms, apart from eight thousand who asked to continue in service. These men would have been best dealt with by awards of land as part of their discharge settlement, and Philippi is a likely candidate for some of them at least. In 30 BC Octavian renamed the city *Colonia Julia Philippensis*, at which point more veterans were settled there. The city was once more renamed in 27 BC when it became *Colonia Augusta Julia Philippensis* in recognition of the name Augustus, which he was awarded that year. The coin is likely to belong to after that date and refers perhaps to the settlement of praetorian veterans there.

What is more certain is that after Philippi the eight thousand troops who asked to stay in service were reorganized into praetorian cohorts and divided between Antony and Octavian.[24] They were technically veterans and thus not only highly experienced but also of proven loyalty. The fragile relationship between Antony and Octavian soon started to fragment, and by 41 BC Antony's brother Lucius Antonius had marched on Rome, determined to support his brother by bringing the triumvirate to an end. He forced Lepidus to leave, but when Octavian approached he fled to Perusia in Etruria. Here Octavian besieged him and he was forced to capitulate. Octavian's force at that time included four legions 'and his praetorian cohorts', which may or may not have been his share from the division of veterans the year before.[25]

A useful idea of the sort of proportions praetorians might be deployed in a war setting alongside legionary forces comes from accounts of Antony's Parthian war. In 40 BC the Parthians had invaded Syria and were joined by some of what was left of the tyrannicide forces. During this war Plutarch describes how Antony confronted the Parthian leader Phraates IV in 36 BC with an army made up of ten legions and three praetorian cohorts. This equates to around fifty thousand legionaries and fifteen hundred or three thousand praetorians, depending on how big a praetorian cohort was at this time.[26] The praetorians at this date are thus better seen still as temporary and ad hoc units, still usually deployed in battle alongside legions as a matter of course. The term *cohors praetoria* was still simply a generic one for any cohort made up of reliable veterans who wanted to remain on the muster and to do so for the extra pay and prestige their proximity to the commander brought them. Since they tended to be veterans it also follows that they were unlikely to be able to remain in the job for anything like as long as they had served as ordinary soldiers. Praetorian units seem to have been raised whenever necessary and, presumably, disbanded or redistributed when appropriate.

Octavian was nearly killed at some point during the time he was dealing with Lucius Antonius at Perusia; the lack of a permanent praetorian escort may have been responsible. Octavian had ordered that a soldier be ejected from a demonstration of games, presumably for committing some misdemeanour. Unfortunately, the man then disappeared, giving rise to the belief amongst the rest of the troops that he had been tortured and killed. A riot ensued, with Octavian only being saved by the sudden reappearance of the soldier.[27] There is no suggestion that any praetorians came forward to protect him, which means either that there were none there at the time or that they were part of the riot. The latter seems less likely but there is no reason to assume that at this date praetorian loyalty was slavish and unconditional;

later on, praetorian loyalty was very definitely fluid. The continual revision of praetorian units is also reflected in the two thousand praetorian troops brought to Greece by Octavia, Octavian's sister, for her husband Mark Antony in 35 BC. Given the rising tension between Octavian and Antony, the gesture seems a strange one. Plutarch explains that Octavian only allowed his sister to take the soldiers, as well as other soldiers' clothing, pack animals and money, in the hope that she would be rebuffed and thus provide Octavian with a pretext for war. Antony had already fallen in with Cleopatra VII in Egypt and was well on the way to abandoning Octavia permanently.[28]

A clear pattern was emerging during these troubled times. Praetorians provided a convenient way of keeping on invaluable experienced soldiers who might otherwise have been tempted to retire after fulfilling their period of service, or gravitate to better offers made by rivals. The extra wages were clearly attractive to some of these men, and enough to entice them to stay. There was also the simple matter of posturing and prestige. The presence of these men on a Roman general's establishment was as much a style statement as it was an important part of his security. Having said that, it is not entirely clear in what way they would have been expected to behave any differently to a general's other troops except to act with a greater degree of loyalty should their leader's position become dangerous. The practical issue of personal security when dealing with the Roman people was also a factor. In 40–39 BC Octavian was stoned by starving rioters in Rome when the grain supply ran low due to the disruption on the seas caused by the civil war, and only just escaped with his life.[29] He had unwisely decided to confront the mob with only a few attendants. Antony came to his help but ended up having to call in troops from outside the city to escort Octavian away. The incident showed how potentially suicidal it could be for a Roman leader to expose himself to the mob without armed protection.

In 32 BC, just prior to his final battle with Octavian at Actium, Antony issued a huge coinage series of silver denarii that commemorated the military units under his command and were presumably designated as pay for the soldiers of those units. They are usually known today as Antony's legionary denarii. With a silver purity of no better than around 85 per cent, they compared badly to conventional issues of the era, which had a standard of around 95 per cent. Consequently, these 'legionary denarii' were liable to remain in circulation for longer since they were spent in preference to being hoarded. So poor was their reputation that Pliny the Elder cited the common perception in the AD 70s when he wrote that their silver had been alloyed with iron.[30] Vast numbers have survived as archaeological finds because they were available to be lost casually over a longer period of time. By the mid-second century AD, imperial issues were declining in purity themselves and as a result Antony's denarii became more eligible for hoarding.

All this has preserved enough of Antony's coins for an interesting link to the praetorians to emerge. One of the rarest varieties of the 'legionary denarii' series, which itself reflects the relatively small number of praetorians involved, bears the remarkably unabbreviated legend *c(o)hortium praetoriarum*, 'of the praetorian cohorts'. Another records the *cohors speculatorum*, or 'cohort of scouts', though the word also means 'investigator' and has connotations of spying. This additional bodyguard component seems to have survived into Augustus' Praetorian Guard, with *speculatores* serving thereafter in the various praetorian cohorts.[31] Interestingly, the other types always designate single legions, such as 'LEG II' for the II legion, whereas his praetorians are here referred to in terms of the cohort fraction rather than as a collective entity. This reflects a situation in which the praetorians were not regarded as a single overall force, as individual legions were. Once the praetorian cohorts were gathered together in Rome during the reign of Tiberius (14–37), this perception changed, even though the Guard remained known as the *cohortes praetoriae*.

Conversely, such information as we have about Octavian's forces at Actium is precise but very late in date and possibly quite unreliable as a consequence. According to a late Roman source, Orosius, Octavian handed over control of his forces, including praetorians, at Actium to Marcus Agrippa. Agrippa dispersed his forty thousand men from eight legions and five praetorian cohorts amongst the galleys he had at his disposal.[32] The information is, however, sufficiently exact to suggest the possibility that it is true or close to the truth.

The outcome of the Battle of Actium in 31 BC was that Octavian succeeded in what he had set out to do as a teenager some thirteen years before. He had destroyed his rivals one by one, avenged Caesar's assassination and secured for himself not only supreme power but also a population that was so heartily sick of war that no meaningful opposition to his rule existed. There was mopping up to do and Octavian did not hold his celebratory triple triumph in Rome until 29 BC, but the civil wars were over. The Roman Republic had ceased to exist in any real sense. The praetorian escorts now found themselves reorganized into an integral part of the new regime. Ahead of them lay over three centuries of power and influence.

CHAPTER 2

FOUNDATION
(31 BC–AD 14)

Octavian turned the praetorians into a regularized, privileged and organized part of his power base as Augustus, Rome's first emperor. The Praetorian Guard enjoyed advantageous pay and conditions, but by dispersing them around Rome and Italy Augustus avoided creating the impression that he ruled at the head of a military dictatorship. Augustus focused far more publicly on his constitutional position and playing down the fact that he had come to power, and remained in power, as the result of naked force. He needed the army and the Guard, and they needed him. This interdependence established a dynamic that would have significant consequences in the centuries to come. The essential post of the praetorian prefect was created, but this involved putting a man, or men, in charge of a potentially very dangerous force. Augustus' attempts to create a dynasty also raised the question of whether the Guard was loyal to the office or to the person of the emperor.

D URING THE CIVIL WAR after Caesar's death in 44 BC an important principle and concept had been established: a Roman general would equip himself with a bodyguard drawn from his most effective, experienced and reliable troops. Now that he had supreme power, Octavian moved fast to make himself a permanent institution. After the Battle of

Actium in 31 BC, Octavian was unchallenged. The permanent Praetorian Guard which he created at this point, made up from both his praetorians and Antony's, emerged before the end of his reign as a far more regularized and coordinated force than anything that had gone before. The praetorians swore an oath of allegiance to Augustus, something that would be transferred to other emperors.[1] In time this would present some praetorians, ordered to carry out killings on behalf of the emperor or confronted by an emperor such as Nero whose behaviour became intolerable, with serious challenges to their loyalty.

Octavian had reorganized the army after the war was over in 31 BC. At that stage he controlled around sixty legions, comprising his own army and what was left of the forces controlled by Antony's faction, as well as praetorians. Later, as Augustus, Octavian would claim to have demobilized approximately 60 per cent (300,000) of the half million troops he controlled after Actium, dispersing these veterans throughout new colonies or back to their own home towns. Dio states that by AD 5 Augustus had twenty-three or twenty-five legions, as well as ten thousand praetorians in ten cohorts. Writing about the situation in 23, Tacitus gives twenty-five legions, though in the interim three legions had been lost in Germany in AD 9, and nine praetorian cohorts (size unspecified). These praetorian cohorts seem to have been part-mounted with the *equites praetoriani*, perhaps in a proportion of four to one in favour of the infantry component.[2]

Unfortunately we possess no piece of evidence in any form that tells us the configuration of the Guard when Augustus founded it, in terms either of total size or the organization of cohorts. All we have to go on is Dio's description of the armed forces in AD 5, and Tacitus' summary of the disposition of the same in AD 23, both of which were written long after the event, and sporadic pieces of evidence that crop up in various contexts across the first century AD. Dio states that the Guard in AD 5 was made up of ten thousand men in ten cohorts, Tacitus that in AD 23 it consisted of nine cohorts, but without specifying either the total size of the Guard or the individual cohorts.[3] Obviously, these figures are incompatible, which means either that one is wrong or that the arrangements had changed since the date of foundation and probably continued to change. The men recruited to the Guard were predominantly aged around eighteen to twenty years at the start of their service, a similar age to that of around two-thirds of legionaries, and drawn from Italian Roman citizens, by far and away the most convenient source.[4] The nature of their individual origins is less certain, for example whether they came from poorer families or were drawn from the better-off. The distinction is unlikely to have made much practical difference once they had been absorbed into the Guard.[5]

A number of modern authorities have made different assumptions about the size of the cohorts, based on the available evidence, and come to a variety of conclusions. One of these is that Dio was actually referring to the configuration of the Guard in his own time in the early 200s, and was therefore mistaken in suggesting that this was how the Guard was organized in Augustus' time. This position is largely responsible for inferring that the nine cohorts referred to by Tacitus was the correct number for the Augustan era. It has also contributed to the assumption by some that these cohorts were quingenary in size, with a nominal 480 men each. This would have made the Augustan Guard similar in size to, but smaller than, a legion.[6] Together with the equestrian tribunes who commanded each cohort, the centurions, *optiones* and standard-bearers, the total in each cohort would have been around five hundred. It is, however, important to stress that nine cohorts is a retrospective estimate based on the figures provided by Tacitus for the army in the year 23 under Tiberius, some fifty years or more after the foundation of the Guard by Augustus. We do not know for certain how many cohorts were involved when the Guard was founded. We also do not know if the numbers changed or, crucially, whether those cohorts were quingenary or milliary (one thousand strong) at this date. Quingenary cohorts are never specifically attested for the Praetorian Guard, now or at any other date, though quingenary cohorts were normal for the legions at the time. The praetorians, however, were not legionaries so there is no particular reason, in the absence of any evidence for praetorian quingenary cohorts, to insist that this was how the Guard was organized.

In fact, there is good reason to support the idea that milliary cohorts are not only possible but even likely for this early date, though there can be no certainty about this. Dio's reference to there being ten thousand praetorians in ten cohorts must imply milliary cohorts, making the Guard close to the size of two legions. The possibilities are that this was the size of the Guard when it was founded, or the size to which it had grown by AD 5, or was a retrospective reference by Dio. If both Dio and Tacitus were correct this would have to mean that the Guard had been reduced by one cohort between 5 and 23. The number of cohorts, however, may also have varied in ways that have gone unrecorded, rendering futile efforts to reconcile the disparate evidence. There were at least nine cohorts on the evidence of tombstones at Aquileia, which specify cohorts up to and including the VIIII (IX) cohort under Augustus, while other evidence suggests an expansion to twelve cohorts by the 30s or 40s. In 76, one of the earliest praetorian discharge diplomas known explicitly refers to nine praetorian cohorts, though this surely reflects the reorganization of the Praetorian Guard after the civil war, during which Vitellius had increased its numbers to sixteen cohorts. Whatever reason there might have been for using nine cohorts under Augustus or at any other time, as opposed to another number, is unknown to us, especially as a graffito from Pompeii, which must predate August 79, refers to a tenth cohort. It is quite clear that arrangements could and did change.[7]

The idea that Dio was mistaken is a convenient, but unsatisfactory, way of refuting one piece of evidence to resolve the discrepancy between Dio and Tacitus. When discussing the division of Rome into fourteen districts for the purposes of firefighting in 7 BC, Dio makes it clear with his phrase 'this is also the present arrangement' that he was fully aware that circumstances might have differed between his time and what had prevailed two centuries earlier.[8] There is no reason therefore to assume as a matter of course that he was wrong about the size of the Guard in AD 5. Since the Guard at that date was not accommodated in a single location, and was widely dispersed, none of the normal methods (such as the size of a fort) by which a theoretical number could be estimated applies.

The figure of ten thousand given by Dio is also the same number given by Appian for Octavian's praetorians in 43 BC. Given the lack of precision in our sources, and the difficulty of reconciling all the disparate pieces of information available to us, it is possible that Octavian did indeed create a Praetorian Guard on the scale described by Dio, based on ten milliary cohorts. After all, it would have been useful to reward especially loyal soldiers towards the end of their careers in the aftermath of the war. Moreover, it would be some time before Octavian could feel completely secure, so a large Praetorian Guard might have seemed a good idea to begin with. The conspiracy led by Fannius Caepio in 22 BC showed that almost a decade after Actium, Augustus could still face danger at home just as Caesar had. The only other early reference to milliary cohorts in the Guard is by Philo for the year 40, who clearly mentions a thousand-strong cohort.[9] In other words, the only specific evidence we have for the size of early imperial praetorian cohorts comes from Dio and Philo; both suggest the cohorts were milliary, at least for the times they were writing about.

The layout of the Castra Praetoria, built in Tiberius' reign by 23 when the Guard was all based in Rome, allows for a very substantial garrison, perhaps in excess of fifteen thousand. This certainly does not conflict with the idea that Dio was indeed right about the size of Augustus' Guard in AD 5, and that the cohorts were milliary from the outset.[10] Even if the Guard was smaller under Augustus, the availability of the Castra Praetoria would have transformed the extent to which praetorians could be accommodated in Rome, making an enlargement of the Guard logistically feasible from at least thereon.

All these speculative possibilities really serve to show is that we simply do not have enough precise information to know how the size of the Guard changed over time from its inception, if indeed it did change, and to resolve the contradictions in the evidence. We do not have to assume that Dio was wrong about the size of the Guard under Augustus, or that his information conflicts with that of Tacitus. It is possible that the cohorts were milliary sized from the beginning, and that the numbers of cohorts fluctuated in ways that we are now unable to pin down with certainty, as indeed has been acknowledged by some authorities.[11] The latter seems certain, the former no better than the balance of probability. As an aside, it is worth noting that the individual cohorts of the Guard did not possess at this date any form of honorific or loyalist name commemorating particular acts or campaigns as the legions did. There was thus no overtly prestigious or privileged praetorian cohort.[12]

There is also the question of the *cohors speculatorum*, 'the cohort of scouts', the subunit of the Guard associated with intelligence and spying, first attested in Antony's forces at Actium. Augustus is even recorded as having remained on social terms with a former *speculator* on his staff. They were still in existence in 68, when they were described by Tacitus as forming a special bodyguard chosen by height, and presumably remained a permanent feature. They did not necessarily serve in separate cohorts, even if they had done so under Antony.[13]

The Guard was, in any relative sense, a tiny part of the Roman world's armed forces but a very definitely privileged one, regardless of how it was organized. In 27 BC Augustus saw to it that the senate passed a decree authorizing the Guard to receive 'double' the pay of the ordinary legionaries. Predictably enough this does not tie up with other evidence for later dates, which suggests that the ratio was modified to 3.33:1. In AD 14 a praetorian was paid two denarii per day, according to Tacitus, whereas a legionary received 10 asses (0.625 of a denarius) per day. The latter figure was a slight approximation, equating to 228 denarii per year. The actual annual rate for a legionary was 225 denarii per year, rising to 300 under Domitian (81–96), so the day rate given by Tacitus is obviously a rounded figure for the sake of simplicity. Soldiers in the Roman army were in theory paid three times a year so the figure needed to be divisible into thirds, which of course 225 and 300 are. Based on this, the differential recorded in AD 14 would probably have to mean that by then a praetorian was perhaps paid 720 denarii per year (that is, 3×240), equal to 1.97 notional denarii per day, in other words the 'two denarii' cited by Tacitus, who had no means even to express the term '1.97'. Another, more likely, possibility is that the praetorians were paid 750 denarii per year (3×250 denarii), equivalent to 2.05 denarii per day. Either approximation would fit with Tacitus and fulfil the need to be divisible by three. Moreover, 250 denarii is equal to 1,000 sestertii, the amount awarded praetorians in Augustus' will, just as legionaries were awarded 75 denarii (300 sestertii). It is of course entirely possible that the praetorians' 'double' pay in 27 BC had been raised to a higher rate by AD 14, though we have no evidence to prove this, other than the discrepancy discussed here.[14]

In 13 BC Augustus fixed the length of service for a praetorian at twelve years and a legionary's at sixteen, modifying this in AD 5 to sixteen and twenty years respectively. These should be seen as minimum figures rather than fixed points at which discharge automatically took place. The gratuity received at discharge for praetorians and legionaries seems to have been set at a related ratio to that for pay. Praetorians received 20,000 sestertii but a legionary received 60 per cent of that amount – 12,000 sestertii. This is equivalent to 1.67:1 or approximately half of the 3.33:1 ratio for pay, which is unlikely to be a coincidence. The amounts left to praetorians and legionaries in Augustus' will were also based on the ratio of 3.33:1. The slight differences are easily explained by the need to have rounded figures divisible by three for the purposes of annual pay, and rounded figures for the single distribution of retirement gratuities and imperial bequests. The idea that the ratios are inconsistent therefore simply does not hold up, since it is quite clear they were very closely related and were rounded for convenience.[15]

These figures correspond well with the likely arrangements for the urban cohorts, discussed below. Nor is there any need to seek precise correspondence either in totals or in those ratios laid out in Appendix 2, Table 1. The Roman world was far more pragmatic than that. Regardless of the detail, the principle that praetorians were paid more, and served less, than legionaries is the important point. We have, however, not the slightest evidence of when and how these sums were paid to individual praetorians in practice, regardless of the theory or theories. The evidence from Egypt, where some military accounts survive on papyri, is that soldiers in the garrison there were only ever paid token amounts of cash while in service. The rest of their accumulated pay, less deductions for equipment, clothing and food, was only given to them on discharge. If this was also usually the case for praetorians then the theoretical rates of pay are no more than that, with the everyday practicalities impossible for us to reconstruct. However, this may explain the added attraction of accession donatives paid by new emperors to praetorians, though we know those were not always forthcoming either, with disastrous consequences for the emperors who had made rash promises.[16]

Some praetorians voluntarily re-enlisted once they had been honourably discharged, and were known as *evocati Augusti*, where *evocatus* means literally 'a man recalled to arms [by the emperor]', carrying vine stick rods as a mark of their status. These men seem to have been chosen to serve as praetorian centurions, sometimes alongside ex-legionary centurions who joined the Guard as praetorian centurions.[17] In consequence, the Guard could at any time consist of soldiers in their late teenage years up to and including men past retirement age, though the latter were more likely to be left in the barracks when the Guard was needed elsewhere. At retirement, praetorians received honourable discharges. Praetorian veterans were also offered land grants. One of the new colonies earmarked for praetorian veterans was Augusta Praetoria Salassorum (Aosta), established on land in north-western Italy captured from the Salassi tribe in 25 BC. The Salassi had just rebelled and Augustus sent Marcus Terentius Varro Murena to crush the revolt. In the aftermath, local men of military age were sold into slavery for a minimum of twenty years and the best tribal lands seized for praetorian veterans.[18] Legionary colonies were more likely to be in frontier provinces.

Praetorian discharges were commemorated on inscriptions displayed in certain prominent places in Rome. Some soldiers commissioned their own personal copies, engraved on bronze plates. Known as diplomas (*diplomata*), some survive and provide evidence for the distinctive formula applied to praetorians. No such diploma is known from an earlier date than the mid-70s but it is unlikely that the special form of address had changed. In a praetorian discharge the emperor addressed the praetorian directly, and referred to his 'courageous and loyal performance of military service' in 'my Praetorian Guard'. This emphasized very much the close personal relationship that was supposed to exist between the emperor and his praetorians, and reflected the oath these soldiers had taken. The praetorian standards reinforced this proximity. Unlike other military standards, praetorian standards incorporated imperial portraits, *imagines*, rather than having them on separate standards. The late-first-century relief of a praetorian standard on the tomb of Marcus Pompeius Asper shows that of the III praetorian cohort. It includes two *imagines* as well as various other devices such as civic crowns and an eagle.[19]

This distinction in length of service from other parts of the Roman army also had an ethnic component. The choice of troops was an important distinction from the later Guard because in the earliest decades praetorians had by definition served with other legions first. Under Augustus and Tiberius they were 'levied for the most part in Etruria and Umbria, or ancient Latium and the old Roman colonies'. This meant that the Guard was recruited in the main from freeborn Italian Roman citizens aged from their mid-teens to as much as thirty-two, a geographical bias that would remain a characteristic until 193 when Septimius Severus cashiered the Guard and switched recruitment to deserving soldiers from any legion.[20] The reasons for the original arrangements must have included confidence that Italians were likely to exhibit more reliable loyalty, and also a straightforward belief in their natural entitlement to superior opportunities and conditions. Like other soldiers, praetorians were not allowed to marry during their time of service. In practice, some acquired unofficial wives, with the proportion increasing over the next three hundred years, but always at a lower percentage compared to legionaries.[21]

The limited amount of available evidence for individual soldiers at this time suggests that whatever the theoretical conditions of service, the reality could be very different. This divergence between theory and practice seems to have affected almost every aspect of life in the Roman world, especially when it involved officialdom. Caetronius Passer joined the Guard in AD 11 but was not released until 29, after eighteen years' service.[22] Extensions of service, voluntary or otherwise, are also attested in the normal army, as the mutiny that arose in Pannonia on Augustus' death showed.[23] The reason for this is probably to be found in Dio's description of the extension to the length of service in AD 5, discussed above. The implication is that the state expected soldiers would volunteer to serve for longer. By 5 it had become apparent that troops were dissatisfied with the bounties they had been paid and declined to put themselves forward for additional service. The formal extension of service at that date appears to have been the result. Caetronius Passer may have chosen to serve for longer or perhaps been effectively forced to.

Dio's account of the army as it was in the year 5 includes, as well as the reference to twenty-three or twenty-five legions and ten thousand praetorians in ten cohorts, an indeterminate number of auxiliary units, six thousand watchmen in four cohorts (not to be confused with the *vigiles* who were only founded after AD 6), the urban cohorts (*cohortes urbanae*) whose numbers are not specified by him, and a unit of 'picked foreign horsemen' described as Batavians. This is a confusing label because during the first century AD the Batavians seem also to have been called by other sources the German bodyguard, the *Germani corporis custodes* (literally 'German guards of the body'). They dated back to when Octavian had called up Caesar's veterans to fight with him against Antony. Thanks, however, to the majority of these in the first century being ethnically Batavian, this became the name by which the unit was generally known. Being non-Roman was a critical distinction from the praetorians and was something they shared with the much later *equites singulares Augusti*, founded by the end of the first century. Suetonius clearly suggests the Germans had formed part of Augustus' bodyguard. They certainly were under later reigns, notably those of Caligula and Nero (Plate 12).[24]

Quite how the Germans were used compared to the praetorians is not entirely clear. The reason for employing them though is much easier to understand. Roman or Italian praetorian troops were always at risk of transferring their loyalty to rivals or other factions, thanks in part to the complex network of client–patron protocols in Roman society. Foreign troops hired directly by the emperor had no such affiliations, owing their loyalty only to him – at least in theory, in spite of the risk that their very existence might have provoked resentment amongst the praetorians. Certainly this was why, over half a century later, Nero trusted them. The destruction of three legions in AD 9 in Germany, however, seems to have provoked Augustus to think again. The German bodyguard was disbanded in 68 by Galba. It was reformed in a different guise by Trajan, but was still known as the Batavian bodyguard in Dio's time.[25]

Regardless of its organization or size under Augustus, the Praetorian Guard did not operate as a single unit to begin with. Only three cohorts at any one time were stationed in Rome but they functioned as a presence and backdrop to Augustus' power all the time that he was engaged in manufacturing his constitutional position. The other praetorian cohorts were dispersed amongst towns near Rome.[26] As we will see, subsequently placing praetorians in Rome at all amounted to a major institutional change and constituted a fundamental watershed in the nature of power during the Roman era.

The Guard had little more strategic military potential than acting as a 'strong escort' for the emperor if he went out on campaign.[27] Inevitably troops appointed to serve in any *cohors praetoria* in the Republic enjoyed a certain amount of prestige by virtue of their privileged status and association with the commanding officer. Clearly, those attached to the emperor's praetorian cohorts were the most prestigious version but they were not specialized soldiers with specific fighting skills. In that respect they were not marked out as different from ordinary citizen legionaries. But if the imperial Praetorian Guard started out as just a bodyguard, it did not remain restricted to that function. It is not unusual for the Roman Empire to be regarded as a form of military dictatorship and to some extent that is a valid judgement. The implication is that this was as much a matter of deliberate policy as a matter of choice or ideology. The truth was much subtler than that.

The formation of the Praetorian Guard by Octavian was a sideshow to a much more significant political rearrangement. Octavian underwent a metamorphosis into the person of Augustus by 27 BC, a leader whose constitutional position was embedded in Republican offices and whose name was imbued with religious symbolism. He ostentatiously gave up the exceptional powers he had been awarded and basked in the gratitude of a population that had had enough of war, factionalism and chaos. His new name, Augustus, evoked a special kind of pseudo-religious sanctity and consecration for which there is no easy English equivalent. It placed him above other mortals but, crucially, without immortalizing him. The choice supplanted an initial suggestion that he be called Romulus, proposed because he was a 'second' founder of the city, since Augustus was considered both to be new and more honourable.[28]

The process by which Octavian became Augustus and settled his constitutional position took at least until 23 BC. It was awkward, contrived and ultimately incongruous since the concept of a sole ruler was not only a total anathema to the Romans but there was also no such position for anyone to occupy. At the time, few had the stomach to return to the disorder of previous decades. It was nevertheless a highly unusual situation: one man had supreme and effectively unchallenged power but he made no public admission of this and sought no single legal position that would confirm or identify it. Augustus emerged as the *princeps*, 'first among equals', with no formal pre-eminence beyond his personal *auctoritas* and the annual grant of the powers of a tribune of the plebs to him which included making him inviolable. It was a brilliant sleight of hand that created a position of pre-eminence in a system now called the principate by scholars of the period. There is no modern equivalent for the term and even in antiquity the Romans continued often to refer to their government as the Republic. Tacitus was well aware that although there had been a major shift in how the Roman world was governed, lip service was still paid to the idea that the old order remained in place. He referred to how Tiberius made sure every measure went through the consuls first, 'just like the old republic'.[29] The position Augustus now occupied, for all its unconventional characteristics, had a new formality and permanence about it. The move away from the ad hoc praetorian units of the Republic to the permanent Guard was a manifestation of this new type of power.

The tribune of the plebs was an extremely significant position established early in the Republic. The plebeians walked out of Rome in 494 BC in disgust at the way the upper class, the patricians, had completely taken over the institutions and offices of the Republic, operating it in effect as an oligarchy. In order to appease the plebs it was agreed that several tribunes would be elected from them annually to protect their interests. These tribunes were able to intervene to prevent any procedure or law that might damage the interests of the plebs, using their power of veto. The problem for Augustus was that an elected tribune could not hold the position in consecutive years. His solution was simple but it twisted the law. By being granted the powers of a tribune annually, rather than the office, Augustus could enjoy the privileges of a tribune but none of the restrictions. The annual grant of the tribunician powers meant that Augustus did not hold them 'permanently'; he was merely awarded them afresh each year, conveniently making it look as if the arbiter of power was the senate. The arrangements were settled by 23 BC; under these Augustus was entitled to veto senatorial legislation and any measures passed by the other tribunes, but they could not veto his.

Consequently, Augustus could pose as the saviour of the citizens, and not as a military dictator. In Gibbon's eyes this 'crafty tyrant' had recognized the need to 'colour' his power with laws, but that 'arms alone' would maintain it.[30] The whole package was a studiedly creative revision of an existing position that suited Augustus' purpose perfectly. Tacitus regarded it as a blatantly cynical ploy that evaded the use of a title like 'king' or 'dictator' but provided something that still made Augustus pre-eminent over everyone else.[31] Augustus was, however, being pragmatic. Caesar's position of perpetual dictator led to his assassination. It was too soon for Augustus to risk anything similar and indeed he never did.

Augustus also had to avoid any overt definition of his position in military terms. The tribunician power had nothing whatsoever to do with the military power that had brought Augustus to where he was. That was conveniently, and literally, swept to the margins, yet of course he enjoyed the protection of his praetorians and the power of the implicit threat they represented while the actual tribunes of the plebs of course had no such privilege. The emperor's 'province' was made up of a large number of frontier provinces where, naturally enough, the vast bulk of the Roman army was dispersed. These included most of the Iberian Peninsula, the three Gaulish provinces, Syria, Phoenicia, Cilicia, Cyprus and Egypt. In 27 BC Augustus made a point of handing these over to the senate, which promptly granted the 'province' back to him along with the power of *imperium* not only there but also with a special dispensation to hold it in Rome too, a neat aside that changed everything but appeared on the face of it to be no more than a minor modification.[32] Moreover, Augustus was also able to force citizens to obey him through the power of *coercitio*, which he obtained through the possession of *imperium*.

There was an important formal point here. Augustus' personal authority only in theory applied to his 'province', with the fiction being maintained that the rest of the Empire was under the senate's control. By 23 BC his *imperium* had become *imperium maius*. In this form it entitled Augustus to intervene on behalf of the state in areas that were not technically under his personal authority. Augustus thus had complete control of the army in his territory and any manifestation of the army in Rome as well. This conveniently also legitimated his control of the Praetorian Guard, though under the circumstances it was improbable that anyone would have been inclined to raise an objection. Nonetheless, fabricating constitutional propriety was an essential component in the Augustan regime.

Accepting all this was, as Tacitus observed, a kind of conspiracy in which everyone willingly engaged.[33] Augustus strived to present himself as normal, ordinary, modest and traditional, but to do so in such a way that advertised his exceptional qualities. He was to be the embodiment of all that Rome stood for. No wonder then that Augustus prevented the clause in the poet Virgil's will that his epic poem, the *Aeneid*, be destroyed from being fulfilled. Virgil had regarded the work as incomplete and unworthy as a consequence. Augustus recognized that the heroic tale of Aeneas leading his Trojan followers to establish a new conflated dynasty of Latins, Etruscans and Trojans as the forbears of the Roman people was an important component in his own myth. In Virgil's tale Aeneas is a proto-Augustus, a worthy progenitor and peace-loving warrior who is shown during his visit to the Underworld a line of future Romans climaxing in the coming of Augustus.

Lurking in the background was the fact that the Praetorian Guard had been made into a permanent institution. Although most of Augustus' contemporaries were breathing a sigh of relief that the years of disorder and civil war seemed to be over, Augustus could not possibly afford to be complacent. Virgil had predicated the story of the *Aeneid* on the notion that Augustus was a heaven-sent saviour, a predestined and glorious leader of the Roman people whose rule would usher in a new golden age of peace and set the Roman people on the path to their destiny as the benign and beneficent rulers of the world.[34] That was the idealism. The reality was the military force that had taken Augustus into power and which would keep him there, of which the Guard was a key component. In Virgil's vision war has given way to peace and there is no sense that any need existed to maintain a powerful military presence.

The game that Augustus played was a charade in plain sight. There can have been no one who did not know that Augustus could not conceivably have come to power without a successful army behind him. He had, after all, persistently presented himself as victorious on his coins during the period up to 31 BC and immediately afterwards. Yet, one factor above all symbolized that a new age had begun: the presence, if not the very existence, throughout all this of the Praetorian Guard in Italy, and in Rome. The Praetorian Guard had one formal purpose and that was to protect the person of the emperor and his family. The Roman Empire was the first ancient western state to take on a scale and complexity that bear comparison with modern nations. It covered a colossal amount of territory and a very large number of subject peoples, all of whom were contained within an administrative system that attempted to encourage, or if necessary impose, a certain amount of cultural homogeneity. That the Roman state managed to accomplish this with relatively primitive communications was a remarkable phenomenon.

Compliance was a key ingredient in the Roman state's ability to govern its territories, as was delegation to local elites who were absorbed into the Roman system of imperial patronage. Beyond this, there were very considerable limits on how Roman government could both have a presence and act in Rome itself and beyond on its subject provincials. It lacked the infrastructure and mechanisms of a complex modern state; but it did not lack the power or will to adapt and evolve. That meant using what was available, and the Praetorian Guard was a conspicuous resource, alongside the rest of the Roman army.

As we saw earlier, although Augustus greatly reduced the size of the army after 31 BC, he maintained a significant part, almost half, of it. Whatever his desire to diminish any public impression of the nature of his power he was perfectly well aware that the presence of the legions in his 'province' (in practice mostly the frontier provinces of the Empire) was a passive warning to any challenge, from either the senate or a pretender. Augustus formalized the idea of a permanent standing army whose loyalty remained principally to him rather than the state, manifest in the army's oaths and other gestures of loyalty. This was a natural development from the last days of the Republic when individual Roman armies focused their loyalty primarily on their individual generals, largely because they were the source of the soldiers' pay.

In the Roman world the only possible large-scale source of trained, disciplined, loyal and equipped government agents was the army. The Roman army was the means by which the state exerted its authority, manifested its presence and symbolized its power. Soldiers were also by far and away the most literate and organized part of the population and this was especially true in the provinces. The evidence for this is conclusive. Military communities, including colonies of veterans, were far more likely than other settlements to leave an epigraphic record of their presence, both in the form of records of the unit involved or individual soldiers. In places where written documents survive, principally Egypt and Britain, the same bias appears to be true.[35] Soldiers, including praetorians, turn up in innumerable capacities, serving for example as police, surveyors and engineers.

In this broader context the Praetorian Guard played an exceptionally important role because its members were the most visible evidence of imperial authority in Rome and Italy. Exactly where they were based in Italy outside Rome is a matter for debate. A concentration of Augustan-date tombstones of members of the Guard at Aquileia in north-eastern Italy makes that a prime candidate for the location of several cohorts. Some were perhaps located at another, as yet, unidentified north Italian settlement though the port of Rome at Ostia is another possibility, as well as Tivoli, Preneste, Anzio and Terracina; so also is a base located near the Campanian city of Nuceria.[36] Evidence from later dates found at, for example, Pompeii, London and North Africa shows that individual praetorians or detachments could be operating on state business almost anywhere.

The emperor, literally, could not do without the Guard. Recognizing this, Augustus had made it permanent. The Guard was essential for his personal protection, to assert his authority and to carry out his commands, which became increasingly varied and pragmatic. Such duties could include suppressing slave rebellions, dealing with public order and even staffing a prison. In time the need for the ruling house to stay in position would involve the Guard more and more in secretive activities including spying on the public, assassinating enemies of the state and other clandestine operations. These went on while the public pretence of the principate as a benign and peaceable restoration of the old order was maintained. Some praetorians enjoyed substantial personal reputations. Vinnius Valens was a praetorian centurion during the reign of Augustus who was memorialized on his tomb for his strongman antics which included holding up wine carts while they were emptied, or using his weight and strength to force wagons to come to a halt with one hand. So famous was Valens that Pliny the Elder included his story in a collection of anecdotes about human physiology, because in Pliny's time Vinnius Valens' tomb was still well known.[37] The anecdote suggests that the centurion's vast strength helped add to the praetorians' more general reputation for power.

It is hard to see how the emperor could have acted without the Guard, especially in times of emergency. The impression is of an organization that acted as a kind of all-purpose state contractor, doing whatever was necessary because there was no one else available or qualified to fulfil the state's requirements. In short, if the Praetorian Guard had not existed it would have been necessary for Augustus to invent it or something very like it. Conversely, the Guard could not do without the emperor. Without him, the Guard had no identity, no purpose and – crucially – no pay. The praetorian soldiers had to back the emperor, or an emperor, or else they would cease to exist, or at the very least find themselves returned to the garrisons whence they had come. In this respect, so long as the Guard existed there would, by definition, be an emperor whom they supported. This loyalty, however, was conditional and transferable.

In this context, the whole nature of the Roman military dictatorship has to be questioned. The Roman Empire better resembles aspects of the modern totalitarian state where military-style authority, order and discipline take on special importance because in practice it is perceived as the only way of creating and enforcing stability. Unlike the twentieth-century Fascist military dictatorships, however, the Roman Empire had no 'ideology' of a militarized corporate state. If the Roman world had any political ideology at all it was of a proto-democratic civilian state in which military power was limited and contained. Although consuls served as generals the award of *imperium* was always on condition of limited tenure and geographical extent. The Roman army was thus in theory emphatically no more than a temporary or occasional adjunct to the civilian Republican state. This does not conflict with the other Roman ideology of a divinely ordained and unlimited Empire won through brilliant military victories. The prize and aspiration of that ideology was the utopia promised by Jupiter of a future world in which war has been set aside in favour of a peace enjoyed by all and overseen by a beneficent Roman power. In his Fourth Eclogue Virgil also wrote of the return of the Golden Age and a new generation that had come down from Heaven to rule the world.[38]

The reason the Roman world relied on the use of the army in so many contexts was because within the limits of the era there was no other way to manage such a vast extent and range of territory. In the older, 'civilized', provinces around the Mediterranean the tradition of urban government was sufficiently well established for the Romans to need to do little more than re-brand the cities that passed under their control, with Greece and Asia Minor being especially good examples of this. Here the need for military reinforcement was limited. In the past the Romans had used the institution of the military colony as a kind of median between garrisoning conquered territory and leaving it to its own devices. When the Samnite town of Pompeii in Campania backed the wrong side in the Social War in the early first century BC it was first besieged and then defeated, and afterwards turned into a colony of military veterans. They provided a form of trained reserve and also a disincentive to any further local risings. Military in nature though they were, colonies were really intended to function as a form of local civil policing and as a demonstration of civilized Roman life.

The frontier provinces were a different story, with Britain (which did not come under Roman control until after AD 43), Germany and other provinces strung out along the Rhine and Danube not only requiring the physical presence of a garrison to guard the frontiers but also to manage the imposition of Roman government on those provinces. In later years, especially from the late first century AD on, the frontier forces were liable to be reinforced with detachments of the Praetorian Guard accompanying the emperor on campaign. Individual legions were commanded by men personally appointed by the emperor from the senatorial class and were overseen by the governor of the province in which each was stationed. The sheer time lag involved in transmitting communications across thousands of miles meant that legionary commanding officers and provincial governors were expected to operate with a certain amount of initiative.[39] Out in remote frontier provinces like Britain or Germany military colonies played an even more crucial role since they might serve from inception as the sole examples of Roman urban government.

Even so, the Roman Empire, compared to a modern state, was small in relative numbers and its army geographically very widely dispersed. The Roman Empire therefore relied far more on compliance than enforcement for control of its territories, even where substantial frontier garrisons were deployed. The most developed and Romanized frontier provinces had minimal garrisons. Even the largest frontier garrisons were in absolute terms small in number compared to the population.

The Roman army's structure and local autonomy allowed Roman imperial authority to operate automatically at vast distances from the centre. Without the army there would have been no other means of achieving this. There was no separate civilian 'police' force and nor, it seems, had the concept even been considered. The city of Rome was not only a state within a state, but it was also the embodiment of the state. It was the template on which the rest of the Roman world was modelled. Its vast size and, by ancient world standards, astronomical population of at least half a million meant that simply keeping the city functioning and maintaining order and stability would have challenged any ruler.[40] The Praetorian Guard, together with the urban cohorts, resolved that problem because military force was the most pragmatic solution. Indeed, military force was the only solution and over time it was used as and when required for any purpose the emperor needed. It was that dependence that also led the Praetorian Guard to recognize its indispensability and its power. Even so, there were limits to what the Guard could have done in a real crisis, beyond protecting the emperor's person, and in that sense its value was vested far more in symbolism than in a practical ability to suppress a popular uprising. Although we do not know the precise figures, as has been discussed, the maximum estimate of ten thousand in Augustus' time equates to no more than one praetorian to fifty civilians. Since we know that at this date only three cohorts were actually stationed in Rome, this means that at most there was one praetorian to every 167 civilians. If the cohorts were quingenary rather than milliary then the ratio diminishes to one to 333 civilians at any given moment.

Once the Guard was established in Italy and Rome after Actium it became immediately less clear precisely what it did during the reign of Augustus, even at the time of the one known conspiracy during the reign (see below). The lack of evidence for the Guard's activities almost certainly reflects the fact that the Guard was doing precisely what it was supposed to do, and with a low profile. Tiberius used the Guard as an escort for every foray he made into the forum or when he attended the senate. Tacitus implies that this was a manifestation of Tiberius' paranoid personality, but it is also quite possible that it was the way that the Guard had served Augustus since its permanent formation.[41]

Any opponent of the regime would have found it extremely difficult to find a way in which he could attack or criticize Augustus and expect to find enough supporters to realize his ambitions. The sheer attractive fact of peace was difficult to refute and resulted in a general mood of acquiescence. The creation of the permanent Praetorian Guard could have become a focal issue for an opposition movement since it was such an overt demonstration of Augustus' military backing, but there is no suggestion that this ever occurred, not least because the Guard appears to have remained in the background.

The most serious known instance of a conspiracy during the reign occurred in 22 BC, though it was not the only one. According to Cassius Dio, a former governor of Macedonia called Lucius Primus was on trial for starting an unauthorized war against a tribe called the Odrysae. His defence, which was being handled by a senator called Licinius (or Varro) Murena, was that Augustus had told him to start the war. Much to Murena's annoyance, Augustus presented himself at court. When Murena challenged him, Augustus said he had come in the public interest. It was a significant moment because what Augustus was saying was that he personally embodied the public interest. This was tantamount to stating once and for all that Rome's traditional institutions, principally the senate, either no longer represented the public interest or were no better than subordinate to Augustus. At this still comparatively early point in Augustus' reign it is hardly surprising that some senators resented their marginalization. Murena joined a group of senatorial conspirators led by one Fannius Caepio but they were rumbled very quickly. It is highly likely that the Praetorian Guard, no doubt equipped with intelligence gathered by the regime's agents, apprehended the plotters, though we do not know this for a fact. No trials followed since it was taken for granted that they had planned to make their getaway, which was seen as synonymous with an admission of guilt. They were all executed.[42]

The Fannius Caepio (or Murena) plot, about which we know very little thanks to the fragmented and minimal available evidence, must have been useful to Augustus. It allowed him to experiment with suppressing dissent in a way that merely made him look like the guardian of order and stability, which in many senses he was. Assuming the Praetorian Guard was involved in crushing the conspiracy, and it is inconceivable that it had not been, this would have emphasized their utility and given them an opportunity to show their loyalty. The same would have applied to other plots that surfaced under Augustus, though we know tantalizingly little about them.[43] Under the circumstances it is likely that in general a blind eye was turned to any other unsatisfactory details of Augustus' rule and his ultimate reliance on military power, however well it was disguised. In any case, as Tacitus later observed, the general acceptance of Augustus' rule derived from the fact that he had enticed everyone with 'the sweetness of inactivity', his disparaging synonym for the lethargy resulting from peace.[44]

Augustus went to a great deal of trouble to diminish any impression that force had played any part in his acquisition or maintenance of power. Up until Actium, his coins frequently bore references to military power. For example, a denarius issued in 32–31 BC shows Octavian on the reverse in military dress and wielding a spear.[45] Within a few years the tone had changed. A denarius of 19 BC showed Augustus as a bare-headed ruler with the legend 'Caesar Augustus' and on the reverse a laurel wreath with the legend OB CIVES SERVATOS ('for saving the citizens'), commemorating the declaration of this by the senate several years earlier. Other coins depicted his legal titles and powers, such as possession of the tribunician power. The army in any form, or any reference to it, became much less common than it had before 31 BC. The Praetorian Guard also went unmentioned on his coinage, a very noticeable difference from, for example, the accession of Claudius in 41. The fact that only three cohorts of the Guard were stationed in Rome and that even then they had to do without any formal or official base was an important tactic.[46] Augustus evidently wanted to avoid creating the impression that he needed the praetorians to maintain power; it also inhibited them from acting as a unified force to oust him should their loyalty have been transferred to someone else – at this early stage of the principate that was surely a realistic risk. The Guard goes without specific mention in his *Res Gestae*, though whether this was a deliberate omission or merely simplification (he does refer to the soldiery more generally) is a matter for debate.[47]

How the praetorians normally appeared in public is uncertain. Uniform seems to have been more the exception than the rule, though our evidence is mainly from later dates.[48] Going about in civilian dress would certainly have accorded with Augustus' own personal image, not only as a citizen but also as someone who proudly claimed to have restored old customs. Indeed, he made a point of encouraging the use of togas, once castigating a group of men dressed in black cloaks with an apposite quote from Virgil: 'Behold Romans, lords of the world, a race clad in togas.'[49] Since the praetorians stationed in Rome presumably spent most of their time standing guard outside Augustus' house on the Palatine Hill, the wearing of togas or tunics with the *paenula* cloak in preference to military uniform would have been perhaps more appropriate, given the regime's image in other contexts. Nevertheless, the evidence for the use of togas or tunics at any time is only occasional, though the praetorians depicted in such garb are also shown as armed.[50]

The imperial Praetorian Guard also differed from the citizen legions in one crucial respect: by whom it was led. To begin with, the military tribunes who commanded each cohort of the Praetorians were apparently under the direct control of Augustus himself. This is scarcely surprising. The events of 43 BC showed that Octavian's bodyguard of ten thousand men was very much his personal force, raised on the basis of the loyalty they had felt to Caesar. Introducing an intermediary as a leader would simply have created a potential rival and focus of loyalty.[51] By 2 BC Augustus was sufficiently secure, and no doubt distracted by other matters, to feel able to delegate command of the Praetorians to, in the first instance, a pair of equestrian prefects.

Augustus had been advised to make specific arrangements for two equestrian prefects to command the Praetorian Guard some twenty-five years earlier by his friend Maecenas as part of wider advice given to him in speeches by Maecenas and Agrippa, described by Cassius Dio.[52] The speeches are recounted in some detail, which means that they take the *form* of an exact record of what was said. However, the speech format was a routine method employed by ancient historians to allow their subjects to articulate their positions, and this makes it almost certain that Dio invented most of the content and indeed possibly all of it. Maecenas is said to have warned against the danger of allowing one man too much power and the advantage of having a second man to retain control should the first fall sick.

The question must be whether Dio was writing with the benefit of knowing about later praetorian prefects, when the post had sometimes come to be held by one man only. This made it possible for the incumbent to acquire too much power and even threaten the state, Sejanus under Tiberius being the most notorious example. It is possible that hindsight played a part in the composition of this speech, if indeed it was written by Dio. But there is no good reason to assume that it was advice that could not have been given at the time – or by the person – to which Dio attributes it. Part of the reason for Augustus' political and military success was that he sought and found good advisers. His entire acquisition and expression of power were a highly successful product of experimentation over time. He, Agrippa and Maecenas were all quite astute enough to see that the loyalty of troops to their commanding officers had been a potent factor in the civil war; handing over day-to-day control of the Guard to one man would indeed have been a risk and probably not one worth taking because it could have created a private army.

Maecenas' suggestion was part of more general advice about the use of equestrians in a wide-ranging number of positions because this maximized the development of administrative expertise. It also allowed these less affluent aristocrats the opportunity to improve their incomes, and made it possible to divide responsibility for military and financial affairs so that men of senatorial rank did not control both. There was also the benefit of extending imperial patronage to as many people as possible and thereby increasing loyalty to the state. Giving more men of rank a stake in the system brought with it the additional advantage of diminishing the impression of Augustus' power.[53]

Augustus had earlier in his reign also followed a deliberate policy of recruiting more provincial men of ability specifically to equestrian military commands of auxiliary units or legionary cohorts.[54] Applying this policy to the command of the Guard could be seen as no more than a straightforward extension of a more general idea. Interestingly, Maecenas did suggest that the Guard prefectures were appointments made for life, as should be the post of prefect of Rome (*praefectus urbi*). Other prefectures were to be for a fixed term only. Expanding his support network would strengthen Augustus' hand, should he be confronted with challenges to his power, as indeed had happened with his daughter Julia (see p. 62).

The information about the appointments to the double prefecture to command the Guard also comes from Dio, who implies that these took place at the same time as Augustus was officially given the title *Pater Patriae*, 'Father of the Country', during the celebration of Mars in 2 BC.[55] This was a purely honorific title and it seems that Augustus was already being unofficially referred to in that way. What happened now was that the senate formalized the title through a vote. It was a significant further stage in Augustus' exalted and unprecedented status. Whether there was any link with the appointment of the two prefects is not clear but it was perhaps a useful way of further distancing himself from any overt link to military power.

The use of two prefects might have been a function of the fact that the Guard was physically dispersed at this date, since it clearly would have been impossible for one man to maintain an equal level of supervision.[56] Legions were routinely split into vexillations, each made up from several cohorts, while on campaign. This did not entail the appointment of two or more legionary legates. Instead, a senior officer such as the *praefectus castrorum*, 'prefect of the camp', might be used to command part of the legion; indeed, such men might command the whole legion during an interregnum of legionary legates (such as when a legate died in post and his replacement had not yet arrived). The equestrian rank of prefect of the camp was held by a man who had risen up through the centurionate and was highly experienced, perhaps even more so than the legionary legate who was of senatorial rank. There was also the most senior tribune, an officer of junior senatorial rank early in his career and the legion's most senior centurion, the *primus pilus*, either of whom might take on temporary command of part of a legion.

The purpose may also have been to prevent any instability resulting from an interregnum should one of the prefects die in office. Comparable provision for the legions would have been very difficult to arrange because of the number of legions involved. Moreover, the Praetorian Guard was far closer to home; maintaining their trust and loyalty under the leadership of someone already known to the praetorians was likely to be more secure. It is possible, although it is not stated, that the first two prefects were in fact a senior and a deputy, with the latter earmarked to succeed the former and likewise to be replaced himself by a new deputy.[57] Maecenas' argument, if it can be accepted as advice given in or around 27 BC, is quite plausible. The pairing also emulated the tradition of senatorial magistracies always being held by multiple incumbents to prevent one man gaining too much power.

Dio gives us the names of the first two prefects of the Guard, though it is not clear if this time the appointments were for life, as Maecenas had advised. One was called Quintus Ostorius Scapula. He was a high-ranking equestrian from a favoured family who must have played a part in supporting Octavian in the civil war and during the earlier part of the reign. A relative of his, perhaps his brother, Publius Ostorius Scapula, was made prefect of Egypt, a governorship reserved for men of equestrian status, so that this fabulously wealthy province and the personal possession of Augustus after Actium did not fall into the hands of ambitious senatorial governors. Such men might use their power to turn off the grain supply and hold the emperor to ransom. So successful were the Ostorii as beneficiaries of the imperial period that later members of the family were promoted to senatorial status, one being appointed second governor of Britain between AD 47 and 51 during its conquest period under Claudius.

The other prefect of the Guard appointed in 2 BC was Publius Salvius Aper. He is only known from this single reference in Dio, though he may have come from Brixia in northern Italy on the evidence of an inscription that records a civic magistrate called Lucius Salvius Aper in 8 BC, who was perhaps a brother. Just one more prefect of the Guard is known in Augustus' reign, Publius Varius Ligur, but he is even more obscure and the dates of his tenure are lost, though he might have come from Alba Pompeia in Piedmont.[58] Presumably this man served alongside another prefect, but no others are known from the reign of Augustus. Regardless of the arguments one way or the other for having two prefects, there was no consistency thereafter in the practice, in spite of the benefits of having two. At times the Guard was led by two prefects, at others by one.

The Castra Praetoria was not built until the reign of Tiberius and, as we will see, it appears to have had no provision either for a headquarters building or a commandant's residence. This suggests that the Guard was already controlled from elsewhere, probably the imperial palace on the Palatine Hill, and is a reminder that being prefect of the Guard was not necessarily a 'military' post. The praetorian prefecture is better seen as a career political appointment, serving as a representative of the emperor. The emperor therefore obviously chose men he could trust, meaning that, depending on specific requirements at any given time, he might use the prefects to take care of issues way beyond simply commanding the Guard. It was in this capacity that the post survived long after the Guard itself was dissolved in the fourth century. By then the prefecture had evolved into an indispensable great office of state, its origins as a military command irrelevant.

The use of equestrians as prefects of the Guard was in theory a useful low-risk way of delegating power. Such men would be unable to use their positions to compete with the emperor. Equestrian prefectures also enabled the emperor to sidestep the senate. In the early Empire the senators were still coming to terms with their loss of pre-eminence and the gradual neutralization of their power and influence. Upward mobility from equestrian to senator did exist but only at the emperor's discretion. The position of praetorian prefect was inevitably one of considerable potential power and influence. It automatically brought the incumbent into extremely close proximity with the emperor, sometimes playing a dramatically important part in influencing the course of Roman imperial rule and not only for the better. The notorious rise under Tiberius of the ambitious Sejanus,[59] whose father had been praetorian prefect too, came within a whisker of toppling the emperor, while Tigellinus under Nero and Perennis under Commodus wielded extraordinary control. Tigellinus, in particular, became quite literally Nero's personal hit man. It is, however, important to distinguish the power of an individual praetorian prefect from the power of the Praetorian Guard as a whole. The two were related, but separate, phenomena, and of course Augustus had had no intention, when he created the prefecture, of facilitating abuse of the office by certain later incumbents.

Each praetorian cohort was commanded by a tribune. Although we have no clear evidence for the career structure of praetorian tribunates in the Augustan period the position is clearer for the mid-first century on. It is quite reasonable to assume that the origins of this were at least being laid under Augustus. A centurion who rose to the height of the centurionate as a *primus pilus* in a legion had acquired equestrian status and was eligible then for promotion to be the tribune of a cohort of the *vigiles*, proceeding from this to command an urban cohort and then a praetorian cohort.[60] From here his career ultimately could lead to a post as a procurator. One of the best known is Marcus Vettius Valens, whose recorded career starts with the note that he was decorated in the British war during the reign of Claudius as a soldier of the VIII praetorian cohort, before being promoted through the centurionate in the VI cohort of *vigiles*, the XVI urban cohort (see p. 113) and the II praetorian cohort. His centurionate with the II praetorian cohort was in the capacity of *exercitator equitum speculatorum*, 'exerciser of the mounted *speculatores*', in other words as a cavalry instructor and a position that took him as high as a praetorian centurion could go. From this he rose to be *primus pilus* of the VI legion and then from there to tribune of the V cohort of, respectively, the *vigiles*, the XII urban cohort and the III praetorian cohort. Subsequently Valens became a tribune in the XIIII legion and finally procurator of Lusitania before dying around the year AD 66. He cannot have held any of these individual posts for more than about two years. Similar careers are attested at later dates. In the post-Hadrianic period Aulus Scantius Aelius Larcianus was indeed a legionary *primus pilus* from which he became tribune successively of the IIII cohort of the *vigiles*, the X urban cohort and the IIII praetorian cohort. With those posts behind him he seems to have served once more as a legionary *primus pilus* and then advanced through three procuratorships, climaxing in the post of procurator of Mauretania Tingitana.[61] However, the progression was by no means standard; it was equally normal not to serve as a tribune successively of an urban and praetorian cohort.

The urban cohorts, which existed alongside the Praetorian Guard, require some explanation since at first glance it is hard to see why there would be any need for an additional force in Rome. The *cohortes urbanae* were created by Augustus to act as a military city police force but were placed under the leadership of the prefect of Rome. In AD 23 there were three urban cohorts, perhaps the original number. It is even possible that they were created by the conversion of some of the original praetorian cohorts, which would go some way to explaining why resolving the number of praetorian cohorts has been such a problem. That they were apparently numbered consecutively from the praetorian series supports this idea. The urban cohorts were increased in number to four cohorts in 69, by which time, if not before, they were milliary.[62]

One of the reasons Augustus created the urban cohorts must have been to inhibit the power of the Praetorian Guard. By creating parallel organizations with potentially similar duties or at least potentially overlapping spheres, Augustus is bound to have created rivalry. This tactic, used to great effect by Hitler when appointing high-ranking Nazis to his staff, diverted energy away from challenging his leadership into squabbling with one another. This would have been exacerbated by the fact that the urban cohorts later occupied barracks in the Castra Praetoria. We can be certain that they would have loathed each other, even if it is clear from tombstone evidence that soldiers in the urban cohorts could be promoted to the Guard in time, since this seems to be an eternal characteristic of military units of different status deployed in proximity to one another. While soldiers in the urban cohorts were paid more than ordinary legionaries, they were not paid as much as the praetorians. The evidence for this comes from Augustus' will in which they received 500 sestertii, equivalent to 125 denarii. On the basis that the legacies to praetorians and legionaries were equivalent to one-third of their respective annual rates of pay, this would mean the urban cohorts received 375 denarii per year, nominally equivalent to 50 per cent of the praetorian rate. The ratio to legionary pay was thus 1.67:1, placing them at half the ratio of praetorian to legionary pay (this is not the same as half the rate of pay).[63]

The picture was further complicated by the recruitment from freedmen of the *cohortes vigilum* in AD 6 to act as the city's night watch and fire brigade. Fires were common in Rome and extremely dangerous in a congested ancient city with many buildings made of wood. A fire in 7 BC had resulted in Rome being divided into fourteen administrative wards. At that stage Rome seems to have relied on six thousand watchmen in four cohorts, but these were not the same as the *vigiles*. A further fire in AD 6 seems to have been the catalyst for creating the 3,500-strong *cohortes vigilum*, raised mainly from freedmen. They were helped by a vast fire wall erected behind the Temple of Mars Ultor in the Forum of Augustus, a building that was dedicated eight years earlier in 2 BC, which was supposed to protect the imperial forums from conflagrations breaking out in residential areas beyond. The *vigiles* were dispersed around Rome in designated bases (*stationes*) so that they could be on hand to deal with fires and also help prevent structural collapse.[64] Organized into normal-sized centuries and cohorts, they were increased in number to seven thousand by the third century.[65]

Dio states that the *vigiles* were organized into seven cohorts and placed under the command of an equestrian prefect. It is clear from a number of prefects' careers that commanding the *vigiles* could result in promotion eventually to the praetorian prefecture.[66] The seven cohorts correspond with the fourteen wards, so a cohort must have been responsible for two wards. An inscription of 205 lists 917 men, divided into seven centuries of variable size, in the V cohort of the *vigiles*, which means it was (at least by then) milliary. At that date, on average 53 per cent of each century are listed as being made up of new recruits. This might suggest that the cohort had just been doubled in size, and coincides with an enlargement of the *vigiles* barracks at Ostia that year.[67] By working backwards, the logical inference could be that until that time the *cohortes vigilum* were quingenary in size which at seven centuries apiece means a nominal total of 3,920 to begin with, rising in 205 to 7,840. These figures are cited in various books, usually without any substantiation or further explanation.[68] It is also quite clear that they might have been milliary from the outset.

The possibility remains, therefore, that the *vigiles* were always organized in milliary cohorts numbering almost eight thousand; if six thousand watchmen had been necessary before AD 6, it is hard to see why only four thousand would have been necessary afterwards. The numbers in the individual centuries of the V cohort of *vigiles* recorded in 205 vary so much that their principal value to us is to act as a reminder that the relentless search for precision, which is such a characteristic of modern Roman military studies, is ultimately futile. The evidence for the *vigiles* is even more limited than it is for the Praetorian Guard. The only reliable rule to follow is accepting that the Roman world, for all its apparent systematization, was prone to very considerable variation in arrangements depending on the circumstances and the time. This explains the variable evidence we do have, even if the result is a frustrating collection of incongruous and conflicting data.

The likelihood is that the *vigiles* took over any firefighting duties the praetorians had been allocated up until AD 6, though in fact there is no specific reference to them at this time fighting any fires in Rome. Moreover, the *vigiles* were actually on site in Rome, whereas the praetorians at this date were still partly dispersed around Italy. An Augustan-date tombstone from Ostia commemorates a praetorian, whose name is lost, of the VI cohort, who was killed while putting out at a fire and was rewarded with a funeral at public expense. The fire is likely to have broken out in one of the port city's vast granaries, thanks to the dry conditions necessary in granaries and the heat generated by grain stocks. It is not clear whether the unnamed praetorian was there in a private capacity or with his unit. The latter is more likely since his cohort is named and he was clearly serving at the time. This incident shows that praetorians could find themselves supporting the state in any emergency capacity as the need arose. While it is possible at this date that the VI praetorian cohort was permanently stationed at Ostia, it is more likely that some sort of rotation existed, with a cohort serving there for a term and then being replaced by another. Claudius specifically ordered that a *vigiles* cohort be based at Ostia to protect against fires, and these subsequently rotated every four months.[69]

The most dramatic military disaster for Rome during the reign of Augustus was when three legions under Publius Quinctilius Varus were wiped out in Germany in AD 9. Quite apart from the humiliation of such a setback, the defeat occasioned a crisis in Rome with Augustus himself reacting particularly badly. He was terrified at the possibility of an invasion of Italy and Rome and that Gaulish and German residents of the city would rise up and join in. Some of these were serving in the Praetorian Guard.[70] Some Germans were also serving in the German (Batavian) bodyguard, which he had kept on from before Actium – though obviously new recruits must have continually been absorbed in the intervening decades. This German unit was now given up by Augustus, presumably because their loyalties seemed to him to be suspect, though according to Tacitus they were still in existence on the accession of Tiberius in 14. They were, however, sent to Pannonia on Augustus' death to help two praetorian cohorts under the command of Tiberius' son Drusus to quash a mutiny in the provincial garrison, part of whose grievances were, incidentally, the superior pay and conditions enjoyed by praetorians.[71] These events show that the role of the Praetorian Guard and other bodyguards was still evolving; in this case, their use was probably precisely because a senior member of the imperial family was involved. The Guard had been created out of a long Roman tradition of raising ad hoc praetorian units in the field to protect a general. This was probably still their theoretical role. Should Augustus have embarked on a campaign in person then their purpose as his escort would have been obvious. Instead, the Guard was gradually becoming more of a domestic protection force for the emperor and his family in Rome, but this brought with it different tensions.

Augustus' main concern for most of the rest of his reign was establishing the image of a restoration of the Republic. He presented himself as the provider and guardian of peace and stability, annihilating any remaining opposition and ensuring a succession despite the fact that he had gone to great lengths to maintain a fiction that no monarchical rule existed. There is no real suggestion after the Fannius Caepio affair that he suffered any meaningful threats either to his person or his rule and this would help explain why so little is known about the Praetorian Guard during his reign. He was able to leave Rome on three occasions between 27 and 12 BC, each time for three years. We can assume some of the Praetorian Guard accompanied him, but leaving the remainder behind would have been a useful reminder and manifestation of imperial power.[72]

The Augustan spin machine also worked overtime to create a Rome in which the methods by which Augustus had secured and retained power were quietly buried. The Forum of Augustus was a showcase of the myth that his rule was preordained and brought about through the force of destiny. A statue in his forum depicted the mythical hero Aeneas in his traditional pose escaping from Troy and carrying his father Anchises and son Ascanius. Nearby was a statue of Romulus, descendant of Aeneas and founder of Rome. The configuration was aped in central locations in other cities, such as in the porch and façade area of the Building of Eumachia in the forum at Pompeii. These loyalist displays were augmented with practical projects that enhanced Rome and the regime. Aqueducts played an important part in these. On Augustus' behalf, Agrippa improved existing water supplies and added new aqueducts. In 19 BC the Aqua Virgo was completed. It had been dedicated a few years earlier when springs were pointed out by a young girl to soldiers looking for water. The soldiers are not specified as praetorians, but since the source is only about 5 miles (8 km) from Rome it is entirely possible, indeed even likely, that they were, given the time and the fact that no other soldiers are likely to have been in the area.[73]

Military power did have a presence in Augustan Rome, albeit a subtle one, apart from the presence of three praetorian cohorts and the urban cohorts. Not only were heroic statues displayed of Augustus in military dress, but the statues of Aeneas and Romulus stood on either side of the Temple of Mars Ultor, 'Mars the Avenger'. Octavian had committed himself to building it after the Battle of Philippi in 42 BC. In doing so he was unequivocally linking his actions to the Roman people and their desire for vengeance after Caesar was assassinated in 44 BC. Caesar might have alienated many of the senatorial elite but he was immensely popular with ordinary Romans and Augustus was well aware of that. Nevertheless, the Mars Ultor complex became an important symbolic location. The senate met on the site to discuss war matters. Generals on their way to war started here and returned with their booty to flaunt it in the Forum of Augustus, and so also did imperial legates being sent to provinces on the grounds that they might have to fight a war.

The Temple of Mars Ultor was counterbalanced by the *Ara Pacis* ('altar of peace'), dedicated by the senate, located to the north of the city in the Field of Mars. It was a monumental homage to the dogma that Augustus was the bringer of peace. Completed a little earlier than the Temple of Mars Ultor, the altar was consecrated in 9 BC. It had been started in 13 BC when Augustus returned from three years in Spain and Gaul. The altar and its surrounding precinct wall depicted appropriate motifs such as Aeneas and the personification of the city, Roma, as well as a parade of members of the imperial family in suitably traditional garb. The figure of Roma nevertheless reminded onlookers that Rome was militarily triumphant. She sits atop a pile of captured arms but the image is still one of war having ceased, with Rome's supremacy being the guarantee of peace. The procession reliefs on the north and south sides, although damaged and incomplete, are entirely traditional, religious and civilian. Augustus appears, along with members of his family and various priestly officials, without a hint here of the reality of how he had acquired and retained his power.[74]

The succession was one of the most serious issues Augustus faced, not least because there was no precedent either for his position or for anything approximating to the dynastic inheritance of office. Whoever followed Augustus, a crucial question was going to be whether the Praetorian Guard's loyalty would be transferable. As Octavian, Augustus had divorced his wife Scribonia, the mother of his daughter Julia, as soon as Scribonia had given birth, to marry Livia in 39 BC. He coerced her husband Tiberius Claudius Nero to divorce her in order to facilitate the union. Livia had much to offer Octavian: she was attractive, highly intelligent and also had impeccable aristocratic origins even though her father, Marcus Livius Drusus Claudianus, had fought with Cassius and Brutus at Philippi, committing suicide afterwards. Tiberius Claudius Nero was an active opponent of the triumvirs and fled with his family away from Italy, fighting with Sextus Pompeius who was then based in Sicily. When the triumvirs negotiated a peace with Pompeius an amnesty followed, at which point Livia was able to return to Rome. Octavian seems to have been transfixed by her and there is no good reason to suppose this was untrue.[75]

The new marriage produced no children, much to Augustus' frustration, even though Livia's sons Tiberius and Drusus by her husband Tiberius Claudius Nero proved she was fertile. This left Julia as the only possible heir of Rome's first emperor, but Augustus needed a male heir. First of all he selected his sister Octavia's son Marcellus who, in 25 BC, was married to Julia. The theatre that bears Marcellus' name in Rome was planned by Caesar who had the site prepared. Construction did not follow until after Caesar's death and it is quite possible, even likely, that it continued in Marcellus' name once he rose to prominence when he married Julia.

Unfortunately, Marcellus inconveniently died in 23 BC at around the age of nineteen, which at least had the advantage of alleviating any jealousy felt by other potential rivals, such as Augustus' principal lieutenant, Marcus Agrippa.[76] No matter. Julia was then married to Agrippa in 21 BC, a union which in dynastic terms seemed to be a far more promising arrangement, earmarking Agrippa and his future children as possible successors. Meanwhile, construction of the theatre carried on and it was officially opened by Augustus in 12 BC, remaining a permanent monument to this now obscure and short-lived member of Augustus' family.

Agrippa and Julia's sons, Gaius (b. 20 BC) and Lucius (b. 17 BC), had already been earmarked as possible future heirs after Agrippa when Augustus adopted them as his sons in 17 BC. This was symbolically commemorated by the entire membership of the equestrian order when they presented honorific shields and spears to Gaius and Lucius Caesar, Augustus' grandsons and adoptive sons, on the occasion they were made consuls at the age of fourteen. This gesture by the equestrian order was a clear expression of fealty to Augustus' dynasty and was recorded on what is probably now the commonest surviving silver denarius coin of the reign.[77] However, Agrippa died in 12 BC, followed by Lucius in AD 2 and Gaius two years later in AD 4. This left only their younger brother Agrippa Postumus, then aged about thirteen, as the last grandson of Augustus. The succession was proving to be a major problem. It also raised the very serious issue of how successfully the loyalty felt by the army, and the praetorians in particular, would be transferred to any new incumbent. There was absolutely no precedent for this beyond the transfer of legions from one victorious general to another, as had happened after the Battle of Actium. In the event, Augustus had no alternative by AD 4 but to adopt both his stepson Tiberius (Tiberius' brother, Nero Claudius Drusus, had died in 9 BC) to whom he had forcibly married Julia after Agrippa's death, and Agrippa Postumus. Agrippa Postumus presented some sort of unspecified problem that made his accession increasingly undesirable.[78] By AD 9 he had been banished and it became clear that by now only Tiberius was being considered as the heir.

Tiberius was held in great esteem for his military and political experience but there is no doubt that seeking to retain power within Augustus' family was a very risky development. In a society where anything resembling a monarchy was regarded with traditional suspicion, and led to the assassination of Caesar, creating a 'royal family' was even more dangerous. It gave rise to a rumour that Livia was responsible for the systematic removal of Augustus' heirs until her own son, Tiberius, was the prime candidate.[79] The arrangements were by no means secured. Augustus' daughter and only child Julia, outraged at being forced to marry Tiberius and already notorious for her promiscuity, became embroiled in a scandalous and potentially bigamous liaison with one Iullus Antonius. This might have compromised Augustus' plan for the succession and indeed seems to have been only one part of a wider faction centred on the family of Augustus' spurned first wife, and mother of Julia, Scribonia. Julia, whose reputation for reckless promiscuity had already scandalized Rome, had been arrested in 2 BC for treason and adultery. She and her mother were forced into exile. The whole incident may have contributed to the decision to appoint two praetorian prefects in order to deflect concerns that power was too concentrated in the hands of Augustus' immediate family.[80]

The latter part of Augustus' reign inevitably involved a process in which Tiberius was awarded duplicated powers in order to ensure a seamless transition after Augustus' death. Tiberius had already been granted the tribunician power for the first time in 6 BC; this followed a triumph he had won as a result of war in Germany. The tribunician power integrated him into the strange fictional political position Augustus occupied. Tiberius, however, for a variety of complicated personal reasons and resentments, which included having been forced to marry Julia, took off for a self-imposed exile in Rhodes. He did not return until AD 2, by which time he had divorced the exiled Julia. Gaius' death in AD 4 left Tiberius now as the only viable heir. His tribunician power was renewed but another decade passed before he followed Augustus as Rome's second emperor in 14. Many questions remained to be answered about the survival of Augustus' great political experiment after his death, one of which was whether the Praetorian Guard would transfer its loyalty to the intended successor or to someone else.

CHAPTER 3

AMBITION

(14–37)

The story of the Praetorian Guard under Tiberius is largely about the prefect Sejanus and his successor Macro, and the power they wielded as the commanders of several thousand soldiers in Rome. Under Sejanus' command, all the praetorians were brought into Rome and established in their own fortified compound, the Castra Praetoria. This turned the Guard from being a potential threat to imperial power into an actual one. Sejanus exploited the vulnerability resulting from an emperor withdrawing from public life and delegating much of the everyday running of the Empire to his praetorian prefect. The dangers of an ambitious prefect were now exposed. Sejanus' fall was followed by the rise of Macro, his successor who, in the interests of securing his future under Tiberius' successor Caligula, hastened Tiberius' death, becoming the first praetorian prefect actively to cause the demise of an emperor.

TIBERIUS TOOK CARE NOT to announce the death of Augustus until the latter's last grandson by Agrippa, Agrippa Postumus, had been killed. He was murdered by soldiers, undoubtedly praetorians, in the form of a centurion and a tribune. According to Tacitus, the instructions sent to the tribune guarding the young man came from Tiberius but with the pretence that they originated with Augustus, ordering Agrippa Postumus be killed on the same day he died.[1] Tacitus regarded this as implausible, and took it for granted that Tiberius was behind it. The actual killing was carried out by a centurion who said that he had been ordered to do the deed, something that Tiberius denied had anything to do with him. Tiberius ordered that the senate be informed. This caused an equestrian called Sallustius Crispus great disquiet; he had carried the original instructions to the tribune and was very worried that the truth now might come out. So he warned Livia that these sorts of goings-on in the imperial household needed to be kept quiet and away from the scrutiny of the senate.[2] The episode illustrated how the Guard was already liable to be used as a kind of private secret service hit squad, engaging in clandestine activities and subterfuge on behalf of the emperor.

Perhaps the most remarkable fact about the accession of Tiberius was that although the two consuls for the year 14, Sextus Pompeius and Sextus Apuleius, swore allegiance to him first, the next to do so were the prefect of the Praetorian Guard, Lucius Seius Strabo, and the prefect of the corn supply (*annona*), Caius Turranius. Only then did the senate take its turn. It was a mark of how important the Guard was already becoming or, to look at it another way, it was indicative of the marginalization of the senate in a system where the head of state was now a dynastic emperor, regardless of the constitutional window-dressing. Tacitus acerbically dismissed this as a time when senators and equestrians were 'plunged into slavery'.[3]

Tiberius was equipped with the same level of formal powers that Augustus had enjoyed, even if he lacked the same extraordinary level of prestige and *auctoritas*. This was in spite of the fact that his career as a general and senator placed him at what would have been in any other circumstances a very high level. In 20 BC, when aged only twenty, it had been Tiberius who received the standards lost by Caesar's then co-triumvir Crassus at the Battle of Carrhae in 53 BC against the Parthians. He had also saved Rome during the Illyrian Revolt of AD 6–9, and led the stabilization of the Rhine frontier after the Varian disaster in AD 9. His military reputation greatly facilitated the transmission of power.

Tiberius' elevation to the principate was thus more or less automatic, despite the process of succession being unprecedented. It was also extremely difficult, fraught with risk and uncertainty. To his credit, Tiberius made no attempt to match Augustus. Instead he posed as guardian of his stepfather's name and reputation. Since Augustus had left each praetorian 1,000 sestertii in his will, twice the amount bequeathed to troops in the urban cohorts, and more than three times that set aside for legionaries (300 sestertii), we can easily gauge how important he felt it was to ensure their loyalty was retained.[4] The figures maintained the differential with the rest of the army that had been established from the inception of the Guard as a permanent body. The rates correspond surprisingly well with the rates of pay estimated from Tacitus' account of the grievances felt by legionaries on the frontier about the fact that praetorians were being paid at a ratio of about 3.2:1 compared to them.[5] At 3.33:1 the ratio for the bequests in Augustus' will was similar and was based on the need to use rounded figures as discussed earlier. If the praetorians were to be awarded 1,000 sestertii (250 denarii), matching the amount they may have been paid then thrice annually, then maintaining the same ratio applied to pay would have meant giving legionaries either 312.5 or 333 sestertii each as a bequest. It was obviously much simpler to round this down to 75 denarii (300 sestertii), which is what they were paid every four months. Given that there were far more legionaries than praetorians, the saving was substantial (around 1.5 million sestertii).

With the Guard's loyalty purchased, Tiberius took no chances. The Guard was instantly mobilized to be with Tiberius wherever he went, accompanying him into the forum or into the senate, in accordance with its primary function. To assert his control of the praetorians Tiberius gave them their new watchword when Augustus died.[6] This was probably the moment, if Tacitus' description of events can be taken at face value, when the Guard first appeared openly as a public display of an emperor's power. The symbolism of being able to grant a military watchword as a mark of the transition of power was considerable and reflected the inherent nature of the principate, however carefully cloaked it had been in civilian and constitutional guise. Tiberius had good reason to use the praetorians like this. The armies in Illyricum and Germany mutinied when they heard about his accession, the latter resenting that they had not chosen the emperor themselves and preferring their then commander, Germanicus. Interestingly, the mutinying legionaries also demanded the same level of pay enjoyed by the praetorians.[7] The mutinies were suppressed but they demonstrated how vulnerable a new emperor could be.

Although Tiberius focused his immediate attention on the funeral obsequies for Augustus, the use of a military guard of forty praetorians at the funeral became a worrying source of possible ridicule; even though Augustus' takeover of the state had been so comprehensive, apparently he had still felt the need to make provision for military protection in order to ensure his funeral went off peacefully. Tiberius also felt sufficiently insecure that he dared not allow Seius Strabo, the praetorian prefect, to leave Rome to help crush a mutiny in Pannonia.[8] This showed a remarkably conscious dependence on the praetorians from the outset and it must have communicated to the Guard how much latent power they might have.

Tiberius, however, had a potentially sound practical reason for placing himself in such an unequivocal position. Although Tiberius had had a very successful military career, his nephew Germanicus, son of his deceased brother Nero Claudius Drusus (d. 9 BC), was not only similarly successful but also extremely popular, especially with the Rhine army, and a good deal younger. In AD 4 Germanicus had been adopted by Tiberius at Augustus' insistence. This implicitly marginalized Tiberius' own son, Drusus, from the line of succession. Germanicus was married to Augustus' granddaughter Agrippina (the Elder), meaning all their children were descended from both Augustus and Livia, a fact enhanced by Agrippina's inspiring fertility. Drusus was married to his cousin Livilla, sister of Germanicus, daughter of Tiberius' brother Nero Claudius Drusus and Antonia Minor, herself daughter of Antony and Octavia and therefore Drusus could only claim descent from Livia. Moreover, Drusus' great-grandfather was an equestrian called Pomponius Atticus, which was something of an embarrassment to the senatorial Claudian family.[9] So, in terms of lineage, it was not surprising that Germanicus and his family were favoured by Augustus. Since Tiberius was already fifty-four when he became emperor, it is obvious that Augustus had foreseen the need to set out plans for the succession, especially having already seen Marcellus, Agrippa and his grandsons predecease him.

Shortly after Tiberius' accession, Seius Strabo's son Lucius Aelius Sejanus was appointed co-prefect. This particular example of nepotism, both routine and completely accepted in the Roman world, was to have devastating consequences. Within a year Sejanus held the position on his own when his father was promoted to the most senior equestrian post, the prefecture of Egypt, where he probably died in office. This is the first clear example where the inconsistency in the number of prefects becomes obvious. Seius Strabo had held the position on his own before his son joined him. The two men made an impact. After Sejanus' fall some eighteen years later, an equestrian called Marcus Terentius defended Sejanus' record to the senate, recalling how impressed he had been by father and son commanding the praetorian cohorts together at this early stage in Sejanus' career. The senator and historian Dio wrote in the early third century and took a different view. He had access to two centuries of imperial Roman history. With this before him he was able to state unequivocally that, with the single exception of Plautianus under Commodus, no other praetorian prefect had come close to Sejanus in terms of power gained.[10]

Sejanus had a trusted pedigree as a member of the equestrian order. This must have contributed to the ease with which he inveigled himself into Tiberius' favour from the moment of his appointment, so much so that the emperor would come to call him *socium laborum*, 'my partner in labours'.[11] His father had been on the staff of Augustus' grandson Gaius before rising to the position of prefect of the Guard, which from AD 12 he held jointly with his son. It is hardly surprising that Tiberius, the most reluctant of emperors, fell into Sejanus' trap, or at least so it seemed.

Sejanus soon had a chance for an outing with part of the Guard. The death of Augustus occasioned a mutiny amongst the Pannonian legions in the Emona (Ljubljana) region in the summer of AD 14. At the time the Pannonian units were under the command of a former consul (AD 10) called Quintus Junius Blaesus, who happened to be Sejanus' uncle. Blaesus suspended normal military routines in observation of Augustus' death but the consequent inactivity led the soldiers to listen to a barrack-room troublemaker called Percennius. Percennius had a sharp eye for what were quite legitimate grievances over ludicrously extended periods of service, poor pay compared to the praetorians and deductions for equipment. Blaesus managed to calm the malcontents down and agreed that his son would lead a deputation on their behalf to Tiberius.[12] Unfortunately, this only achieved a very brief respite before the mutiny erupted again, this time over Blaesus' personal troop of gladiators whom he employed to execute soldiers. Before long the chaos led even to the VIII and XV legions planning to fight each other.

When this news reached Tiberius, he sent his son Drusus with two praetorian cohorts and a group of 'first citizens' (these included senators who had reached proconsular rank) to find out what was going on and make appropriate decisions on the spot. This is the first attested use of imperial praetorian cohorts 'in the field'. It is possible that Drusus collected the praetorian cohorts from Aquileia, on the route from Rome to Pannonia. Drusus and the two praetorian cohorts were also accompanied by a unit of praetorian cavalry and the best troops in the German unit, called by Tacitus 'the guards of the emperor'. Sejanus was sent too, so that he could watch over Drusus; this was a mark of his already conspicuous influence over Tiberius. Dealing with the mutiny proved far from straightforward. Ringleaders openly threatened praetorian soldiers, while the praetorians themselves, along with the legionary centurions, killed soldiers who strayed outside the camp.[13] In the end, filthy weather in the winter of 14–15 brought the mutiny grudgingly to an end.

From 15 Sejanus was serving as sole prefect. He was the first of the praetorian prefects to experiment with the power and influence the position enjoyed, and thereby also with the potential power of the Guard as a political force. For the moment, Sejanus' grand ambitions were not evident, if they even yet existed. Theatres in Rome were becoming more frequently associated with violence. In 15 the violence became worse. In one incident an unnamed tribune of the Guard was injured and a centurion and a number of soldiers, presumably also praetorians, were killed. The senate discussed the problem and decided that praetors could order performers to be whipped. A tribune of the plebs, Decimus Haterius Agrippa, vetoed the proposal as was his privilege, following an earlier decision of Augustus to treat such people as sacrosanct. Haterius Agrippa was related to Germanicus by marriage, so this might have been seen as a sideswipe at Tiberius since the praetorians were by definition his supporters. Gallus' actions might have led to a split in the imperial family. In fact, no such split occurred, not least because, according to Tacitus, Tiberius regarded Augustus' decisions as sacred. Nevertheless, it was a significant risk because there was a real possibility that the Guard could have regarded this as a betrayal of mutual loyalty. The Guard was, however, becoming more and more obviously an imperial dynastic protection force, or at least so it appears to us. With so little information about the use of the Guard during Augustus' reign, one cannot rule out the possibility that practices and usage attested under Tiberius had already been established.[14]

In 16 the senator Marcus Scribonius Libo Drusus was put on trial, accused of conspiring to start a revolution. An adjournment was agreed so that the investigation could be pursued by interrogating his slaves. Libo was allowed home, but soldiers surrounded his house and disrupted his final dinner party. If the purpose was to spur Libo Drusus on to take his own life, it worked. The soldiers must have been praetorians, here acting as the intimidating and unconstitutional force of the principate.[15]

Tacitus made much of the idea that there was intense rivalry at the imperial court between the supporters of Drusus and Germanicus. Tiberius undoubtedly promoted his son's interests, sending Drusus to Illyricum in 17 to improve his military experience. In reality Tiberius also gave Germanicus opportunities to enhance his own popular standing. Soon after Augustus' death, Germanicus had quashed mutinies in the frontier garrison in Germany. The dangerous situation was primarily defused when Germanicus sent his pregnant wife Agrippina, Augustus' granddaughter by Agrippa and Julia, and their son Gaius (the future emperor known as 'Caligula') away from the volatile legions. The legions concerned were horrified – both mother and son were held in enormous esteem by the soldiers, who liked to think of themselves as their guardians. Chided by Germanicus, the mutiny collapsed in short order, enhancing his prestige even further. The soldiers begged that he would lead them against the German tribes.[16]

The war commenced with an assault on the Marsi. Germanicus began the war with a nocturnal assault on the tribe after they had enjoyed a festival. With characteristic ruthlessness, the murderous destruction involved killed everyone and anyone his legions encountered over a fifty-mile area. Determined to expiate their mutinous crimes, the legions were easily whipped up by Germanicus in the fighting that followed when other tribes joined in. The following year Germanicus reached the location where Varus and his three legions had been destroyed in AD 9. In 16 Germanicus crossed the Weser and fought the Cherusci at Idisiovisa. At this battle Germanicus advanced with auxiliary units of Gauls and Germans, four legions and two praetorian cohorts. It is likely the two praetorian cohorts had been with him all along.[17] In this capacity they were acting as if they had escorted the emperor on campaign – which, with Germanicus as Tiberius' proxy, to all intents and purposes they had. This single episode is a useful indication of how praetorians could be deployed for military purposes. Since we cannot be certain of the size of praetorian cohorts at this time, these two amounted to either one thousand or two thousand men. Even the upper estimate equates to only 10 per cent of the legionary force of around twenty thousand men. We might also assume therefore that at least seven praetorian cohorts remained in Italy and Rome, but given the piecemeal evidence there is every possibility that some of them had been deployed elsewhere as well.

Despite the violence and the victories, Germanicus' war in Germany was inconclusive and expensive in terms of Roman losses, so he was recalled. Tacitus believed that Tiberius was simply jealous and sought to frustrate Germanicus, who thought he was within sight of a major success. This was typical of Tacitus' depiction of Tiberius as a paranoid, jealous and vindictive emperor, but Tiberius may well have had a simple and practical reason. If Germanicus was the principal heir and the war had achieved all it really could, then perhaps the time had come when Germanicus could gain other useful experience and be withdrawn from danger. Tiberius allowed Germanicus the privilege of a triumph in 17.[18] Had he and Drusus survived long enough to be rival candidates for the succession after Tiberius, it would have been interesting to see which of them was backed by the Guard. In the event, neither had many more years to live.

Germanicus' triumph in Rome in 17 advertised and enhanced his prestige, belying the idea that Tiberius had set out to damage his nephew and adopted son. Germanicus was then sent to the east to act as an imperial deputy in the region. Unfortunately, he fell out with the new (and thoroughly corrupt) governor of Syria, Gnaeus Calpurnius Piso. The dislike may have been purely personal but it became impossible for them to work together; Tacitus was content to put all the blame for this on Piso. By 19 Germanicus had come back from a trip to Egypt but fell ill on his return to Syria, believing that Piso was operating black magic against him. According to Tacitus, various clues such as human body parts, spells and curses were found in Germanicus' room. Germanicus denounced Piso and then died. Piso is reputed to have engaged in an unseemly 'orgy of celebration' when the news reached him on the island of Cos. When he subsequently made something of a triumphant arrival in Rome to face retribution, even mooring his ship beside the Mausoleum of Augustus, he provoked popular outrage. Piso, however, committed suicide during his trial when it became clear that Tiberius was not going to support him.[19]

In the meantime Agrippina headed to Italy with the ashes of Germanicus. She was met at Brundisium by two praetorian cohorts.[20] Their presence at this moment symbolized both the significance of Germanicus' passing and their role as a prestige escort for members of the imperial family. It has never been clear, however, whether any specific criteria were applied when members of the imperial family received praetorian protection.[21] The Guard was becoming an integral part of the everyday expression and manifestation of the emperor's power, status and public image. Accordingly, the praetorians accompanied Agrippina and her husband's ashes across Italy, the Guard's officers carrying the urn themselves. With Germanicus dead, Drusus now became the obvious heir, with his own son Tiberius Gemellus (b. 19) next in line. He faced an obstacle in the form of Sejanus.

It was apparent as soon as 21 that Sejanus was a force to be reckoned with. That year a new proconsular governor of Africa was required. One of the candidates was Marcus Aemilius Lepidus, a man with a substantial aristocratic pedigree. The other candidate was Junius Blaesus, Sejanus' uncle. Aemilius Lepidus offered a number of family and personal reasons why he should be passed over, fully recognizing that Blaesus' connection to Sejanus made him far more powerful. Blaesus was duly given the job.[22]

As is the case so often in history, a chance event now helped Sejanus, who had the wit to capitalize on the opportunity. The huge theatre built by Pompey the Great in 55 BC burst into flames in the year 22. The fire was contained, thanks to quick work by Sejanus, and spread no further. Tiberius heaped praise on Sejanus for his assiduous efforts in controlling the conflagration and thereby delivering Rome from what could have been a catastrophe. There is no specific mention that the praetorians were involved in dousing the flames, but it must have been the case that they were, acting feverishly alongside the *vigiles* either under Sejanus' orders, or at the very least in his name. Either way he took the credit as men like Sejanus always do. The senate, presumably with an eye to the sort of crawling adulation that might save their own skins, voted that a statue of Sejanus be erected out of gratitude next to the theatre.[23] One dissenter to this sycophantic gesture would pay with his life a few years later.

The career of Sejanus now began to expose for the first time how dangerous the commander of the Guard could become. For the moment Tiberius seems to have been wilfully unconcerned. Sejanus made his first significant move the year after the fire at Pompey's theatre. His ambition in the post was unprecedented, but it was his reorganization of the Guard that turned out to be the most important permanent change, and it would last until the year 312. By 23 Sejanus had installed all the praetorian cohorts in the Castra Praetoria in the north-eastern part of the city. This vast complex, begun in 20 and surrounded by four walls in the manner of a permanent fortress in one of the frontier provinces, transformed the significance of the prefecture of the Guard, 'up till now of slight importance'.[24] It is worth noting that Tacitus specifically says at this point that until this time the praetorian cohorts had been *dispersas per urbem*, 'dispersed throughout Rome'. He makes no reference to them being anywhere else in Italy, even though we know this was the case under Augustus. This must mean that the Praetorian Guard had *already been* brought into Rome in their entirety, perhaps when Tiberius became emperor and made overt use of the praetorians, billeting them in various locations round the city (notwithstanding the fact that some were almost certainly allocated to various ad hoc duties in Italy). If so, the creation of the Castra Praetoria at this point would have seemed more pragmatic and less radical (Plates 3, 4 and 5).

The new base would have resolved at a stroke the everyday problems of organizing the Guard, distributing duties, keeping order and storing equipment. The Castra Praetoria, which would remain a permanent feature until the Guard's disbandment under Constantine almost three centuries hence, meant also that the 'soldiers were placed in his [Sejanus'] hands'.[25] Sejanus had some very sound practical reasons for this which no doubt assisted in securing Tiberius' approval for the new installation. It now became possible to maintain reliable discipline throughout the whole Guard and also be confident that any orders reached them all at the same time. Locating them in their own dedicated barracks would also keep them out of trouble in Rome. Of course it also made the Guard a more obvious force, inspiring 'everybody with fear', and this would have been most obvious to the praetorians, as it clearly already was to Sejanus.[26] This also went some way towards improving the ratio of praetorians to members of the city population and thus the practical prospect of controlling any disturbances.

The move into the Castra Praetoria amounted to the Guard being refounded by Tiberius. This may explain the appearance of the distinctive scorpion emblem that can be seen on some depictions of praetorian shields and standards, along with more routine devices such as lightning bolts. It has been suggested that the scorpion must be connected with Tiberius because it was his birth sign.[27] The mostly likely time for the inception of this device then would be the time all the Guard was moved into Rome. The praetorians were around this time joined by some of the men of the Misenum fleet, the *Classis Misenensis*, also founded by Augustus. Occasionally described as the naval wing of the praetorians, its manpower was largely drawn from the eastern Mediterranean area.[28]

Sejanus' ambitions were, for the moment, frustrated by the fact that not only was Drusus alive, but he also inconveniently had a living son in the form of Tiberius Gemellus. Moreover, Drusus bitterly resented the way an upstart in the form of Sejanus was being regarded as the emperor's 'partner in labours'. With breathtaking audacity, Sejanus was already having an affair with Livilla, Drusus' wife. This was a course of action he adopted allegedly as the best means of securing Drusus' death, by convincing Livilla that her husband's murder would open the way for the pair of them to seize power. Dio claimed that sleeping with the wives of important men was a key technique Sejanus employed in order to find out what was going on and who was saying what about whom.[29] Whether Sejanus genuinely operated to quite that reckless extent matters probably less than the fact that it was clearly believed; certainly it would have helped maximize his perceived power and ability to find out crucial and incriminating information. According to Tacitus, Sejanus was not prepared to leave his future to chance, not least because his indiscreet comments about his ambition were openly talked about by his wife, Apicata.

Sejanus decided therefore to assassinate Drusus, using poison to be administered by a eunuch on his staff called Lygdus. The reason Lygdus obeyed was because Sejanus, apparently covering all possible avenues, had been sleeping with him as well as Livilla, and by these means had beguiled them both into his designs.[30] However, we should be careful with such claims. The allegations made about Sejanus' youthful pimping and sleeping with Lygdus may be true, but they may also fall into the more general ritual of character assassination that ancient historians were so inclined to indulge in. Since Sejanus had turned out to be so thoroughly rotten, corrupt and cynical, he would have been regarded by those historians as a lost cause from the day he was born. Therefore any scurrilous rumour, however obscure, was likely to be gleefully incorporated into a canon of malignant criticism of his malevolence and opportunism.

As the poison took hold, Drusus' health deteriorated and he died, much to Tiberius' horror, though at this time the emperor had no idea that foul play might have been involved (if indeed it had been). Such was his trust in Sejanus that he believed the prefect's story that Drusus had been planning to poison Tiberius.[31] Drusus' death was extremely convenient and it is not therefore surprising that it was believed he had been murdered both at the time and afterwards.[32] Sejanus had divorced Apicata in 23 in order to encourage Livilla's belief that his intentions towards her were sincere and to allay any suspicions that he had an ulterior motive.[33]

Explaining why Tiberius had fallen so easily under Sejanus' control is difficult. Tacitus is not particularly helpful here, dismissing Sejanus' cunning as the principal cause, since it was precisely that which led to his downfall. Tacitus preferred to attribute Sejanus' rise to the wrath of the gods. His description of Sejanus' ambition and his assiduous efforts to achieve supreme power makes for a more convincing explanation. If Sejanus was calculating and very convincing, then so was Tiberius vulnerable and very susceptible (or so it appeared). Sejanus also realized that his command of the Praetorian Guard had provided him with the means and status to pursue his intentions. The phrase Tacitus used was *magna auctoritate*, meaning 'great influence' of a kind magnified to the extent that it was almost venerated.[34] On the other hand, such was Sejanus' ambition that it is no less plausible that he was readily exploited by Tiberius, whose disdain for the senators might have stimulated him to use Sejanus as bait. Certainly, given how the story of Sejanus ended, there is circumstantial evidence to suggest that this was what was really going on.

Sejanus had successfully managed to set behind him his youthful career as a pimp in association with Gaius, Augustus' grandson. That his uncle, Quintus Junius Blaesus, was a friend of Tiberius seems to have helped. While Sejanus clearly had some loathsome characteristics, he must have had sufficient charisma and charm to extricate himself from his disreputable past. One problem Sejanus potentially faced was the simple fact that he was an equestrian. This inevitably excluded him from the high office open to those of senatorial rank, but emperors were prone to be suspicious of ambitious senators and this turned out to be no obstacle to proximity to Tiberius. Tiberius selected a small number of equestrians to form part of his most intimate circle. In addition to Sejanus, another was Curtius Atticus, later killed by Sejanus. Sejanus also had unusual connections. It seems that he had been adopted by the senator Gaius Aelius Gallus, which explains why his name differed from his real father's.[35] Technically, the adoption would have legitimated Sejanus having a senatorial career, but he must have decided that the prefecture of the Guard offered him more real power, and personal access to the emperor. If so, he was right on both counts.

With Drusus dead in 23, the way was open for Sejanus, at least in the short term. Germanicus' brother Claudius was regarded as totally unsuitable to serve as a successor because of his physical and mental ailments, while Germanicus' sons, Nero (b. AD 6), Drusus the younger (b. AD 7) and Caligula (b. AD 12), were still too young. It was clear though that before too long the elder two would reach adulthood and present an insurmountable challenge to Sejanus, so long as they lived. There was also the less pressing question of Tiberius' grandson, Tiberius Gemellus (b. AD 19). All these boys shared one inalienable fact: they were members of the imperial bloodline, which Sejanus obviously was not. Agrippina's children were descended from Augustus through her mother Julia, Augustus' daughter. Gemellus was descended from Octavia, Augustus' sister.

In the meantime, in the summer of 24 the Guard found itself dispatched to deal with the treacherous actions of one of its own former members. Titus Curtisius (or Curtilius) is described by Tacitus as 'formerly a soldier of the praetorian cohorts', rather than expressly as a veteran, making it possible that he was dishonourably discharged.[36] If this was the case, it would perhaps help explain his actions. Curtisius had started to stir up a slave rebellion, something most free Romans were terrified of because of the rising numbers of slaves. Curtisius led meetings in Brundisium (Brindisi) and then published his manifesto, posting it in public. The rebellion was crushed by the timely intervention of the quaestor Cutius Lupus, who was in the area. He took advantage of a marine force that happened to make port, presumably at Brundisium. When the news reached Tiberius, he sent a praetorian force under a tribune called Staius down to arrest the ringleaders and bring them to Rome.[37] Clearly the Guard was also being used to protect the wider public and not just the emperor.

Meanwhile, Agrippina also presented a threat, not least because of the remarkable cachet she had established with the army.[38] The hostility between Sejanus and Agrippina and her family worsened, with Tiberius contributing to deteriorating relations.

Sejanus insisted on warning Tiberius of the existence of a *partium Agrippinae*, 'Agrippina's faction', which needed resisting. The occasion was early in 24 when priests were offering vows for Tiberius' preservation; they decided to add Nero and Drusus to the vows, apparently in the interests of advertising their loyalty to the imperial house. It turned out to be a bad idea. Tiberius was infuriated that his two great nephews might now develop ideas above their station, but his fury was deliberately cranked up by Sejanus and his talk of the Agrippinian faction.[39]

The next consequence that year was at Sejanus' behest, when he decided to prosecute key friends of Germanicus. Their fall would then spread fear amongst other members of the 'faction'. The first target was Caius Silius, commander of an army in Germany. It was alleged he had wildly bragged that his soldiers had stayed onside while the others mutinied; had his men not stayed loyal, then, so he said, Tiberius would have fallen. His wife, Sosia Galla, was also arrested on the specious grounds that she was friends with Agrippina.[40] Silius took his own life and Sosia Galla fled into exile.

Further proscriptions followed and Sejanus' confidence grew as he realized that being praetorian prefect gave him the power to destroy whomsoever he chose so long as he held the emperor's unwavering trust. He could also simply obstruct ambitions. The Numidian leader Tacfarinas was defeated by the general Publius Dolabella. Not unnaturally, in return for terminating this protracted war, Dolabella asked for a triumph. He was denied, according to Tacitus, because Sejanus did not want his uncle Blaesus' glory dented. Blaesus had fought against Tacfarinas in previous years.[41]

It was starting to look as if the position of prefect of the Guard was, under Sejanus, evolving into an executive post that propelled the incumbent potentially to the heart of imperial rule, with the praetorians themselves being of marginal significance. Part of that impression is down to Tacitus who was far more interested in the relationship between Sejanus and Tiberius. The existence of the praetorians was of course a vital part of that relationship, and so was the fact that all of them were now physically based in one place in Rome from where Sejanus could, at a word, send them anywhere he or Tiberius wanted. Tiberius perceived the praetorians as the physical manifestation of his power in Rome and Sejanus as the medium through which that aspect of his power was operated. Accordingly, Sejanus took care to make sure the power of the Guard was laid out for all to see. His efforts to destroy potential rivals or enemies were experiments in what a praetorian prefect could do, and get away with. Each move he made merely seemed to make another possible.

In 25, not long after the Guard had been brought into Rome in their new camp, Tiberius ordered the praetorians to put on an exhibition of their drill for the benefit of senators. This was apparently with the express purpose of discouraging anyone from considering a conspiracy.[42] If that was Tiberius' intention it must also have made it very clear to the senators just how integral a component of his principate Sejanus was and that making an enemy of him would also mean making an enemy of Tiberius, and vice versa. As it happens, the preceding part of Dio's accounts lists various individuals who were accused of treasonous crimes in a campaign orchestrated by Sejanus. They included the historian Cremutius Cordus, who was accused of praising Cassius and Brutus and showing insufficient praise for Caesar and Augustus in an account of the civil war and the rise of Augustus. He had even gone so far as to suggest that the tyrannicide Cassius had been 'the last of the Romans'.[43] These were the specious charges laid against him, when in reality he had merely fallen out with Sejanus, whose clients Satrius Secundus and Pinarius Natta prosecuted him. Cordus' mistake had been, three years earlier, to be the sole voice of criticism when the statue of Sejanus was erected in the Theatre of Pompey after the fire. Cordus had announced, 'now the theatre is indeed ruined'. Presented with the new charges, Cordus took the opportunity to starve himself to death, succeeding before a plan was initiated to have him force-fed so he could be put to death in a more appropriate way.[44]

So by the year 25, just over ten years into the reign of Tiberius, to fall out with Sejanus was enough to occasion a death sentence. It was a mark of the sort of place Rome was turning into. Sejanus reached the point that year where his growing confidence led him to overstep the mark. He decided to propose marriage to Livilla, Drusus' widow, and followed protocol by writing to Tiberius but misjudged the moment. His brazen audacity had gone too far, although it is easy to see why by this stage he thought he could get away with such an outrageous proposition. Sejanus' oleaginous letter to Tiberius not only emphasized his personal devotion to the duties of a soldier but also how much he valued his connection with Tiberius. Moreover, the marriage would help protect him against Agrippina. It would also of course provide him with an enhanced sense of purpose and fulfilment in the glory of the relationship, given his modest status as an equestrian, which, he claimed, he had no ambition to improve on. Sejanus even pointed out that Augustus had considered marrying Julia to an equestrian.[45]

It was obvious that Sejanus was trying to integrate himself into the dynasty: by marrying the emperor's niece he could sire another possible heir to Tiberius. This blatant move exposed his ambitions, regardless of how he dressed up the request. Tiberius' preference for his grandson Gemellus and the children of Germanicus remained firmly intact. He replied to Sejanus in an equivocal fashion. The most obvious reason he provided for refusing was simply one of status. It was inconceivable that Livilla would be content to spend the rest of her life married to an equestrian.[46] The emperor darkly warned Sejanus that senators were already complaining to him that Sejanus' advancement went way beyond what was appropriate for an equestrian. In the event Tiberius did no more than delay the marriage, which eventually took place in 31, and said that he planned to make him and Sejanus inseparable, but would not disclose (as yet) the means by which he would do that.

Concerned apparently by the revelation that he had enemies in high places, though it is hardly credible that this had not occurred to him already, Sejanus now encouraged Tiberius to withdraw from the centre of government. This appears to have been the point at which he started to contemplate becoming emperor himself, if he had not already done so. Once Tiberius was installed in a suitably remote place, he, Sejanus, would control access to the emperor who would inevitably have to hand over more and more responsibility for ruling to him. That he had several thousand soldiers under his direct command made Sejanus' plans more than a foolish conceit; he had a very real prospect of seizing power and becoming emperor if a coup was carefully timed.

Sejanus tried to manipulate events but was also helped by circumstance. Agrippina tried to secure general permission to remarry, though no specific candidate seems at the time to have been mooted; Tiberius declined her request anyway. This was scarcely surprising – had she remarried, the inevitable consequence would have been a man brought into the imperial orbit who might have presented a new threat. Sejanus would have been as unhappy about that as Tiberius, but that possibility seemed now to have been removed. In 26 he decided to tell Agrippina that Tiberius was planning to poison her at a banquet. Agrippina spurned the food only for Tiberius to be offended at the thought that he might be planning such a dark deed.[47]

Sejanus had successfully increased Tiberius and Agrippina's mutual paranoia. Not long afterwards, Tiberius and Sejanus dined in a seaside grotto near the Villa Spelunca. During the meal a rock fall buried some of the staff, to everyone's horror. Sejanus leaped to his feet and placed himself on all fours over Tiberius in the manner of a protective canopy. This conveniently created the impression that he was selfless and demonstrably more trustworthy. Meanwhile he continued to work on Agrippina's family, encouraging allegations to be made about her eldest son Nero while claiming to Nero's younger brother Drusus that their mother preferred Nero. These suggestions were neatly enhanced by the idea that should Nero be removed then Drusus' own prospects of becoming emperor would be greatly improved.[48]

By 27 Sejanus' dreams had come true. Tiberius had moved to the island of Capri, off the southern tip of the Bay of Naples. Sejanus' power in Rome was now effectively unchallenged, and even extended effectively to approving candidates for the consulship. Doubtless he exploited his position to use *speculatores* in the Guard to maintain secure communications between the island and Rome. The potential threat posed to the principate by a sole prefect of the Guard was on the verge of being realized. In 28 an altar was voted by the senate to 'friendship' (*amicitia*); it was set up with statues of Tiberius and Sejanus on either side. We have no knowledge of the feelings of the individual praetorian soldiers at this time, but it is difficult to believe they were unable to bask in some reflected glory as their commander blazed his way across the firmament. The drill display put on some three years earlier must have impressed the participating praetorians as much as it intimidated the senators. Perhaps this was when the praetorian tradition of intimidating the inhabitants of Rome, so memorably recounted by Juvenal the best part of a century later, was established.[49]

Tiberius certainly had praetorians on hand in Capri, doubtless on the face of it to protect him but also surely ordered by Sejanus to keep him fully informed of any developments. One stole a peacock and was executed on Tiberius' orders, while another was flogged within an inch of his life simply for clearing brambles in the emperor's way. Sejanus also allegedly assigned soldiers to Agrippina and Nero, ordered to spy on them and their correspondence, and record their findings in minute detail. These men are not identified as *speculatores* but it is difficult to believe they were not, since the justification for their presence must surely have been that they were part of the bodyguard for the imperial family. If there had been any restraint on Tiberius and Sejanus it had been the presence of Livia but she died in 29. A letter emerged immediately after her death in which Tiberius, thoroughly convinced by Sejanus of Agrippina and Nero's malicious intentions, accused the pair of various nebulous misdemeanours. Any further plans to follow the allegations through were thwarted for the moment by popular protests that the letter could not possibly be true.[50] But within a short space of time Agrippina and her sons had been neutralized.

Sejanus responded to this setback by aggrandizing himself even more. His birthday, on a senatorial decree, was to be publicly celebrated. Anyone who was anyone recognized the self-preserving utility of supporting Sejanus. The result was that innumerable statues of him were commissioned and set up. Since none of these survives it is impossible to know either what he looked like or whether the accompanying inscriptions made much of his position as prefect of the Guard. His prefecture was looking increasingly nominal. In some respects Sejanus was effectively operating a parallel court. Separate representatives of the senate, the equestrians and the ordinary people were sent to both Tiberius and him.[51]

It was hard to see where this could lead other than to Sejanus being declared co-emperor or seizing power for himself. In Capri the penny finally dropped, unless the reality was that Tiberius had been giving Sejanus a rope to hang himself with for years. For some time, Agrippina's youngest son, Caligula, had been resident with Tiberius on Capri. Sejanus' position was now putting Caligula at risk, quite apart from the danger to Tiberius' grandson Gemellus. If Caligula was to succeed Tiberius then it was obvious that Sejanus could not be tolerated any longer. Moreover, Caligula was the only eligible living male of the imperial family who could claim descent from Augustus himself, through his grandmother Julia, Augustus' daughter.

Whatever the truth about Tiberius' relationship with Sejanus, when he heard reports of the way Sejanus was operating in Rome, he realized that there was a genuine risk of the senate turning against him and declaring Sejanus emperor. He had been wrong-footed by the prefect's manipulation of Tiberius' associates such that they kept Sejanus informed about Tiberius' actions but not vice versa. Some of the senate had received Sejanus' favours, the rest had been intimidated by him; they all knew that he had a loyal Praetorian Guard.[52] The key question at this stage must be whether the Guard was the decisive factor. The prefecture of the Guard had been the route to the top for Sejanus. In some respects he perhaps no longer needed it since he had long exceeded his remit in that capacity. On the other hand, the simple fact of the potential force and that no one, now including even Tiberius, had anything to rival it must have rendered him apparently inviolable.

What happened next was attributed by Dio, who had presumably harvested more contemporaneous accounts, to Tiberius' dissimulation. If this was the case, then Tiberius showed remarkable presence of mind. If not, we must assume that Tiberius was still so beguiled by his prefect's attributes that he continued to shower him with favours. We cannot verify the story either way, since the account by our principal source for the period, Tacitus, is missing for part of 29 on into 31. In Dio's version Tiberius was smart enough to see that he could not thwart Sejanus by openly confronting him. Instead, he elevated Sejanus to the position of consul, though it is not certain if he continued officially to be prefect of the Guard at the same time. Through his adoptive father, Gaius Aelius Gallus, Sejanus was theoretically eligible to become a consul one day, even though he had not held any of the other senatorial magistracies and had remained an equestrian. This was also the time when, according to Dio, Tiberius started calling Sejanus 'partner in my labours', though Dio regarded this as another way in which the emperor sought to put Sejanus off his guard. According to Josephus, it was Livilla's mother, Antonia, who realized what Sejanus was up to and informed Tiberius.[53]

Naturally enough, the career of Sejanus is not mentioned on Roman imperial coinage. Indeed, there was no reason why it should have been. Such appointments never usually were. Sejanus' name does, however, appear on a copper *as* of Tiberius struck at Bilbilis (*Augusta Bilbilis*) in Spain, a local product in the Roman provincial coinage series. The obverse depicts Tiberius and his titles and on the reverse are the names and titles of the two Roman consuls for the year 31 – the emperor, and Lucius Aelius Sejanus (Plate 6).[54]

Sejanus' celebration by Tiberius as his partner was widely accepted as sincere. Since Roman society operated with a system of allegiance and deferential respect in return for protection, Sejanus was awarded the same honours as the emperor. It was agreed that the two would share the consulship every five years and, even more extraordinarily, that Sejanus' *imago* would be sacrificed to as part of the imperial cult.[55] Meanwhile proscriptions against senators who were suspected of being treasonous proceeded apace. Sejanus apparently had no idea he was to be accused of treason himself, something which conflicts with the accounts of the inside information he had been able to amass. Around the beginning of 31 Sejanus was instructed by Tiberius to go to Rome ahead of him on the grounds that he was ill. This was accompanied by a grand show by Tiberius of what a wrench this parting would be.

Sejanus also seems to have courted popular support amongst the Roman mob. A fragmentary inscription from Rome appears to quote a speech from Tiberius after Sejanus' fall. It refers explicitly to how 'Sejanus' wicked incitement' had destroyed sixty years of peace after he held 'evil assemblies on the Aventine when he was made consul'. Tiberius bemoaned the fact that he was reduced to being the companion of a walking stick, a reference to his advanced years, and to being a suppliant.[56] The significance is not entirely clear but the Aventine Hill was the traditional setting of the early Republican 'conflict of the orders' between the patricians and plebeians. In 494 BC the plebeians seceded from the Republic and withdrew to the Aventine Hill in Rome. The occasion had been mythologized in Roman lore and perhaps Sejanus had sought in some way to challenge the notion of the ruling elite by presenting himself as some sort of popular leader. This is a great deal to read into one inscription, the reading of which is not even certain. What can be inferred from the text suggests it is authentic, but the occasion to which it refers goes completely unmentioned in the extant sources. One of its greatest values is to support the Roman historians' depiction of Sejanus as someone who had gone far beyond being a mere praetorian prefect. He was in every sense a major and notorious political figure whose career was to echo down the centuries.

Once in Rome, Sejanus and the senate became the bewildered recipients of a series of increasingly bizarre correspondence from Tiberius. Some of the letters offered unctuous praise for the prefect, some denunciations, while others rewarded or punished some of Sejanus' friends. Sejanus was left thoroughly disorientated but nothing really changed. He was awarded proconsular powers, as any consul would expect to be. Although it is plain that Tacitus and Dio assumed Sejanus planned to become emperor all along, this is difficult to accept without question. Sejanus was clearly a slick operator and he must have been intelligent enough to see that his best option was to act as a protector during the principate of Tiberius Gemellus, the emperor's grandson, or that of his great-nephew Caligula who now looked as if he was being earmarked as one possible successor. Agrippina and Nero were exiled. Nero then died in early 31, probably either being killed or committing suicide, leaving only Drusus, then in prison for allegedly conspiring against Tiberius, as a potential obstacle. He was also killed in 33.[57]

Tiberius also started banning any honours that might have to be given to Sejanus as well as himself. This occasioned the perception that Sejanus' power was beginning to slide. In order to prevent Sejanus realizing the game was up, Tiberius put it about that Sejanus was to be given the tribunician power. This was tantamount to naming him as a successor, just as had happened with Tiberius himself in 6 BC. He had also offered the prefecture of the Guard to Quintus Naevius Cordus Sutorius Macro and given him instructions. Macro had served at some point as prefect of the *vigiles*, a position that would have brought him to the emperor's attention, though there is no evidence he held the post in 31.[58] Macro entered Rome at night and made contact with one of the two consuls for 31, Memmius Regulus (the other was Tiberius), and the prefect of the *vigiles*, Graecinius Laco. Critically of course the *vigiles* were not under Sejanus' direct control. On the morning of 18 October 31, Macro found Sejanus and told him that he brought news of the tribunician power that was to be awarded him.[59] Sejanus fell for it and entered the senate, now assembled in the Temple of Apollo on the Palatine Hill, delighted at this news.[60] Outside, Macro instructed the praetorians who had been guarding Sejanus and the senate to return to the camp. He achieved this by the simple expedient of showing them a letter from Tiberius granting him the emperor's authority. Sejanus was about to be hoist with his own petard. In bringing all the praetorians into Rome, he also made it possible for the loyalty of the entire Guard to be transferred to someone else in one stroke. And indeed it was.

The Guard was kept out of what followed. Under Graecinius Laco's command, the *vigiles* surrounded the Temple of Apollo to guard the senate while Macro headed off to the praetorian camp to take control there before the news reached the Guard. Meanwhile, the emperor's letter was read out in front of the senators and Sejanus, presumably by Memmius Regulus.[61] The text is not extant in any form but instead of praising Sejanus and heaping honours on him, the letter simply ran him down little by little with a litany of minor criticisms that led finally to the senate itself denouncing him. Crucially, it had been expected by the whole senate that Sejanus was about to be awarded the tribunician power. When it became apparent that no such privilege was on offer the mood changed. His supporters abandoned him and some senators restrained him from leaving. It took time to establish whether Sejanus had a dangerous support base in the senate. Memmius Regulus was worried that a vote would bring out Sejanus' supporters. Instead, he asked a single senator whether there was any good reason not to imprison Sejanus. The answer was that there was indeed no reason, so Sejanus was led out to prison by Regulus, along with other senators and Laco (Plate 7).[62]

Some, perhaps most, of the senators turned on Sejanus like dogs that had smelled blood. He was assaulted by them and by the mob outside who had followed the proceedings. With not a praetorian soldier in sight, the senators assembled in the Temple of Concordia Augusta and condemned Sejanus to death.[63] Sejanus was executed and his body cast down the Gemonian Stairs, which led down from the Capitoline Hill to the Roman Forum, a location that could not have been more prominent or public. He was followed shortly afterwards by his children. These included his son Strabo, named after his grandfather.[64] Mayhem ensued, with anyone believed to have collaborated with Sejanus being attacked. A few days later, Sejanus' former wife, Apicata, committed suicide, having told Tiberius that Sejanus had murdered Tiberius' son Drusus at the behest of Livilla, though this contradicts Tacitus' suggestion that Livilla had not been in on the plans.[65] Sejanus' remaining children were also put to death, his virgin daughter Junilla apparently being raped by the executioner in order to legitimate the execution of a female. Their bodies were also dumped on the Gemonian Stairs. Other members of Sejanus' family were hunted down and killed, including his uncle Blaesus.[66] Livilla was subsequently either killed by Tiberius or starved to death by her disgusted mother Antonia.[67] The killings were a massive act of revenge against Sejanus for coming so close to overturning the system established by Augustus (Plate 8).

As has been demonstrated by Robert Graves in his novel *I, Claudius*, it is easy enough to depict Sejanus as exclusively focused on supplanting Tiberius in order to become emperor, and Tiberius as calculating and underhand in wrongfooting the ambitious prefect. Such a depiction depends on taking at face value the way both Tacitus and Dio portrayed the two men. In reality, Sejanus' ambitions may have been less focused and Tiberius' scheming rather more strategic. It is just as possible that Sejanus' ambition increased by increments as he felt his way forward and detected what was possible in the light of the latent force he had at his disposal in the form of the Guard. Tiberius' letter to the senate, although damaging, really acted as a kind of catalyst for a great deal of pent-up resentment, but whether he really expected the outcome that occurred is a moot point. The fall of dictators, and Mussolini is an excellent example, is often accompanied by a cathartic explosion of revenge from followers who feel betrayed, usually as a result of the self-loathing occasioned by realizing they have been fooled. Today, no statue or likeness of Sejanus is known; they were all destroyed in the eruption of *damnatio memoriae* that followed. The coins struck at Bilbilis in Spain bearing his name were liable to be defaced, with the letters L AELIO SEIANO carefully chiselled off.[68] In Rome there was a palpable sense of fear amongst senators who had at least pretended to support Sejanus that they would now be the victims of vengeance. Not surprisingly, some over-compensatory gestures were manufactured in the form of a statue of Liberty to be erected in the forum, an annual festival of horse racing and wild-beast hunts to be held on the day of Sejanus' death. Awarding honours similar to the ones Sejanus had been awarded was now banned, but in short order they were soon bestowing privileges on Macro. Macro had succeeded Sejanus, presumably as part of his reward, though we do not know for certain that this was the deal. He was even awarded senatorial propraetorian status and the right to wear their toga.[69]

The Praetorian Guard, meanwhile, now found itself in a potentially very vulnerable position. The praetorians were by definition Sejanus' men but they were disgusted that the inferior *vigiles* troops had been treated as if they were more loyal to Tiberius.[70] This would have been hugely offensive to their sense of honour, given the oaths they would have taken. Enraged, they started looting Rome. No doubt, however, the favours so swiftly awarded to Macro must have helped assure them that their status was secure. This is a reminder of the difference between the office of the prefect and the praetorians themselves. Sejanus had used the prefecture as a vehicle. His behaviour depended in part on the potential force the praetorians offered; the threat was very real – Tiberius had allegedly been worried that Sejanus would take control of Rome and then sail with a naval force down to Capri to attack him. Had this happened, Macro was under orders to release Drusus from prison and declare him emperor to sidestep Sejanus.[71] Tiberius also moved to secure the loyalty of the praetorians, fully aware that despite the support they had shown Sejanus he had no choice but to buy them. He was more suspicious of the duplicitous senators who were now swearing loyalty to him when but a short time before they had been actively fawning around the very man who had betrayed him. Tiberius won the praetorians over with 'words and money', a principle that would play a decisive part in imperial events in years to come. Each received 1,000 denarii for staying loyal to him. He also secured a senatorial decree that the praetorians be paid from the public treasury. This was a very useful means of making it appear more credible that the praetorians were public servants rather than the emperor's personal staff.[72]

The real issue here is whether the outcome was what Tiberius had planned all along or whether Sejanus had been the driving force until he was rumbled. After all, the whole Sejanus affair had exposed the senators, Cremutius Cordus being one of the very few exceptions, as mealy mouthed, unreliable, self seeking and duplicitous. It is feasible that Tiberius had seen Sejanus for what he was from the outset. Easily tempted to self-aggrandizement, Sejanus was lured into a trap along with most of the senate. Tiberius had all the proof he needed, and with the praetorians secured he had the means to keep the senators under control. The truth lies probably somewhere in between. Sejanus seems, by all accounts, to have been a particularly good example of a nauseatingly greedy, ambitious and cynical opportunist, so it is difficult to believe that he was merely a victim of Tiberius' dissimulation and cynicism. On the other hand, once Tiberius had the measure of Sejanus, his response showed that he was in every respect Sejanus' equal, if not even more duplicitous.

After the fall of Sejanus, Macro remained praetorian prefect until he was removed during the first year of Caligula's reign. Tiberius' generosity towards the praetorians was short-lived. In 67 BC the Roscian Law had set aside the front fourteen rows of the theatre for the equestrian order. In AD 32 a senator called Junius Gallio proposed that this section of seating be additionally opened to praetorians who had completed their term of service. Tiberius was furious, outraged not only that a senator should deem it fit to interfere with the terms of service for soldiers when that was the prerogative of their commander (that is, himself), but also as this was not something Augustus had suggested.[73] Tiberius accused Gallio of being a Sejanus-supporter who had set out to corrupt the simple-minded soldiers by giving them ideas above their station. The incident is primarily interesting for showing that even though the praetorians were under the charge of a prefect, their real source of authority and position remained the emperor. Gallio was forced into exile on Lesbos, which proved too comfortable, and so he was brought back to Rome to be placed under house arrest.

Sejanus still cast a long shadow. Tacitus was disgusted by the hypocritical way in which so many of Sejanus' former friends denied their association with him. Informers, who in one case at least included a tribune of an urban cohort, were used to bring charges against those guilty of being involved with Sejanus. Only one, an equestrian called Marcus Terentius, was prepared to own up honestly to his relationship with Sejanus, freely admitting that he had been a friend and that he recognized this admission would now do him damage.[74] The equestrian body as a whole selected Tiberius' nephew Claudius (the future emperor) to be their special representative to carry their best wishes to the consuls.[75] Nevertheless, before the year was out Tiberius ordered the execution of anyone still in prison who was accused of association with Sejanus. He even went so far as to order the death of his great nephew Drusus, still malingering in prison.[76] Agrippina took her own life shortly afterwards, having given up hope that the death of Sejanus would bring about a reversal of her fortunes. Her tombstone, set up in the Mausoleum of Augustus during the reign of her son Caligula, survives and recounts her astonishing career (Plate 9).

Beyond Rome itself other communities asserted their loyalty to Tiberius. To fail to do so might have raised questions, though Sejanus had now become subject to *damnatio memoriae* – and could not be named. So, at the colony of Interamna Lirenas (near modern Pignataro Interamna) in central Italy an inscription was set up in 32 to the 'perpetual safety of Augusta and the public liberty of the Roman people'. The text also added a dedication to the foresight (*providentia*) of Tiberius 'now that the most deadly enemy of the Roman people [Sejanus] has been removed'.[77] It was commissioned by Faustius Titius Liberalis, a local priest of the imperial cult (*sevir Augustalis*). Such men were usually successful freedmen who had professional connections with the freeborn decurial class. Evidently, Liberalis thought it worth his while to assert his affiliations in the new climate. Further afield, in Gortyn in Crete, an even more cryptic inscription was set up by the proconsular governor Publius Viriasius Naso to the 'divine majesty and foresight' of Tiberius, specifically to the 'foresight of 18 October', the day Sejanus was toppled.[78]

Early in 33 Macro first appears in the extant text of Tacitus as prefect of the Guard. He was instructed to escort Tiberius, along with selected tribunes and centurions, on his way to the senate house.[79] This is the first description we have of the senior officials of the Guard being deployed in a practical everyday way as part of the emperor's entourage. Tacitus presents it as a new development. What was not so new was that by 37 Macro seems to have headed some way down the same road as Sejanus. Caligula, the younger brother of Nero and Drusus, and Tiberius' co-heir with Tiberius' grandson Tiberius Gemellus, had been married to a woman called Junia Claudia in 33, but she had died in childbirth not long after. Caligula next embarked on an affair with Macro's wife, Ennia Thrasylla. It is not clear whether Macro instigated this in order to ingratiate himself, or whether Caligula started the affair to beguile Macro into believing that acquiescence in his wife's infidelity would be to his advantage and that he would therefore help Caligula get rid of Tiberius. Either way, providing his wife to the emperor was a new duty for a praetorian prefect.[80] Caligula even went to the extent of promising to marry her if he became emperor. Tiberius was aware of Caligula's scheming but had a problem: his grandson Gemellus was too young to succeed. Caligula was tainted by association with Germanicus, according to Tacitus, who was convinced that hatred of Germanicus had dictated many of Tiberius' actions. The only other candidate, Tiberius' nephew Claudius, was regarded as mentally impaired. Tiberius decided to leave the future to fate, sure that Caligula would succeed him, but appeared to be resigned to the inevitable fact that Caligula would kill Gemellus and then be killed himself.[81]

Macro was clearly engineering his position for after the death of Tiberius (and was criticized by the emperor for doing so), and secured evidence to facilitate the disposal of his opponents through interrogation of witnesses and the torture of slaves.[82] Quite what Macro's motivation was is unclear. There is no sense, as there was with Sejanus, that he might have planned to take supreme power for himself. Tacitus believed that Macro had been chosen to topple Sejanus because he was even more depraved than the latter.[83] Macro seems to have acted in a more conspicuous fashion as the emperor's personal attendant. He was clearly on hand in March 37 when Tiberius was fading and received personal updates from the emperor's doctor, Charicles. Tiberius expired on 16 March, or so it was believed, and Caligula prepared to succeed him. Tiberius had, however, only plunged into a temporary bout of unconsciousness, his breathing being so light that it was assumed he had died. He rallied and called for food, causing instant panic. If Tacitus can be believed, Macro ordered Tiberius to be suffocated and everyone else to leave. Dio suggests that Macro actually participated in the smothering as a way of ingratiating himself with Caligula.[84]

The death of Tiberius thus became, allegedly, the first moment when a praetorian prefect proactively and deliberately influenced the course of history – if, of course, the reports are true. In reality his advanced age made a natural death quite possible, but such a turn of events would not have helped Tacitus or Dio. Since Tiberius was seventy-seven and ill, his death sooner or later was inevitable anyway. In practice, it made no difference: Tiberius was dead and a new age dawned.

The increase in the number of praetorian cohorts to twelve may have happened as early as the reign of Tiberius, or by 47. Typically, the evidence is as confusing as it is enlightening. An inscription, found at Marruvium (Lecce nei Marsi) in Abruzzo in Italy, concerns the career of one man, Aulus Virgius Marsus, who rose from being *primus pilus* with the III legion Gallica. He appears to have finished his military career by serving in the Guard as tribune of the XI cohort and then the IIII cohort under Augustus and Tiberius.[85] The text reads COHORT(IUM) XI ET IIII PRAETORIAR(UM), 'of the eleventh and fourth cohort of the praetorians'. Since eleven cohorts seems a strange total, and a twelfth praetorian cohort is known to have existed by 65, it is reasonable to suggest that the Tiberian increase involved three additional cohorts, taking the nine cohorts attested in 23 by Tacitus to twelve. If so, the urban cohorts, hitherto numbered X–XII in the same sequence as the praetorian cohorts, would have had to be renumbered initially XIII–XV. There is evidence for this. By 66, for, example there was a XVI urban cohort, reflecting the fact that by

69 the number of urban cohorts had been increased to four.[86] However, as is pointed out below, this all relies on the assumption that a regular numbering sequence was in use.

Conversely, it has been suggested that the XI cohort of which Marsus was tribune was in reality one of the urban cohorts, also created by Augustus.[87] The inscription was produced in a provincial town at the behest of local magistrates who might only have been dimly aware of the technical difference between the praetorian and urban cohorts which were, by then, all housed in the Castra Praetoria. If so, then Marsus had actually progressed to be tribune of the XI *urban* cohort and then to tribune of the IIII *praetorian* cohort. This would have been a natural promotion from an urban cohort to a praetorian cohort reflected in numerous other praetorian tribunate careers recorded on tombstones. Under such circumstances the word *praetoriarum* on the inscription needs to be interpreted as just generally descriptive of troops 'of the emperor's *praetorium*', and indicative of a time when specific qualification of the cohort or cohorts concerned had not yet become the standard formula.[88] In other words, there remained nine praetorian cohorts for the moment, with Marsus' XI cohort being an urban cohort. What is not in doubt is that the number of praetorian cohorts was indeed eventually increased to twelve, at least nominally. The evidence of the tombstone of Gaius Gavius Silvanus is relevant here. He died in 65 but at some point in his career he had served as tribune of the XII praetorian cohort, showing that a cohort (or at least one that bore the number XII) was created before that date.[89]

Just to complicate matters further it has also been suggested that perhaps the Augustan Guard originally consisted of twelve cohorts, with three being subsequently detached to form the urban cohorts, only for three more praetorian cohorts to be created later.[90] Although the urban cohorts were paid at half the rate of the praetorians, we do not have any evidence for that differential until the will of Augustus when the praetorians were left 1,000 sestertii and the urban cohorts 500. Certainly there is much evidence to suggest both praetorian and urban cohorts were administered in this way, operated together and were even buried together.[91] This means that it is possible the urban cohorts were created out of the praetorians during Augustus' reign. Whenever it happened, the expansion of the Praetorian Guard must have involved reorganizing the urban cohorts.

As with the praetorian cohorts, it is quite obvious that the system of numbering urban cohorts probably changed on more than one occasion and may or may not have been tied up with the system for the praetorians; it is simply not now possible to identify a single arrangement that explains the disparate evidence we have. All such discussions are generally based on the assumption that a logical and continuous numbering system was used. This was not necessarily the case. Gaps and duplications in the numbering sequence of legions are well known. The numbers XVII, XVIII and XIX were not reused after the disaster of AD 9 in which all three were destroyed. Conversely, in the 70s Britain was home to both II Adiutrix Pia Fidelis and II Augusta, distinguished by their titles rather than their numbers. Similar issues affected the auxiliary forces. Vindolanda seems to have been home at various times to the I, III and VIIII cohorts of Batavians. A II Batavian cohort is attested in Pannonia and Moesia Inferior, but nothing whatever is known of the theoretical IV–VIII cohorts which may well therefore never have existed or, if they did, may have been disbanded before they had time to leave any record. It is therefore entirely possible that for periods in the Guard's history some cohort numbers were disused or revived as the need arose, making technical discussions about precise numbering sequences futile. Evidence for a XII praetorian cohort does not necessarily mean that twelve active praetorian cohorts were in existence then and continuously thereafter. The Roman army, like much of the Roman world, seems to have been content with systems that were sometimes both illogical and irregular.

CHAPTER 4

MAKING HISTORY
(37–51)

*The accession of Claudius in 41 as the nominee of a Praetorian Guard,
agitated at the thought they might no longer have a job, was occasioned by
the assassination of Caligula in 37. Caligula was the victim of a plot in
which praetorians and senators were implicated; ironically, other praetorians secured the perpetuation of the Empire, rather than a restoration of
the Republic. Claudius, the uncle of Caligula, was thus the first emperor
whose elevation was secured at the hands of the praetorians, marking a
significant diminution in the power of the senate. Claudius' overt recognition of the reality of his succession, and the participation of praetorians in
the invasion of Britain, showed that the Guard's significance was increasing.
The nature of imperial rule was itself changing, largely under the influence
of Agrippina the Younger, Claudius' last wife, and niece, who intervened in
the praetorian prefecture appointments.*

IN THE YEAR 41 in the heart of Rome a middle-aged man stood trembling behind a curtain. His full name was Tiberius Claudius Nero
Germanicus, known to us as Claudius. He was fifty years old and the son
of Nero Claudius Drusus, son of Augustus' wife Livia by her first marriage,
and his wife Antonia Minor. Through his mother Antonia Claudius was
descended from Mark Antony and Augustus' sister Octavia. Claudius'
long-dead brother was the celebrated general Germanicus, so beloved of

94

the Roman people. Claudius was another sort of person altogether. He probably suffered from cerebral palsy, though of course no one understood that at the time. The resultant stammer and limp, and other characteristics such as a tendency to dribble when under stress, meant that he was widely regarded as an idiot and as a family embarrassment. He had held some official positions, such as the consulship under Caligula in 37 and even represented the emperor sometimes at the games.[1] Significantly, that consulship was the only one he held before he became emperor and, in his late forties by then, he was unusually old for the position. Instead, most of his life had been spent in comparative obscurity while he devoted himself to historical research and writing. In consequence, unlike so many of his relatives, he was still alive.

Claudius was trembling behind a curtain in an apartment called the Hermaeum in the imperial palace, where he lived, because the whole place was in uproar. His nephew, the emperor Caligula, had just been assassinated at the hands of an officer of the Praetorian Guard, Cassius Chaerea, and others.[2] Chaerea was a member of a conspiracy that included disaffected senators. It was a decisive moment. One of the imperial bodyguard had killed the very man he had sworn an oath to protect. On the orders of the conspirators, Caligula's wife Caesonia and their daughter were also murdered. It was clear that the plan was to obliterate the imperial family and bring to an end the age of the emperors. Claudius got wind of the assassination so he went to a balcony where he could hide behind the window curtains. One of the praetorians passing through the palace saw his feet and hauled him out. Claudius was proclaimed emperor by the praetorians. Desperate to secure their jobs, they carried him off to the Castra Praetoria.[3]

That, at least, is the story as told by Suetonius. It is vivid, ironic and dramatic. Whether it is true or not is another matter altogether. Another version, by Josephus, says the praetorians had met in advance of the assassination and decided on Claudius as a replacement so that they could put forward a candidate of their own choosing. That way they would guarantee their positions.[4] It makes no practical difference: the praetorians chose the new emperor, even if they did select someone from the imperial family rather than anyone else. Claudius was only the fourth incumbent and he was chosen because he was the only available male link to the family of Augustus. It seems that already the Praetorian Guard had reached the point where they could exert an enormous influence over historical events. Conversely, perhaps Claudius was already in on the plans to assassinate Caligula and these stories were circulated simply to avoid any accusations that he had somehow seized power. Again, it makes little practical difference to the importance of the praetorians in what occurred. Their implicit power had lain behind Sejanus' ability to pursue his ambitions but they played no collective or institutional part in determining the end of Tiberius' reign or the accession of Caligula. Within four years the praetorians had reached the point where circumstances conspired to make it possible for them to act as kingmakers.

The accession of Caligula four years earlier in 37 was, under the circumstances, what Augustus would have wanted, and the nature of the end of his reign the last thing. Through his mother Agrippina, Caligula was descended from Augustus, and through his father Germanicus he was descended from Livia. He was also descended from Agrippa and Octavia. Caligula's pedigree was therefore impeccable. Caligula appears to have been operating to some sort of premeditated schedule when it came to the end of Tiberius' life. The Praetorian Guard was clearly part of this plan, both in a straightforward practical sense and as a display of power, but it was also essential to bring the senate on side immediately. Therefore, it seems only logical to see the cuckolded Macro acting here as a source of counsel, helping and advising Caligula during the first few critical hours and days. In the first instance Tiberius had to be buried and his body was brought up from Misenum, where he had died, so that the funeral could be organized. The deceased emperor was brought in at night by praetorians.[5]

Macro was dispatched immediately to the senate with Tiberius' will and instructions that the senators should reject it on the grounds that Tiberius had lost his reason. Caligula had a very good reason for choosing this course of action. Tiberius had left the Empire jointly to Caligula and his grandson Tiberius Gemellus. At still only seventeen Gemellus was too young to enter the senate and Tiberius' decision to choose him as an heir was taken by Caligula as indisputable proof that Tiberius was mad.[6] This was obviously no more than a convenient interpretation and by having the will publicly read and rejected by the senators (rather than suppressing it altogether) Caligula achieved a public display of legitimacy. Gemellus was adopted by Caligula, an act that would have demonstrated unequivocally that the boy was not of an age to be given office, but created *princeps iuventutis* ('the first amongst the young') which made it clear he was a designated heir.[7] Why the senate acquiesced so easily is less obvious, unless the senators believed that they now had a youthful and inexperienced emperor whom they could manipulate. If so they were wrong, and when Caligula's reign had reached the point that made his removal unavoidable it was members of the Praetorian Guard, rather than the senate, who took matters into their own hands.

However, Caligula was only doing what the Roman people wanted, or so at least it seemed. On his way to Rome onlookers, delighted at the thought that their marvellous boy was to rule, showered him with proprietorial and affectionate compliments. He was acclaimed as emperor by the senate and the people as soon he arrived in the city.[8] A brass *dupondius* was issued then or shortly afterwards with an unprecedented design showing the deified Augustus on the obverse with the very prominent letters SC ('Senatus Consulto'), and on the other a seated male and the legend:

CONSENSU.SENAT.ET.EQ.ORDIN.P.Q.R

which means 'by consent of the senate, the equestrian order and the people of Rome'.[9] The SC device was a clear statement that the coin was being issued in the name of the senate and not the emperor. The reverse, which probably depicts a seated Augustus or Caligula, was an equally clear statement of the common consensus of every tier of free Roman society and without any explicit or even implicit reference to military backing. A *dupondius* was a base-metal denomination coin; its choice indicates the desire to promote the message widely and quickly.

This popular consensus may have been genuine. It was certainly very convenient and Macro must have known that it would be. Naturally, Macro's position and that of the Guard could only gain from a clear affirmation of Caligula's succession. In choosing to utilize Macro as a source of guidance, Caligula ensured not only Macro's support but also that of the Guard. The dynamic was clearly reciprocal, at least for the moment. Moreover, Caligula already enjoyed enormous popularity amongst the military thanks to his father Germanicus' enduring reputation, his mother Agrippina's unprecedented rapport with the army, as well his own childhood career as a military mascot in his father's entourage, dressed in military costume and earning his nickname *Caligula*, 'little boots'.

Caligula took care to pay out all of Tiberius' bequests to soldier and civilian alike. Crucially, this included 1,000 sestertii to every praetorian, handed out at a parade of the Guard, a sum that matched Augustus' bequest. For good measure, just in case any of the praetorians remained unclear about Tiberius' intentions, Caligula doubled the sum at his own expense. The praetorians had not been singled out for special treatment in the sense that other recipients included the urban cohorts, the *vigiles*, and the rest of the army; but they would certainly have received the most as befitted their special status. The payouts were indicative of what was regarded as appropriate behaviour and helped establish the protocols of accession. Caligula issued a brass sestertius showing himself haranguing five soldiers with the legend AD LOCUT COH, which refers to a speech (*locutio*) apparently being delivered to the praetorians.[10] Like the consent *dupondius*, it was an issue never produced before and it almost certainly records the address and payout Caligula made on his accession. It was another sign of the rising significance of the Guard and established a ritual no later emperor could risk overlooking.

Caligula was also particularly respectful to the deceased members of his immediate family. He personally recovered the remains of Agrippina, Nero and Drusus from overseas and had them re-interred in the mausoleum of Augustus. Agrippina's tombstone, erected there about this time, has survived and shows how important it was to Caligula to record his dynastic lineage. His grandmother Antonia was honoured as Augusta and, together with his sisters, was awarded the privileges of the vestal virgins.[11] These included places of honour at public games and accordingly Julia Drusilla (d. 38), Agrippina the Younger and Julia Livilla appeared with their brother when he attended the circus. They were also depicted and named on the reverse of a remarkable sestertius issued about this time. No other emperor ever had his female siblings portrayed this way. Claudius was elevated to the consulship in 37 alongside Caligula. Caligula also issued coins in memory of his parents and elder brothers, as well as a remarkable series of gold and silver coins with his own portrait on one side and that of the deified Augustus, his great-grandfather, on the other. His own conventional issues included types with legends that made specific reference to his status as Augustus' great-grandson, *pronepos Augusti*.[12] There was a very clear agenda. Caligula was asserting his right to rule on a dynastic basis. He was in power by virtue of his birthright. In reality he had no choice. Caligula was only just approaching twenty-five and, unlike both his predecessors, he had no achievements he could use to legitimize his claim. The development of this dynastic component of imperial rule would have important implications for the relationship with the praetorians. Family lineage and praetorian loyalty would play a crucial role in the transmission of the principate to Claudius when Caligula was assassinated in 41 (Plate 9).

In the meantime, one of the enduring mysteries of Caligula's reign is his degeneration into increasingly volatile, manic and unpredictable behaviour. By September 37 he had fallen gravely ill. By late October he had recovered but was a changed man. Shortly afterwards, Gemellus was murdered, allegedly for praying for Caligula to die when the latter fell sick; it appears that a tribune 'of the soldiers', presumably a praetorian tribune, was sent to kill him. According to Philo, Gemellus intended to save face by committing suicide, but was ignorant of how to do the job. He had to ask the centurion and tribune to assist him with the technicalities.

Philo's reference to the death of Gemellus includes one important incidental comment. He mentions the involvement of a centurion and the commander of 'a thousand [troops]'. Since it is clear Philo was referring to praetorians, this appears to be evidence for the fact that a praetorian cohort was milliary in size.[13] If this is correct, then it strengthens the case for praetorian cohorts having been milliary from the outset. Philo's account comes from his description of an embassy to Caligula in the year 40 and in which he participated, only two years after Gemellus' death. It is therefore likely to be broadly accurate and based on personal research in Rome.

Meanwhile, by 38 Drusilla, Caligula's favourite sister, was dead. The praetorians played a prominent role at her public funeral. Caligula and her husband, Marcus Lepidus, presided over the obsequies while the praetorians paraded around the funeral pyre.[14] The occasion was used as another dynastic showcase and reinforced the role of the praetorians. Nevertheless, Caligula's relationship with his extended family deteriorated. Allegedly, in revenge for some slight, he forced the aged Antonia to take her own life, and is said to have conducted incestuous relations with his sisters. After Drusilla's death in 38, he exiled the other two in 39, accusing them of being involved in a conspiracy led by the governor of Germany, Lentulus Gaetulicus.[15] The unparalleled issue by Caligula of the sestertius depicting his three sisters on the reverse suggests an unusual closeness, but the alleged unnatural relations may well have been a later elaboration based on rumour and hearsay, which conveniently accentuated his despotic reputation. Josephus, Suetonius and Dio all allege that Caligula slept with one or more of his sisters.[16] However, this was just one aspect of an unprecedented personality cult that Caligula gradually built up around himself. He was the first emperor to be consistently portrayed on his coinage in all denominations and all metals. This was a later development; to begin with Caligula was more accommodating, adopting a deferential approach to the senate as well as running down the treason (*maiestas*) cases that had so characterized the latter part of Tiberius' reign. He increased the number of equestrians and then promoted some to the senate, a move that was welcomed.[17]

If Macro believed that the role he had played in helping Caligula to become emperor was to be repaid with a career as a trusted and rewarded senior member of the regime, he was wrong. Macro had been transferred to the prefecture of Egypt, a position that removed him from the seat of power to almost as far away as it was possible to be, and once there he was forced by Caligula to commit suicide on the basis that he had been involved in a scandal. Why Macro was moved is unknown. When Caligula recovered from his illness, he may have decided he distrusted Macro because of some action the prefect had taken during the emperor's indisposition. However, given the arbitrary nature of so much of Caligula's behaviour from now on there is no point in assuming any coherent rationality was responsible for the change in duties.[18]

Caligula floundered around trying to find ways to assert his power and status, using the praetorians as part of the performance. He ordered that ships be moored in a line between Baiae and the mole at Puteoli and buried in earth to create a road along which he paraded in various different ways. These included riding in a chariot, with the entire Praetorian Guard and his friends in chariots of the Gaulish or British style as his personal escort. It was one of the first occasions on which the praetorians were utilized as a sort of imperial set dressing. The story sounds frivolous but it was deadly serious. For Caligula, asserting his status in this sort of way had become a desperate substitute for real personal prestige. The barbarian chariots had become part of Roman pomp, and so too it seems had the praetorians. Nonetheless, Caligula was quite capable of seeing the praetorians as a practical and economical tool. When he raised new taxes he used praetorian tribunes and centurions to enforce collection, simply cutting out the tax-collection contractors (*publicani*) and saving their commission. The praetorians were, after all, being paid anyway. The new tasks reflected the evolving role of the praetorians into an all-purpose instrument of the Roman state. Being soldiers they were doubtless more intimidating than civilian tax collectors.[19]

Caligula also courted the mob with games, and indulged his fanatical support of the Green circus team. Caligula's restoration of popular elections was, on the face of it, a reactionary move that went some way to appeasing residual republican sensibilities. Candidates for election needed to win votes, and the traditional way of doing that was to compete with one another in putting on the best and most extravagant games. All this achieved was damage to his relationship with the senators, who regarded the entertainments as a shameful debasement of an emperor's status. Caligula's promise to make his horse Incitatus consul was probably no more than a calculated and fanciful insult to the senate rather than a serious intention. The arbitrary nature of his behaviour, which meant that those guilty of significant crimes could escape censure while innocent men were executed, created an environment of uncertainty and destroyed any possibility of his rule being regarded as one based on sound judgement. As a result he even destroyed his relationship with the people, reversing his earlier efforts to provide them with what they wanted and instead actively denying them.[20] It was not really very surprising that a conspiracy to remove him eventually developed, with praetorian officers amongst the key players.

Meanwhile, Macro had been succeeded by two prefects of the Guard. One was Marcus Arrecinus Clemens; the other may have been a man called Arruntius who was subsequently responsible for helping praetorian tribunes pacify the mob after news of Caligula's assassination broke. Clemens' part in the degeneration of Caligula's rule is unknown, since his name only comes down to us in a retrospective reference by Tacitus, and by Josephus when describing the assassination of Caligula in 41.[21] The praetorians must have been deployed in Rome, along with the urban cohorts, to enforce Caligula's increasingly arbitrary decisions that seem to have had no purpose beyond experiments in the enforcement of power. Certainly it is inconceivable that he would have been able to do so without them. State granaries were closed so that the grain dole could be suspended, for no apparent reason other than to present the people with the prospect of starvation. Although some of the tales about Caligula's cruelty seem to bear the hallmarks of stock depictions of tyrannical behaviour, such as burning a comic playwright alive and forcing parents to watch their sons being executed, the alleged and even attested behaviour of latter-day tyrants suggests that at least some of the stories about Caligula are plausible.[22]

Caligula also proceeded to institute a cult of himself as a living god. Given that he lacked any recognizable achievements or credentials, his problem was not having any rationale for his pre-eminence beyond his birth. He could not pose as an equal amongst senators, some of whom had commanded legions and governed provinces, let alone as a 'first amongst equals', as Augustus and Tiberius had. To begin with, Caligula toyed with titles that alluded to more abstract qualities, such as 'the best and greatest Caesar', and 'Son of the Military Camps', a clear allusion to his childhood fame as the son of Germanicus.[23] None of these satisfied his need to mark himself out as a supreme being.

Caligula thus promoted himself to the pantheon of Roman state deities, posing as one or other of the gods as the mood took him, as well as commissioning temples to his own divine spirit.[24] In such an exalted position his power was unlimited, legitimated and unchallengeable. His current wife, Milonia Caesonia, was made a priestess of the cult, and his uncle Claudius was made a priest, incidentally being charged eight million sestertii for the privilege.[25] Together with his baby daughter Drusilla, Caligula was fabricating a divine nuclear family. He was also very well aware that by now he had a potential rival. His sister Agrippina had married Cnaeus Domitius Ahenobarbus and in 37 she gave birth to a son, the future emperor Nero, at this time still called Lucius Domitius Ahenobarbus. Three years later, when Lucius Domitius' repellent father died, Caligula seized the entire estate.

Caligula's declaration of himself as a god was more or less taken for granted by ancient historians as an expression of outright insanity. But in some respects it was only a marginal leap in the context of an era when Augustus and before him Caesar had claimed descent from Venus. In the Eastern Empire it was entirely acceptable and in those cities dignitaries regarded it as a privilege to serve as priests in the cult of Caligula.[26] This does not, however, take into account the unique problems Caligula faced as a man in possession of supreme power but not the temporal qualifications or credibility to hold it. Flaunting his status as the great-grandson of the deified Augustus was simply not enough. Crucially, it was also not enough for some of the praetorians.

Caligula's only attempt to acquire a military reputation came to nothing. He appears to have embarked on a project to campaign somewhere in the north-west, perhaps in order to revisit the world of his childhood and emulate the achievements of Germanicus. In 39 he set out for Gaul on the pretext that German tribes were threatening trouble, and also because he wanted to recruit a special bodyguard of Germans ('Batavians'), in the manner of Augustus. This was the occasion when he also dealt with the governor of Germany, Lentulus Gaetulicus, which may have been another motive. Gaetulicus was held in rather too high regard by the soldiers for Caligula's liking, and so he was executed. Also killed was Marcus Aemilius Lepidus, husband of Drusilla but accused of adultery with Caligula's other sisters. The two men were accused nebulously of 'wicked plots'. Lepidus was ordered by Caligula 'to offer his neck to the tribune Dexter'.[27] There is no suggestion that the accusation of Lepidus and his execution took place in Germany alongside Gaetulicus.[28] Wherever it happened, the question is whether Dexter was a praetorian or legionary tribune and, if the former, whether he was in Germany with Caligula.

Either way, the expedition appears to have taken place on impulse and resulted in Caligula taking with him a bizarre troupe of actors, women and gladiators, as well as an army.[29] Any military activity was confined to a brief foray beyond the Rhine, and a speculative and fleeting conceit that he might invade Britain, before turning his attention to extorting as much money as possible out of wealthy citizens in Gaul. Caligula was accompanied on his rapid march by several praetorian cohorts, who were forced to leave their standards to be carried by pack animals so they could keep up. The praetorian cavalry were also obliged to take part in what can only be described as a mock battle. Lacking anyone obvious to fight, Caligula ordered some of his German bodyguards (perhaps ones he had just hired) to be taken over the Rhine and to pose as the enemy. When 'news' was brought that the 'enemy' were approaching, Caligula sallied out with the praetorian cavalry and secured tree branches as trophies. Perhaps the praetorians' memories of this unusual and pointless campaign contributed to the events of early 41.[30]

Caligula also made use of the praetorian *speculatores* to carry a dispatch from his campaign headquarters back to Rome, but they were ordered to be as ostentatious as possible instead of being secretive. They were to carry the letter into the imperial forums and hand it to the consuls at a meeting of the senate in the Temple of Mars Ultor. It was important to Caligula to show off the trappings of power. Back in Rome Caligula also appears to have gone about the city with an escort of mounted soldiers, presumably as part of his display of status.[31] It is not possible to identify whether these were praetorian cavalry or the German mounted bodyguards, but being accompanied by soldiers was something Caligula would have recalled from childhood on campaign with his parents. By 40 the senate had voted that Caligula be even more conspicuously protected, decreeing that not only would he enjoy a military guard in the senate house but also that his statues be similarly guarded.[32] There is a small possibility therefore that the increase to twelve praetorian cohorts occurred under Caligula to facilitate the extension of duties. A praetorian called Gaius Julius Montanus died at the age of thirty, after serving eleven years in the XII cohort.[33] If he was enfranchised under Caligula, and his name makes this possible, then the twelfth cohort ought to have been created by 41. This, however, is far from conclusive and, as was discussed earlier, evidence for a twelfth cohort is not proof on its own that twelve active cohorts were in existence.[34]

It was, as Dio said, inevitable that Caligula would be the victim of a plot if he continued to rule this way. Caligula had already begun to fear the prospect of challengers, resulting in the execution of Lentulus Gaetulicus (see above).[35] However, real conspiracies now started to take shape, threatening the very existence of the principate. Back in Rome, the plot of Anicius Cerealis and Sextus Papinius was discovered and the members executed, but this did not resolve the problem. Betilienus Bassus seems to have been another of the conspirators, and his father Capito was obliged to watch his son's execution as part of Caligula's policy of forcing parents to witness the killing of their children. Capito wanted to close his eyes, for which he too was sentenced to death. Capito then decided to offer to name other conspirators to save his own skin and included what Dio called 'the prefects', one of whom must have been the praetorian prefect Marcus Arrecinus Clemens, as well as the prefects of the urban cohorts and *vigiles*. Caligula confronted 'the prefects' and invited them to kill him. They swore blind that they had had no intention of harming him. Caligula distrusted them and they presumably concluded that if they did not kill him then he would have them executed if not now, then soon enough. This was probably the point at which his assassination became certain.

Some of the principal conspirators in the decisive and final plot were drawn from the Praetorian Guard in the form of one of the prefects (probably Clemens), the praetorian tribunes, Cassius Chaerea, Cornelius Sabinus, Papinius, and Julius Lupus, the imperial freedman Callistus and a senator called Annius Vinicianus. The soldiers were hardly likely to tolerate being the bodyguard of someone so manifestly unsuitable for the role either of commanding them or ruling the Empire. For his part, Chaerea bitterly resented that Caligula had constantly accused him of being effeminate, though the conspiracy was more widely spread. It conferred an aura of legitimacy on the plotters that they were carrying out the killing for the common good. Caligula was stabbed to death on 24 January 41 during the Palatine Games being held in the imperial palace complex. The last straw for the tribunes had been when Caligula wanted to dance and act. They killed him when he went out to listen to a song composed in his honour.[36]

The aftermath of the killing occasioned a new outbreak of chaos. It had been easy enough to plan Caligula's death but it was a great deal more difficult to decide what to do next. Caligula's German bodyguard dissolved into infighting and the killing of anyone they suspected of being implicated in the assassination, infuriated by the prospect of the loss of their privileges that was bound to follow. Three senators were killed by them quite randomly. They even burst into a theatre and threatened the entire audience. This was the moment when 'Arruntius', possibly one of the praetorian prefects, pacified them.[37]

Notwithstanding the involvement of praetorian tribunes in the assassination, the praetorian troops seem to have had no inkling of what was up. When they heard the news they 'became excited' and demanded information. Only the quick thinking of a former consul called Valerius Asiaticus calmed things down. He addressed them with the assertion that he wished he had killed Caligula himself. This pacified them while the senators removed state funds to the Capitoline Hill, a place with steep sides that could be more easily defended by the three urban cohorts that accompanied them under the command of the city prefect Lucius Scavius Saturninus. Here the senators assembled and debated what to do next.[38]

They floundered around, some proposing a democracy, others a monarchy, and then argued over who the monarch might be.

While the senators engaged in inconclusive debate, presumably beginning to appreciate that the death of Caligula had brought absolutely no useful consensus about what to do next, some of the praetorians took the initiative themselves. They were determined that there would be an emperor and that he would be a man of their choosing. They also recognized that a return to the Republic would not be to their advantage, deciding that Claudius had unmatched ancestry and education and would be likely to reward them. In the meantime, Cnaeus Sentius Saturninus appealed to the senate to seize this opportunity to capitalize on their deliverance from rule by the emperors. Another senator, Trebellius Maximus, tore a ring from Saturninus' hand that bore an image of Caligula. Cassius Chaerea symbolically asked the consuls for the watchword for the night, to their delight. The word chosen was 'liberty' and he gave it to four cohorts of the praetorians who had remained on the senate's side.[39] To ensure that Caligula's line was wiped out, his wife Caesonia and his daughter Julia Drusilla were killed shortly afterwards by praetorians commanded by the tribune Julius Lupus on Chaerea's orders.

Claudius, having witnessed the assassination, made himself scarce. The praetorians were not overly distressed about the death of Caligula on the basis that he had probably deserved it, but were rather more concerned about their own prospects.[40] As things were, their futures were on a knife-edge. They went looking for Claudius. One of their number, Gratus, located the terrified middle-aged man and declared that he should be made emperor. It was clear that being the brother of the late and still-beloved Germanicus was an enormous asset, as was a total lack of confidence in the ability of the senate to govern the state. It is worth pointing out that almost seventy years separated this moment from Augustus' constitutional settlement of 27 BC: not a single senator alive had any meaningful experience or memory of a world when the senate had held real power.

If the senate was not already aware of the power of the Praetorian Guard, it was about to become so. Claudius was carried to the praetorian camp. A disagreement broke out between the senate and the people. The senators had spotted an opportunity to recover their 'former dignity', while the people regarded imperial rule as a bulwark against the arbitrary and oppressive nature of senatorial rule that had led to such destructive civil wars the best part of a century ago.[41] The disarray continued for hours. Claudius had acquiesced (or posed as acquiescing) in being taken to the praetorian camp but for a brief moment the consuls tried to coerce him to back off so that any decision could be made in the name of the senate, the people and the rule of law, just as Caligula's accession had been. The praetorians guarding the consuls, however, withdrew their protection, leaving them isolated and vulnerable. The client king Herod Agrippa, a confidant of the imperial family and former friend of Caligula, who was then in Rome, played an important role in realizing there was no turning back. He moved to convince the senate of this. His irrefutable argument was that the praetorians knew how to fight and the senators did not. So, in the face of latent force the consuls acquiesced too and, in an effort to maintain some of the dignity of their office, voted that Claudius be granted all the powers of an emperor. In return for an oath of fidelity, Claudius promptly offered the praetorians the remarkable sum of 15,000 sestertii each, which, as Suetonius observed, was the first occasion that outright bribery was used to secure the Guards' loyalty.[42] It could of course be said that this merely advertised what had been the case ever since the praetorians were given much higher pay and handouts than any other soldiers.

The real issues underlying these remarkable circumstances, made more confusing by differences in detail between the accounts of Josephus, Dio and Suetonius, are whether the Praetorian Guard, or at least part of it, made a decision to elevate Claudius *before* they found him, and whether Claudius was fully aware of the praetorians' intentions in advance instead of it being what Suetonius called 'an extraordinary chance'.[43] That he promptly paid out so much money gives some credence to the theory that Claudius was already aware of the praetorians' plans (and perhaps even playing an active role), as does the speed with which everything was resolved, but there is nothing specific to substantiate either. It would have suited Claudius' purposes to be presented as an entirely innocent party, magnanimously accepting office out of a sense of duty and responsibility, just as Augustus had pretended to be the recipient of powers granted by the senate.

What is apparent from all the accounts is that the night following Caligula's death was utter chaos. During the night Claudius' credentials and support from the praetorians formed one of the very few certainties. Using Herod Agrippa as an intermediary he promised the senate fair government and told them that he fully understood their reservations after the experience of Caligula's rule.[44] In the midst of senatorial equivocation, the sheer force of circumstance and decisiveness of the praetorians offered a relatively clean and conclusive outcome in spite of Claudius' physical defects and other shortcomings. The detail does not really matter. Claudius was made emperor and, however the consuls and the senate dressed it up, the Praetorian Guard had dictated what happened. In essence the praetorians had discovered that they could force everyone else's hands.

Not surprisingly, there was a considerable amount of mopping up to do. Claudius got rid of one praetorian prefect. This could have been Marcus Arrecinus Clemens. Josephus implicates the prefect in the plot to kill Caligula, and Clemens was related to one of the known conspirators, Julius Lupus.[45] However, he was also advanced in years and his son, a man of the same name, enjoyed a successful senatorial career under the Flavians. The prefect in question was replaced by a new prefect of the Guard, Rufrius Pollio, who is named by Josephus.[46] It seems that Claudius maintained the policy of having two prefects because by 43 another, Catonius Justus, is also attested.[47]

Chaerea and the other conspirators might have liberated Rome from Caligula, and Claudius recognized that, but it was essential to discourage any repetition. Moreover, it was obvious that they had not planned to make Claudius emperor and so they presented a threat. Chaerea and others were executed on the basis that they had planned to kill other members of the imperial family, including Claudius, but senators who were involved were set free. Nonetheless, Claudius delayed entering the senate in person for another thirty days and made sure that no one could approach him without being searched.[48] It is sometimes said that Claudius entered the senate on this occasion with soldiers, but this is not specifically stated by the sources, even if it is probable. He did, however, secure the senators' agreement that he could bring the praetorian prefect and the praetorian tribunes to the senate with him. That they acceded to so blatant a display of the real basis of power showed much had changed from Augustus' reign.[49]

Claudius ordered the immediate issue of two new coin types, struck in gold and silver. They had no precedent and amounted to the first open and public acknowledgement of an emperor's dependence on military force, regardless of how lacking in enthusiasm Claudius had seemed at being elevated. One shows the praetorian camp and the abbreviated legend IMPER(ATOR) RECEP(TUS), 'the emperor received'. The other depicts Claudius grasping the hand of a praetorian soldier with the legend PRAETOR(IANI) RECEPT(I), 'the Praetorians received'.[50] The soldier is evidently a *signifer* because he sports a lion skin over his head, neck and shoulders, wears a tunic and carries a standard. The coins were exercises in mutual back-scratching and almost certainly formed part of the payout Claudius had promised the praetorians, as well as almost suggesting that Claudius was only able to rule through the praetorians.[51] No other part of the army or Roman society was similarly honoured, and the coins continued to be issued at least until 46 or 47. Claudius continued to commemorate his accession with the inception of annual games, appropriately held in the Castra Praetoria. He also gave the praetorians the chance to perform in public by providing panthers for the praetorian cavalry to hunt down under the command of the prefect and tribunes (Plates 10 and 11).[52]

The increase in the size of the Guard to twelve cohorts has always been difficult to date precisely. The inscription discussed earlier that records the career of Marsus and his tribunate of an eleventh cohort, apparently under Tiberius, is not conclusive. This still does not tell us when the change occurred. There is nothing whatsoever to confirm that the expansion happened under Claudius, but the circumstance of his accession and his continual promotion of the praetorians' profile do suggest themselves as an appropriate context.[53]

Other coin types reinforced new claims for the imperial regime. A brass sestertius was also issued around this time, with the legend SPES

AUGUSTA, 'Augustan Hope', on the reverse. It clearly marked out the new emperor as a promising and optimistic dawn for the principate. A copper *as*, one of the lowest-value denominations, showed Constantia Augusti, the 'Constancy of the Emperor', in an attempt to demonstrate the 'unchanging steadfastness' of the principate. A LIBERTAS type promised that Claudius would protect the people's liberty; there was implicitly no need to look to the senate for that, a gesture that might have been provoked by knowledge of Saturninus' exhortation to the senate on the night of the 24/25 January 41 to seize the chance to retake the people's liberty.[54]

The accession of Claudius was a true watershed moment. Not only did it ensure the continuation of the principate, but it also demonstrated that the power of the Praetorian Guard was decisive. It was 'the key to the future'.[55] This power may also have contributed to a new style of imperial rule in which the pretence of working in cooperation with the senate became of little importance, though Claudius sustained a professional and deferential relationship with it. Claudius preferred to seek counsel and assistance from his trusted freedmen, Narcissus, Pallas and Polybius. He also relied far more openly on his wives, first Messalina and then Agrippina, than any of his predecessors, including Augustus. It was a convenient way of neutralizing residual opposition to his rule in the senate, which was now treated as effectively irrelevant.

There remained the danger that senators could build up support amongst the military and use it as the basis of a coup. Obviously, it was essential to ensure the Praetorian Guard were prevented from assisting in any such plans. Claudius obliged the senate to pass a decree that banned soldiers, which in practice meant praetorians, from attending the morning *salutatio* ceremony held by senators.[56] Roman society depended on a complex web of patron–client relationships. A patron received into his house in the morning his clients, men who supported him in any necessary way in return for protection and help with their own problems. These relationships were based on reciprocal obligation and, in consequence, a soldier attending a senator could find himself being drawn into playing an active role in that senator's ambitions.

Claudius also modified the membership of the senate through the simple expedient of incorporating wealthy Gauls. He presented this as a natural development of a long-standing tradition but it also created a small body of senators who owed their new status to Claudius and his vision, rather than to the republican system. The change was symbolic more than anything else but perhaps the established senators recognized that the emperor could pack the senate out with more such provincials if he chose to. Claudius applied the same principle to the Alpine tribes of the Anaunians, Tulliassians and Sindunians. The tribes behaved as if they were Roman citizens but this had never actually been enacted in law. On 15 March 46 Claudius issued an edict granting them Roman citizenship. The edict made specific reference to the discovery that a number of men serving in Claudius' Praetorian Guard belonged to these tribes. Claudius appears to suggest that this revelation was a deciding factor. He stated, 'I am all the more inclined to do this because a number of this group are said to be serving in my Praetorian Guard, several indeed even serving as officers.' He would have had little choice but to incorporate the tribes: given the circumstances of his elevation to the principate, he was hardly likely to want to make enemies of any of his supporters by declaring they were aliens.[57]

Having made their choice, the praetorians must surely have been pleased with the events of the next few years. Not only did Claudius embark on major building projects in the form of the new harbour at Ostia, installing drainage systems at the Fucine Lake to control its level, and constructing aqueducts, but he also provided the opportunity for the army, including praetorians, to participate in military campaigns. The development of Ostia's port had become a critical requirement. As the Tiber's estuary silted up it became impossible for grain ships from Egypt and Sicily to dock, especially in winter. The ships had to moor off the coast in the hope that lighters could take off the grain and land it. The ordinary population of Rome had become so dependent on the grain dole that any disruption to its supply could be extremely dangerous to the emperor, who would be held responsible. Claudius was attacked by a furious mob in the forum during a drought, an episode that only further emphasized the practical need for a bodyguard. The construction of the harbour involved creating a mole to protect the entrance, using a ship that had brought an obelisk (now standing in the Vatican piazza) for Caligula. The inspiration for this idea may very well have come from the time when a killer whale became stuck in the sand while foraging in a wreck. Claudius decided to make the most of the occasion, ordering that nets be thrown across the mouth of the harbour. He then sailed out with members of the Praetorian Guard so that the soldiers could throw lances at the unfortunate animal. The whole event seems to have been presented as a public entertainment, with the Guard centre stage.[58]

The conquest of Britain, initiated in the late summer of 43, was the first campaign of the principate that set out specifically to add territory to the Empire. Like the harbour at Ostia, it was something that Caesar had not succeeded in seeing through. In tackling both, Claudius was showing his mettle, though in truth the campaign was calculated opportunism. Not only could Claudius take advantage of whatever arrangements were left of Caligula's plans to invade Britain, but also if the invasion went wrong there was no chance of the enemy marauding through continental Europe. Suetonius dismissed the British campaign as a trifle, but in reality its symbolic importance was considerable and it allowed some men the chance to embark on the greatest adventure of their military careers. Gaius Gavius Silvanus was to end his days as tribune of the XII praetorian cohort, forced to commit suicide for his part in the Piso conspiracy against Nero in 65. He had probably served as an *evocatus* in the Praetorian Guard when he was decorated by Claudius for his performance in the British campaign of 43, receiving 'necklets, armlets, medals and a gold crown'. His career is of importance because of the evidence that a twelfth praetorian cohort was in existence before the civil war of 69. Marcus Vettius Valens was decorated twice in Britain, firstly on the staff of the praetorian prefect as a *beneficiarius*, presumably under Rufrius Crispinus (prefect 43–7), and secondly as an *evocatus*. The climax for Claudius was the opportunity to travel to Britain and lead the march on and into the Catuvellaunian tribal capital at Camulodunum (Colchester). While we might reasonably assume that he did so in the company of his praetorians, their presence with him on this triumphant entry is not attested.[59]

Britain was not the only place in which soldiers had the chance to fight. Gnaeus Domitius Corbulo prosecuted a campaign in Germany in 47, and another followed in 50, though there is no specific evidence that praetorians were involved in either and nor did these campaigns result in significant expansion of the Empire.[60] Moreover, having won a victory in Britain, Claudius neither needed another great conquest nor could spare the troops – Britain had absorbed four legions and at least the equivalent in auxiliaries, which, despite Caligula's raising of additional forces, still represented a net loss to continental forces, not counting reinforcements that had to be sent to Britain under Nero after the Boudican Revolt of 60–1.

The opportunity to win decorations on campaign was an important one for any soldier; it was certainly more exciting than swaggering around Rome and provided the opportunity to prove oneself, earn tales to tell and generally bask in the glory of having been to war. It also reinforced a form of patron–client relationship between Claudius and his praetorians. Typically, these men's achievements were inscribed on their tombstones, which were erected in their home towns – in Vettius Valens' case Rimini – with this episode forming one part of their respectable and successful careers. Thus each became a man of note in his family, with his descendants basking in the inherited kudos of their heroic forbear. Such achievements tied the praetorians ever more closely to the person of the emperor. If an emperor turned out to be inadequate in playing his part in providing opportunity and the sense that one was working for a glorious regime, then the consequences could be very significant. Within two years of becoming emperor, Claudius had taken the Guard past a point of no return.

Part of cementing the loyalty of the Guard involved building up the profile of the imperial family, past and present, as the centrepiece of the imperial court. Caligula had of course tried this, but his behaviour outweighed any achievements he made in that area. Claudius honoured his parents, Antonia and Nero Claudius Drusus, with games on their birthdays, and rescheduled existing festivals for those days. Livia was honoured in various ways, including games, a statue in the Temple of Augustus and the use of her name in oaths. Caligula's sisters, Livilla and Agrippina, were recalled from exile, though Claudius' wife Messalina secured Livilla's re-banishment and subsequent murder the same year on trumped-up charges that she had committed adultery with, amongst others, Lucius Annaeus Seneca, later Nero's tutor, and spent time indiscreetly alone with Claudius. Claudius also issued a series of coins that commemorated his father, his mother, his brother Germanicus, his sister-in-law Agrippina and his son Britannicus (named for the British invasion).[61]

Claudius' wife at the time, Messalina, was in fact his cousin by virtue of the fact that his grandmother Octavia was also her great-grandmother. She produced two children (at least supposedly) by Claudius: Britannicus and Octavia. A powerful and independent-minded woman, Messalina built up a power base of her own. She used her sexuality to secure a clique of influential and useful male acolytes, creating for herself a reputation as a prostitute. One of her former lovers was Decimus Valerius Asiaticus, one of the members of the plot to kill Caligula. In 47 Messalina seems to have taken a fancy to gardens that Asiaticus was developing, so she denounced him as someone bent on aggrandizing himself. Claudius sent a praetorian prefect, Rufrius Crispinus, to apprehend Asiaticus at Baiae, for which Crispinus was generously rewarded. Crispinus would pay a price for this as he remained permanently scarred as a possible Messalina-loyalist and lost his position in 51.[62]

By 48 the principal player in this curious drama was the consul-designate, Caius Silius. The plan he and Messalina cooked up involved going through a bigamous marriage ceremony while Claudius was inspecting the works at Ostia, in advance of seizing power and presumably eventually assassinating Claudius.[63] This recklessness had not gone unnoticed by Claudius' freedmen and Narcissus therefore decided that a prostitute called Calpurnia, whom Claudius trusted, would tell him. Failure to act immediately would have ensured that Silius would have held Rome, and securing the Guard would have played a crucial part in that. When Claudius found out, one of his principal concerns was that he distrusted one of the then praetorian prefects, Lucius Lusius Geta, who had served alongside Rufrius Crispinus since 47. In an unprecedented move, at the insistence of Narcissus, Claudius transferred command of the

Guard for one day to Narcissus.[64] Claudius initially despaired, declaring before the Praetorian Guard that he had given up on marriage after his various experiences of wives, and if he went back on his word he would not resist if they decided to kill him.[65]

Remarkably, Narcissus appears to have had no problem in securing the day as interim commander of the Guard. He took Claudius first to the house of Silius, showing him that imperial heirlooms had been stolen and taken there. Next they went to the Castra Praetoria where a furious and embarrassed Claudius addressed the praetorians. It had the desired effect. The soldiers acclaimed him and demanded to know the names of the guilty, promising that they would be punished. Silius, who had by then been apprehended in the forum, was displayed to them. He knew the game was up and simply asked that his execution be expedited. Messalina was also executed, ironically in the very gardens she had coveted.[66] Others who had been in on the conspiracy included the prefect of the *vigiles*, Decrius Calpurnianus, which only serves to show how very close Claudius had come to losing his position and his life, though this does not necessarily mean that the night watch would have followed their prefect. It is not known whether Calpurnianus' behaviour contributed to the decision to redistribute the *vigiles*. A rotational system was introduced during the reign to station one cohort at the port cities of Puteoli (Pozzuoli) and Ostia where the vast granaries presented a colossal fire risk. The practical value of such a move is obvious, but it also served to split up the *vigiles*.[67]

The story of Messalina and Silius seems impossibly foolish and ill starred, but it is also quite plain that Claudius had unwittingly permitted a great deal to go on without his knowledge. The Guard might have made him emperor seven years earlier but it now had come close to being the decisive factor in ending his rule; crucially, the conspiracy failed to secure the support of the Guard and in the end its loyalty proved decisive in the collapse of the plot. But it cannot be assumed, and Claudius did not assume, that their loyalty would prove durable had events unfolded even slightly differently. There is no good reason to suspect that the overall story is untrue since the existing accounts are compatible and detailed, and trace such a remarkable narrative that they are beyond the bounds of mischievous anecdotes.

With Messalina gone, the way was open for a new twist in the structure of Claudius' imperial family in the form of his niece Agrippina, whom he married in spite of his recent insistence that he would never have another wife. Fortunately for Claudius, the Guard did not kill him as he had suggested they could. The widow of Cnaeus Domitius Ahenobarbus, and mother of Lucius Domitius Ahenobarbus, the younger Agrippina offered a pedigree that Claudius' children lacked. Lucius Domitius was descended from Augustus because this Agrippina, like Caligula, was the great-grandchild of the first emperor. Britannicus and Octavia lacked the crucial bloodline because they were not descended from Augustus; moreover, thanks to Messalina's endless infidelities it could not even be certain that they were truly descended from Octavia. In the evolving dynamic of the imperial family, and the increasing importance of the Guard's slavish dynastic affiliations, keeping the Julio-Claudian bloodline both secure and unadulterated was now a major priority.

The promotion of Agrippina to empress was by no means certain. Claudius' freedmen squabbled over their rival nominees for the position of Claudius' next wife. Narcissus favoured one of Claudius' earlier wives, Aelia Paetina, and mother of his daughter Antonia on the grounds of continuity and accommodation of Britannicus and Octavia. Callistus preferred Lollia Paulina, a childless woman who would come with no need to be partisan about her own offspring by another man. Pallas preferred Agrippina on straightforward and irrefutable dynastic grounds.[68] The stumbling block was the uncomfortable and unavoidable fact that she was the emperor's blood niece.

The legal obstacles to the marriage were managed by Lucius Vitellius, one of Claudius' most trusted friends, who had already served as consul three times. Vitellius addressed the senate, emphasizing Agrippina's pedigree and also the advantages of creating for an emperor a state-sponsored marriage. He dismissed objections to an uncle marrying a niece on the grounds that other societies allowed it, and proposed a permanent change in the law.[69] Agrippina had already been planning that her son Lucius

Domitius was to be married to Claudius' daughter Octavia, supplanting the man who had been lined up to marry her, Lucius Junius Silanus.[70] Agrippina moved very fast to consolidate her position. By 50 she had been named Augusta by Claudius. The captured British tribal leader Caratacus was brought to Rome in 52 and displayed with his entourage on the parade ground outside the Castra Praetoria in a ceremony to which the Roman people were summoned. Caratacus' trophies were put on show and also the members of his family, at which point he addressed the Romans and sought their clemency. Claudius was so impressed he released them. In a striking gesture, the Britons accorded Agrippina the same respect as they accorded Claudius, coming from a tribal tradition in which women were quite able to hold high office and lead armies. Tacitus observed that this was a novelty for the Romans but that Agrippina was indeed presenting herself as Claudius' partner in every way.[71]

Meanwhile, Agrippina's thirteen-year-old son Lucius Domitius had already been adopted in 50 by Claudius and renamed Nero Claudius Caesar Drusus Germanicus, declared consul designate, and awarded the title *princeps iuventutis* that marked him out as heir designate. For good measure he offered a handout to the people, provided a payout to the soldiers and paraded with the Praetorian Guard, even holding a shield as he did so.[72] In adopting Nero perhaps Claudius was merely formalizing a line of succession he suspected the praetorians would take it upon themselves to enforce anyway.

Agrippina also saw to it that the praetorian prefecture came under her control. She dismissed the joint prefects of the Praetorian Guard, Rufrius Crispinus and Lusius Geta. They were, according to Agrippina, suspected of residual loyalty to Messalina, and mostly to Messalina's children. She claimed that the two men's separate ambitions were splitting the Guard; this had always been a potential problem but her ulterior motive was clear. Agrippina wanted her own nominee in charge. Sextus Afranius Burrus was appointed as sole praetorian prefect in the year 51, effectively bringing the entire Guard into Agrippina's orbit.[73] Britannicus, during this time, was marginalized and removed from public life. At four years Nero's junior, he had inevitably been reduced to a secondary heir, but his continued existence remained a threat to Nero. Agrippina also removed her son's teacher Sosibius and had him executed. By 52 Agrippina had made Claudius proclaim Nero capable of running the state, should anything happen to Claudius. The following year Nero married Octavia, reinforcing the dynastic union.[74] The scene was set for the remarkable reign that was to follow but it went in a direction Agrippina could never have planned.

CHAPTER 5

A TALE OF TWO PREFECTS
(51–68)

By 51 the praetorian-sponsored emperor Claudius had three years to live. Power had drifted increasingly into the hands of his wife and niece Agrippina who was determined to see her son Nero safely on the throne with herself still in the driving seat. Claudius' death in 54, probably at Agrippina's hands, indeed saw his stepson become emperor. The praetorian prefect Burrus and Nero's tutor Seneca played a critical role in maintaining stability. Agrippina's murder in 59, ordered by a frustrated Nero, still left Burrus and Seneca as crucial restraining influences. By 62 Burrus was dead, with Seneca following soon after. The appointment of Tigellinus, another ambitious and cynical prefect, transformed the way Nero ruled. Permitted to indulge himself in any way he wished, Nero destroyed the relationship between the principate and the senatorial class. The critical moment came in 68 when the praetorians themselves abandoned Nero and he realized there was no hope. The withdrawal of praetorian backing in 68 was as decisive as praetorian support had been in 41.

I{N ROME, A SHORT} distance east from the vast brooding mass of the Colosseum, a gate leads up a winding path to a park where masonry protrudes from a grassy hillside. It is a relatively quiet spot, despite its proximity to one of the city's greatest tourist attractions. It is difficult to believe that the masonry forms part of the nerve centre of one of the ancient world's most notorious regimes. This was Nero's Domus Aurea (Golden House) or, rather, what is left of it. The enormous sprawling complex covered as much as 350 acres (142 ha) in the heart of Rome, land which Nero seized after the Great Fire that destroyed huge parts of the city in the year 64. Throughout Nero's reign, the praetorian prefects played a hugely important and defining role, first Burrus as a benign and paternal guiding hand, and then Tigellinus as a wicked and cynical opportunist. It was when the Guard gave up on Nero in 68 that his reign finally came to an end.

The Colosseum was built by Vespasian (69–79) on the site of the Golden House's ornamental lake. Much of the palace was demolished or buried under new public buildings. The amphitheatre, the largest in the Roman world, was designed to enhance the city for the benefit of the general population rather than the conceit of a single man. Perhaps it was only fitting that from the time it was dedicated in 80 the mob could be entertained with gladiatorial bouts and other extravagant displays where Nero had once planned to enjoy languid afternoons in a boat with his coterie of admirers and flunkies.

The surviving section of the Golden House was chanced upon in the late fifteenth century during the Renaissance and soon became a sensation. By sheer luck it had been built over by the Baths of Titus and then the Baths of Trajan, burying and preserving over 140 rooms, which were incorporated into the substructures of the baths. Even Michelangelo came to wonder at the find. Today the building is in a parlous state, suffering collapse and decay. Within are darkened chambers, corridors, alcoves, arches, stucco and the remains of exuberant frescoes depicting mythological figures. The torch picks out flashes of colour, which just as quickly retreat to the shadows as the torch moves on. The air is still, cold and damp.

Walking round this grand dereliction in the gloom is now more like a journey into the Underworld. But even in its decrepit state this crumbling and crepuscular ruin still has echoes of the place it used to be. It represents just one wing of Nero's vast indulgence, with most of its lower floor given over to dining rooms once adorned with marble, pools and fountains. The palace even included an octagonal domed court and a circular dining room with revolving roof described by Suetonius. The remains of this remarkable feature may have been identified during archaeological work in 2010.[1] This luxurious accessory epitomized what Suetonius called Nero's wastefulness. It also epitomized the moral dereliction of Rome's ruling dynasty that Nero, the last of the Julio-Claudians, should seek to live like this with a total disregard for the hundreds of thousands of ordinary Romans displaced by his needs. He was helped to live and rule as he did by his last praetorian prefect, Tigellinus.

Nero's descent into theatrical, asinine and perverted self-indulgence almost resulted in the very end of the imperial system. His reign has gone down in history as the template of tyranny and infamy, even though in many ways the worst aspects of his rule really belong only to the last four of his fourteen years as emperor. The first five, and often forgotten, years of Nero's reign were regarded then and afterwards as the five good years. Even so, Nero's common touch meant that he enjoyed a remarkable level of popularity amongst the Roman mob.

Sextus Afranius Burrus was chosen as praetorian prefect in 51 by Agrippina for his military reputation, but he was also very aware of who had nominated him and what her expectations might be. Agrippina did nothing without careful calculation. Burrus seems to have been a member of the Gaulish Vocontii tribe and came from the city of Vasio (Vaison) in the province of Gallia Narbonensis. He had been a military tribune, then a procurator for Livia, Tiberius and Claudius in succession before being made sole praetorian prefect in 51 and awarded honorific consular regalia.[2] He was probably about fifty years old in 51. He would serve as praetorian prefect for eleven years, covering the rest of the reign of Claudius and from 54 the first eight years of Nero's reign.

The Guard had already helped Claudius entertain a crowd at Ostia by killing a whale that had been washed up there. In 52 Claudius came up with another way of using the praetorians in a manner Augustus is unlikely to have anticipated. The drainage works he had commissioned for the Fucine Lake were designed to regulate its level. To celebrate their completion he ordered that a naval battle, *naumachia*, be held for the benefit of a gigantic crowd that gathered around the lake to watch. Battleships floated around on the lake with nineteen thousand convicts aboard them to fight, hemmed in by a ring of rafts manned by praetorian infantry and cavalry to contain the action and prevent any ship sailing away.[3] Although Nero is not mentioned, he is likely to have been present. It was perhaps the time the future performer realized praetorians could be useful manpower on such occasions.

The latter part of Claudius' reign saw Agrippina gradually eclipse the ageing emperor. She also used her position to marginalize Claudius' son Britannicus in favour of her own son Nero. When the boys appeared in public at circus events, Nero wore triumphal clothing while Britannicus was condemned to wear the praetexta, the boy's toga. Any centurion or tribune suspected of having sympathy for Britannicus' lot was removed; it seems that Agrippina was responsible. Agrippina also took advantage of her unique status, riding by carriage into the Capitol, a right normally only enjoyed by priests. Agrippina was the daughter of the celebrated general Germanicus, the sister of an emperor, the wife of an emperor, and the mother of an emperor-in-waiting; no wonder she expected to enjoy unprecedented privileges. Dio claims that Claudius gradually became aware of her actions and grew angry.[4] However, it is hardly plausible that her behaviour was a surprise to him. Since 50 she had started to appear on coins alongside him, in the manner of joint monarchs, unprecedented in Rome. This reflected the fact that she participated in state occasions and ceremonies with Claudius. Gold and silver coins issued at Rome (or Lyon) from 51 on show Claudius on one side and Agrippina on the other.[5] Coins depicting Claudius and Agrippina were also issued at a number of places in the Eastern Empire where cities enjoyed the privilege of producing their own local Roman coinage, such as Ephesus in Ionia and Mostene in Lydia. These provincial issues typically have jugate portraits of Claudius and Agrippina on the obverse with Claudius in the foreground and Agrippina behind and slightly offset. This was an unequivocal representation of joint rulers.[6]

The joint rule was not to last long. On 13 October 54 Claudius was killed by Agrippina, who fed him poisoned mushrooms.[7] The story is generally accepted as being true. There was no question of Agrippina succeeding in her own right, but it was now possible for her to rule through Nero who, as a youth, would in theory be easily manipulated and controlled. The Roman world was in practice replete with examples of how official protocols and legal obstacles were simply sidelined. This was a curiosity of a society that superficially appeared to be founded on rigid social structures.

As a woman, Agrippina could not claim any political status whatsoever. With Nero holding the necessary privileges she could act through him, Roman propriety being satisfied by a blatant charade of legality. This curious incongruity of the Roman world had already permitted Agrippina to determine the choice of Burrus as praetorian prefect. His appointment was clearly designed to make sure that the Praetorian Guard was on side from the outset. On 13 October 54 Nero emerged at midday from the palace with Burrus where as usual the allocated praetorian cohort was on guard duty. Burrus indicated to the praetorians that they should cheer, and so they did. A few asked what had happened to Britannicus, but evidently the rest were quite happy to accept the situation as it was and Britannicus was forgotten. Nero then headed off in a litter to the Castra Praetoria where he delivered a speech to the rest of the Guard, who promptly hailed him as emperor. The speech had been written for him by his tutor, Lucius Annaeus Seneca, and was followed by a promise that whatever Claudius had given them, he would match.[8] This clearly meant that the donative of 15,000 or 20,000 sestertii handed out in 41 was to be repeated, which makes it easy to understand why Britannicus had been so readily consigned to constitutional oblivion by the Guard. There was even more for the praetorians: Nero subsequently founded a colony for veterans of the Guard at Antium (Anzio) and also provided serving praetorians with a monthly free grain allowance.[9]

With the praetorians taken care of, the same process of delivering a speech written by Seneca was applied to the senate as well. Nero's accession was being systematically stage-managed by Agrippina. In practice she oversaw the administration of the Empire and even took precedence over Nero as they went about. Moreover, it is clear that it was her intention to continue to do so with a praetorian escort, as she had as Claudius' wife. Nero gave a tribune of the Guard the watchword on the first day of his reign; it was to be 'Best of Mothers'. Agrippina's apparent pre-eminence continued to manifest itself on the coinage, this time with her son. Early issues in the reign featured the pair facing each other, with Agrippina labelled as NERONIS MATER, 'mother of Nero'. Another showed the two on one side and on the other statues of the deified Augustus and Claudius being towed by four elephants in a clear advertisement of their shared lineage.[10] Agrippina's dominance was to be short-lived. The subsequent loss of her Guard escort, preventing her from nurturing a cult of loyalty amongst any of them, naturally made her vulnerable.

Seneca and Burrus seem to have operated a remarkable partnership from the outset. Their qualities were different but complementary, Burrus being inclined to austerity and restraint and Seneca with his eloquence and affability. Dio described them as the 'most sensible and influential' men at court.[11] Burrus was also given to extreme bluntness, once telling Nero not to ask him for his opinion on the same matter twice. His uncompromising firmness reflected the years spent on the parade ground and dealing with young soldiers. Burrus revealed himself to be different in a crucial way from Sejanus. Lacking Sejanus' self-serving ambition, but possessing the same post, he (and Seneca) simply did a good job. They were recognized to be competent and fair and had no problems with Nero, who had no interest in governing anyway.[12]

If there was any failing it was that Nero was allowed to indulge himself more and more. Alternatively, perhaps Nero was exercising sound judgement on his own part anyway by relying on them. Burrus and Seneca were concerned at the power Agrippina had amassed. Having managed to divert her away from greeting an embassy of Armenians, they then took over running the Empire themselves. An important component in the way Agrippina was sidelined was the fate of the imperial freedman Pallas who had been her principal advocate when the question of Claudius re-marrying was raised. But in 55 Pallas, who was also in charge of the imperial accounts, was made to retire. Nero had become resentful of his mother's demands and recognized that one way of solving the problem was to remove Pallas. Pallas agreed to go once he had cut a deal which meant he was immune to prosecution for any past act.[13] Agrippina found herself suddenly without her principal ally and also all her honours. These included the praetorian and German escorts she had become accustomed to going about with, without necessarily being entitled to them in the first place.[14] Nero took objection to her use of a Guard escort, declaring that only an emperor should enjoy this privilege, forcing her to do without one; so worried were ordinary people of the consequences of being caught in her vicinity that they went out of their way to avoid being anywhere near her.[15] The removal of her praetorians was a very distinct mark of the loss of Agrippina's status. The German bodyguard she had used was presumably taken over by Nero. The tombstone of one, a soldier called Indus, describes him as by nationality a Batavian, of the German fraternity, in Nero's bodyguard, the *Germani corpori custodes*. This record shows that the terms German and Batavian were synonymous in this context. By this date they were based in their own barracks near to the Gardens of Dolabella; neither location is now known (Plate 12).[16]

The existence since 23 of the Castra Praetoria did not mean that the Guard was all there or that they had ceased to be a presence in Italian cities. There is evidence from Pompeii that suggests praetorians were part of the fabric of the region for what remained of the city's life. It is inconceivable that this was a local phenomenon; it is merely the unique circumstances of Pompeii's preservation that have provided us with the evidence. A writing tablet, dated to 56 and in the name of Publius Alfenus Varus, a *trecenarius Augusti* (the most senior centurion in the Guard), concerns the sale of property of a cavalry officer (*decurion*) called Publius Alfenus Pollio and another individual called Numerius Eprius Nicia, which realized 25,439 sestertii paid to Varus. The auction was managed by the freedman banker Lucius Caecilius Iucundus, serving as Varus' agent. The tablet states that it was *actum Juliae Cosstatiae* [sic] *Nucheriae*. This can be translated as 'enacted at *Julia Constantia* at Nuceria', a place taken to be a military encampment. Constantia was a title adopted by Claudius on his coinage soon after his accession in 41 and may therefore be named for him, though of course the installation could easily have been in place for longer.[17] The tablet seems to suggest that not only were praetorians based at Nuceria but were clearly sufficiently longstanding to have become embroiled in local affairs and, remarkably, even act as creditors. The similarity of Varus and Pollio's names suggests also that they were relatives. The remarkable survival of this tablet at Pompeii must suggest that this sort of scenario and local involvement were far more widespread than we will ever know.

Praetorians were also dispatched to the Bay of Naples area in 58. The town council of the city of Puteoli, on the north side of the Bay of Naples, sent representatives to the senate in Rome to complain about the behaviour of the Puteoli city mob. The people of Puteoli, however, sent their own deputation to complain about the greed of the magistrates. As the city was at boiling point there was a very real risk of violence breaking out. In spite of that the townsfolk refused to accept the strident measures the senator Gaius Cassius, appointed to deal with the dispute, wanted to impose. The commission was transferred to two other senators, the brothers Scribonius Rufus and Scribonius Proculus, who with the assistance of a praetorian cohort set out to terrorize the people of Puteoli and impose a few executions. The Guard was clearly being used in this instance as a militarized police force to maintain public order ruthlessly. What is not clear is whether the cohort was sent from Rome or was already in the area, perhaps at Nuceria. The presence of a number of tombs of praetorians at Pompeii suggests that they were a well-established presence in the region by 79, if not long before.[18]

Agrippina's ambitions were intolerable to Seneca, Burrus and even her son. Women were regarded as too volatile and too capricious to fulfil a position of political responsibility. In the *Aeneid* Mercury tells Aeneas that women are 'ever fickle and changeable'; it was a common perception of women in Roman society that meant Agrippina would never have been allowed permanently to act as a co-ruler.[19] She had gone too far. Nero was flexing his muscles and doing so in a way that would have ingratiated him with the senate. By then he had already, with Seneca's guidance, paid due deference to the senate's ancient traditions and responsibilities, and allowed them considerable freedom when it came to conducting trials.[20]

Within a year of his accession, Nero's latent ruthlessness started to emerge. In 55 he had Britannicus poisoned at the dinner table, fearing that one day his step-brother might become more popular than him. The death was arranged by securing the services of a notorious criminal poisoner called Locusta who was currently incarcerated in, probably, the prison at the Castra Praetoria. Nero used a praetorian tribune called Pollio Julius as his agent, which must mean that Julius obtained the necessary poison from Locusta and appropriate instructions and then brought it down to the palace. To begin with Britannicus' tutors were supposed to administer it, but this did not work. Nero was furious with Pollio and Locusta and told them they were threatening his personal security while trying to protect themselves. A new, quicker-acting poison had to be prepared. As Britannicus dined, his food was sampled by a taster as usual so that he would not suspect anything. He was then handed a scalding hot drink, which he complained about, and was handed cold water to which the poison had been added. Britannicus died on the spot, his seizure provoking panic amongst the other diners except Nero, who languidly attributed it to Britannicus' epilepsy.[21] Agrippina recognized that Nero had set a precedent by killing a close relative. The involvement of a praetorian tribune showed how the Guard was becoming an essential tool for an emperor in every possible capacity, even if this meant participating in the most nefarious crimes.

The death of Britannicus was a moment of realization for Burrus and Seneca. They decided to adopt a lower profile when it came to managing public business and thereby hoped to stay alive. Unfortunately, this merely allowed Nero to realize that he was freer to do as he pleased, and so he did.[22] By 58 Nero had taken up with Poppaea Sabina as his mistress. She had formerly been married to the praetorian prefect Rufrius Crispinus and then embarked on an affair with one of Nero's friends, Marcus Salvius Otho.[23] This brought her to Nero's attention, at which point Agrippina is alleged to have tried to engage Nero in incestuous relations in order to divert his attentions from Poppaea. It is not certain whether this actually happened. What is beyond dispute is that in 59 Nero had his mother murdered.[24] However, the plans did not go smoothly. Anicetus, prefect of the fleet at Misenum, hated Agrippina and she him. Anicetus offered to create a booby-trapped ship so that she could be drowned on the return voyage after sharing a banquet with Nero near Misenum. The plans went wrong because the detachable component of the ship did not operate properly and she survived. When the news reached Nero he panicked and wondered how he would possibly be able to explain himself since, he reasoned, Agrippina was bound to work out who was behind the scheme. He fled to Seneca and Burrus, desperate to know what to do. Seneca promptly turned to Burrus and asked if the praetorians would finish her off. Burrus rejected this on the grounds that no praetorian would harm the progeny of Germanicus. His advice was that Anicetus should finish what he had promised. Anicetus obliged, using manpower from the fleet. Burrus stepped in to encourage the gang to grasp Nero's hand and fortify his resolve that he had been delivered.

In the aftermath Nero decided to give the praetorians a cash gift. Perhaps it was to compensate them for the loss of a daughter of Germanicus, whom they had once escorted. After all, Burrus had said there was no chance that they would assist in the crime. Dio's view was that it was to encourage them to associate such crimes with gratuities.[25] Perhaps it was just a generic precaution. Nero wrote to the senate to list Agrippina's crimes, which included allegedly plotting against him, and attributed her death to suicide when she was found out.

Nero had engineered his liberation from Agrippina but not yet from the steadying hands of Seneca and Burrus, though he was working on it. He took a fancy to the idea of competing in chariot races and also of performing as a singer with a lyre in the manner of Apollo. Presented with the prospect of an emperor behaving inappropriately in two different ways, Seneca and Burrus decided to allow Nero to ride in a chariot in private across the Tiber in the Vatican valley.[26] The plan went wrong because in the event a crowd turned up and, far from being appalled at the indignity of their emperor taking part in a profession regarded as little better than semi-criminal by Rome's aristocracy, were greatly impressed that he shared their tastes.

Nero, not unnaturally, was galvanized by the response and proceeded to embark on even more eccentric thespian and musical activities. This propelled the praetorians downwards into one of the most humiliating episodes in their history. Nero arrived on stage with his lyre and voice-trainers, and a cohort of praetorians, complete with their centurions and tribunes, to pack out the audience. Even a 'sorrowful Burrus', as Tacitus put it, had been compelled to come along and add his praises. Dio suggests that Burrus and Seneca put on a rather more convincing performance of guiding and supporting Nero, orchestrating the crowd to join in. Dio also reports that Nero had organized a claque of five thousand soldiers, whom Nero called 'the Augustans', to lead the applause. Most of them must have been praetorians. If the Guard was by this date made up of twelve cohorts, quite possibly milliary in size, plenty of them would have been available, as well as the urban cohorts and the *vigiles*, depending on how many were physically in Rome at the time.[27]

Despite his desire to perform in a profession traditionally despised by the Roman elite, Nero was acutely conscious of the structure of Roman society. He felt a need to enhance the differential between different classes, though he was no less motivated by financial reasons. For example, the estates of deceased freedmen were subject to 50 per cent going to the emperor. Nero changed the rate so that he took five-sixths.[28] This was part of a wider policy of clamping down on slaves and ex-slaves. In 61 Lucius Pedanius Secundus, the prefect of Rome, was killed by one of his slaves. The motive is not clear; the slave had either been denied his freedom after it had been agreed or had challenged his master for the affections of another male slave in the household. The traditional legal response to such a dramatic situation was to execute all the slaves on the grounds of collective guilt. This excited a popular protest, which degenerated into riots after the senate ordered that the law must take its course. Nero stood fast and ordered praetorians to line the route along which the condemned slaves were led.[29]

In 59 a senator called Rubellius Plautus had been sent into exile. Plautus was descended from Tiberius, making him a potential rival. In 55 Nero had become suspicious that Agrippina might transfer her favours to his distant cousin and replace him. In 60 a comet arrived, and was interpreted as an ominous portent of monarchical change, with Plautus being the name cited as the most likely candidate. In 62 Tigellinus sent sixty praetorians to kill the exiled Plautus as part of a policy of his to associate Nero ever more closely with the purges and thereby gain the emperor's approval.[30] The soldiers were reluctant, giving a freedman of Plautus time to alert him to his father-in-law's advice to take his own life before being killed in the manner of a coward. Plautus did not act and was killed by a centurion, and his head returned to Rome to be handed to Nero.

In 62 Nero decided to divorce Octavia and marry Poppaea. Since he was plainly infatuated with the latter, this was an inevitable development, even though Octavia represented a far more suitable dynastic union, which Poppaea could not offer at all. Octavia was subsequently executed on the spurious grounds of adultery and sorcery. Burrus was appalled by the idea that Nero was to marry Poppaea and told him that if he did so, then effectively the young emperor was giving up his right to rule.[31]

Perhaps this was the point at which Burrus gave up. The praetorian prefect had, by then, withstood over a decade of putting up with Nero. From soon after he became emperor Nero had learned to nod compliantly at the advice Burrus and Seneca gave him and then increasingly ignore it, being encouraged to do so by his disreputable friends. Eventually, he ceased even to pretend to listen, subscribing to the view that an emperor should outdo everyone else, even in wickedness. By 62 Burrus, an old man by the standards of the era, had disappeared from public life due to his health. He died soon after. He had been struggling with breathing, but whether this was down to a genuine condition or simply the effects of poison was unknown at the time. Burrus' objections to the marriage to Poppaea had led Nero to order him poisoned. It made no difference – whatever the explanation, he was gone. Nero returned to the idea of two praetorian prefects, choosing the very popular Faenius Rufus who had been the *praefectus annonae*, 'prefect of the grain dole', since 55 without ever taking a cut for himself, and Ofonius Tigellinus. Tigellinus, formerly prefect of the *vigiles*, was the complete antithesis of Rufus; Nero admired him for his dissolute behaviour, for which Tigellinus was generally regarded as having no equal. He was also assiduous in using every mechanism the state afforded to keep his eye on any potential enemies of the state. The reasons for the choice seem to have been straightforward. In Rufus, Nero wanted a prefect who would earn him popular support and in Tigellinus he wanted someone who would assist him in even more infamous and immoral carryings-on.[32] It was the first time that being a scoundrel was treated as the primary qualification for holding the esteemed office of prefect of the Praetorian Guard.

The death of Burrus left Seneca dangerously exposed and Nero strengthened. The 'good' praetorian prefect Rufus was to all intents and purposes marginalized. The principal influence over Nero's last six years as emperor was Tigellinus. By 64 Nero's desire to perform had resulted in him appearing in public venues, most notably at Naples, rather than principally only at his own house and gardens. He selected Naples for his first such outing because, as a Greek city, it would be a suitable place to start before he crossed to Greece. Nero left the stage when his performance was over, only for an earthquake to cause the theatre to collapse, which he regarded as a providential deliverance. Shortly afterwards he also performed in Rome, participating in his Neronia festival. This was a quinquennial event he had established in 60, and was therefore not due to be repeated until 65. Unable to wait any longer Nero ran it in 64, and took part himself allegedly at the request of both the people and a 'guard of soldiers'. He was added to the list of lyre players and came forward to perform with Rufus and Tigellinus in attendance, who were carrying his instrument together, and tribunes of the Guard. The ancient sources are explicitly or implicitly hostile to what Nero was doing, but the ordinary people of Rome appear to have welcomed Nero as one of their own. He played to the crowd. Some of his behaviour was appallingly self-indulgent, but his gesture seems to have been appreciated by at least some of the Roman people. Spies were on hand to detect anyone less than enthusiastic, or even to make a note of absentees. These were almost certainly praetorian *speculatores* 'disguised' as civilians.[33] The theatrical performances were also of course another variant on parading Nero's status, though in a thoroughly unconventional way that completely disrupted traditional Roman moral standards and social conventions.

The praetorian prefects, the tribunes and therefore the Guard had been recast as the chorus in the extraordinary performance that was Nero's life.

This mandatory participation, also forced on other members of the elite and ordinary people, meant everyone had been drawn into the world over which he presided. Some of the equestrians, for example, were chosen along with five thousand ordinary men to learn special styles of choreographed and coordinated applause, which they would carry out while he sang. In 64 Tigellinus threw a banquet for Nero, using the pool of Agrippa as the venue. It was part of the Baths of Agrippa complex at the southern end of the Field of Mars. Floating pontoons created platforms, while taverns and brothels had been built around the edge. Both Tacitus and Dio describe the occasion as a full-scale orgy of indulgence and obscenity, with Dio adding details of unlimited promiscuity and perversion. Not entirely surprisingly, the episode led to the deaths of a number of the partygoers. Nero sometimes presented himself to the Roman public in a more appropriate manner. A sestertius issued in 64 with one of the most artistically successful designs of the whole Roman coinage series shows him on a prancing horse accompanied by a pair of foot soldiers, and in another version with a mounted soldier. The only legend is the word DECVRSIO, 'military manoeuvre'. The most plausible context in which this might have occurred is if Nero trained with the praetorians, but it is no less likely that the design is an entirely fictitious attempt to portray Nero as a military performer, with praetorians as members of the cast (Plate 13).[34]

At some point in 65 Poppaea was killed by Nero. She was pregnant for the second time and for some reason he became enraged. According to Suetonius this was because she had complained about the time he spent at the races, though Tacitus suggests it was simply a fleeting outburst of anger. Nero kicked Poppaea and the ensuing internal injuries led to her death shortly afterwards.[35] Precisely when this happened in 65 is not clear but the outcome was the same: whatever restraining influence she might have exerted over Nero had now been lost. Moreover, the loss of Poppaea and her unborn child compounded the loss of their daughter Claudia, who had died as an infant. Nero now had no dynastic line of descent to offer the Roman people, or (perhaps more crucially) the Praetorian Guard. His death, whenever it came, would inevitably occasion a crisis and leave the Guard looking for a champion.

In any case, by 65 some of those who mattered had had enough of the emperor's behaviour. Seneca and Faenius Rufus, Tigellinus' co-prefect, joined a plot headed by a celebrated lawyer Lucius Calpurnius Piso to topple Nero. It was the first time that a praetorian prefect had demonstrably joined a conspiracy to bring down an emperor. No doubt Rufus nursed resentment for the way Tigellinus had systematically tried to damage him. They were all sick of Nero's behaviour, but since Piso had no dynastic claim to be emperor, the plans were fatally flawed. Nonetheless, it illustrated the value of having two praetorian prefects; had Faenius Rufus been sole prefect then there would have been a significant risk of losing the entire Guard to the services of the plotters. As well as the senators involved, a number of the key conspirators were members of the Guard. They were experienced men who had had plenty of opportunity to witness Nero's rule at first hand and had doubtless been obliged to participate in some of the more demeaning duties ordered by the emperor. Those attested are three tribunes, Subrius Flavus, Gaius Gavius Silvanus and Statius Proximus, and three centurions, Sulpicius Asper, Maximus Scaurus and Venetus Paulus. Flavus and Asper seem to have been on board from the outset, and perhaps helped draw in their colleagues, though it was unclear when Tacitus was writing exactly who had instigated the process, though he was certain that Faenius Rufus was the most committed and dedicated of the conspirators. Silvanus is attested on an inscription from Turin recording his career. After reaching the position of *primus pilus* with the VIII legion he had progressed on to several posts as tribune in Rome, starting with the II cohort of the *vigiles*, next the XIII urban cohort and, finally, the XII praetorian cohort.[36]

The conspiracy then began to take shape with various ideas being bandied about. Subrius Flavus liked the idea of attacking Nero on stage or while he went on one of his nocturnal forays into Rome. Another idea was to kill Nero at Piso's villa at Baiae, but Piso objected, believing that an assassination in public or in Nero's Golden House, paid for by extorting money from citizens, would be more appropriate. The plan they decided on was to kill him at the circus on the last day of the Games of Ceres, because he would be easier to attack. A senator called Plautius Lateranus would trip Nero up, at which point the praetorian tribunes and centurions would lead the assault on him. With the deed done, Piso was to be rushed to the Castra Praetoria to secure praetorian and popular support.[37] So far so good. Naturally, nothing went according to plan. Had it succeeded as conceived, the Piso conspiracy would have been the third occasion in which praetorians in some capacity were involved in the death of an emperor.

The plot started to unravel when Volusius Proculus, commander of the fleet at Misenum, decided to act on his grievances. He had helped in the murder of Agrippina but felt he had not been appropriately rewarded for his dirty work. So, he offered himself and the fleet to a woman called Epicharis who was one of the conspirators. His real reason seems to have been to try and gain information by ingratiating himself with Nero. Epicharis tried to draw him in with promises of a great reward but sensibly withheld the names of the other conspirators. Proculus reported back to Nero but without names his information was of limited value, though it did reveal that a conspiracy was afoot. Part of the attraction was Nero's negligence. He often went to the baths and banquets without any kind of bodyguard. It was probably part of his sense of self-importance, at least when public appearances were involved. Going about unprotected was a mark of his inviolable status as emperor, and emulated Caesar's self-confidence. Nero took no such risks when out on one of his private nocturnal ventures into the city. On those occasions he went with an escort, part of whose duties was to rough up passers-by.[38]

One of the conspirators, Flavius Scaevinus, upset everything by behaving very oddly. The plotters had managed to maintain absolute secrecy but Scaevinus started apparently seeing to his affairs as if he expected to die. He also ordered a knife to be sharpened and gave it to his freedman Milichus. Milichus went to an imperial property called the Servilian Gardens where Nero was currently residing and reported his concerns. Torture, orchestrated by Tigellinus and in Nero's presence, followed and the names started to pour forth. Those conspirators who had not yet been named toyed with the idea of rushing Piso to the Castra Praetoria on the basis that this could trigger a popular rising against Nero. Piso declined and went home to wait. Meanwhile Faenius Rufus decided to bluff his way out. For the moment unnamed, he acted as outraged as Tigellinus during the interrogations and threatened his fellow plotters, even thwarting Subrius Rufus' impulsive plan to leap up with his sword and kill Nero during the interrogation. Statius Proximus, one of the tribunes and likewise not yet revealed as a plotter, went even further and carried out the orders to kill Plautius Lateranus to protect himself.[39]

Meanwhile, Gavius Silvanus, also as yet unnamed, was sent to tell Seneca that he had been implicated. He surrounded Seneca's house 4 miles (6 km) outside Rome with praetorians. Seneca's equivocal response was conveyed back to Nero, who asked if Seneca was preparing to commit suicide. Silvanus said that Seneca had given no such impression, which was almost certainly a misunderstanding of Seneca's Stoic affiliations. These would have led Seneca to expect whatever was to happen, including death. Silvanus was sent back with the death sentence but along the way he diverted to go and find Faenius Rufus. Rufus told him that since the plot had been uncovered, there was nothing to be gained now by going against any of Nero's orders. This was something Tacitus regarded as a chronic weakness of the whole conspiracy – they had ended up actually making Nero's crimes worse by complying with his instructions. Nonetheless, Silvanus told a centurion to pass on the bad news to Seneca rather than going himself.[40] Seneca committed suicide, though his end was hastened by the praetorians who were in attendance.

In the final stages of the investigation it was inconceivable that the praetorian conspirators could remain undetected. Faenius Rufus' attempt to be first a conspirator and then an investigator was too much. Scaevinus exposed him and he was seized, and the rest followed. Subrius Flavus damned Nero to his face with faint praise, saying that he had been loyal until Nero had killed Agrippina and Poppaea, and been a charioteer, actor and arsonist. The centurion Sulpicius Asper said it was the only way left to him in which he could help Nero. Other participating centurions maintained their dignity in death, but Faenius Rufus was not so steadfast. According to Tacitus, even his will contained wailing.[41] A loyalist tribune, Veianius Niger, decapitated Flavus in a nearby field. Gaius Silvanus, remarkably, was acquitted but committed suicide just the same; Statius

Proximus was pardoned but then died in some unseemly way, and several other tribunes called Pompeius, Cornelius Martialis, Flavius Nepos and Statius Domitius were thrown out of the tribunate on the grounds that they were believed to hate Nero. Regardless of what individual praetorians privately thought of what Nero was doing, or of their sympathy with the conspiracy, they were all collectively once again in receipt of a payout from Nero, this time of 2,000 sestertii each and free grain. Tigellinus was rewarded with a statue in the palace. Rufus was succeeded in the joint prefecture by Gaius Nymphidius Sabinus, who would play a decisive part in the end of Nero.[42]

Although the Piso conspiracy was inchoate and included too many people for its own good, it was only uncovered by chance. The discovery showed Nero that the fears of plots he had been developing for some time were well founded. In 59 a senator called Thrasea Paetus had left the senate in protest at how his colleagues had acquiesced in the murder of Agrippina, even agreeing to ban the celebration of her birthday. Thrasea remained a thorn in Nero's side until he was sent for trial in 66 and killed himself. Nero's paranoia compounded the terror. Caius Cassius Longinus, an elderly and blind senator, was sent into exile because he had kept a bust of his ancestor, the tyrannicide Cassius, in his house. Even knowing one of the Pisonian conspirators was a crime. Publius Gallus, an equestrian, was exiled for being a friend of Faenius Rufus. At least one option, however, remained for any man who faced prosecution. Tigellinus was happy to receive a vast bribe in return for letting a man go.[43]

In late 66 or 67 Nero removed the three most important generals of the era, Corbulo and the brothers Sulpicius Scribonius Rufus and Sulpicius Scribonius Proculus. They presented an obvious threat because they had the means to overthrow and kill Nero. Nero had grave reasons in the aftermath of the Piso affair to doubt the loyalty of the senators and equestrians, so the deduction that these men represented a significant threat was fairly logical. In 66 the Parthian Tiridates, king of Armenia, had arrived in Rome to be crowned by Nero. It marked the symbolic end to the war against Parthia that had begun in 58. Henceforth the king of Armenia would be a Parthian, but only with Roman approval. The gates of the Temple of Janus were closed. Nero presented him to the people with the Praetorian Guard in attendance. The occasion was a highly formalized one with appropriate speeches of extravagant mutual respect, climaxing in Nero crowning Tiridates king of Armenia. Despite all this pomp, the event was rounded off with something that left Tiridates incredulous and disgusted: Nero sang, and then rode round in a chariot, dressed as a member of the Green circus faction. Tiridates could only praise Nero's general, Gnaeus Domitius Corbulo, for putting up with such a master.[44] Corbulo would not have long to wait.

The praetorians present at this bizarre display wore full armour, and the fact that the point needed to be made is a reminder that for most of the time the Guard did not appear in full military attire, more usually wearing a tunic. At the trial in 66 of Clodius Thrasea Paetus, a Republican opponent of Nero, two armed cohorts of praetorians acted as security. They took control of the Temple of Venus Genetrix in the forum of Julius Caesar. Tacitus says that praetorians wore togas as they stood guard over the entrance to the senate and others were distributed through the fora and basilicas. It is not clear whether all the soldiers wore togas. It may be that it was only those guarding the senate entrance, out of deference to the senate and to avoid creating the impression they were trying to force the outcome on behalf of the emperor. In general, it is likely that there was no fixed rule, with dress being chosen as appropriate to the occasion.[45]

Nero set out for Greece that same year, where he participated in games and performed. He was inevitably accompanied by some of the praetorians, and Tigellinus. Crucially, this meant that the other praetorians were left in Rome under the control of Tigellinus' new co-prefect, Nymphidius Sabinus. The praetorians accompanying Nero may have been delighted at the prospect of a foreign tour, but rather less impressed by the order to start digging a canal through the Isthmus of Corinth.[46] While he was still in Greece, in late 66 or 67, Nero ordered the brothers Sulpicius Scribonius Rufus and Sulpicius Scribonius Proculus, joint governors of the two German provinces, to join him, along with Domitius Corbulo. The Scribonii committed suicide when it became apparent they had fallen foul of Nero, and Corbulo killed himself before he was executed on Nero's orders.[47] These were only some of a dramatic series of deaths that followed in the aftermath of the Piso conspiracy and would presage the end of Nero's reign, with the Praetorian Guard playing a decisive role.

One curious episode involving the Guard seems to belong to the latter part of Nero's reign. Nero is reported to have considered a campaign against Ethiopia. In order to prepare for this, he dispatched a reconnaissance party of praetorians to Egypt under the command of a tribune. They were sent up the Nile but reported back that there was nothing but desert.[48] It is impossible to know now whether the unit concerned, perhaps a whole cohort, was sent out from Rome, whether it was already temporarily stationed in Egypt, or was sent directly from Greece while Nero was on tour there. The expedition shows the Guard being deployed not as a bodyguard, but simply as a state-owned force carrying out the emperor's wishes.

In this general context, Nero's Domus Aurea must have seemed strangely appropriate. Capitalizing on the extensive damage caused by the fire of 64, Nero had ordered the clearance of a vast area and the construction of his monumental and sprawling palace. By the time he returned to Rome the work was well advanced. It was a theatrical setting for Nero's power. The work had cost astronomical amounts of money, adding to the vast costs of other projects such as the canal in Greece. Dio attributes the purging of prominent men as much to the need for money as to Nero's fear of plots against his person. Anyone who was executed had his entire estate confiscated by Nero, and if anyone left a will that had failed to bequeath the due amount either to Nero or Tigellinus then that will was overturned and everything taken. This extended far beyond Rome, even with enormously wealthy Roman landowners in Africa being targeted and executed.[49]

By 68 Nero was still in Greece, and his prospects at Rome had deteriorated. He had left Rome to be administered by a freedman of his called Helios. Helios had been given carte blanche to rule in as arbitrary a fashion as he liked and to do so without reference to Nero. Helios organized further rounds of executions and confiscations. These inevitably led to threats of a conspiracy so Helios hurried to Greece to persuade Nero to come home. Nero did so with a self-conscious but ill-considered display of himself as a grand potentate, entering Rome in the manner of a triumph with a military escort and a crowd, including the beleaguered senators, heaping praise on him all the while. This was followed by games.[50]

The nascent conspiracy extended well beyond Rome. Gaius Julius Vindex, believed to have been governor of Gallia Lugdunensis, had been trawling for support amongst his fellow governors. One of them was an elderly senator born in 8 BC called Servius Sulpicius Galba, governor of Hispania Tarraconensis, whom Vindex suggested should declare himself emperor. Galba had discovered from correspondence he had acquired that his murder was being planned by Nero. The sequence of events was complicated and is very unclear in the surviving sources. Vindex's putative rebellion collapsed when he was attacked by Verginius Rufus, one of the two new German governors. Galba, who had enough prestige to have rallied support amongst the senate, had far too limited access to troops to have mounted a full-scale rebellion, though this was no consolation to Nero who was horrified, reportedly fainting to begin with and then declaring that he was finished.[51] Rufus' troops declared him emperor, but he declined. Whatever the reason for this, the way was thrown open for Galba as Nero's grip on power deteriorated.

The mere fact that these rebellions had occurred seemed to have played a decisive role in demolishing any residual belief that Nero could survive. Nero realized this himself and briefly indulged himself with absurd plans to wipe out the senate, burn Rome and go to Alexandria. Even Tigellinus had abandoned him, and seems to have played an active part in betraying him.[52] Now the Praetorian Guard, once more, played a decisive role. Floundering around for options, Nero made his way to the Servilian Gardens and tried to persuade tribunes and centurions of the Guard to come with him into exile. The soldiers equivocated or point-blank refused, one even quoting from Virgil with the line, 'Is it so dreadful to die?' By the following day Nero woke up to find that his bodyguard had gone. This may be what Dio meant when he said that the senate withdrew his bodyguard and went to the Castra Praetoria to declare that Galba had been appointed emperor.[53] On his way to a villa offered him by his freedman, Phaon, Nero overheard praetorians shouting their support for Galba and declaring that Nero was doomed. They had been encouraged by their prefect, Nymphidius Sabinus, who knew that Nero's case was hopeless; Nymphidius even promised a ludicrous 7,500 denarii to each praetorian soldier. Nero tried to make his escape to Egypt but was spotted by a retired praetorian, who inopportunely offered him a loyal salute. Shortly afterwards and before he could be caught and executed, Nero committed suicide with the assistance of his secretary, Epaphroditus, just before a praetorian centurion arrived to administer the coup de grace.[54]

It was evident that the fact that the praetorians had turned against Nero played a vitally important part in his own realization he was finished. The consequence was devastating because, in search of a reward promised by Nymphidius Sabinus if they went over to Galba, they abandoned Nero but only because Galba seemed a better financial prospect. When Galba failed to deliver they turned against him too, which as it turned out seemed to have been part of Nymphidius' plan.[55] The outcome was even more disorder as the Guard sought some sort of suitable and acceptably high payout. The date was around a century after Octavian had defeated Antony at Actium and then, in its aftermath, formalized the Praetorian Guard. By 68 a very distinct pattern had formed. The praetorians had emerged as the single group of people whose support, or lack of, could make or break an emperor. Their headquarters, the Castra Praetoria, was turning into the place where emperors and senators went to seek support. Nevertheless, the end of Nero's reign marked a new twist. This was the first time the praetorians had broken their oath to a living emperor. This was an age when many hitherto secret facets of the principate were being revealed. The revelation that the Praetorian Guard's loyalty was transferable was an uncomfortable discovery, firstly for Nero. The next was that an emperor could be made in a place other than at Rome.[56] The Guard was to play an extremely important part in the events that followed.

CHAPTER 6

CIVIL WAR
(69)

Nero's demise was accompanied by a collapse into civil war. How the candidates dealt with the Praetorian Guard played an extremely important role in a turbulent and destructive year. Galba failed entirely to court the praetorians, providing an opportunity for his rival, Otho, to exploit with ease. With the Guard now behind him, Otho's bid for power was greatly helped. Otho actively indulged in buying praetorian support and used the Guard in his war against Vitellius, also now trying to secure the principate for himself. Otho's short reign ended in suicide as Vitellius' bid gathered pace. Otho's defeat led to Vitellius disbanding Otho's praetorians and forming his own hugely inflated Guard. The Othonian praetorians now simply became potential supporters for the fourth and last candidate, Vespasian. When Vespasian's advance forces secured Rome and defeated Vitellius, the climax was a battle for the Castra Praetoria. Securing the Guard and its headquarters proved to be the final turning point in the battle for Rome in 69.

A CENTURY AFTER OCTAVIAN had brought the years of civil wars to an end at Actium, the epigonistic tendencies of the Julio-Claudians had brought the fighting back. With Nero's death, the Julio-Claudians effectively came to an end. Since the Praetorian Guard had been institutionalized as the Julio-Claudians' bodyguard, the praetorians now found themselves without a dynastic champion who could act as their benefactor and protector.

It was a remarkable moment, and the day they had made Claudius emperor in 41 was now more than a quarter of a century ago. Now it was time to be kingmakers once again.

However infamous Nero might seem to posterity, the fact remains that he had enjoyed immense popularity with many of the ordinary Roman people who had exulted in his insulting disdain for old elitist traditions. Galba's age and authoritarian nature provoked unflattering comparisons with Nero's youth and reckless love of glamour.[1] This was partly responsible for the emergence of the phenomenon of the Pseudo-Nero. In 69 the first one popped up in Greece. Not entirely surprisingly, the chaos that followed Nero's death had meant there was a great deal of confusion in some places about whether Nero really was dead and, even if he was dead, what had happened. Nero had only recently been in Greece and it probably seemed implausible that this remarkable character had been extinguished. The strange thing was that in spite of the celebrations after Nero's death in 68 he had retained a coterie of devoted followers. They decorated his tomb with flowers and even went to the remarkable extent of installing statues of him in the forum, along with Neronian edicts, as if the emperor was still alive.[2] The Parthian king Vologaesus said he was sorry that Nero was dead and asked that honours continued to be paid to his memory.

The first impostor was, according to Tacitus, either a freedman from Italy or a slave from the province of Pontus in Asia Minor.[3] This must mean either that no one knew for certain or perhaps that two impostors became conflated into one. The man apparently looked like Nero and was able to play the cithara and sing. The vast majority of the population would have seen no more of Nero than his coin portraits. Vivid though these are, it is entirely possible that any overweight musical youth with a quiff and stubble could have passed himself off as Nero so long as he had sufficient chutzpah. At any rate it worked and this first Pseudo-Nero began to gravitate towards Syria, armed with a band of gullible ne'er-do-wells, and reached the island of Cythnus. He recruited military deserters and slaves whose masters he killed and, remarkably, his fame grew, fuelled by people who were terrified by the chaotic Roman civil war that had started after Nero's death. This Pseudo-Nero's plans only collapsed when the governor of Galatia and Pamphylia, one Calpurnius Asprenas, arrived at Cythnus with a detachment of the imperial fleet. The Pseudo-Nero had been trying to beguile various sea captains in the harbour there but they told Calpurnius what they had seen. On his orders they killed the impostor.

None of these men managed to secure the support of the Praetorian Guard and there is no evidence that they even tried. Nonetheless, it is worth speculating on what might have happened had the Guard decided to resolve their problem of whom to follow by manufacturing their own emperor especially as a Nero, any Nero, could have been passed off as a Julio-Claudian, the dynasty to which they were most loyal. In the event, the praetorians made do with what was available and forgot about the Julio-Claudians. The praetorian prefect Nymphidius Sabinus had been content to transfer his loyalty from Nero to Galba. He was also very well aware that Galba was an old man, in his early seventies, and would struggle to reach Rome from Spain.

Nymphidius Sabinus must also have been aware that under the circumstances, as prefect of the Guard, he was the only person capable of maintaining a semblance of order in Rome until Galba arrived. Nymphidius had cultivated the praetorians' loyalty by making sure that since the massive handout had been offered by Galba, the praetorians would bear a grudge against Galba and not him if it went unpaid. As well as obliging Tigellinus to give up the prefecture, he also tried to persuade the praetorians to demand that a deputation be sent to Galba to insist that he be made sole prefect for life.[4] Nymphidius sent his friend Gellianus to Spain to try and find out what Galba was up to. Gellianus returned, obviously several weeks later at the very earliest, and told Nymphidius that Galba had appointed his own praetorian prefect, Cornelius Laco, a man dismissed by Tacitus as 'most idle'.[5] This naturally caused Nymphidius considerable disquiet. Galba had also fallen under the spell of a man called Titus Vinius. Vinius maintained that Tigellinus had saved his daughter during the period of executions under Nero. As a result Tigellinus remained under Galba's protection until after Galba's murder, and was only subsequently killed on Otho's orders.[6]

The real issue is whether Nymphidius' intentions were to keep order in Rome or whether, now that Galba had appointed his own praetorian prefect, to try and make a bid for supreme power. Plutarch thought that was what Nymphidius was planning now to do.[7] There was even a rumour that Nymphidius was Caligula's son by a woman named Nymphidia, the daughter of Caligula's freedman, Callistus. Plutarch argued that this was impossible on the grounds that Nymphidius was already born when the affair started, but that the prefect was only too happy for the story to circulate.[8] Given the dynastic affiliations of the Praetorian Guard, it was worth taking advantage of. Regardless of the truth about his pedigree, or his intentions, Nymphidius rapidly lost control. The praetorians decided briefly to declare him emperor in the Castra Praetoria. Unfortunately, a tribune called Antonius Honoratus made an impassioned speech pointing out that while there had been very sound reasons for abandoning Nero, there were no similarly good reasons to abandon Galba in favour of Nymphidius, the very man who had persuaded them to give up on Nero. The outcome was inevitable. The praetorians declared for Galba. Nymphidius, who was preparing to deliver a speech to the praetorians, was killed. Galba was outraged when he heard and ordered the execution of any conspirators. These included the consul-designate Cingonius Varro for writing the speech that Nymphidius had been about to give.[9]

These killings were seen as arbitrary and despotic and began the process of undermining Galba's support almost as soon as his reign began. He had compounded his problems by singularly failing to recognize the importance of courting the Praetorian Guard from the outset. Instead, Galba openly declared that he chose his troops rather than buying them. As Tacitus observed, this was an admirable principle to espouse in the interests of the state but would only lead to danger for Galba. This factor added to further complications for the Guard. In addition, Nero's special German *custodes corporis* had been disbanded earlier by Galba. He suspected their reliability, regardless of the fact that all the previous emperors had used them and found them completely loyal.[10]

Meanwhile, Rome was in a potentially explosive state as Galba laboriously made his way to the city from Spain. The praetorians had rivals. In June 68 Galba's VII legion arrived, joining detachments from other legions brought to Rome by Nero in preparation to send against

Vindex. Galba had been declared emperor by legions, and not by the Guard, meaning they had lost the initiative and the chance to ingratiate themselves with the new emperor. Naturally, this created an opportunity, and it was seized by Marcus Salvius Otho, from whom Nero had helped himself to Poppaea some six years previously. Otho had expected to be named as Galba's heir, but in the event that honour went to a young senator called Licinianus Piso on 10 January 69, when Galba publicly adopted him in the Castra Praetoria.[11]

Otho was now in Galba's faction in Rome. He had ingratiated himself with the soldiers while marching from Spain with Galba. Once in the city Otho exploited every chance that came his way, helped by Laco's indolence. Using an agent in the form of Mevius Pudens, an associate of Tigellinus, any praetorian susceptible to persuasion or who had money troubles was courted and finally bribed with cash gifts every time they stood guard over a dinner at which Galba was dining with Otho. One praetorian called Cocceius Proculus was engaged in a land dispute with a neighbour, of itself an interesting insight into the lifestyle of a member of the Guard. Otho purchased the neighbour's estate and gave it to Proculus.[12]

The plot against Galba progressed with members of the Guard drawn in ever deeper. Galba's failure to invest in praetorian loyalty was now leading inexorably to an inevitable conclusion. It was a remarkable oversight, given that Galba was so old that in childhood he had met Augustus and had been the principal intended beneficiary of Livia's will. This experience of witnessing the reigns from Augustus to Nero, including a close friendship with Claudius, ought to have taught Galba the importance of keeping the Guard on side.[13] Otho's scheming expanded along with his ambitions. He delegated administration of the plot to his freedman Onomastus, who brought in a couple of accomplished crooks from the praetorian *speculatores*, a *tesserarius* called Barbius Proculus and an *optio* called Veturius. Otho was suitably impressed and bankrolled a scheme to bring the whole Guard over. Those who had been promoted by Nymphidius were warned that they needed to prove their loyalty to Otho. The general resentment that Galba had failed to pay the promised bounty was whipped up. There was some substance to these grievances. A number had been discharged by Galba on the grounds that they were Nymphidian allies. Anyone not on message now with the plotters was informed that posting to other units, which meant less money and inferior terms of service, would follow once Otho was in power.[14]

Corruption in the Praetorian Guard seems to have been well established by this date. One of the practices was paying centurions in return for time off duty. Praetorians either stole the money they needed for the bribes or took second jobs with the unfortunate effect that the better-off they were, so the more duties were allocated to them to coerce them into paying up. The whole set-up provoked indiscipline and dissent, making it more likely that they would participate in a rebellion.[15] The prospects looked promising, especially as anti-Galba feeling was spreading more widely in the army throughout the Empire, particularly in Germany, but a coup had to be planned. On 11 January 69 one nearly occurred but the realization that the praetorians and other units in Rome were too widely dispersed to coordinate at short notice suspended a scheme to carry Otho to the Castra Praetoria and declare him emperor. Under the circumstances it was remarkable that Galba managed to avoid finding out about Otho's machinations, but the prefect Laco was so disconnected from what was going on with the troops he was supposed to be leading that nothing got through.[16]

Onomastus and his praetorian cronies were as much a part of determining the agenda as Otho. On 15 January Otho attended a sacrifice at the Temple of Apollo on the Palatine, the very place where Sejanus had fallen, in the company of Galba. Onomastus arrived with a fictitious message that Otho's architect and builders were waiting for him. This was the pre-arranged signal that the coup had begun. Otho made his excuses and left with Onomastus. They walked down from the Palatine and into the forum where, close to the Temple of Saturn, twenty-three praetorians acclaimed Otho as emperor. Otho was horrified to be declared emperor by such a tiny fraction of the Praetorian Guard, but he was placed in a chair and carried off, joined by a couple of dozen more soldiers, not all of whom even knew what was going on.[17]

At the Castra Praetoria Julius Martialis was the tribune serving as officer of the day. Whatever his understanding of the situation when the news reached him, Martialis decided to go along with the plot and was joined by the other tribunes and centurions. It was a remarkable feat, achieved more by force of circumstance and opportunism than anything else. There is no suggestion that the praetorians as a body were about to go over at that moment, even if they had been carefully groomed by Onomastus and his team in the preceding months. It appears also that they did not even know at that point who was seizing power. Eventually the news arrived that Otho was on his way.[18]

There was a serious problem. Galba had with him on the Palatine the duty cohort of praetorians, dressed as normal for them while on that detail in togas, and thus (incidentally) clearly not ready for fighting.[19] It was essential to find out whether they would join the coup or not. Licinianus Piso, Galba's adoptive heir, addressed the praetorian cohort on the emperor's behalf. He talked up the challenges faced by Galba, embarked on a character assassination of Otho, appealed to them not to fall in with a conspiracy led by so few men, and inevitably offered a bounty. The *speculatores* amongst them seem to have disappeared at this point, presumably to join Otho, while the others prepared for action against the rebels by sounding out other military units in Rome. The problem was the rest of the praetorians. Three tribunes were sent to the Castra Praetoria to find out how the land lay. They were not welcomed. Cetrius Severus and Subrius Dexter were threatened, and Pomponius Longinus, notorious for his personal friendship with Galba, was attacked and arrested. The praetorians were joined by the navy, some of whose number had been killed by Galba when he arrived in Rome and others sent back to rowing on galleys, while other units remained uncommitted.[20]

Events moved extremely fast – too fast for Galba and his advisers, though they recognized that once Otho had secured the support of the praetorians and also taken control of the forum and Capitoline Hill then all would be lost. Nevertheless, there was indecision about whether Galba should go and try and take control of the praetorian camp.[21] Extraordinarily, for a brief moment the crisis seemed to be over. A spurious rumour erupted that Otho, incredibly, had been killed by the praetorians in the Castra Praetoria. Loyalists, including the mob and even senators, dropped their guard and burst into the palace. Galba was confronted by a praetorian called Julius Atticus who claimed to have killed Otho. Ever a stickler for protocol, the aged emperor, who might reasonably have been delighted by the news, demanded that the soldier tell him on whose authority he had done this.

The rumours of Otho's death had been greatly exaggerated. How the story emerged that he had been killed is unknown but can probably be put down simply to the chaotic circumstances and an element of wishful thinking. It seems to have been the ordinary praetorians who really took charge. They placed Otho on a pedestal, brought any soldier who came over to them to Otho to swear allegiance, and warned off the tribunes and centurions, whose loyalty to the coup they doubted. Otho spoke at length to the praetorians and other soldiers, running down Galba's regime for its corruption and arbitrary executions and explaining that there was no turning back now for the coup. The armoury was thrown open and arms and equipment distributed indiscriminately, regardless of whether the soldiers were praetorians or others. They now faced an armed mob of Galba's supporters. A rebel force, including the cavalry, evidently left the Castra Praetoria and made for the forum. As they approached, Atilius Vergilio, one of the standard-bearers with Galba's cohort, ripped off Galba's likeness from the standard, indicating that they had gone over to Otho. The mob fled. Galba was thrown from his chair and brutally murdered beside the Lake of Curtius in the forum by soldiers of unknown identity.[22] At less than seven months, Galba's tenure was the shortest principate to date. Within a year that record had been broken twice.

The praetorians had not all gone over to Otho. A praetorian centurion called Sempronius Densus stood fast so that Licinianus Piso could escape. Piso fled down through the forum and took sanctuary in the Temple of Vesta. One of the soldiers who hauled him out and killed him was a *speculator* called Statius Murcus. Meanwhile, the senators and the mob fled to the Castra Praetoria, falling over themselves to swear allegiance to Otho.[23] The Praetorian Guard had played a major role in toppling a short-lived emperor. Had Galba secured their support from the outset then he may have lived long enough to ensure that Licinianus Piso succeeded him and change the course of history. The Guard had now tasted power in an unprecedented way. The Castra Praetoria had become the epicentre of a watershed moment in Roman history, and the praetorians knew it. The soldiers appointed their own praetorian prefects, Plotius Firmus and Licinius Proculus, Laco being murdered to make way for them. The soldiers also chose for prefect of Rome one Flavius Sabinus, brother of the senator and general Titus Flavius Vespasianus who was even now waiting in the wings for his own chance to become emperor. It was not all ominous. Otho did away with the corrupt practice of soldiers paying centurions for time off, but avoided alienating the centurions. They now received a payment direct from the state for each soldier awarded leave.[24]

The fall of Galba left Rome shaken. The forum was strewn with dead bodies. Worse, news arrived that Aulus Vitellius, governor and therefore commander of the army in the province of Germania Inferior, had led a mutiny, egged on by some of his legionary commanders, Alienus Caecina and Fabius Valens. The crucial day had been 1 January 69 when the legions were supposed to renew their allegiance to the emperor. Many of the soldiers declined, and some openly attacked Galba's image and name.[25] In the next few days they were joined by armies in other north-western provinces, including Britain and Gaul, all declaring for Vitellius. Vitellius had been appointed to the governorship by Galba, and Tacitus ruminated on how fate had decided that the future of the Empire was to be determined by two of the most repellent men available. The only hope lay with Vespasian, then commanding an army in the east. But it made no difference to the fact that the only prospect seemed to be civil wars like those of a century earlier.

In Rome, Otho responded to the news by trying to step up to the mark of what was required of an emperor. He pardoned one of his opponents, the consul-designate Marius Celsus, but also took the decision to order the death of Tigellinus, Nero's deposed praetorian prefect who so far had escaped retribution thanks to Galba's protection. Tigellinus was ordered to commit suicide, which he did after hesitating, using a razor to slit his own throat. He had lived badly, but in Roman terms he died well.[26]

Otho tried to negotiate with Vitellius, offering him the money and opportunity to lead a quiet life. The gesture was reciprocated but the correspondence soon degenerated into mutual abuse, with each even sending assassins to his rival's headquarters. Otho then ordered a senatorial deputation to go and try and win over part of Vitellius' army. They were given an escort of praetorians. The diplomatic venture went completely wrong. The senatorial envoys threw in their lot with Vitellius and the praetorians raced back to Rome, armed with a letter given them by Fabius Valens, addressed to the praetorian and urban cohorts. The letter was strangely ambivalent. On one hand Fabius argued that the Vitellian forces were so large that the praetorians and urban cohorts should come over. On the other he castigated them for making Otho emperor when Vitellius had already been declared emperor in Germany.[27] Of course, Otho enjoyed a crucial advantage. He held Rome and was in control of affairs of state at the hub of the Empire with the praetorians as his sponsors. Vitellius was on the periphery and he had no choice but to march on the city. Otho's grip on Rome was not absolute. The 'XVII cohort', probably one of the urban cohorts, was ordered by Otho to relocate from Ostia to Rome. When they arrived, a praetorian tribune called Varius Crispinus was detailed to issue the arriving troops with arms. Crispinus decided to do this after dark because the barracks would be quieter. The armoury was duly opened but the time chosen merely led some of the rest of the praetorians, including some drunks, to assume that Crispinus was organizing a coup. The soldiers convinced themselves they had chanced on a plot by the tribunes and centurions to murder Otho, so they threw themselves into the melee, helping themselves to equipment and cutting down some of their officers before hurtling off to the palace to find Otho.[28]

Otho was hosting a banquet. His guests were terrified but tried to stay calm while they worked out what was going on. Otho told his praetorian prefects, Plotius Firmus and Licinius Proculus, to calm the soldiers down who were now busily cursing the centurions and tribunes and threatening the senate. Otho then advised guests to leave the dining room, a decision that occasioned a mass panic as they exited. Meanwhile the enraged praetorians burst in and demanded to see Otho. In the chaos, Otho panicked too and resorted to pleading with the soldiers. This worked, but not well. The praetorians returned to the Castra Praetoria feeling frustrated, resentful and guilty. The following day the sullen soldiers were told off by their praetorian prefects, but any ill feelings were swiftly mollified by the granting of a donative of 5,000 sestertii to each. Otho then spoke to the men himself. The tribunes and centurions offered to retire in return for their lives and the regular praetorians went back to work after insisting that the ringleaders be executed.[29]

It was twenty-eight years since the Guard had brought Claudius to power, which meant every one of the praetorians was a member of an organization that knew what it could do. Since Otho had become emperor, he knew he had to keep the praetorians both on side and under control. It was a very difficult proposition. He decided to attribute recent events to misguided loyalty on the part of the Guard and hope that by flattering their vanity they would be more inclined to accept that they needed to obey orders without question, and not act unilaterally. They were certainly not to take it upon themselves to threaten the senate, whose support was what legitimized Otho's regime.[30]

Precisely two praetorians were punished and an illusion of calm followed. The others remained apprehensive and suspicious. Claudius had passed a law banning praetorians and other soldiers from waiting on senators as their clients. This seems to have been overturned now by praetorians who, posing as civilians, infiltrated the houses of aristocrats in order to find out if the families concerned were Vitellian sympathizers.[31] Otho's coin issues were limited to gold and silver, ideal for paying troops. They depicted some of the usual imperial personifications, virtues and aspirations. One type, unique to his reign, depicted a Victory with the legend VICTORIA OTHONIS, 'Othonian Victory'; it was clearly designed to promote confidence that his forces would prevail over Vitellius.[32]

The prospect of Vitellius' advance added to Otho's problems, which now involved tackling natural disasters including major floods. These caused bridges in Rome to collapse, tenement blocks to be undermined, and a famine. Otho decided to make a move by using his loyal naval force to invade Gallia Narbonensis, since all the land routes were blocked by

1. Camp gate.
Fragment of marble relief now close to the Portico of Octavia, depicting a stylized fort with gates. The way the fortifications have been used as a wreath surrounding a victorious eagle atop the globe symbolizes the Roman state's militarized identity. It is possible it represents the Castra Praetoria, but may well be of earlier date.

2. Philippi Praetorian coin.
Of uncertain date and purpose, but probably struck between 27 BC and AD 68, this bronze issue produced at Philippi appears to commemorate the battle of 42 BC. It also seems to honour the praetorians either at the battle or as settled veterans in the colony established by Augustus. The coin depicts three praetorian standards and the legend COHOR PRAE PHIL.

3. Castra Praetoria north gate.

The Castra Praetoria's north gate Porta Principalis Dextra, filled in probably by Maxentius, is still quite easily visible from across Rome's Viale de Policlinico. Like the east gate, and probably also the south and west gates, it was single-portalled. Three filled-in windows are noticeable in the gate tower. The remains are of multiple periods including the Tiberian lower walls, the gate tower of c. 238 and the upper sections from c. 270–5.

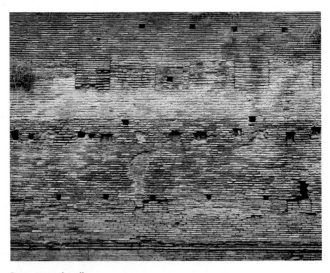

4. Castra Praetoria north wall.

Close-up view of a section of the Castra Praetoria's north wall showing how the original 3.35-metre wall with crenellations was subsequently raised to 5 metres by the simple expedient of filling in the crenellations and building upwards. The walls exhibit evidence of numerous modifications, repairs and heightening.

5. Castra Praetoria NE corner. The Castra Praetoria's northeast corner retains its tower and also evidence of the precautions taken by the Tiberian builders of the original structure. A weight-relieving arch is clearly visible at the bottom, designed to help stabilize the wall on unreliable patches of ground.

6. Sejanus coin, Bilbilis.
Bronze coin of Tiberius issued at Bilbilis, Spain. On the reverse, the names of the two consuls in Rome for the year 31 are given, in this case the emperor and also Lucius Aelius Sejanus, the then praetorian prefect. This is a unique instance of a serving praetorian prefect being recorded this way.

7. Temple of Apollo, Palatine Hill, Rome.
These fragments are all that is left of the Temple of Apollo on the Palatine Hill. It was here, on 18 October 31, that the senate was gathered when Sejanus was tricked by Macro into attending, in the belief that he was to be promoted. As Tiberius' speech was read out, it became clear he was in fact being publicly denounced.

8. Temple of Concordia Augusta, Rome.
The foundations to the right mark all that remains of the Temple of Concordia Augusta. Shortly after the arrest of the praetorian prefect Sejanus on 18 October 31, this was where the senate met and condemned him to death. Behind is the Tabularium (record office), now part of the Capitoline Museum, and, to the left, the remaining columns of the Temple of Vespasian and Titus.

9. Tombstone of Agrippina the Elder.
The tombstone of Agrippina the Elder, granddaughter of Augustus, daughter of Agrippa, wife of Germanicus, and mother of Caligula. Beloved by the army, when she returned to Italy with her husband's ashes in 19 she was met by two praetorian cohorts at Brundisium, who accompanied her to Rome. She died in 33. Her ashes were deposited in the Mausoleum of Augustus, from which this stone comes.

10. Claudius and the Praetorian Guard.
A gold aureus of Claudius (41–54). The reverse depicts Claudius greeting a praetorian *signifer* and the legend 'the praetorians received'. This example struck at Lyon, 44–5.

11. Claudius and the Castra Praetoria.
A gold aureus of Claudius (41–54). The reverse depicts the Castra Praetoria and the legend 'the emperor received'. This example struck at Lyon, 44–5.

12. Tombstone of Indus, German bodyguard.
The tombstone of Indus, a soldier in Nero's *Germani corporis custodes*, here described as being of the Batavian nation. The stone was erected on his behalf by his 'brother Eumenes' and his heirs from the 'guild of Germans'.

13. Nero sestertius.
Reverse of a brass sestertius depicting Nero on horseback alongside a mounted praetorian and the legend DECVRSIO, 'military manoeuvre'. The design appears to be an effort to portray the emperor as an action man, an extension of his other public performances, and was borrowed from earlier Greek types such as coins issued by Thessaly. Rome, 64.

14. Pompeii, Titus Suedius Clemens.
Inscription erected under Vespasian (69–79) to commemorate the resolution of a dispute over the illegal appropriation of public lands by various locals outside Pompeii, presumably in the vicinity of the Nucerian Gate cemetery where the stone is located. The matter was dealt with by Titus Suedius Clemens, described as a tribune. On the basis of how praetorians were liable to be used for this kind of local policing and surveying activity, it is likely Clemens was a praetorian tribune.

15. Tombstone of Marcus Naevius Harmodius. Marcus Naevius Harmodius was a doctor attached to the X praetorian cohort. He died aged fifty-five and was commemorated by his son Marcus Naevius Naevianus, his daughter Naevia Harmodia, and his freedwoman wife Naevia Gluconis. Found by the Via Nomentana in Rome. Note that for all the careful lettering, the first line of the main text was misplaced, requiring the clumsy insertion of an 'M' for the first part of Harmodius' name. Late first/early second century AD.

16. Tombstone of Lucilius Proculus. Lucilius Proculus had served as treasurer of the VI praetorian cohort for thirteen years when he died in 33. He had come from Siscia in Pannonia. Although the text is hard to read now, thanks to the texture of the stone, the memorial is remarkable amongst praetorian tombstones for carrying a likeness of the deceased. Late first/early second century AD.

17. Trajan's Column.
A section of the Trajan's Column reliefs, which illustrated the emperor's Dacian wars of 102–3 and 105–6. This scene depicts legionaries and praetorians crossing two parallel pontoon bridges, and usefully records their joint participation in the campaign. The praetorians, shown to the right and on the farther bridge, are distinguished by their wreathed standards. From the cast now in the Victoria and Albert Museum. Rome, 113.

18. Lucius Laelius Fuscus. The marble funerary urn of the centurion Lucius Laelius Fuscus. His career began as an *eques* in the Praetorian Guard. A series of centurionates included command of the X praetorian cohort and culminated in a transfer to the position of *trecenarius* with the VII legion Claudia. Late first/early second century AD, with the latter being more likely due to the participation of both the Guard and the VII legion in Trajan's wars.

19. Tombstone of Caius Caristicus Redemtus. Caius Caristicus Redemtus, from Brixellus (Brescell) in Cisalpine Gaul, was a soldier of the III praetorian cohort who died at the age of forty after sixteen years' service. He is described as a *plumba(rius) ordina(rius/tus)*, a term that indicates he was a lead-worker of a rank equivalent to that of a centurion. Late first/early second century AD.

20. Forum Baths, Ostia.
The Forum Baths at Ostia form one of the largest public facilities in the port town. They appear to have been built at the expense of Marcus Gavius Maximus, praetorian prefect under Antoninus Pius (138–61). The scale, sophisticated architecture and lavish decoration exemplify the wealth and status enjoyed by the praetorian prefects by this date.

21. Freedman of Marcus Gavius Maximus.
Tombstone of Marcus Gavius Amphion Mus ('the
Mouse'), a freedman of the praetorian prefect
Marcus Gavius Maximus, whose name and title are
proudly included. Gavius Maximus was prefect for
around twenty years, an exceptional length of time.

22. Palatine.
The remains of the imperial palaces on the Palatine Hill, Rome. The cohorts of the Praetorian Guard
spent much of their time in and around the palaces, rotating on a daily basis in order to fulfil their
primary duty as the emperor's personal bodyguard.

23. Marcus Aurelius and praetorians.
Marcus Aurelius (161–80) is shown here in a triumphant arrival being greeted by at least two praetorians in full armour to the right. From a relief originally on his arch and now in the Capitoline Museum, Rome. About 176–80.

24. Praetorian standard.
Relief showing a praetorian standard, depicted on the Arch of the Moneylenders (*Argentarii*) in Rome. Dedicated in 204 under Septimius Severus by cattle merchants and bankers of the Cattle Market. The inclusion of a praetorian standard seems to have been just one in a series of decorative elements designed to invoke Rome's military greatness and piety.

25. Praetorian standard detail.
Detailed on a relief showing a praetorian standard, on the Arch of the Moneylenders in Rome, depicting a stylized representation of, perhaps, the Castra Praetoria. 204. (See also Plate 24).

26. Lucius Septimius Valerinus.
The funerary monument of a praetorian of the VIIII cohort, Lucius Septimius Valerinus, depicting the deceased in the praetorian tunic and *paenula* cloak. He had formerly served with the I legion Adiutrix, and had presumably obtained citizenship under Severus. Early third century AD.

27. Praetorian diploma.
Bronze diploma fragment recording the honourable discharge on 7 January 246, during the reign of Philip I (244–9), of Nebus Tullius Ma[…], a soldier of the V praetorian cohort. The text specifies that soldiers from cohorts I–X were involved. Height 140 mm, diameter 102 mm. Reputedly found at Piedmont, northern Italy.

28. Philip I, 'the Arab' (244–9). All too typical of the era, Marcus Julius Philippus served as praetorian prefect in 243, seized power as emperor in 244, only to be killed along with his son by praetorians in 249.

29. Maxentius (306–12).
Maxentius, the last emperor to deploy the Guard in a military context. From a statue found at Ostia.

30. Battle of the Milvian Bridge.
Section of relief on the south side of the Arch of Constantine in Rome, depicting the Battle of the Milvian Bridge on 28 October 312. Maxentius' fleeing *equites singulares* in their distinctive scale armour are shown falling into the Tiber as the pontoon bridge over which they were making their escape collapses. This left Maxentius' infantry praetorians alone on the north bank to be defeated by Constantine.

31. Milvian Bridge, Rome.
The Milvian Bridge, where the Via Flaminia heading north from Rome crosses the Tiber. Built originally in 115 BC, the structure has undergone many significant repairs and alterations, and now only the lower parts of the piers are Roman. On 28 October 312, Constantine I defeated the army of Maxentius here, which included part of the Guard.

32. Constantine I (307–37).
Constantine I, 'the Great', who defeated Maxentius at the Battle of the Milvian Bridge and disbanded the Praetorian Guard immediately afterwards.

Vitellian forces. A force would lead the way under the overall command of the praetorian prefect, Licinius Proculus. This seems to have involved five praetorian cohorts, plus cavalry and, even more remarkably, two thousand gladiators, as well as the I legion. Proculus had no experience of campaigns, and so was accompanied by three senatorial generals who included Suetonius Paulinus, who had defeated the Boudican hordes in Britain almost a decade earlier. Tacitus, with predictable senatorial venom, accused Proculus of slating his far more experienced assistants in order to remain in charge.[33] The use of praetorian and urban cohorts in such a prominent position in warfare was a worrying sign of the times and reflected the enormous impact on the Roman world of the growing crisis. That one of Galba's coin issues in the summer of 68 had been a widely circulated *dupondius* with PAX AUGUSTA ('Augustan Peace'), and Otho's gold and silver types included one with PAX ORBIS TERRARUM ('peace of all the lands of the world'), must have seemed cruelly ironic.[34]

In the middle of March 69 Otho handed over civil government to the senate, his own duties to his brother Salvius Titianus, and prepared to leave for the war. There was no time to be lost. Vitellian forces were advancing over the Alps. Otho headed out to join the army of five legions and the praetorian contingent of five cohorts. He brought with him what Tacitus describes as the rest of the Praetorian Guard, praetorian veterans (presumably *evocati*, thereby serving as a solid body of experienced troops), and a 'large number' of naval troops.[35] The praetorians first saw action during Otho's invasion of the Ligurian coast, securing the territory between the inland hills and the sea, while the legions and auxiliaries bore the brunt of the fighting.[36] The outcome was inconclusive and Vitellian forces were already making their way into Italy. Three praetorian cohorts had been assigned to Vestricius Spurinna who was holding Placentia (Piacenza) for Otho, along with a detachment of a thousand legionaries and some cavalry. Recognizing that his force lacked experience and would have been hopelessly outclassed by seasoned troops, Spurinna decided to keep the men safely behind the city's fortifications. They ignored him out of sheer terror that Vitellian forces under Caecina were on their way. They left Placentia and Spurinna had no choice but to go with his men. The soldiers headed west and after 17 miles (27 km) reached the Po where they decided to make a camp for the night. Creating an overnight base was routine for Roman military forces, but for the effete praetorians the task proved impossibly onerous and demoralizing. Finally, the centurions and tribunes managed to persuade the men that Spurinna had been right all along and back they went to Placentia.[37] The incident is a fascinating vignette of the real quality of praetorian soldiers whose comfortable life in Rome, for all their posturing and political interference, had really left them little more use than weekend military poseurs. On the face of it, these louche Hectors lacked the discipline, coordination and even basic physical ability to function as soldiers in a war setting. This was not a problem peculiar to praetorians; legionaries stationed in the comfortable setting of a peaceful province could easily lapse into indolence and incompetence as Corbulo had found in Syria in 58.[38]

In spite of this, the prestige of Rome and the praetorian cohorts with the Othonian army became part of the morale-boosting preamble to the two-day fight that followed when Caecina and his Vitellian force arrived. The Vitellians, for their part, dismissed the defenders as circus fans and theatregoers, an allegation that probably had a great deal of truth in it. In the event, the praetorians, for all their apparent lack of moral fibre, turned out to be more than equal to the occasion. They defended Placentia bravely, even hurling millstones down the ramparts on to the attackers to great effect. Caecina was forced to withdraw towards Bedriacum (Calvatone, near Cremona).[39]

Otho was struggling with leading an army. He was disorientated by the way his troops criticized his senatorial generals, Annius Gallus, Suetonius Paulinus and Marius Celsus, with those responsible for Galba's murder being the most disruptive. Otho handed over command to his brother Salvius Titianus.[40] However, more positive news lay ahead. Caecina, infuriated by his humiliation at Placentia, was bent on recovering his reputation. At a place called the Castores, a shrine site 12 miles (19 km) from Bedriacum, he set up an ambush and laid plans to entice the Othonian forces into it. Unfortunately, someone in Caecina's army passed the information on to the Othonians. Paulinus and Celsus prepared for the battle by using a combination of legionaries, auxiliaries, praetorians and praetorian cavalry. Three praetorian cohorts were to hold the road, and a force of a thousand cavalry drawn from praetorians and auxiliaries was organized to mop up at the end of the battle.[41]

To begin with the battle did not go too well for the Othonians. Part of the praetorian cavalry was wiped out when the Vitellians counter-attacked from the safety of a wood. This setback was rapidly overcome when the main Othonian infantry force charged and routed the Vitellians.[42] In the aftermath, though, the Vitellian armies' prospects improved when Fabius Valens and his force joined up with Caecina. There was now a risk that the combined Vitellians would attack quickly. Otho sought advice from his generals. Paulinus, supported by Celsus and Gallus, counselled waiting because the Vitellians were likely to be undone by supply problems as they made their way into Italy. The Vitellian forces could not count on the rest of Britain's huge garrison crossing over to join them since the province was proving so troublesome to keep under control. Conversely, the Othonian army had plenty of resources and still held Rome.[43]

Otho was more inclined to listen to his brother Titianus and the praetorian prefect Proculus. They recommended going for an attack on the basis that luck and the gods were on Otho's side. Otho, preferring superstition to reason, decided to attack but also accepted a decision that it was too dangerous for him to stay. He was to withdraw to Brixellum (Bresello). It was a fateful decision. Otho set out with 'cohorts of praetorians and *speculatores*, and some cavalry', but his departure demoralized the troops who were left behind. None of this escaped the notice of Valens and Caecina. Tacitus raised the possibility that the two forces toyed with the idea of negotiating a peace rather than fighting it out for two men, each of whom was so obviously unsuitable for power. But Tacitus also rejected that theory as implausible on the basis that as the Roman world had grown stronger so the thirst for power won by violence had superseded anything else.[44]

Either way, the war continued. The Othonians were now commanded by Titianus and controlled by the praetorian prefect Proculus. The tribunes leading two of the Othonian praetorian cohorts left on campaign made their way over to enemy territory and tried to speak to Caecina. Before they could explain what they wanted, whether to sue for peace, to go over to Caecina or initiate some ruse to trick him, he was warned by his own lookouts that the Othonians were approaching. Caecina returned to the main force where Fabius Valens was preparing for battle. The fight that followed near the city of Bedriacum (Cividale) on 14 April 69 was bloody and chaotic, but the Vitellians prevailed. It is known to history as the First Battle of Bedriacum, or the First Battle of Cremona. The Othonian praetorians vented their fury by blaming the defeat on treachery, almost certainly a reference to what Tacitus described as hand-to-hand fighting between troops who had known each other. This must have been the praetorians, and I legion Italica, both of which were based in Italy.[45] The news filtered through to Otho at Brixellum; it had been a comprehensive disaster. Otho's supporters tried to bolster his resolve. The praetorian prefect Plotius Firmus begged him to stand fast in the face of adversity, and was backed up by other soldiers who insisted that reinforcements were on their way. Otho, however, recognized that the game was up and the price of carrying on too much. He settled his affairs and arranged for his inner circle of friends and attendants to be transported away. Despite his calm and collected approach, Otho still had to settle down his troops who were threatening to kill his staff as they left.[46]

At dawn on 16 April 69 Otho committed suicide. It was an honourable death that went some way to ameliorating his tarnished reputation. Praetorians carried the body to the funeral pyre, some remarkably even choosing to take their own lives too, so impressed had they been by his dignified end. At least the praetorians showed an appropriate level of loyalty, having brought Otho into power and continuing to hold him in high esteem.[47] In the event his reign had lasted only into its ninety-fifth day, or just over three months. Once more, the Praetorian Guard was without an emperor. Soon there would be no Othonian Praetorian Guard at all.

Vitellius, at this juncture, had no idea that he was effectively emperor of the whole Roman world. He expended most of his efforts on preparing for more fighting with Otho's forces, completely unaware that this was unnecessary. The impact of the previous fighting had been bad enough on civilian communities in Italy but now his troops in Italy simply capitalized on the opportunity to run riot, sacking rich villa estates.[48] When Vitellius learned of what had happened to Otho his reaction was a mixture of magnanimity and revenge. He met his supporters and former enemies at Lyon. He executed Otho's principal centurions, which immediately alienated some of the army, but acquitted Suetonius Paulinus and observed proper legality when it came to the wills of Otho's deceased supporters. Tacitus indulged himself with a depiction of Vitellius as an otiose and repellent glutton who was far more concerned with rich food and luxuries than with disciplining and organizing his forces The regime appears to have become more brutal in fairly short order, with summary and arbitrary executions.[49]

One of Vitellius' problems was how to deal with Otho's legions, now thoroughly resentful at the humiliation of defeat. The soldiers of the XIIII legion Gemina Martia Victrix, a unit with a significant military reputation after its defeat of Boudica in Britain in 60–1, were very embittered and even insisted that most of them had not been at Bedriacum. So, therefore, technically the legion had not been defeated. Vitellius ordered them to return to Britain but until the transfer went ahead they were stationed in the Augusta Taurinorum (Turin) area with some auxiliary Batavian cohorts. This was an exceptionally bad decision since the Batavians and the legionaries loathed each other. A fight broke out when a legionary backed a local civilian whom a Batavian said he had been cheated by. The violence was set to get a great deal worse except that two praetorian cohorts, presumably also billeted nearby, joined in on the side of the legionaries and forced the Batavians to back off.[50]

This incident demonstrates that Othonian praetorians were still operating alongside the rest of the defeated army, and also capable of dangerous partisanship. Vitellius' solution was two-fold. Firstly, the men were 'separated', which could either mean that they were now to be kept apart from the rest of the army or that the individual praetorian cohorts were now dispersed so that they could not act together. Secondly, Vitellius offered them an honourable discharge, which in practice amounted to presenting them with the opportunity to end their service early on the same terms as if they had completed their full sixteen years. Suetonius suggests that the process was more punitive, saying that Vitellius disbanded the Othonian praetorians by edict on the grounds that they had treacherously abandoned Galba for Otho. In addition, he ordered that one hundred and twenty praetorians who had requested a reward from Otho for helping to murder Galba be hunted down and punished.[51] This was not wholly unreasonable and, indeed, Suetonius considered it a responsible act since it was quite plain the Othonian praetorians had acted without honour in abandoning and killing one emperor in favour of another. Either way, the demobilization of the Othonian praetorians started out well from Vitellius' perspective, since the praetorians had clearly not transferred their loyalty to him, though his failure to secure their loyalty would play a crucial part in his downfall. The demobilization process started with praetorians handing over their equipment to the tribunes and preparing for retirement, but this simply provided Vespasian with an opportunity. Unfortunately for Vitellius, news started to reach the dismissed praetorians that Vespasian in the east was commencing his own bid for power.[52]

Titus Flavius Vespasianus had been sent out to the east in 66 by Nero to settle the Jewish Revolt with his son Titus. A tough and experienced general, Vespasian had played a major role in the invasion of Britain in 43, commanding the II Augusta. He took over the campaign against the Jews from the governor of Syria, Gaius Licinius Mucianus, but the two remained important allies, though Mucianus was even keener on Titus.[53] Mucianus played a crucial role in persuading Vespasian to challenge Vitellius. On 1 July 69 in Alexandria, Vespasian was declared emperor with the assistance of the prefect of Egypt, Tiberius Julius Alexander, who obligingly organized his garrison to take the oath of allegiance. When the news reached Syria, Mucianus had his troops take the oath too. By 15 July 69 the whole of the wealthy province of Syria was behind Vespasian, with Asia, Greece and other important provinces onside.[54] However, apart from Syria, not all these places had garrisons so it was crucial for Vespasian to bring over as much of the Roman armed forces as possible. Vespasian prepared extremely carefully. He started by striking his own bullion coinage at Antioch so that he could pay his forces and offer rank and position to men who came over to him. He also secured the Empire's eastern borders so that his campaign could proceed without placing the eastern provinces in danger from Armenia and Parthia. Titus would finish the war against the Jews. Vespasian would settle affairs in the east, securing Egypt so that he could starve out Vitellius,[55] and Mucianus would march against Vitellius. Vespasian made a particular point of targeting the praetorians whom he knew were hostile to Vitellius. He wrote to all the various Roman armies he could, requesting that they encourage the praetorians to come over to him, dangling the carrot of readmission to the Praetorian Guard.[56]

In the meantime Vitellius marched towards Rome with an army of sixty thousand men, Vitellian senators and equestrians, hangers-on and entertainers. Like a plague of locusts this motley crew made its way through Italy, taking whatever it needed from the hapless communities unfortunate enough to lie in the way. Eventually, the Vitellian entourage reached Rome but his advisers had the wit to discourage Vitellius from marching in as if he were a conquering general. He donned a toga for his big moment, but was still followed in by his forces. Tacitus conceded that it was a very impressive moment, or, rather, would have been, had it not involved Vitellius.[57]

Now safely ensconced in Rome, Vitellius adopted the trappings of an emperor. He accepted the title Augustus, became *pontifex maximus* (chief priest), and attended the senate, though it appears that the two men really running the show were Valens and Caecina. Vitellius also chose two prefects to command the Praetorian Guard, though at that point there were no Vitellian praetorians to command. Vitellius selected two associates of Valens and Caecina respectively, a centurion called Julius Priscus and a prefect of an auxiliary cohort called Publilius Sabinus.[58] Valens and Caecina were increasingly preoccupied with their own rivalry, so the praetorian prefectures are best seen as an extension of that tension. Rome was already in a dangerous state. Since Vitellius had brought sixty thousand troops with him it was patently clear that the Castra Praetoria could not possibly accommodate them, so they ranged dangerously through the city without any semblance of discipline or organization.

In the event, sixteen milliary praetorian cohorts were formed by Valens on Vitellius' behalf, along with four urban cohorts, using soldiers taken from Vitellius' legions. It is quite possible, as was discussed earlier, that this was already the size of the praetorian cohorts. If so, then the principal point of interest is the increase from twelve to sixteen praetorian cohorts, taking the Guard at least from twelve to sixteen thousand men. If the praetorian cohorts had only been quingenary up to this date then the increase was even more dramatic. Quantity was more important to Vitellius than quality. He allowed soldiers to choose the unit in which they wished to serve, regardless of their personal attributes or motivation. The result was that the new Vitellian praetorians included disreputable individuals and damaged the Guard's prestige.[59]

There were now effectively two groups of praetorians: Vitellius' sixteen thousand new praetorians recruited from his legions, and Otho's old (and now discharged) praetorians. In the context of the chaos at Rome, Vitellius' profligacy and the attractive prospect of Vespasian, the Vitellian supporters started to drift away. It began with the III legion, which went over to Vespasian. Vitellius dismissed the reports in a speech to his forces, blaming the discharged Othonian praetorians for spreading rumours of civil war.[60] Other commanders waited to see which way the tide would turn. By September 69 the game was nearly up for Vitellius. The first wave of Flavian forces, under Antonius Primus, reached northern Italy, ready to secure the Alps and open the way in to the peninsula for Mucianus, then following up from the rear.[61] Vitellius ordered Valens and Caecina to march north to meet them, which they did, setting out for Bedriacum. Caecina decided to betray Vitellius. His associate was the disaffected Lucilius Bassus, commander of the Vitellian fleets at Ravenna and Misenum. Despite this prestigious command, Bassus was embittered that he had not been made praetorian prefect. Bassus then turned the fleet over to Vespasian, and would have been followed by Caecina had the latter not been imprisoned by his own soldiers.[62]

The Second Battle of Bedriacum (Cremona) followed shortly afterwards on 24 October 69. The old praetorians fought alongside the III legion for the Flavians where they would help play a crucial role.[63] The battle did not start well for the Flavian forces and Antonius Primus was forced to call them up to help hold his line. Even so, Vitellian artillery proved extremely dangerous to the Flavian forces. A Vitellian ballista belonging to the XV legion proved particularly lethal. Two soldiers, possibly praetorians, dashed forward, disguising themselves by picking up shields from dead legionaries of the XV, and wrecked the machine by cutting its ropes. Obviously that gave the two men away and they were killed immediately by the Vitellians. Their heroic effort seems to have gone down in Roman military lore even though their names remained unknown. If they were praetorians then the episode suggests that in battle they were otherwise indistinguishable from legionaries. Primus spoke to all his forces, selecting the praetorians for special treatment when he said that if they did not win that day then there was no one else who would have them.[64] When the III legion hailed the sunrise this kicked off a rumour that Mucianus had arrived to reinforce the Flavians. This was not true but the Flavians were galvanized and rallied. The Vitellians collapsed and the Flavians had the day. A horrific sack of Cremona followed, lasting four days, in revenge for the city's support for Vitellius.

In Rome, Vitellius was understandably disorientated by events. He sent Valens off to fight at the front and turned on one of his praetorian prefects, Publilius Sabinus, because he had been Caecina's nominee. In his place Alfenus Varus, an ally of Valens, was appointed. The Vitellian praetorians might now have played an important role in helping bolster Valens in the war; indeed, this was mooted, but he rejected the plan.[65] Perhaps he knew they were not up to the job. Valens went to the province of Alpes Maritimae (Maritime Alps) where the procurator, Marius Maturus, warned him not to head into neighbouring Gallia Narbonensis. At this point Valerius Paulinus, procurator of Gallia Narbonensis and a supporter of Vespasian, weighed in. He had called up the old praetorians whom Vitellius had discharged, cashing in on his popularity with them since he had once been a tribune of the Guard, and stationing them in Forum Julii (Fréjus). Valens had to leave, taking with him just four *speculatores* from the Maritime Alps but, thanks to a storm, was washed up on some islands near Toulon and captured by a force sent after him by Valerius Paulinus. He was subsequently executed on or around 10 December 69.[66]

In another passage Tacitus mused on the extent to which chance, rather than fate and circumstance, dictated events. Valens' end could not have been a better example.[67] The chance storm that washed Valens up on the Îlles d'Hyères meant that, for him, the war was over. With Valens removed, the whole Vitellian edifice started to collapse. The process was not instant, nor was it straightforward, but it was relentless. The legions gradually began to tranfer their allegiance to Vespasian. Nevertheless, Vitellius had not yet given up, though he seems to have been a man inclined to change his mind; one of his habits was to dismiss the praetorians and then promptly call them back again.[68] Antonius Primus made his way into Italy, slightly concerned to hear a rumour that Vitellian praetorians had been sent north from Rome to meet them. In fact Vitellius had sent almost twenty thousand troops in the form of fourteen of his praetorian cohorts and a legion's worth of naval troops under the command of Julius Priscus and Alfenus Varus.[69] The remaining two praetorian cohorts and, presumably, the urban cohorts were left behind to protect Rome under the command of Vitellius' brother, Lucius. Vitellius then headed off to his army in the field at Mevania (Bevagna in Umbria), in spite of his lack of experience as a military commander.

News arrived that the Misenum fleet had abandoned Vitellius. The reason was sheer trickery. A Flavian sympathizer, a centurion called Claudius Faventinus, circulated a forged letter which he claimed had been sent by Vespasian. The 'letter' offered the fleet a reward in exchange for abandoning Vitellius. In the ensuing confusion the Campanian cities of Puteoli and Capua became involved, the latter being pro-Vitellian but not for long. Capua went over to Vespasian too and the rebel forces ended up taking control of Tarracina. Vitellius divided his forces. He ordered Priscus and Alfenus Varus to stay at Narnia with, presumably, eight praetorian cohorts, and sent his brother Lucius with the remaining six cohorts and five hundred cavalry to deal with the Campanian threat. The onset of winter was a distinct advantage to Vitellius, but the Flavians also had luck on their side. They were joined by the general Petilius Cerealis, who had managed to find his way to them disguised as a peasant.[70]

At Interamna (Terni) a Vitellian force of four hundred cavalry was garrisoning the city. A Flavian force under Arrius Antoninus Varus, Antonius

Primus' cavalry commander, attacked them but most immediately surrendered. A few got away and headed back to the main Vitellian army where they bewailed the size of the Flavian force in order to explain their defeat. The praetorian prefects Julius Priscus and Alfenus Varus immediately left to go to Vitellius. That had the effect of persuading the rest of the Vitellian force that there was no shame in giving up.[71] As the Vitellian cause collapsed, the Flavian forces under Antonius Primus and Antoninus Varus offered Vitellius his life in return for capitulating to Vespasian, though this was really a hopelessly unrealistic prospect. It was an offer Vitellius considered but while he was doing so Rome was about to fall to Vespasian. The prefect of Rome was Titus Flavius Sabinus, elder brother of Vespasian. Senior senators assured Sabinus of their support, and pointed out that with the urban cohorts and the night watch at his disposal, it would be easy to bring Rome over and win credit for helping to end the war.[72]

On 18 December 69, Vitellius abdicated. He said it was in the interests of peace. Sabinus, with whom Vitellius had been negotiating, sent instructions to 'the tribunes of the cohorts' to keep the men in their barracks. This may or not be referring at least in part to the tribunes of such praetorians who were still in Rome. Unfortunately for Sabinus and the Flavian supporters amongst the senators and equestrians, the general public in Rome was still distinctly pro-Vitellian and a fight broke out between them and Sabinus' forces. Sabinus, angry that the agreement with Vitellius had broken down, took the Capitol with his men. Here he was joined by Vespasian's younger son, Domitian. In the ensuing fight, the Temple of Jupiter Capitolinus was burnt down. The Vitellians captured the Capitol. Domitian escaped but Sabinus was captured and brutally murdered. This was an enormous shock to the Flavian army, now at the city of Ocriculum (Otricoli), just 44 miles (71 km) north of Rome. More bad news followed when it turned out that Petilius Cerealis and a cavalry force had been defeated in the city suburbs.[73]

Despite these setbacks, an attempt by the Vitellians to negotiate peace collapsed. On 20 December 69, the Flavian army entered Rome and an orgy of violence followed, climaxing in the battle for control of the Castra Praetoria, which Vitellians were determined to hold as their last stand.

Since the Flavian army included former praetorians who were determined to recover the barracks from the usurpers, the fighting was all the more vicious. The Flavians organized themselves into the *testudo* formation and brought up artillery to assault the Castra Praetoria. When the camp fell, it did so with dead Vitellians hanging over the walls and those left alive charging the attackers in a last and futile gesture of defiance. The fall of the Castra Praetoria was the climax of the fighting and its collapse marked the end of the reign of Vitellius. He planned an escape but was apprehended by a tribune called Julius Placidus, only to be attacked by soldiers from the German garrison who killed him on the Gemonian Stairs.[74] Vitellius' reign of nine months had ended in a cavalcade of destructive violence that had torn the Roman Empire apart. Throughout those desperate months the praetorians, on whichever side, had played important roles, but it was the way in which the Castra Praetoria, yet again, acted as the stage on which so much of the drama unfolded that epitomized the importance of the imperial bodyguard to Roman history.

CHAPTER 7

TO THE VICTOR, THE SPOILS
(69–98)

The aftermath of the civil war left the Flavians in complete control of the Roman world. The chaos of the fighting and rival regimes had left the Praetorian Guard inflated, and an inchoate collection of cohorts whose loyalty and affiliation could not be relied on. Reduction and reform were needed to reorganize the Guard, which was fully established in the Castra Praetoria. For the first time, the Guard came under the personal control of the emperor's son and heir. The praetorians had been tamed and, in an age of military campaigns, began to appear more often in the field. In spite of Domitian's unpopularity, the Guard seems to have played no part in his downfall.

WITH ROME AT THEIR mercy, the Flavian forces did nothing immediately to cover themselves in glory. They toured the city seeking out anyone suspected of Vitellian affiliations. In advance of his father's arrival, Domitian was declared Caesar by the leaders of the Flavian army and took over the palace.[1] The title 'Caesar' was evolving into one used by the heir or heirs apparent, the emperor being the 'Augustus'. A new praetorian prefect was appointed. Arrius Varus took the position, though Antonius Primus was the man really in charge. The senate proceeded to vote all the necessary and customary imperial powers to Vespasian but Rome was still in a very unsettled and volatile state. It was not until the arrival of Gaius

Licinius Mucianus, the governor of Syria and Vespasian's main ally, that the situation started to settle. Antonius Primus and Arrius Varus abruptly lost their influence and Mucianus took centre stage. Vitellius' praetorian prefects came to different ends. Julius Priscus committed suicide, but Alfenus Varus seems to have escaped censure, despite the witch-hunt for Vitellians.[2]

A serious problem remained with what to do about the praetorians. Not surprisingly, the Othonian praetorians, sacked by Vitellius, wanted their jobs back. The Flavian forces, however, had a number of legionaries who had been chosen as praetorians and were looking forward to the money and privileges that came with the job.[3] There was also the problem of Vitellius' praetorians. It was impossible to accommodate or pay them all. It began to look as if fighting was about to break out. Mucianus decided to review every soldier's individual claim and relative seniority and make appointments on that basis. A very curious episode followed. Mucianus ordered the Flavian claimants to parade in full armour and equipment and the Vitellians, who had been rounded up across Rome, were told to parade in whatever rags they were wearing before being separated into groups depending on whichever garrisons they had come from originally. This caused the Vitellians considerable disquiet, with some believing they were about to be executed. Meanwhile, Mucianus had a subtle plan in operation. Once they had all calmed down, he spoke to them as if they were all equals and took them onto the praetorian complement. That defused any chance of fighting or a mutiny and allowed him to initiate a process of working through this new Praetorian Guard one by one, discharging individual soldiers if they were of retirement age or sacking those who had a record of misconduct.[4]

This occasion poses the problem of just how many praetorian cohorts existed by the early months of 70. An undated tombstone from Rome, stylistically attributed to this period, of a praetorian called Metilius Pudens says that he died at the age of forty-three, having served for twenty-three years. His final unit was the nineteenth praetorian cohort. On the assumption that a continuous numbering system had been maintained, in spite of the various manifestations of the Guard during the civil war era (and, as has been discussed already, there is no guarantee that this was so), this ought to be a minimum number which would mean nineteen thousand troops. Yet, a diploma of Vespasian found in Moesia Inferior (Romania), dated to 2 December 76, refers to the soldiers who had served in 'the nine praetorian and the four urban cohorts'. This suggests Mucianus had succeeded in bringing the numbers down to a manageable level and/or that there had never been nineteen praetorian cohorts at any one time.[5]

What remains unresolved is whether the Flavian praetorian cohorts were milliary, as those of Vitellius had been, or quingenary. There is no specific evidence to settle it either way, and the existing arguments merely rely on what individual authorities regard as the more probable.[6] The only contemporary circumstantial evidence is that by the late first century the first cohort of a legion seems to have consisted of five double centuries of 160 men (eight hundred in total). The organization of forts was explained in a document called *On the Fortification of Camps*, which belongs to the late first or early second century. This source allocates twice the space for a praetorian cohort as for an ordinary legionary cohort: 60 x 720 feet (18.3 x 219 metres), compared to 30 x 720 feet (9.1 x 219 metres).[7] This appears to suggest that by the time of writing, if not already, praetorian cohorts were routinely twice the size of a regular legionary quingenary cohort. It is therefore possible, and even probable, that Flavian praetorian cohorts were also a thousand in size and had continued on in that form from the Vitellian units, remaining so to Dio's time and beyond, by which time they had been organized into ten cohorts.[8] However, it is also possible this additional space was simply required by praetorians because their prestige demanded that they had larger tents, more equipage, more slaves and so on. Nevertheless, it seems inherently unlikely that a new emperor, especially after the massive disorder of 68–9, would have risked a dramatic reduction of the Guard. Milliary cohorts would have meant only having to dispose of around half of Vitellius' praetorians. Reducing the Guard to nine quingenary cohorts would have meant removing three-quarters. Appointment to the Guard represented privilege and reward; Vespasian had a very large number of troops who would be seeking recognition of their service, and these were shortly afterwards followed by Titus' veterans from the war in

Judaea.[9] However, regardless of the degree of likelihood either way, it is impossible to resolve the problem conclusively.

The disorder in Rome was followed by a rebellion led by Julius Civilis, a Batavian chieftain who had been co-opted into the Roman auxiliary forces. He had been falsely accused of treason and as a result he turned against Rome. Initially he supported Vespasian so that he could pose as a loyalist and attack the Vitellians; his real purpose was to draw the German tribes into fighting alongside him and attack the frontier Roman garrisons. Two Treveri chieftains in Gaul, Julius Classicus and Julius Tutor, joined him. Before long the frontier legionary fortress on the Rhine at Vetera (Xanten) had fallen. Mucianus now had to organize an army to quash the rebellion because the fall of Vetera was a very serious development. In order to secure Rome while he was away, Mucianus had to make sure the city was left in safe hands. Mucianus removed Arrius Varus from the position of praetorian prefect, allowing him to save face by being appointed to be prefect of the grain supply. This was a potentially risky adjustment since Domitian favoured Varus. Suetonius' portrait of Domitian at this time in Rome is of a tyrannical young man flexing his muscles as he explored the powers available to him.[10]

So, in Varus' place Mucianus appointed Arrecinus Clemens, son of Marcus Arrecinus Clemens who had been one of the two praetorian prefects appointed under Caligula after the fall of Macro. Clemens, incongruously, was actually of senatorial rank and the first such individual to hold the praetorian prefecture, but his sister, Arrecina Tertulla, was also married to Vespasian's elder son Titus until her death, probably at some point in the late 60s. In addition, another sister, also called Arrecina, was married to Titus Flavius Sabinus, son of Vespasian's brother of the same name. Domitian was extremely fond of Arrecinus Clemens the younger.[11] Mucianus had successfully removed someone who might have helped Domitian become even more overbearing, and ensured that the Praetorian Guard was now likely to support Vespasian. Clemens may have had a co-prefect in the form of Tiberius Julius Alexander. Alexander had been prefect of Egypt under Nero, transferring his allegiance to Vespasian in July 69. The post was a normal stepping stone towards being prefect of the

Guard, but his tenure of the praetorian prefecture is only known from a papyrus, which does not specify a date.[12]

Around this time Mucianus presented Domitian 'to the soldiers'. Domitian addressed them, and presented them with the paltry sum of 100 sestertii each. The amount was so small it constituted no more than a token gesture and must reflect the fact that the Flavian campaign had, by then, cost so much that it was impossible to pay more. In 68 Nymphidius Sabinus had offered, on Galba's behalf, 7,500 denarii.[13] Domitian's ambitions started to become more obvious when he travelled on campaign with Mucianus in the Batavian War against Civilis. Domitian explored the possibility of persuading Petilius Cerealis to turn his army over to him; this was dismissed and Domitian backed off.[14] This is a turning point in the story of the Praetorian Guard. The remainder of Tacitus' *Histories* is lost. This deprives us of any further detailed information about the Guard under the Flavians. Indeed, there is no equivalent chronicle for the rest of the Roman period. The story hereafter has to be pieced together from very occasional references.

Vespasian, meanwhile, continued to wait in Egypt where he could control the grain supply to Rome and, if necessary, force the Roman people to accept his rule. He finally arrived in Rome in the summer of 70. Once there, he immediately set about establishing not only his rule but also surrounding himself with a solid underbelly of support. Additionally, he took care to entice the Roman people into accepting him. A great deal of public building followed, including the notorious Colosseum.[15] The next year Titus arrived in Italy following the Jewish War. After sharing a triumph with his father, Titus rapidly became Vespasian's virtual co-emperor, holding the tribunician power and also sharing the consulship. Titus even became commander of the Praetorian Guard, an incongruous move that had the advantage of diminishing the chances of the prefecture being held by someone disloyal.

This was entirely consistent with Vespasian's policy of appointing to any senior position only men with whom he had family connections or whose loyalty was beyond question.[16] Titus seems to have been inclined to abuse the position somewhat. Anyone whom Titus suspected of disloyalty or a misdemeanour was liable to be denounced in public by members of the Guard sent down to the theatre or barracks by him. This technique made it look as if the victim was widely unpopular, rather than being persecuted on a ruler's whim.[17] Putting Titus in command of the Guard, which he held on his own from 71 to 79, had the unfortunate effect of removing a prestigious post from the equestrian career structure even if at the same time it very firmly placed the Guard under the command of a highly experienced military man. Obviously, like Arrecinus Clemens, Titus was of senatorial rank but this anomaly was discontinued under Domitian. Pliny the Elder implied that Titus had done a good job, but since this was in the preface to his *Natural History*, published in the mid-70s and dedicated to Titus, he was hardly likely to say otherwise.[18]

By the time Titus took over command of the Praetorian Guard in 71, the Castra Praetoria had been in existence for just under fifty years.[19] In the context of the regeneration of Rome after the end of the civil war it would be as well now to consider what sort of place the Castra Praetoria was. The huge amount of archaeological evidence for Roman forts and fortresses in frontier provinces, especially Britain, Holland and Germany, has created an impression that Roman military establishments were all based on essentially the same template. Apart from the fact that every fort and fortress is unique in detail and precise layout, that image is generally true. The Roman legionary fortress invariably featured the central buildings of the headquarters (*principia*), the legate's house (*praetorium*) and other official structures such as a hospital (*valetudinarium*), granaries (*horrea*) and, in the permanent fortresses, sometimes a substantial baths. The rest of the fort area was largely made up of accommodation for the tribunes, the centurions and of course the soldiers.[20] Smaller forts, either used by legionary vexillations, auxiliary cavalry wings or single cohorts of auxiliary units, were simply smaller versions but included many of the same features on a reduced scale.

It appears from its ruins in Rome that the Castra Praetoria bore no resemblance to the normal Roman fort layout whatsoever, apart from having a defensive wall and barracks. When it was built, the Castra Praetoria lay outside the old Republican Servian Walls of the fourth century BC. By the first century AD these old walls were largely obsolete. A modern visitor leaving the railway station at Termini can walk along a stretch of the Servian Wall before heading out another 500 metres north-east towards the site of the Castra Praetoria. The fort was located in the north-eastern part of the city's urban sprawl on the Viminal Hill, with the old Via Tiburtina running along its south rampart. This road led down into the political and economic centre of Rome. A praetorian walking along it would find himself continuing down over the Esquiline to reach the imperial forums.[21] The distance was around 1,500 yards, or about 1.4 kilometres. Today, the walk takes around twenty minutes.

Unlike the *vigiles*, whose *stationes* were distributed around the city in the places where they were most likely to be needed, the Castra Praetoria was comparatively remote. It was far enough from the imperial palaces and forums where most of the praetorians' official duties would have been carried out to mean that an instant response to a crisis would have been impossible. One cohort at a time acted as the guard at the imperial palace on the Palatine, probably rotating at eight-hour intervals, and exchanging watchwords as they did so. One of the changeovers was at the eighth hour of daylight (early afternoon – around two o'clock). Martial refers to how one cohort, 'armed with spears', was replaced with another at this point in the day, the relieved cohort returning to its barracks.[22] The city of Rome must therefore have been accustomed to praetorian cohorts marching back and forth between the Castra Praetoria and the Palatine at set points throughout a normal day from the year 23 on. There is, however, every possibility that some of the Guard was accommodated in barracks closer to the heart of the city, and this certainly seems to have been the case in the second century.[23]

In the first century AD the camp's location meant that it was right on the edge of the built-up area. Pliny the Elder, when explaining the size of Rome in the mid-70s, described the praetorian camp as being *ad extrema vero tectorum*, 'at the extremes assuredly of the dwellings'.[24] One possibility is simply tact. Locating the Guard's headquarters so far out may have helped encourage the population to acquiesce to its existence.[25] Equally, the fort's size would have made it virtually impossible to find a plot for it in Rome without having to clear away housing. The location chosen was level and enjoyed a commanding position on land that was scarcely built on when the camp was laid out, avoiding the necessity to evict large numbers of civilians. Moreover, since the Tiber essentially flows from north to south along the west side of the city, the Castra Praetoria served the useful function of overseeing the eastern approaches to Rome. Rome's growth would eventually mean that the camp was incorporated into the new city walls built by Aurelian (270–5).

The Castra Praetoria was about 440 metres long and 380 metres wide. This equates to about 167,200 square metres (16.72 hectares) or a little over 40 acres. This was smaller than the legionary fortresses, which range around 17–20 hectares.[26] The footprint is not symmetrical because the southern wall projects outwards to a point that was three-quarters along its length towards the east. This created an eccentric five-sided plan but was clearly caused by the camp being inserted between two roads as they converged towards Rome. The camp had to accommodate the Praetorian Guard and probably also the urban cohorts. So far as is known, legionary fortress barracks were single-storey but the excavated barracks found within the Castra Praetoria included blocks with at least two storeys. Moreover, the Castra Praetoria does not seem to have had the full collection of major internal buildings found in conventional forts or fortresses.

Conversely, additional accommodation had been inserted into the walls in the form of well-appointed cells, something not apparently found in other forts.[27] The stabling for the mounted praetorians and *speculatores* has not yet been located.[28] It is possible that they were accommodated in an annexe that remains to be identified. It is also self-evident that offices and other facilities for everyday administration would have been needed. Each tribune had a hierarchy of personal staff including *cornicularius* (senior clerk), *beneficiarius* (clerk), *singularis* (assistant), *librarius* (accountant) and *exactus* (keeper of records). Medical facilities and staff were also an obvious necessity. Sextus Titius Alexander, probably of Greek origin, was doctor (*medicus*) to the V praetorian cohort in 82 when he made a dedication to Asklepios. Marcus Naevius Harmodius was the doctor attached to the X cohort when he died at the age of fifty-five, probably in the late first or early second century. His name is more obviously Greek in origin.[29] However, since not all the plan of the Castra Praetoria has been traced, let alone excavated, and there is no parallel whatsoever for any of these arrangements, it follows that there is no means of calculating with any reliable accuracy whatsoever how many troops could be housed. It is, however, possible to estimate a minimum. There seems to have been enough space for at least ten to fifteen thousand men. Moreover, it is even possible that a fleet detachment was accommodated there too (Plate 15).[30]

The internal road system of the Castra Praetoria bears some superficial resemblance to a conventional fort or fortress in the way the layout was bisected by two principal routes running at right angles across the camp. Even a casual glance at what is known of the Castra Praetoria's plan, however, will show that the resemblance went no further. Another complication is that the coins issued by Claudius depicting the Castra Praetoria seem to show a very prominent building behind the walls. This resembles a headquarters building: the coins show a structure with two wings flanking a central hall with pitched roof housing standards in the manner of a *principia*. This was described in the early third century as being 'the temple where the standard and images of the soldiers are worshipped'.[31] It is possible that such a building lay in the area of the Castra Praetoria that has yet to be excavated. There was also a temple of Mars, though this may be the same building. Titus Aelius Malchus was a mounted praetorian of the III cohort and also served as a priest in 'the Temple of Mars of the Praetorian Camps', though his tombstone, which records this, is of much later date and probably belongs to the third century.[32] There may have been a baths but a reference by Josephus to the arrangements in 37 suggests that praetorians used facilities in the city; this of course may have changed over time.[33]

The camp's walls were made of brick with a concrete core, a type of construction that resisted fire and became increasingly common in the first century AD. The Castra Praetoria's own walls do survive in part, thanks to their incorporation into the late third-century Aurelian Walls of Rome, though the south and west walls were demolished by Constantine after the Guard was disbanded, and the remaining gates blocked. Originally around 3.35 metres (11 feet) in height with crenellations – around one metre lower than similar military fortifications – the walls were subsequently raised to almost 5 metres (a little over 16 feet). These elevations are still detectable in the extant sections. The Tiberian walls were built on a plinth around 1.82 metres (6 feet) high on a concrete foundation. Up to sixteen towers were located along the walls, though these did not project either externally or internally.[34] No evidence has been found for any form of external ditch, a feature so ubiquitous in Roman forts that its absence here is a curiosity in its own right. The second-century London Cripplegate fort, which housed the governor's bodyguard, and the military compound at Dura-Europos in Syria, are amongst the very few known Roman military installations in an urban setting. So far as is known, the London fort and others in similar contexts seem to have had all the normal structural features, including an external ditch, unlike the Castra Praetoria.[35]

The absence of a ditch combined with the non-projecting towers at the Castra Praetoria shows that it was not conceived of as a defensible military stronghold. It was, instead, literally no more than a stoutly walled compound designed to present an image, provide accommodation, control access and define an area of land. Instead of having its own internal water supply the camp was dependent on water being piped in from aqueducts, which of course would make it vulnerable in a siege.[36] A single-portal gate is known in each of the north and east walls. The other two walls were demolished after the disbandment of the Guard under Constantine but were probably similar. The known gates are simple and small compared to normal fortress gates. Neither had flanking towers and would have been unable to withstand sustained assault. There was good reason for all this. There was always the risk that the Guard, under rebellious leadership, could have used a more fortress-like Castra Praetoria from which to mount a rebellion and withstand assault from other forces loyal to the emperor. It also probably reflects the fact that, whereas in a conventional fort the commanding officer would expect to be resident and administer the troops from the headquarters building, the praetorian prefect was more likely to spend his time in the imperial palace. The overwhelming impression gained from what is left of the Castra Praetoria is that it was essentially just a modestly fortified accommodation compound.

This, at any rate, was the Castra Praetoria insofar as we can understand it by the late first century AD. It is unlikely that Titus spent much time there, though we know almost nothing about what the Guard was used for during the reign of Vespasian beyond Suetonius' description of how Titus used it to weed out people of dubious loyalty. In truth, the civil war and the accession of Vespasian had marked a downturn in the Guard's fortunes. The praetorians had been inextricably linked to the Julio-Claudian dynasty for around a century, but the short-lived regimes of 68–9 had seen fluctuations in the Guard's size, personnel and affiliations. Although the Guard had been settled by Mucianus on Vespasian's behalf, it had played no significant part in bringing the Flavians to power. The retention of some Vitellian praetorians must have left Vespasian with residual concern about their loyalty. Unlike Claudius, who had so explicitly acknowledged the praetorians on his coinage, Vespasian made no such gesture even to his legionary armies that had defeated Vitellius' forces. Apart from a substantial issue of coins commemorating Titus' victory in the war in Judaea, Vespasian's coins concentrated on optimistic themes such as Pax (peace) and Spes (hope), or patriotic nationalism like Roma and the Flavian dynasty.

Soldiers were not always resident in the barracks; the corruption that had become so engrained by Galba's time, involving praetorians taking second jobs, suggests precisely that. Evidence from other locations proves it. In Britain at the end of the first century, the strength report from Vindolanda on the northern frontier of the I cohort of Tungrians records the wide dispersal of the soldiers, some as far away as London. At Pompeii several tombstones of praetorians have been found, three outside the so-called Porta Nola gate on the city's north-east side, and one outside the Porta Stabia on the south side. By definition these burials cannot have taken place after 24 August 79. The Porta Nola burials include Lucius Betutius Niger of the II praetorian cohort who died at the age of twenty after serving only two years. Lucius Manilius Saturninus and Sextus Caesernius Montanus are both described on their stones as *speculatores*, while outside the Porta Stabia Gaius Caelius Secundus served in the VIII praetorian cohort.[37] The obvious question is: what were they doing there?

In all cases it is evident these praetorians were serving soldiers, which implies they were present in the city on official business. It is inconceivable that Pompeii, where conditions of preservation are unique, was the only such place to which praetorians were sent. It is far more likely that they were frequently deployed here and elsewhere, perhaps on rotation, for a number of different reasons. No military installation has been identified at Pompeii, though one probably existed at Nuceria.[38] In 59 a riot broke out at the Pompeii amphitheatre during a gladiatorial event. So serious was the affair that the amphitheatre was closed to gladiatorial bouts for a decade on the senate's orders and measures were taken to ban illegal guilds. It is possible that praetorians were dispatched to help police the settlement after this event. It is also likely that praetorians operated in that capacity in small numbers in the area anyway, but not necessarily always as police. These evidently included cavalrymen. Gaius Annaeus Capito was a trooper with the X praetorian cohort who recorded his name in a graffito by a bedroom door in a Pompeii house.[39] Crucially, his graffito is also interesting evidence for a tenth praetorian cohort in existence by 79. As a graffito it is unlikely to have been old when the city was destroyed in 79 and may therefore either be a Vitellian cohort or a tenth cohort created by Vespasian.[40]

Other praetorians at Pompeii include Titus Crasellius and Marcus Nonius Campanus of the VIII cohort, Sextus Decimius Rufus of the V cohort, and Caius Valerius Venustus of the I cohort.[41] No such similar evidence survives at Herculaneum, which, as a rather more peaceable, affluent and smaller settlement, perhaps needed less supervision, though far less has been explored. Nevertheless, amongst the bodies recovered on the beach in excavations during the early 1980s was one of a man in his late thirties wearing a military belt and *gladius* sword. He was not wearing armour and therefore must have been dressed in an everyday tunic. He was also equipped with an adze and three chisels which were slung over his back. He had suffered a serious wound to his left thigh, but the recovery and healing to the bone indicated a man who was in excellent condition and well nourished. It is obviously not possible to identify him conclusively as a member of any military unit but it is, surely, more likely than anything else that he was one of the praetorians on duty in the region. If he was a praetorian, then his presence in Herculaneum with his tools must indicate that he was engaged in some sort of building project, presumably on behalf of the state. He reinforces the impression of the way the Roman government's presence in everyday life was so often manifested in military form, with the praetorians being a prominent part of that, just as the other praetorians in Pompeii did.[42]

All these individuals suggest an image of Italian Roman cities in many of which praetorians were simply part of the fabric of everyday life. Pompeii and Herculaneum's remarkable circumstances of preservation and destruction in August 79 have allowed these pieces of evidence to survive. A recent discovery in London of a writing tablet dated to c. 65–80 that refers to an *emeritus Augusti* almost certainly means a veteran of the Praetorian Guard serving there in some official capacity. He may have worked on the governor's staff or perhaps been involved in training either the governor's garrison or other units of the provincial army in Britain.[43] We can only make one of two assumptions: that these examples were individually unique and were not matched anywhere else, or that we have here evidence for how praetorians were routinely dispersed throughout Italy and elsewhere in a number of different capacities to serve the state's interests. The tombstone evidence from other dates of praetorians with specialist skills does raise the possibility that individual soldiers had been detailed to perform particular duties on the state's behalf but in a civilian context. The lead-worker praetorian Caristicus is a case in point (Plate 19).[44]

One other small possible vignette of Guard personnel survives in the form of an inscription discovered in the Nucerian Gate cemetery at Pompeii. At some point during Vespasian's reign a tribune called Titus Suedius Clemens was sent to Pompeii to sort out a local dispute. Public lands had been appropriated by various private individuals. Clemens presided over various arguments in court and then arranged for the land to be handed back to the control of the city. Apart from stating that he was a tribune on the inscription that records this episode, Clemens does not specify in what capacity he held the post. It is possible, even likely, that he served as tribune of a praetorian cohort, since a praetorian land surveyor sent to determine a settlement's boundaries is attested under Antoninus Pius.[45] If correct, this is an interesting example of how serving in the praetorians could involve a surprisingly wide range of administrative duties.[46]

All we have to tell us about other individual praetorians apart from Clemens and the praetorians at Pompeii are a few discharge diplomas that name members of the Guard from this time. Part of being able to build a new life after praetorian service involved being awarded the legal right on discharge to marry. In 76 Lucius Ennius Ferox, from the city of Aquae Statiellae (Acqui) in Liguria (north-western coastal Italy), was honourably discharged from the VI praetorian cohort under Vespasian. The discharge included the grant of *conubium*, meaning Ferox could contract a marriage with a non-Roman woman but any children would still enjoy the status of those born to two Roman parents. His diploma, which is one of the earliest praetorian examples known, was found in Tomi (Constanta) in Moesia Inferior (Bulgaria), though this does not necessarily mean Ferox had moved there.[47] There is an incongruous element to this because praetorian diploma texts appear to say that a praetorian's children by a non-Roman woman only received citizenship if they were born after he was discharged. This was unlike those serving in the auxiliary forces and the fleet, who appeared to have been on better terms: their existing children by non-Roman women were enfranchised on discharge. One possible explanation is that originally it had never been considered that praetorians might have consorted with non-Roman women; over time ambiguous wording was developed to compensate for a situation that had arisen as a result of the ad hoc evolution of the Roman armed forces and their different components.[48]

A papyrus from Egypt, dated to the year 63, summed up the disparate arrangements concerning different parts of the Roman army. The papyrus was concerned with the legal rights and entitlements of veterans from legions, auxiliary cavalry wings and infantry cohorts, and fleet personnel; these had caused sufficient grievance to lead the men to make a representation to the prefect of Egypt, Caius Caecina Tuscus. Realizing that the men were so angry that the situation was bordering on rebellion, Tuscus pointed out that the legal rights differed for each branch of the service and that this would affect what was due to each man; he would see to it that those individual rights were established and guaranteed.[49] Praetorians are not included, which is not surprising given the location, but the point is not affected. This is a useful reminder to modern students of the Roman world that individual pieces of evidence, whether they concern the structure of a military unit, the legal status of soldiers or their families, and so on, are not usually a reliable basis on which to form general and long-term conclusions about how the Roman army operated in practice. Clearly, members of the Roman armed forces found themselves in an organization that was hugely complicated by different legal arrangements, terms and conditions, custom and practice, precedent, and ad hoc circumstances. The Praetorian Guard was affected just as much, and this would not change for the rest of its history.

Vespasian's death on 24 June 79 was followed by a seamless transition of power to Titus. Barely two months later Titus was confronted by the catastrophic eruption of Vesuvius that destroyed two cities, untold numbers of rural settlements, and buried Titus Suedius Clemens' inscription (Plate 14). Titus was to rule for just over two years and we know little else about the Guard during that time, including even the name of the prefect(s), assuming that Titus gave up command when he became emperor. Titus does seem to have taken the opportunity to offer at least some of the praetorians a special privilege. A diploma of 30 December, probably in the year 79, preserves the name of Staius Saturninus of the II cohort. The rest of the diploma's text records that, along with the standard grant of the legal right to marry a foreign woman, the property owned on this date by the praetorian concerned is to be exempt from tax and also any land given him by the emperor. This presumably also applied to any other praetorian discharged on that occasion.[50]

It is not until the reign of his brother Domitian (81–96), Titus having left only a daughter, that we know more about the praetorians. Domitian assumed the title of emperor even before Titus died. Titus had contracted a fever while visiting Aquae Cutiliae (near Cittaducale) in central Italy, the place where his father had also expired little more than twenty-six months previously. A rumour continued to circulate that Domitian arranged for Titus' demise to be expedited by insisting that his brother be placed in a container with ice, on the grounds that the fever required cooling. Either way, Domitian then left for Rome without waiting and made straight for the Castra Praetoria where he repeated any gifts that Titus had awarded them. This was the product of the endless plotting that Domitian had engaged in against his brother, frequently focusing on trying to wind up the armies to revolt against Titus.[51] Needless to say the praetorians, their loyalty purchased, promptly acclaimed Domitian as emperor in late September 81.

Although praetorians had always been available for use in warfare, it was not until the civil war of 68–9 that they had been deployed more systematically in this capacity. Domitian was more prepared than his predecessors to take advantage of their potential as an active military force in the field. There were at that time two praetorian prefects, Cornelius Fuscus and Lucius Julius Ursus, showing that he had reverted to the system of two prefects. Domitian was given to an arbitrary style of rule, showing particular hatred towards any friends or supporters of Vespasian and Titus.[52] He was married to a woman called (coincidentally) Domitia Longina, daughter of the general Gnaeus Domitius Corbulo. It was a union that had perhaps been intended to associate Domitian with Corbulo's milieu. In 80 they produced a single child, a son, who died around the year 83. This tragedy coincided with Domitia's adultery with an actor called Paris. When Domitian found out he resolved to execute Domitia but was dissuaded from doing so by Ursus. He contented himself with having Paris murdered and cohabiting incestuously with his niece, Julia, Titus' daughter. This single incident alone illustrates how the praetorian prefects could function more as an emperor's companions and closest advisers than as military commanders. Ursus' advice seems not to have been particularly welcome. He was promoted by Domitian to the senatorial order, becoming consul in 84. This was not quite the privilege it seems, since the promotion to *ornamenta consularia* was honorific, rather than an entitlement to sit in the senate.[53] Moreover, Domitian had taken on the position of censor in 85 on a permanent basis. This means that he was now able to scrutinize and control eligibility to the senatorial order continuously, as well as supervise public morals.[54]

Remarkably, a papyrus letter from Domitian appointing a new praetorian prefect to replace Ursus is known. It was written in 83 or 84 and was addressed to Lucius Laberius Maximus, then prefect of Egypt. The elevation of Ursus created a vacancy in the praetorian prefecture to which Domitian wished to appoint Maximus. The letter explicitly states that Maximus and Cornelius Fuscus are to participate in 'equal sharing of duty', and Domitian looks forward to Maximus leaving for Rome the moment the seas permit his departure. The letter, which was probably found in Egypt, is both official and personal, with Domitian assuring Maximus that he knows of his piety, loyalty and diligence.[55]

Cornelius Fuscus thus continued in post and was duly joined by Lucius Laberius Maximus. A war in Dacia against Decebalus experienced two setbacks. The Dacians first defeated a force under a proconsul called Oppius Sabinus, and secondly another under Cornelius Fuscus in his capacity as praetorian prefect. It is not clear whether Fuscus was sent to replace Oppius Sabinus or whether the defeats occurred around the same time. In the event Fuscus was killed in 86 or 87, and buried on the spot. The poet Martial decided to memorialize him in one of his epigrams, which may have been inscribed on his tomb.[56] Fuscus is described as 'the guardian of the sacred life, of Mars in the toga [i.e. the emperor]' and the one to whom the army had been entrusted. The description is an interesting one because it invokes a sense that the praetorian prefect was effectively leading the army as not only the representative of the emperor but also as if he was a symbolic manifestation of him. By 83 Domitian was actively participating in wars in person; he left for Gaul and led the army across the Rhine against German tribes, probably with praetorians but this is not known.

Domitian also further ingratiated himself with the army by raising military pay. According to Dio the instalment paid three times a year to a legionary went up from 300 to 400 sestertii (equal to 75 to 100 denarii). This meant that annual pay went from 225 to 300 denarii per annum (900 to 1,200 sestertii). Suetonius gave the pay rise as an annual increase of three gold *aurei*, three aurei being equal to 75 denarii, confirming Dio's figure. Praetorian pay is not mentioned in either source, but if the differential of 3.33:1 prevailing in the year 14 was maintained then their remuneration would have gone up to 999 denarii, conveniently divisible into three instalments, each of 333 denarii (which of course do not add up to the rounded figure of 1,000, though in practice this was probably the notional rate).[57] As was noted earlier, and like other soldiers, it is improbable the praetorians received most of this pay until their day of discharge, less deductions for food, equipment and clothing over their years of service.

A sestertius issued in 85 depicts on the reverse Domitian in a toga clasping hands with an officer over an altar while three soldiers stand behind. The coin bears no reverse legend but the reverse design is quite possibly a representation of Domitian parting with Fuscus and the praetorians at the beginning of the campaign. It must have been the case that Fuscus took some of the Guard with him, though the only information we have is that he was accompanied by 'a large force'.[58] It would, however, have been a valuable opportunity to allow the praetorians to win prestige and associate that with Domitian, though of course the death of Fuscus may have been associated with the death of praetorians too.

During one of Domitian's wars, Marcus Arruntius Claudianus served as a commander of praetorian cavalry, winning a number of decorations. He came from Lycia in western Asia Minor, where his career is recorded on an inscription from Ephesus. His name suggests that his father was made a citizen when Marcus Arruntius Aquila was procurator of Pamphylia in AD 50. This places Claudianus' career approximately in Domitian's reign. The lack of any reference to Domitian in the inscription makes this even more likely since after Domitian's murder in 96 his monuments and inscriptions were destroyed, deleted or altered. Claudianus had served as 'a prefect of a cavalry wing and detachment of praetorians' and rose to a senatorial career.[59] A diploma of February 85 was issued to a veteran called Gaius Latinus Primus on the date of his honourable discharge. It refers to the VI, VII, VIII and VIIII praetorian cohorts, and the X, XI, XII and XIII urban cohorts. Latinus Primus came from a city called Sebastopolis, probably in the province of Pontus in Asia (now Turkey). This may have been because Primus was originally in one of Vespasian's legions and benefited from being transferred first to the urban cohorts as reward for loyal service in the reorganization managed by Mucianus after the death of Vitellius. The principal oddity about the diploma is that, unlike other examples, this one omits any mention of praetorian cohorts I–V. One possible explanation is that honourable discharges were only being issued to certain cohorts on this occasion. Another is that cohorts I–V were not available for honourable discharges. Although no demonstrable connection exists, it is clearly feasible that cohorts I–V had already been sent to Dacia with Fuscus, even though the war involved did not start until later in the year. The diploma also lacks the phrase *in meo praetorio*, 'in my [the emperor's] Praetorian Guard', which was otherwise the convention. This can be explained if the whole Guard establishment was not present.[60] Although these arguments are interesting they are no more than circumstantial and far from conclusive, as is so often the case with the organization of the Guard.

Although Domitian had concentrated much of his attention on securing the army's support, he was also wary of how much of a threat the army could pose. He prohibited the quartering of two legions in the same base, presumably out of fear of a potential mutiny; if he applied the same principle to the praetorians then this might explain the decision to send half the Guard on campaign.[61] The Praetorian Guard played a significant role in one form or another in the deaths of Tiberius, Caligula and Nero. Its role in the accession of Domitian had been more passive; it was Domitian who was the active component in his own elevation, rather than the Guard. When it came to the death of Domitian, assassinated on 18 September 96, the Guard did not do anything, in spite of the fact that Domitian was widely hated for his arbitrary, egotistical and insulting style of rule. His adoption of the titles 'Master and God' caused particular disquiet. To this could be added the litany of murders that he ordered after a rebellion led against him by Antonius, a governor of one of the German provinces, and the large numbers of people he had flung into prison on charges of treason.[62] The praetorian prefect Lucius Laberius Maximus was sent against Antonius, defeating and killing him. After that Maximus then searched through all of Antonius' papers to destroy them so that Domitian could not use them to pursue anyone else. This did not stop Domitian who embarked on a killing spree anyway. Domitian's paranoia extended to ceasing to place trust in anyone, including the 'prefects' (which we can assume included the praetorian prefects) whom he had committed for trial in their first year of office. Casperius Aelianus, Maximus' colleague in the office, seems to have been more of a loyalist, leading a rebellion against the next emperor, Nerva, for failing to pursue Domitian's murderers.[63]

On an everyday basis at this time, the average praetorian probably went about dressed in an ordinary military tunic, gathered at the waist with a military belt, wearing socks and sandals, and also sporting the hooded cloak (*paenula*) in the manner of the body found at Herculaneum (Plate 26). Praetorians wore a spear and sword but did not use helmets unless actually fighting. The Cancellaria relief shows Domitian in or around 83 being accompanied by bareheaded praetorians wearing this garb, including one equipped with a pair of socks.[64] However, it was a good idea to be on the lookout for praetorians disguised as civilians. Praetorians dressed in togas or tunics could mingle with ordinary people and try and inveigle them into criticizing the emperor, only then to break cover and arrest the unsuspecting civilian. This procedure was described by the philosopher Epictetus, and written down in the early second century. He was probably recalling how some praetorians had been used by Domitian, but it had echoes of what also seems to have gone on in Nero's reign, when theatre audiences were infiltrated by spies.[65] The anecdote is sometimes used as evidence that praetorians were commonly seen in togas in Rome, but it is quite clear in this case that the praetorian concerned was in disguise for special circumstances and we should not conclude that praetorians routinely wore togas on the basis of this reference. Epictetus is also more likely to be referring to a *speculator* than to a regular praetorian.

In the event, Domitian was murdered in a plot led by his 'friends and freedmen' rather than disaffected praetorians or a praetorian prefect.[66] By 94 the praetorian prefectures had been filled by Titus Flavius Norbanus and Titus Petronius Secundus. They were aware of the plot, it seems, but took no part in it. In 96 the assassins decided to kill Domitian because he had kept a hit list of names, which included theirs, but this was stolen by one of the emperor's catamites and fell into the hands of his wife Domitia. Domitia, already terrified for her own life, passed on the information to those named. They discussed what to do and eventually selected Marcus Cocceius Nerva, sometime friend of Nero and co-consul with both Vespasian and Domitian, and asked him to be the figurehead of a conspiracy to kill Domitian and create a new emperor.[67]

We have an interesting example at this point of a specialist praetorian whose remarkable military career spanned the Flavian era. Gaius Vedennius Moderatus came from Antium (Anzio) in Italy. He served in the XVI legion Gallica for ten years in which he did well enough to be rewarded with a transfer to the VIIII praetorian cohort probably in 69, clocking up a further eight years. XVI Gallica threw in its lot with Vitellius during the civil war. No doubt this was the time that Moderatus acquired invaluable experience with artillery. The transfer to the Guard for Moderatus may therefore have come about as a result of Vitellius' policy of allowing his soldiers to choose whichever part of the army they wished to serve in. Those soldiers who wanted to were allowed to join the Praetorian Guard, 'however worthless' they were.[68] Alternatively, Moderatus may have been transferred to the Guard by Vespasian precisely because of his artillery skills, making him too useful, in spite of having fought for the wrong side. Either way, when he retired in or around 78, Moderatus was then signed up once more as an *evocatus Augusti*, serving for a remarkable further twenty-three years, this time as an engineer in the imperial armoury with specialist artillery skills.

Moderatus' military service thus extended to over forty years, during which time he was decorated by both Vespasian and Domitian. Moderatus must have been well into his sixties when he died, some time early in the reign of Trajan. His tombstone advertises his special skills by, for example, depicting a *ballista* on one side.[69] Moderatus was unusual. He stayed with the Guard for an exceptionally long time and presumably reached the point where the idea of leaving was unimaginable for him. More often, veteran praetorians would return to their homes and this must have been even more likely to happen once praetorians were recruited from the whole army, as happened under Severus in 193. Sextus Quinctilius Seneca was a veteran of the IIII praetorian cohort when he made a dedication to Jupiter on the island of Arba (Rab) in Dalmatia (Croatia). Gaius Terentius Mercator, veteran of the III praetorian cohort, expired at Como where he was buried according to the instructions in his will. Gaius Carantius Verecundus, a veteran of the VII praetorian cohort in Flavian times, was buried at Reate (Riati) in Italy by his freedmen. Moderatus, however, was in for the long haul and had a ringside seat to history during an epic period in which the Roman world staggered from the chaos of civil war right through to the stability of Trajan's reign, a very different time for the Praetorian Guard.

An undated tombstone, but also belonging approximately to this period, provides us with another example of a specialized praetorian, this time Caius Caristicus Redemtus, recorded as a *plumbarius* (lead-worker) on his tombstone (Plate 19).[70] He was sufficiently important to be ranked as an *ordinarius*, a term of uncertain precise meaning. It seems to have indicated an equivalency with the centurionate, even though this particular man served in a century under the centurion Longidus Maritus. In the Roman world lead was an essential resource, not only in hydraulic engineering as an important material for the manufacturing of pipes, but also in the production of some armaments such as sling-bolts, and in roofing. There is no indication of his precise duties but Caristicus is further evidence of the Praetorian Guard as a source of specialist skills which might be called on in either civilian or military contexts on behalf of the state. Other praetorians contented themselves with administrative duties. Marcus Lucilius Proculus, a soldier of the VI cohort, was *curator* (treasurer) of the cohort but gave instructions before his death at the age of thirty-three that he be commemorated unusually with a tombstone that seems to bear a portrait. His is one of very few instances where we seem to have a likeness of a praetorian (Plate 16).[71]

CHAPTER 8

CONCORDIA EXERCITUUM

(98–180)

*The Praetorian Guard had played an enormously important part in the
imperial politics of the first century AD. This also coincided with our richest
body of written evidence for the Roman Empire. The second century is
entirely different. A succession of strong and competent emperors contributed
to a period of unprecedented stability for the Roman world. In this context,
the praetorians had no opportunity or, it seems, wish to play any part
in toppling or appointing emperors. The written canon of evidence also
dramatically declines in quantity and quality, leaving us principally with
only a series of much later biographies of the emperors, and the epitome of
Cassius Dio. The picture that emerges is of a Praetorian Guard that took part
in imperial campaigns, such as Trajan's Dacian wars, and also continued to
operate as a police force in Italy.*

DOMITIAN'S UNPOPULARITY AMONGST THE wider public meant that his
assassination caused little or no disquiet. Only the army seems to have
been bothered. His use of praetorians to help fight the Dacian war meant
that their first response to news of his death was to demand his deification.
The only factor that prevented an immediate military uprising in Rome was
the lack of any obvious leader.[1] In the event, that position was filled by the
prefect Casperius Aelianus in a brief return to the days when the praetorians
shaped the course of Roman history, but he took his time before acting.

Marcus Cocceius Nerva's accession as emperor was clearly a stopgap. In the summer of 96 Nerva was approaching his sixty-fifth birthday and he had no children. There was therefore no question of a new dynasty, though he did have relatives. The ageing new emperor reappointed Casperius Aelianus to the praetorian prefecture, probably to calm down the Guard and the rest of the army. It seems to have worked to begin with. Nerva issued coins in gold, silver and brass, showing two clasped hands grasping a legionary standard with the legend CONCORDIA EXERCITVVM, 'Harmony of the Armies'.[2]

Nerva emptied the prisons of those accused of treason, condemned informers, returned property that had been appropriated by Domitian, and sought out sound advisers. Despite this, he was still the victim of plots, his age at accession being the main reason for unrest. The first was led by a senator called Calpurnius Crassus. An informer told Nerva what was happening, so Nerva outfaced the plotters by providing them with a chance to kill him, even handing them weapons. This was followed by another, led by Casperius Aelianus, who had whipped up the praetorians to demand the execution of his immediate predecessor, Titus Petronius Secundus, and Domitian's freedman Parthenius.[3] He next encouraged the praetorians to mutiny. Nerva's considerable personal courage won out again, this time when he bared his neck and invited them to slit it. He survived, but at the expense of Petronius and Parthenius. Nerva knew he was vulnerable and came up with a solution. He selected a promising soldier, a Spaniard called Marcus Ulpius Traianus (known to us as Trajan), and adopted him as his heir. Trajan had a family connection through being the son of Marcia, sister-in-law of Titus.

The behaviour of the praetorians during this time was strangely muted, despite Aelianus' efforts. They never successfully avenged Domitian, for all their demands that he be deified. Given the time and effort Domitian had expended on massaging the sensibilities of the army, and the role the praetorians had played in acclaiming him in 81, their relative inertia is a little surprising. On the other hand, the crucial factor was perhaps the one Suetonius had observed: there was no obvious champion they could plant on the throne, like Claudius in 41. Moreover, the actions of Aelianus had made him a marked man along with the praetorian mutineers. Pliny the Younger, writing in his Panegyric of Trajan, referred to the mutiny with unequivocal horror: Nerva's authority had been 'snatched', thanks to the breakdown of military discipline. Nevertheless, this does not explain why Aelianus remained in post. Nerva probably feared risking a further confrontation with the Guard by disposing of him, unless Aelianus was involved in the arrangements to appoint Trajan as Nerva's heir. Indeed, the appointment of Trajan may have formed part of Aelianus' demands.[4]

Nerva died on 25 January 98 after a reign of a few days over sixteen months. Trajan, who was still with the frontier armies in Germany, did not actually reach Rome until late 99, apparently preferring to consolidate his hold on the vital Rhine and Danube garrisons. Aelianus and the mutineers were summoned, on the pretext that Trajan had a job for them. This ruse not only removed them from Rome, but was also a trick. Aelianus' only hope would have been to topple Nerva and replace him with his own choice of emperor. Since that had not happened, Trajan was confronted with a praetorian prefect of suspect loyalty, or at any rate someone associated with an emperor (Domitian) who was now being popularly demonized as part of the establishment of the new regime. Aelianus and the mutineers were 'put out of the way', an ambiguous term that might mean they were executed or simply cashiered and dispersed, regardless of whether or not Aelianus had helped facilitate Trajan's adoption.[5] Trajan replaced Aelianus with Sextus Attius Suburanus Aemilianus. He handed Suburanus his sword of office and told the new prefect to use it on his behalf if he ruled well, and use it to kill him if he ruled badly. Suburanus held the post until c. 101, when he was replaced with Tiberius Claudius Livianus who was sole prefect until possibly as late as c. 112.[6]

Trajan's first public appearance in Rome in 99 was attended by an enormous crowd. According to Pliny, 'the soldiers present', who must have been praetorians given that this was in Rome, were dressed as civilians and consequently indistinguishable from everyone else. This may of course have been relatively normal for praetorians but the point being made by Pliny is surely that the praetorians represented no military threat or presence because there was no need to under an emperor who was completely in control. This of course reflects Pliny's obsequious relationship with an emperor and benefactor he revered, but there was probably some truth in it. Interestingly, Trajan decided to pay only half the accession donative to the soldiers, whereas the amount promised to civilians was paid in full. The reason appears to have been to make a public gesture that Trajan was not seeking to bribe the soldiers into supporting him, whereas the civilians 'who could more easily have been refused' were therefore the more deserving.[7]

The question arises here of whether the *equites singulares Augusti*, the 'imperial mounted bodyguard', belong to this date and even whether Trajan brought them with him to Rome from the frontier. They served with the Praetorian Guard in the same way as mounted auxiliary units did with the legions, forming an elite mounted praetorian wing, and had a base on the Caelian Hill. This does not mean they necessarily got on with the ordinary praetorians.[8] They certainly existed by 118 because an unprovenanced and fragmentary diploma refers to the unit with a consular date for this year, though no veteran soldiers' names are preserved.[9] It is possible that the unit existed even earlier, on the evidence that some attested soldiers' names include Flavius, which would suggest a foundation under Domitian. What is not clear is whether the *equites* pushed the praetorians into a subordinate role or operated in a collaborative function, providing a fast mobile bodyguard for an emperor in the field and freeing up praetorians for fighting.[10] The career of Ulpius Titus, although he lived in the late second or early third century, is of interest here. He was selected for the *equites singulares Augusti* after having served as a cavalryman in a Thracian auxiliary cavalry wing. Thracian cavalry had served in the Roman army's auxiliary forces for centuries and provided some of the most experienced and important mounted troops in the whole Roman army.[11]

The praetorians themselves seem also to have increased in number by this time, if not already under Domitian or even as early as Vespasian. A diploma from Vindonissa (Windisch) in Germania Superior dated to the year 100 under Trajan clearly refers to the existence of the X praetorian cohort, which presumably had been added at some point between 76 and 100, most likely by Domitian.[12] This makes it possible there were now ten praetorian cohorts from this date. However, a tenth cohort does not help us by confirming the total number of praetorians, or the size of individual cohorts, now or at any other time. Nevertheless, some authorities have assumed that it does, for example arguing that the Guard was made up of ten milliary cohorts thereafter.[13]

Indeed, the praetorians seem to have enjoyed Trajan's favour. A fragmentary relief from Puteoli, stylistically attributable to the early second century and probably from an arch of Trajan, depicts two praetorians with shields embellished with scorpions associated with praetorians.[14] This is a stylized representation of the Guard in a symbolic setting, and quite unlike the way praetorians are featured at war on several panels on Trajan's Column in Rome. The reliefs represent the start of a period when artistic representations of praetorians become more frequent and an impression can be gained of how they might have appeared. Of course, the sculptures also tend to depict the praetorians on campaign. There must have been several reasons for this. Such images flattered the praetorians' vanity, showing them as the emperor's right-hand men in action. They also showed the praetorians as a military force, and in this capacity were a useful reminder that the emperor ruled with powerful military backing (Plate 17).

The Trajan's Column reliefs depict his Dacian wars against Decebalus and show the praetorians taking an active part in the campaigns. This was a trend that continued and become the norm during the second century. In the 'first battle', praetorians, identifiable from their wreathed standards, stand in the background behind legionaries. Later, a squad of praetorians accompanies Trajan as he is about to embark on a galley; they are his only accompanying troops. Subsequently he reaches a military base with his praetorians in tow, where they are met by legionaries and auxiliaries.[15] Although it is impossible to tell how many praetorians were involved (our principal source, Dio, provides only a brief account of Trajan's campaigns), there are some attested examples of individuals. Lucius Aemilius Paternus had a distinguished career as a centurion, serving at one point in the IIII praetorian cohort when he was decorated for his service in Dacia. He went on to fight in Parthia for Trajan too. Gaius Arrius Clemens served as both an infantry and mounted praetorian in the VIIII cohort in the Dacian war.

He was also decorated, receiving 'necklaces, armbands and ornaments'. Clemens was later to rise to be an aide to the praetorian prefects, and subsequently a centurion in the VII cohort under Hadrian, when he was decorated again.[16]

During Trajan's reign these men served under the prefect Tiberius Claudius Livianus who is attested in Dacia being sent by Trajan to negotiate with Decebalus.[17] These men's careers, and the depictions on Trajan's Column, show that the Guard was functioning now really as part of the general Roman army rather than as a distinct and privileged separate unit based in Rome. By the late first century and thereafter, the Praetorian Guard was the only Rome-based military unit to participate alongside conventional troops in the field; the urban cohorts and the *vigiles* routinely stayed in Rome where of course their services were essential for public order and safety.

Since the purpose of the Guard was to protect the emperor's person, it was only logical that they would participate in wars in which he was personally involved, but the way they were used does illustrate how the Guard was evolving into a part of the regular army.[18] Lucius Laelius Fuscus expired at the age of sixty-five after forty-two years' military service. From being an *eques* in the Praetorian Guard he had progressed through various positions to serve as centurion of the I cohort of the *vigiles*, centurion of the military police (*statores*), centurion of the XIIII urban cohort, centurion of the X praetorian cohort and, finally, holding the prestigious position of centurion *trecenarius* of the VII legion Claudia. The style of the inscription on his marble urn is late first or early second century as far as the reign of Hadrian. The VII legion Claudia participated in Trajan's Dacian and Parthian wars, raising the possibility that Fuscus had been transferred from the Guard during one of those occasions, though there is nothing to substantiate this (Plate 18).[19]

From hereon there is little mention of the Guard in any other capacity until the reign of Commodus, under whom they seem to have degenerated into institutionalized indolence until they were cashiered by Septimius Severus in June 193.[20] However, evidence from Marcus Aurelius' reign half a century after Trajan shows the praetorian prefects operating as police in

Italy, and it is quite possible that this role was already by then well established as the much earlier evidence from Pompeii before 79 suggests. The single most conspicuous problem with the Praetorian Guard after the reign of Trajan until the reign of Commodus is that it is rarely referred to in the extant sources. For this period we are mainly reliant on what remains of Cassius Dio, which for this era only exists in the form of a later epitome, and the biographies of the emperors known as the *Scriptores Historiae Augustae*, which were not composed until the fourth century. For the long period of the reigns of Hadrian (117–38) and Antoninus Pius (138–61), the Guard as an organization is virtually ignored. More is known about praetorian prefects, but otherwise the story can only be pieced together from fragments.

Trajan died in Cilicia in 117, suffering from a sickness that was followed by a stroke that left him partly paralysed. His successor Hadrian was the grandson of Trajan's aunt, Ulpia. Although his side of the family was originally Italian, they had settled in Italica in Spain, where Trajan was from. After his father died when he was ten, Hadrian was placed under the guardianship of Trajan. Hadrian pursued a successful senatorial military and administrative career and early in Trajan's reign married the emperor's great-niece, Sabina, becoming a particular favourite of Trajan's wife Plotina. Hadrian went on to fight in Trajan's Dacian campaign and proceeded through a number of other posts, including the tribunician power in 105 and then governor of Syria, the post he held when Trajan died. It was an extremely unusual situation. Although Hadrian's position as heir looks obvious, at the time it was anything but. Other candidates were believed to be favoured by Trajan, such as the famous lawyer Lucius Neratius Priscus. In the end a rumour circulated that Plotina fabricated the claim that Hadrian had been adopted by Trajan on his deathbed. The letter that confirmed this was sent to Hadrian, arriving on 9 August 117, and he was promptly acclaimed emperor by the army in the province, just as Vespasian had been in 69. This equivocal situation made it all the more necessary that Hadrian assert his position extremely quickly. He requested from the senate the deification of Trajan and tactfully apologized on behalf of the troops for acting presumptuously in acclaiming him as emperor.[21]

Publius Acilius Attianus had been praetorian prefect for about five years by 117 and was with Trajan when he died. As far back as 86 Attianus had been the guardian of the ten-year-old Publius Aelius Hadrianus (Hadrian), along with Hadrian's cousin, Trajan. He seems to have shared the prefecture since around 112 with Servius Sulpicius Similis, a modest man who had taken the post reluctantly after he had been prefect of Egypt; earlier in his career he had risen to the heights of *primus pilus*. When he was still only a centurion Similis was once summoned by Trajan ahead of the prefects. The deferential Similis said 'it was a shame' for him to be called in while prefects waited outside.[22] Sent ahead by Hadrian, Attianus returned to Rome with Trajan's ashes, which were to be placed at the base of his column in the forum, accompanied by Plotina and her niece Matidia (the mother of Hadrian's wife, Sabina). Attianus seems to have written to Hadrian with the advice that he should order the execution of Baebius Macer, prefect of Rome, on the grounds that there was reason to believe he might object to Hadrian being emperor. Perhaps Macer was known to prefer Neratius Maximus. Other potential objectors were cited by Attianus. Whatever the truth, the outcome is unknown, though Macer was probably at least removed from post.[23]

A senatorial plot to murder Hadrian soon after his accession was thwarted, but it resulted in the senate ordering the execution of four senators. Hadrian denied that he had wanted this, but it marred the beginning of his principate and had implications for the praetorian prefecture. Hadrian hurried to Rome, arriving there on 9 July 118, and offered a large handout to the people in order to offset the unpopularity the executions had caused, and made a number of other conciliatory gestures such as remitting private debt owed to the state.[24] Attianus was awarded the honorific promotion to senatorial status of consular rank in 119. Hadrian appears to have had an ulterior motive. He allegedly believed that Attianus had been behind the execution of the four senators, and resented his power, which of course included the potential power of the praetorians themselves. Supposedly reluctant to be associated with any more executions and also wishing to transfer all the blame for the senatorial executions, Hadrian coerced Attianus into resigning. It is equally possible that Attianus was a loyalist who had carried out Hadrian's secret wishes and been prepared to take the blame on the emperor's behalf. If so, it would have made him a good example of how useful the position of praetorian prefect could be to an emperor in a way that had nothing to do with commanding the Guard. The position with Similis is harder to understand. Hadrian's biographer implies that Similis was another victim of what is described as Hadrian's plan to remove the men who had smoothed his path to power. Dio, however, suggests that this unassuming man had some trouble in persuading Hadrian to release him. Similis went on to enjoy seven years of retirement, regarding these as the only years he had enjoyed life; all the years of his career he dismissed as being no more than merely existing. This was recorded on his tombstone.[25]

Attianus and Similis were replaced as prefects in or around 119 by Gaius Septicius Clarus and Quintus Marcius Turbo. Turbo, who had a very significant military reputation, seems to have had a longer personal association with Hadrian. As a young man Hadrian served as tribune of the II legion Adiutrix while it was stationed in the province of Pannonia Inferior. Turbo, at some point in his career, was a centurion with II Adiutrix since the tombstone found at Aquincum (within Budapest) of a soldier called Gaius Castricius Victor states that he was in Turbo's century.[26] There is no certainty that Turbo's time in II Adiutrix coincided with Hadrian's, or even that this is the same man. But they might have served with the legion simultaneously, and if so then they might have come into contact and the future emperor been impressed by Turbo, though a personal connection may have played a more important part in Hadrian's decision.

Turbo was to have a remarkable military career both before and after his appointment as praetorian prefect. He made some of the previous incumbents seem like dilettantes. By 114 Turbo was commanding the imperial fleet at Misenum. Next under Trajan he seems to have been sent to lead an assault on Jewish rebels in Egypt and Cyrene, leading a naval force and one of combined infantry and cavalry. The action was successful and involved the death of a large number of rebels. Soon after Trajan's death, Hadrian sent Turbo to crush a rebellion in Mauretania. This was evidently also so successful that Hadrian, exceptionally, appointed Turbo temporarily to be an equestrian prefect governor of the important frontier garrison provinces of Pannonia and Dacia. This was so unusual that it must reflect Turbo's remarkable skills. The only major governorship normally allocated to an equestrian prefect was Egypt, reflecting that province's nature as the personal property of the emperor; indeed, as governor of Dacia Turbo was considered to hold a rank equivalent in prestige to being prefect of Egypt. The appointment came rapidly after the execution of the four senators and will have involved Hadrian dismissing the consular governor, Lucius Minucius Natalis. The practical effect was to place his own man in charge of an important component of the army. Perhaps Hadrian had in mind Maecenas' advice to Augustus around 150 years previously on the advantages of distributing patronage amongst the equestrians.[27] Turbo rearranged Dacia into two provinces. Dacia Superior was demoted to the status of requiring only a governor of praetorian, not consular, rank, and Dacia Inferior was to be governed by an equestrian procurator.[28]

Turbo took his new post of praetorian prefect extremely seriously. He lived like an ordinary citizen and passed the day in the vicinity of the palace, even punctiliously checking up on everything late at night. He transferred his morning salutation (*salutatio*) to the late evening, greeting his friends and clients then, rather than during the day when he was far busier doing his job. Accordingly, the lawyer Cornelius Fronto dropped in to pay his respects after a dinner party, paradoxically greeting Turbo with the evening departure *vale* ('farewell'), rather than the morning *salve* ('good health'). Turbo was said to have operated on the principle that as prefect he 'should die on his feet'.[29]

The prefect Gaius Septicius Clarus had been a friend and correspondent of Pliny the Younger. He also had a senator for a nephew. Clarus had urged Pliny to publish his letters and was rewarded by having the collection dedicated to him. Suetonius also dedicated part of his *Lives of the Caesars* to him. Although Clarus' earlier career is completely unknown to us, he had probably served in some capacity as an equestrian commanding officer, perhaps commanding an auxiliary infantry unit. His personal tastes and interests were more literary. This probably formed the basis of Hadrian's decision to appoint him to serve as a convivial and interesting companion rather than as a military official. Hadrian set out for the northern frontier in 121, accompanied by Clarus, presumably with part of the Guard too, as well as Suetonius, his imperial secretary.[30]

Hadrian was away until 125. During this time he paid particular attention to military discipline. While we have no specific information that this was applied to the Guard it must have done, especially with Turbo in charge of those left in Rome. The choice of Septicius Clarus and Suetonius as travelling companions seems to have backfired. Around 122 Hadrian visited Britain where he initiated construction of the wall that bears his name 'to separate the barbarians from the Romans'. At this point in his biography we are told he dismissed both Septicius Clarus and Suetonius, along with several other unnamed people, for being too familiar with Sabina. He was even tempted to divorce Sabina but stopped himself on the basis of the dignity of his office. It is clear from the structure of the biography that this event is placed during Hadrian's stay in Britain, but since the biographies of this period are notoriously confused in detail in some places, the actual sequence of events may have been different. Quite what had happened is unclear, but there was a suggestion of sexual impropriety, even if it amounted to no more than indiscreet flirting. Aurelius Victor includes a reference to Sabina's claim that she had deliberately avoided becoming pregnant by Hadrian because she considered him so 'inhuman' that she wished to save the human race from any of his offspring. Hadrian had clearly found out about the carryings-on from his spies, the *frumentarii*, whom he used for all sorts of private investigations in his household and circle of friends. Septicius Clarus had been added to Attianus and others whom Hadrian had once trusted and now regarded as enemies.[31]

An occasional instance of a military career that included a spell in the Guard is available at around this time. Titus Pontius Sabinus was a career legionary who, as *primus pilus* of the III legion Augusta, was placed in charge of detachments of the VII Gemina, VIII Augusta and XXII Primigenia sent on 'the British expedition' around this time, perhaps accompanying Hadrian. The province had been in considerable difficulties since around the end of Trajan's reign.[32] After this foray into the wilds of Britain, Sabinus was promoted to be tribune of the III cohort of the *vigiles*, tribune of the XIIII urban cohort, and then tribune of the II praetorian cohort, before becoming *primus pilus* once again and finishing up as pro-curator of the province of Gallia Narbonensis. This shows how much experience was considered necessary for a man to hold the tribunate in the Praetorian Guard. His time as tribune of the II praetorian cohort probably occurred under the latter part of the reign of Hadrian.[33] A praetorian denied the chance to accumulate any experience at all was Lucius Marius Vitalis. He joined the Guard when he was around sixteen or seventeen years old during the reign of Hadrian. He left Rome with the Guard, headed for some unknown destination, perhaps with Hadrian, but died aged seventeen years and fifty-five days.[34] Marius Vitalis illustrates how the original Republican tradition of hiring praetorians from experienced soldiers had been at least partly replaced by recruiting very young men. Men of Pontius Sabinus' calibre therefore found themselves knocking into shape youths with little or no experience at all of soldiering, and who would have taken some time to turn into praetorians with the right skills to serve the emperor either in Rome or in the field. This goes some way to explaining the rationale behind the decision over half a century later in 193 to cashier the Guard and replace it entirely with legionaries who had considerably more to offer in the way of experience.

Meanwhile, the man who replaced Septicius Clarus and continued to command any members of the Guard in Hadrian's retinue is unknown. That Turbo had remained in Rome is only likely, and not an attested fact. The most obvious choice to replace Clarus would have been the former prefect of Egypt (117–19), Quintus Rammius Martialis; however, not only is there no information to that effect, but unless he was with Hadrian already there would have been something of a delay before he could either fill the post or join him. Hadrian was to remain abroad until 125, finishing up in Sicily by way of Greece before returning to Rome.[35]

For all his skills and experience, Turbo also fell foul of Hadrian's capricious inclination to turn against those he had trusted, even though Turbo, like Similis, had been honoured with a statue. He was said, along with others, to have been 'persecuted', though what that means, or its consequences, is unknown to us. This may not have occurred until Hadrian returned to Rome in 134.[36] The same applies to the Praetorian Guard at this time. We seem to know a remarkable amount about Turbo's career before he became praetorian prefect and the manner in which he conducted himself in the post, but little or nothing about the praetorians themselves or how he led them. We can only assume that praetorians accompanied Hadrian on his journey between 121 and 125 because Clarus went with him. In 128 Hadrian visited North Africa, returned to Rome and then headed off to the eastern provinces, including Greece, Syria, Arabia and Egypt.[37] We can do no more than speculate on how the praetorians regarded being removed from the privileged comforts of the Castra Praetoria in Rome. If Septicius Clarus had not been replaced, which is quite possible, then Turbo may have been out of Rome with Hadrian on some of his later travels serving as sole prefect; equally, he may have remained in the city with the prefect of Rome, Annius Verus, with a tribune instead commanding a detachment of the Guard accompanying the emperor.[38]

The governor of Britain, like any provincial governor, enjoyed the prestige of having his own military staff, *singulares*, drawn from soldiers in the provincial garrison, including the auxilia, and serving on detachment. These men were known as *beneficiarii*, literally because they benefited from the privileges and status afforded by the job, and carried out the governor's orders. They were not praetorians but they were the governor's equivalent. Just as the praetorians amplified the status of the emperor, so the governor's bodyguard enhanced and advertised his status and made it possible for him to allocate soldiers from his guard to other deserving officials. While governor of Bithynia and Pontus, Pliny the Younger was asked by a visiting imperial freedman procurator for an escort of six soldiers on a corn-procuring mission, to which Pliny added two mounted soldiers.[39]

Under Hadrian, if not before, additional barracks were built in Rome. In 2015 during work on a new metro line a substantial and well-appointed barrack block of Hadrianic date was discovered around half a kilometre south-east of the Colosseum in the vicinity of four other barrack blocks, together with associated burials.[40] It was clearly a dedicated military zone. It is difficult to imagine who the occupants might have been other than some of the praetorians, and in this case it was probably the *equites singulares*

Augusti. The remains uncovered included a corridor around 100 metres long with thirty-nine rooms opening off it. Some of the floors had mosaics that had existed long enough to be patched and repaired. Such decoration was not typical of legionary fortresses and reflects the higher standard of living to which praetorians were accustomed. These facilities were roughly half the distance from the centre of Rome compared to the Castra Praetoria, making them much more convenient and also made a quicker response in a crisis possible. We know so little about the internal layout of the Castra Praetoria that there is every possibility it was not fully used at this time.

It is therefore interesting that around the same time, by c. 120 or not long after, a fort to accommodate the governor of Britannia's guard was built in the north-west part of the settled area of London, perhaps connected with Hadrian's visit to the province and to ensure his protection. The location and purpose of the Cripplegate fort resembled those of the Castra Praetoria in the sense that it was a freestanding military base on the outskirts of what was otherwise a civilian and administrative settlement. London, although tiny compared to Rome, was still the largest city in the province of Britannia. The new fort, which may have replaced an earlier timber one, covered 4.5 hectares and was thus far smaller than a legionary fortress, but it was more than twice the size of most ordinary forts. It was large enough to accommodate the equivalent of a milliary infantry cohort, probably with a cavalry component. The location of known gates, defences, and fragmentary traces of barracks suggest that unlike the Castra Praetoria it was conventional in plan, resembling other forts.[41] Evidence from tombstone inscriptions in London indicates that soldiers were detached from all three legions to serve on the governor's bodyguard, for example Flavius Agricola of the VI legion, which only arrived in Britain under Hadrian, who died in London aged forty-two.[42] The London fort was by no means typical. Roman forts in a civilian context are very unusual, Carthage being an exception.[43] It survived long enough to be absorbed into London's later Roman walls, just as the Castra Praetoria was absorbed into the Aurelian Walls of Rome in the late third century. All provincial governors had bodyguard units, so far as we know, for obvious reasons of security and prestige. London's fort suggests that special conditions prevailed in Britain, necessitating a fortified headquarters in the manner of a provincial castra praetoria, but in this case requiring full military defences because of the residual instability in the province.

Back in Rome, by the end of Hadrian's reign or shortly after the accession of Antoninus Pius in 138 two new praetorian prefects were appointed: Marcus Gavius Maximus and Marcus Petronius Mamertinus.[44] The reign of Antoninus Pius is even less well known than Hadrian's since Dio's account is more or less completely lost, leaving us only with the *Historia Augusta*. It is both conceivable and probable that praetorians participated in wars during the reign of Antoninus Pius, but there is nothing to confirm that.

Hadrian's original intention had been to be succeeded by Lucius Ceionius Commodus, adopted by the childless emperor in 136 and renamed Lucius Aelius Caesar. The occasion of his adoption was accompanied by the distribution of 300 million sestertii amongst the soldiers. This must have included the praetorians, and at a preferential rate compared to the rest of the army. Aelius, in the event, predeceased Hadrian, dying on 1 January 138. His demise occasioned a crisis for the ailing Hadrian, who selected Antoninus Pius, a highly regarded senator whose wife Faustina was the great-granddaughter of Trajan's sister, Marciana. Antoninus and Faustina adopted Aelius' son, Lucius Verus, along with Marcus Aurelius, the husband of their daughter, Faustina Junior, providing a cash handout to the soldiers on the occasion of that marriage in 145. This complicated web of relationships successfully created a dynasty but for the most part had relied on selecting suitable men rather than on a direct bloodline. Hadrian had even initially considered Marcus Aurelius as his heir, but rejected him on the grounds that at eighteen he was too young.[45]

The principal praetorian prefect of the new reign was Marcus Gavius Maximus, who in or around 158 was said to have served in the position for twenty years, so therefore must have been appointed either by Hadrian in early 138 or by Antoninus soon afterwards (Plate 20). With one exception Antoninus Pius kept men in the posts in which they had been placed by Hadrian until they died. The other prefect, Marcus Petronius Mamertinus, served 138–143, after which Gavius Maximus held the sole prefecture for the rest of his life. The two men are cited on an inscription of 1 March 139 recording the honourable discharge of thirty-nine *equites singulares Augusti*. The inclusion of the names of both praetorian prefects suggests a closer link between the office of the prefecture and the emperor's mounted bodyguard than might otherwise have been obvious.[46] In the same year a mosaic floor was installed in the Castra Praetoria with an inscription that commemorated the *vicennalia* (twentieth anniversary of the accession) of Antoninus Pius. It was an appropriate recognition of the mutual dependence of emperor and his bodyguard.[47]

Little is known about Marcus Petronius Mamertinus. His tenure as praetorian prefect is otherwise only known from a letter of Marcus Cornelius Fronto. He may have previously been prefect of Egypt. After his praetorian prefecture he was awarded honorary consular status by 150, leaving only Gavius Maximus in post. Marcus Gavius Maximus was apparently 'a very stern man'. He also seems to have been extremely rich. A fragmentary inscription from the port town at Ostia, and another one in the Vatican Museum, suggest that Gavius Maximus had paid for the lavish Forum Baths, which remain one of the most conspicuous and largest ruins at the site today.[48] The structure is imaginatively designed so that the bath chambers, which all face south-west, received sun throughout the middle of the day and afternoon, reflecting the most popular time of the day to visit the baths. Although the building, like all such structures at Ostia, is built largely of brick, it was expensively faced throughout with marble, much of which has since been robbed away. It is difficult to know what to make of this. Gavius Maximus may have paid for the baths at his own expense, but it is also possible that Antoninus Pius subsidized the costs on his prefect's behalf. Why Gavius Maximus would have wanted or needed to pay for the baths, or indeed how he became wealthy enough to fund them, is unknown. Civic munificence was virtually ubiquitous in the Roman world but we know of no particular connection that Gavius Maximus had with the port town; perhaps he had come from there or his father had made his name in the thriving commerce of the settlement. Either way, there is no obvious connection with the praetorians themselves. Instead we have an image of the praetorian prefect as a member of the imperial court rather than as a military commanding officer, and encouraging public popularity through his gifts to the community. Whether or not he is representative of the praetorian prefects at this date cannot be said. This was certainly what the office had evolved into when the Guard was disbanded in 312 (Plate 21).

Marcus Gavius Maximus was succeeded briefly in 158 as praetorian prefect by Gaius Tattius Maximus, who had been prefect of the *vigiles* since 156. The prefecture was then once again restored to a joint position, with Sextus Cornelius Repentinus and Titus Furius Victorinus being appointed. Cornelius Repentinus' promotion from his position as imperial secretary did not last long. His reputation was destroyed in 158 when a rumour emerged that he had been appointed with the assistance of Galeria Lysistrata, one of Faustina's freedwomen and mistress of Antoninus Pius.[49] It should be noted in the emperor's defence that Faustina, highly esteemed though she was, had died in 141.

One inscription from this era gives us an example of a praetorian operating in the broader community in an official capacity as a surveyor. Blesius Taurinus was a praetorian land surveyor (*mensor agrarius*) serving with the VI praetorian cohort during the reign of Antoninus Pius. Taurinus was sent on imperial authority to Ardea, 22 miles (35 km) south of Rome, where he determined the boundaries of the settlement. With that done, Tuscenius Felix, serving for the second time as *primus pilus* of an unspecified unit, delivered a decision (what it was is unknown).[50] As so often in the Roman world, military personnel exhibited the greatest concentration of professional expertise available. In this case Antoninus Pius had used these men to resolve something that had been brought to his attention, perhaps a property dispute. The army was the most convenient, and perhaps the only source of the necessary skills and manpower the emperor could call on.

Antoninus Pius was succeeded in 161 by Marcus Aurelius, who since 145 had been his son-in-law and earmarked as his heir by awarding him the tribunician power at the same time. As he lay dying, Antoninus Pius called together all his friends and prefects, who must have included Titus Furius Victorinus, and told them that Aurelius would be succeeding him.[51]

When he assumed power, Marcus Aurelius immediately appointed Lucius Verus, the son of Hadrian's originally intended successor Aelius, as his co-emperor and had him marry his daughter Lucilla. The reasons were both dynastic and practical. Verus was younger and more interested in participating in the frontier wars that were to be increasingly a characteristic of this reign, and was soon dispatched to fight the Parthians in the east.[52]

The joint emperors' first act was to head for the Castra Praetoria where they allegedly offered the soldiers 20,000 sestertii each, and proportionately more to the centurions and tribunes. This figure is generally regarded as an obvious exaggeration – though it matched the amount awarded on discharge as far back as Augustus' time so there is no overwhelming reason to assume it is wrong.[53] In 162 the praetorian prefect Titus Furius Victorinus accompanied Lucius Verus to the Parthian war, where he was to die either by fighting or from plague in 167. He was commemorated in the forum at Rome by a statue with an inscription that recorded his exploits and how he had been awarded honorary consular status.[54] Furius Victorinus must have commanded several cohorts drawn from the Praetorian Guard, presumably another occasion when praetorians were now routinely forming part of imperial armies in the field when necessary.[55] This war was to be successful. Verus returned to Rome in 166 where his inclination to luxurious and indulgent living annoyed Marcus Aurelius.

In January 168 veteran praetorians were offered improved support for starting families. In order to help these men acquire wives, any sons born of the marriage would count for their fathers-in-law when it came to seeking a claim for intestate property or claiming exemption from *tutela* (legal guardianship). In other words, the boys' maternal grandfathers would now be able to use their grandsons by their daughters (so long as these daughters married a praetorian veteran) in the same ways, legally, as they would have done their grandsons by their sons.[56] Praetorians, like all other soldiers, were not allowed by law to marry while in service and this had been the position from the inception of the Guard under Augustus. In practice, unofficial unions did take place and it is apparent from a number of sources that during the second century such arrangements were sometimes accepted by the authorities, right up to and including the emperor. This was far from guaranteed. In 117 the prefect of Egypt, Marcus Rutilius Rufus, denied a wife the right to a claim on the estate of her deceased soldier husband on the simple grounds that 'a soldier is not permitted to marry'.[57]

Whatever the legality and unofficial liaisons, praetorians do not appear to have embarked on such relationships to anything like the same degree as ordinary soldiers. On the evidence of funerary epitaphs and who dedicated them, only 3 per cent of praetorians in the first century had unofficial wives; the majority of deceased praetorians were commemorated by fellow soldiers. This rises to over 10 per cent in the second century and to over 25 per cent in the third century. By comparison, a third of the legionaries on the Danube in the second century were likely to be commemorated by a wife – three times as many as a praetorian of the same period.[58] The praetorians may have been subjected to sterner discipline because of their location and involvement in imperial security, but it is no less possible that frontier legionaries found that acquiring unofficial wives was the easiest way of securing female company, whereas praetorians, being based in Rome, had more casual opportunities.

There is some suggestion that the Praetorian Guard also evolved its own distinctive traditions of a more formal military presentation and terminology in which, perhaps, publicly acknowledging the existence of an unofficial wife was less 'the done thing' than it might have been amongst legionaries. Praetorians were much more likely to describe themselves as the *commanipularis*, 'comrade of the same maniple', of a colleague than legionaries were. For example, Marcus Paccius Avitus of the V praetorian cohort died at the age of thirty after five years' service. His tombstone was erected by his *commanipularis*, Lucius Valerius. Whether this is really evidence of a fundamentally different culture or merely different style is a moot point. Legionaries were more likely to call each other *commilito*, 'co-soldier', or *contubernalis*, 'tent-party comrade', which seems more a matter of style than evidence of different levels of formal military culture. Unless a praetorian had a wife whose name is mentioned on his tombstone, we cannot assume that more praetorians had wives who were excluded from the epigraphic tradition and that therefore, for whatever reason, praetorians were less likely to form unofficial unions while the law remained in force.[59] Moreover, Paccius Avitus had died young and this seems to be common to many of the praetorians we happen to know about. Praetorians of the second century were also more likely to be discharged early than legionaries. Up to 58 per cent had been discharged within seventeen years, whereas legionaries had served 'much longer periods of time' before being discharged at this rate. Various factors might explain this, including a possibly higher rate of loss in combat and disease in Rome.[60]

Those who lived long enough to benefit from the shorter terms of service were likely to be awarded an honourable discharge and then move on to prestigious civic jobs such as municipal magistracies in their home towns. Gaius Com[. . .] Secundus, a veteran of the V praetorian cohort, returned to what was probably his home town of the colony of Minturnae (Minterno) where he served his community as an *aedile*, a magistracy that would have entitled him thereafter to a seat on the town council (*ordo*) as a *decurion* (councillor).[61] Gaius Arrius Clemens, who had served with distinction in Dacia under Trajan while with the VIIII praetorian cohort, proceeded to a series of posts as centurion before ending up as a *duumvir* (one of the two senior magistrates) in the town of Matilica (Matelica) in Umbria, and as patron of the community.[62] Such men were primarily memorialized in their prestigious positions of later life, their service as ordinary praetorians being brushed over if mentioned at all. They would have been more likely to marry during this later time in their lives, having both the money and legal opportunity, as well as having age on their side, unlike legionaries.[63] This would also explain why praetorians received discharge certificates which noted their right now to marry, an essential document if they were to marry non-citizen wives.

The outbreak of war on the Danube frontier, when the Germanic tribal confederation known as the Marcomanni invaded in 168, caused Verus and Aurelius to head out to fight, but Verus died in 169 during their return to Rome.[64] Marcus Aurelius carried on as sole emperor until 177 when his son, Commodus, was elevated from the position of Caesar that he had held since 175, to joint Augustus with his father. During that period, between the years 169 and 172, there is clear evidence of praetorian prefects serving

206

in a capacity we would most easily recognize as commissioners of police. An imperial freedman called Cosmus wrote to the praetorian prefects Bassaeus Rufus and Macrinius Vindex, who had succeeded the deceased Furius Victorinus in or around 167, with Vindex probably being appointed a little later. Bassaeus Rufus came from modest origins and reached the praetorian prefecture via the prefecture of Egypt, but Macrinius Vindex's earlier career is unknown.[65] The purpose of the letter was to appeal to the prefects for their help in stopping the magistrates at the cities of Saepinum (Attilia) and Bovianum (Boiano), and *stationarii*, from troubling lessees of sheep flocks on an imperial estate. The *stationarii* were armed police installed in specific locations, and had been established by Augustus. It is not clear in this instance if praetorians were being used as *stationarii*, though some inscriptions show that praetorians could be used in this role and sometimes far beyond Italy. Titus Valerius Secundus of the VII praetorian cohort, for example, was a *stationarius* at Ephesus where he died in service at the age of twenty-six.[66]

Cosmus alleged that the magistrates and *stationarii* had been accusing the lessees of being runaway slaves, and appropriating the sheep accordingly. This meant that the magistrates and *stationarii* were stealing imperial property. Rufus and Vindex obliged. They wrote to the magistrates, attaching a copy of Cosmus' letter, and it is the text of this that has survived. It was a warning to the magistrates and other suspects to desist, on pain of further investigation and punishment. Although the outcome is not known, the document is one of the most specific records of the praetorian prefects operating in a way more akin to a civilian police force, though urban cohorts seem to have been included as well.[67]

In the meantime, the Marcomannic War continued. For all their responsibilities in homeland policing, the praetorian prefects also continued to serve as military commanders in the field. Both Bassaeus Rufus and Macrinius Vindex travelled with Marcus Aurelius on campaign in the early 170s, though we do not know how often or the numbers of praetorians involved. Since both prefects were participating it is possible that a large proportion of the Guard had accompanied them, the remainder perhaps being left under the command of a tribune in Rome, apart of course from those dispersed on various duties around the Empire. In the event Macrinius Vindex was to die leading in battle in or around 172.[68]

Macrinius Vindex was not replaced immediately. Marcus Aurelius was said to have had a particular favourite candidate in the senator Publius Helvius Pertinax, praising him both in the senate and also at military assemblies, but regretted that as Pertinax was a senator he would have to pass him over.[69] Of course, given the appointment of Titus as commander of the Guard by Vespasian, this was a technicality which could have been overlooked had Marcus Aurelius really wanted to. Bassaeus Rufus continued in post in the meantime, possibly as sole prefect. He attended the trial of Herodes Atticus before Marcus Aurelius at Sirmium in 173 or 174. Herodes had been accused of tyranny by the Athenians. During the trial Bassaeus Rufus, described as being praetorian prefect by Philostratus, said it was clear Herodes wished to die. Herodes retorted by saying that at his age there was very little he feared. Bassaeus was still in post in July 177, but probably for not much longer, after which he received honorary consular status.[70] His name is recorded in this capacity. Publius Tarrutenius Paternus became praetorian prefect in or around 179, having been a former imperial secretary. He led a force against the Marcomanni in 179 so he must have been in post by then, but is not specifically attested in it until after the death of Marcus Aurelius when in c. 182 he participated in a plot to kill Commodus.[71] The only other possible evidence we have for the Guard in action at this date is the sculpture on the Column of Marcus Aurelius in Rome depicting the Marcomannic War. Unlike Trajan's Column, the identification is a good deal more tenuous and depends on the belief that scale armour is the distinguishing factor. There is some verification for this in Dio who refers to this feature of praetorian equipment when describing the Guard under Macrinius in 218. Other scenes on the column also show the *equites singulares Augusti* with Marcus Aurelius on campaign.[72]

This single example highlights the central issue when it comes to dealing with the Praetorian Guard between the accession of Trajan in 98 and the death of Marcus Aurelius in 180. These eighty-two years were more than long enough for no one to have any living memory of the power the Guard could choose to exert as emperor-breakers and makers. The reality was that none of the emperors in that period was deficient in any of the key qualities required. Their successions were largely undisputed, their judgement was respected, and their personal qualities for the most part sufficient to ensure that they stayed in power and died in their beds. The Avidius Cassius episode in Egypt in 175 was a rare exception.[73] The state was thus not vulnerable and in these circumstances there was no opportunity or need for the praetorians to try and influence events. They took part in wars, and their prefects served the emperors as advisers, chiefs of police or generals as and when needed. It must have been for the most part an easy, complacent and privileged lifestyle. This was to change dramatically under Commodus who was the first ruler for almost a century to exhibit serious shortcomings in his ability either to rule or to choose suitable men for key commands, amongst which was of course the praetorian prefecture. This was to result in the revival of a badly led and dysfunctional Praetorian Guard which would culminate in one of the most degenerate episodes in its history (Plates 22 and 23).

CHAPTER 9

THE AGE OF IRON AND RUST
(180–235)

The death of Marcus Aurelius marked a turning point not only for the Roman Empire but also for the Praetorian Guard. The accession of his weak and reckless son Commodus created a power vacuum into which the praetorian prefects and the praetorians themselves, as the most significant force in Rome, were inevitably sucked. The emergence of opportunistic and self-serving praetorian prefects of a type unseen since the days of Tigellinus under Nero added to the problems caused by a greedy, lazy and indulgent Guard. The murder of Commodus in 192 heralded a protracted age of instability, beginning with a massive power struggle, orchestrated in part by the Praetorian Guard. It would culminate in the whole Guard being cashiered in 193 by Septimius Severus, and its reformation. The Guard of the third century increasingly found itself operating as an integral part of the emperor's field army in an era of unrestrained military ambition and chronic frontier instability.

COMMODUS WAS THE FIRST weak emperor for more than eighty years.[1] As the blood son of Marcus Aurelius he was also the first filial heir since Titus a century earlier. Whereas Titus was up to the job, Commodus was not. In 177 he had been made joint Augustus with Marcus Aurelius so the legitimacy of his sole reign was never in doubt. Aurelius recognized that Commodus, then aged only about nineteen, would be susceptible to poor advice because of his inexperience. On his deathbed he urged his advisers and relatives to support him, and recommended him to the support of the army, something Commodus claimed his father had done ever since he was a boy.[2] Aurelius died shortly afterwards, on 17 March 180 in Vindobona (Vienna).

A few days later, Commodus was taken by those same advisers to the camp at Vindobona so that he could address the soldiers and offer them a donative. The troops were summoned to the parade ground outside the fort where Commodus made his speech. He appealed to their loyalty, experience and support. One of the great values of the evidence for this period is that our principal sources, Cassius Dio and Herodian, had not only lived through the times they were describing, but had also known the emperors concerned, though this does not mean that their accounts always accord; all too often they do not. Dio entered the senate during Commodus' reign and thus witnessed events as they unfolded. Herodian was only a teenager when Commodus died, but his proximity to the period and its records make him equally invaluable. Dio's opinion was that Commodus was not innately evil, but that he lacked guile; as a result he was easily led astray by his companions.[3]

Commodus immediately made peace with the Marcomanni, a decision that instantly alienated the army. On his arrival in Rome, which was eagerly awaited, he boasted to the senate about his exploits. He thanked the soldiers who had been left in Rome, presumably the rump of the Praetorian Guard, for their loyalty. He was immediately the focus of plots. He had inherited Publius Tarrutenius Paternus as praetorian prefect, but by 181 or 182 had also appointed Tigidius Perennis to the post. Paternus became involved in the first of a series of plots against Commodus. The conspiracy was a complicated one, and not made easier to understand by the piecemeal references in the sources, which provide quite disparate detail. Commodus' sister Lucilla was married to Claudius Pompeianus, a man whom she hated and who was also an adviser to Commodus.[4] Pompeianus had a son, Claudius Pompeianus Quintianus, by (probably) a previous marriage. Egged on by Lucilla in the hope that her husband would be permanently ruined by the association, and apparently all under the guiding hand of

Paternus, Quintianus attacked Commodus. Herodian, however, attributes the plot to Lucilla's lover Quadratus, who was desperate to please her because she resented the precedence now awarded Crispina at her expense. Either way, Quintianus made a physical assault on Commodus, claiming it was being done in the name of the senate, but failed to kill him.[5]

In the aftermath, Commodus forced Lucilla, and then his wife Crispina, into exile. He removed Paternus from the prefecture by awarding him honorary consular status and then killed him anyway in c. 182.[6] Commodus decided that he hated the senate and also now fell under the influence of the remaining praetorian prefect, Tigidius Perennis, who turned out to be only the first in a record-breaking series of new praetorian prefects for a single reign. On the face of it, Perennis ought to have been the perfect candidate: he was both Italian and considered to have an excellent military reputation, though this has proved impossible to substantiate. He was presented with an extremely challenging job because it appears he was expected to do a great deal more than manage the Guard, with Commodus effectively delegating to him all the duties of the emperor. This exposed him to resentment. This is Dio's perspective and, although critical of Perennis, the blame is also laid squarely on Commodus. Conversely, Herodian depicts Perennis as a cynical opportunist who identified Commodus' vulnerability and capitalized on the chance to maximize his own power.[7] There is more than a passing resemblance to the portrayals of Sejanus and Tigellinus here, even if the nature of the emperors involved was different. It is possible that this version of Perennis is therefore effectively a redrawing of the Sejanus episode, but it is just as likely that the circumstances of a vulnerable emperor and an ambitious prefect could generate similar consequences. There is no suggestion that the praetorians themselves were involved. Herodian describes Perennis as maintaining Commodus in a state of licentious intoxication. This would allow him to run the Empire in order to make as much money out of it as possible in preparation for seizing it by offering the army a huge payout. Perennis began by encouraging Commodus to believe he was surrounded by enemies in the form of rich senators, who could be executed and their property seized. This appears really to have taken hold after the crushing of the plot involving Paternus, Pompeianus, Quadratus and Lucilla. Perennis is said to have persuaded Commodus to transfer the army in Illyricum to his sons, though these are unknown, as the next stage in his plan to seize power.[8]

The fall of Perennis followed shortly afterwards in 185. Herodian's version is that Commodus was chastened by a theatregoer 'dressed as a philosopher' who publicly criticized him for attending a performance while Perennis was plotting his coup. The man was executed but Commodus turned on Perennis. In Dio's account, fifteen hundred soldiers arrived in Rome from the garrison of Britain to alert Commodus to Perennis' machinations; the implication is that they were bitterly resentful of how Perennis had been managing the army. This had been orchestrated by Commodus' chamberlain, Cleander, who is discussed in more detail below. The story is amplified in the *Historia Augusta*, where Perennis is said to have been installing equestrians, instead of senators, as legionary commanders in Britain during a war in 184.[9] This remarkable breach of a long-established tradition was probably a device to ensure the army was under the control of men who would owe their allegiance to Perennis and not be troubled by his non-senatorial status. Commodus apparently believed them and handed Perennis over to the praetorians themselves, who killed him, his wife and their children. In Herodian's version, Perennis was killed by someone sent secretly on Commodus' orders. This was followed by sending two agents to Perennis' son, before he heard the truth about his father, to pretend they brought orders for him to come to Rome. Perennis' son, whose name is unknown, fell for the ruse and was murdered when he reached Rome.[10] The various problems with the details do not alter the fact that Commodus permitted his sole praetorian prefect to become far too powerful at his expense. The dangers were the same as under Tiberius and Nero, although the timescale was considerably shorter. Clearly, as with Sejanus, Perennis' power began with commanding the Guard, though in his case he went a great deal further in his attempts to secure control over the legionary forces dispersed around the Empire. Britain's garrison was an interesting and intelligent choice. With three legions concentrated in a geographically small area, along with a large number of auxiliary units, it presented significant opportunities to men of ambition.

Commodus decided to appoint two praetorian prefects, believing that this would be safer. If he was aware of the story of Sejanus, and he must have been, the two episodes would now have functioned as very salutary warnings. The names of the prefects concerned are not certain, complicated substantially by Commodus' mercurial nature, which led him to hire and fire prefects in rapid succession, sometimes after only a few hours. Pescennius Niger seems to have been one of the replacements, and Titus Longaeus Rufus the other, but Niger lasted only six hours. Marcus Quartius lasted five days, and it appears a number of other, unnamed, incumbents may have followed in the reckless days of 185.

The driving force seems to have been Marcus Aurelius Cleander, a freedman and chamberlain (*cubicularius*) of Commodus. Cleander was responsible for selling all sorts of positions under Commodus' nose and effectively took over the metaphorical vacancy of opportunist-in-chief created by the execution of Perennis. In or around 187, Publius Attilius Aebutanius was made prefect but was also executed; it is not known if he secured the position by simply bidding for it. At that point Cleander became praetorian prefect, an appointment (or, perhaps, self-appointment) with no precedent, along with two others whose names are unknown, creating another precedent in their being three praetorian prefects. It is inconceivable that the Guard had done any more than look on in consummate disgust, but Commodus had perhaps allowed Cleander's advancement on the basis that he distrusted the Guard already, and any prefects appointed by the conventional route. Cleander had gone too far. He engineered the execution of a popular official called Arrius Antoninus. Even Commodus realized that Cleander would have to be sacrificed. The occasion in 189 or 190 appears to have been a food riot caused by a famine that was exacerbated by the prefect of the grain supply, Papirius Dionysius. He put it about that Cleander had been stealing from the stores to enrich himself so that the mob would believe Cleander was responsible for the shortage. The riot broke out in the circus with the mob cursing Cleander. Commodus ordered the *equites singulares Augusti* to attack them, but the crowd's resolve was bolstered by praetorians fighting with them, the praetorians allegedly hating the *equites singulares*, though not before a large number of civilians had been killed. A terrified Commodus handed Cleander over to be torn to pieces on the spot.[11]

Two of the last praetorian prefects of the reign were Lucius Julius Vehilius Gratus Julianus and Regillus. They lasted so little time that nothing is known of them apart from the fact that they were executed in short order. Another, Motilenus, followed shortly afterwards when he was fed poisoned figs. Commodus descended further into delusional grandeur, depicting himself as Hercules on numerous statues in Rome and some of his coins while toying with the idea of renaming Rome Colonia Commodiana. He engaged in increasingly reckless bouts of murdering prominent men. The accounts of his profligate expenditure on horseracing, chariot-racing, gladiatorial bouts, grandiose costumes and other indulgences seem impossible. Dio, however, insisted that he had seen and heard everything he described. He pointed out that it was precisely because he was an eyewitness and knew no one else who had his own level of access to what was going on that made his account reliable. Dio and the other sources, however, were susceptible to the tradition of depicting 'bad' emperors as bad in every possible way.[12]

The end, when it came, was the result of a plot by his mistress, Marcia, and the then praetorian prefect, Quintus Aemilius Laetus. Aemilius Laetus, and Eclectus, Commodus' *cubicularius*, had been obliged to wait on Commodus as he fought as a gladiator in the arena. Commodus would compete, and inevitably win, and then kiss Laetus and Eclectus through his helmet. The two men tried to dissuade Commodus from his more extreme acts, but they were terrified of what might happen to them. Commodus was planning to kill the two consuls on 1 January 193. Laetus and Eclectus took Marcia into their confidence and persuaded her to poison him. Commodus' consumption of alcohol meant that he vomited some of the poison up and instead the conspirators had to persuade an athlete called Narcissus to throttle Commodus. He was killed on the last day of December 192.[13]

The plotters had taken the precaution of planning for the succession in advance. Their choice was Publius Helvius Pertinax, a man of similar vintage to Nerva almost a century earlier. At the age of sixty-seven he was a wealthy senator, having risen from being the son of a freedman through a series of military commands to provincial governorships. These included being sent by Commodus to Britain to pacify the troops there after the death of Perennis. In 192 Pertinax was consul for the second time when Laetus and Eclectus approached him. With Commodus dead they informed Pertinax, and he went to the Castra Praetoria to present himself to the Praetorian Guard so that the all-important oath of loyalty could be secured. The praetorians already seem to have tried to elevate their own nominee, a senator called Triarius Maternus Lascivius, but he fled, perhaps wisely.[14] The oath was secured, but at the price of 12,000 sestertii, economizing on the 20,000 sestertii allegedly paid on the accession of Marcus Aurelius and Lucius Verus, despite Pertinax's claim that he had matched their handout. In one version of the events Pertinax allegedly only paid half the 12,000 sestertii anyway.[15] Moreover, the people of Rome had been so worried the Guard would refuse to be ruled by Pertinax that a huge crowd had gone to the Castra Praetoria to coerce the soldiers to accept Pertinax, who had earned their respect thanks to his military reputation and time as prefect of Rome.[16]

A very dangerous development followed. Pertinax informed the Guard that he would be setting right all sorts of distressing circumstances, which formed part of a more widespread and popular programme of reforms. The praetorians had become accustomed to various indulgent privileges that Commodus had allowed them. They now grew concerned that these were about to disappear in Pertinax's new age of discipline and order.[17] For the moment they suppressed their resentment, largely because Pertinax sold off or melted down everything he could that had belonged to Commodus to raise the money after he discovered that the deceased emperor had emptied the imperial coffers. Ending their freedom to do as they pleased alienated both the praetorians and imperial freedmen. The result was that Laetus became embroiled in another plot to topple an emperor, this time with the active participation of the Guard. Their first plan was to seize power while Pertinax was at the coast inspecting the grain supply, and to place a consul called Falco on the throne. The plot was uncovered but Pertinax refused to execute Falco because he was a senator, even though Dio and the other senators were fully prepared to condemn him to death.[18]

Laetus, perhaps to divert attention from himself, turned on the praetorians and started executing some of them, claiming that Pertinax had ordered him to do so. Two hundred praetorians promptly headed off to the Palatine Hill and forced their way into the imperial palace. Pertinax made no attempt to use the *vigiles* or the *equites singulares Augusti* to protect himself, preferring instead to try negotiating with the irate praetorians. But one praetorian stopped him from going out while palace staff let the soldiers in through all the other entrances. When they confronted Pertinax they were momentarily stopped in their tracks; one praetorian darted forward and stabbed Pertinax and Eclectus, announcing that 'this sword is sent you by the soldiers'. Pertinax's body was decapitated and the head displayed on a spear.[19] What followed was the unedifying auction of the Roman Empire, conducted by the Praetorian Guard and described at the start of this book. The long period of silent acquiescence and discipline that had ended during the reign of Commodus gave way fully to a period in which the praetorians were the kingmakers. They were motivated by greed and a reckless disregard either for their own interests or the emperors' and those of the Roman people. This set in train a disastrous series of events that would last for decades.[20]

Didius Julianus secured his position as emperor by promising the Praetorian Guard 25,000 sestertii each. It was a generous offer, but proved too generous because Julianus had failed to consider whether he could pay it. He was gathered up by the praetorians who, displaying their standards, escorted the new emperor to the forum and the senate. The public display of power was deliberate and obvious and had the desired effect. Julianus indulged the conceit that he had come alone to address the senate while a large number of armed troops secured the building outside and a number came with him into the senate. It was a clear demonstration of where the real power lay, reminiscent of the accession of Otho in 69.[21] Under the circumstances it was hardly surprising that the senate confirmed by decree that Julianus was emperor. He also ingratiated himself, or tried to, with the

Guard by acceding to their personal nominees for the prefecture, in this case Flavius Genialis and Tullius Crispinus. His limited coinage focused to some extent on the army, with 'Harmony of the soldiers' being the principal offering. Conversely, Pertinax's coinage had been far more general in its themes. Unfortunately for Julianus, not only did he lack the personal resources to fund the donative, but the imperial treasuries also remained barren after Commodus' reckless reign. The praetorians were infuriated and started publicly humiliating Julianus, who was already gaining a reputation as greedy and indulgent.[22]

Didius Julianus' short-lived regime was already crumbling. In the east, Pescennius Niger, governor of Syria, had been declared emperor by his troops after news of the murder of Pertinax reached them. News of Niger's ambitions reached Rome, where a frustrated populace started to protest in his favour. Part of the reason appears to have been a belief that Pertinax had been capable of arresting the rot that had set in under Commodus but had not been allowed to finish the job by the otiose and wasteful Julianus. Fighting broke out between the crowd and 'soldiers', which probably included the urban cohorts and the praetorians. Niger was by no means the only potential challenger. Lucius Septimius Severus, governor of Upper Pannonia, had allied himself to Pertinax, but on the latter's death Severus had been declared emperor on 9 April 193 by his own troops. There was an irony in Severus' status. He had been made one of twenty-five consuls appointed by Cleander, just before the latter was made praetorian prefect.[23] In the west, Decimus Clodius Albinus, the governor of Britain, had also thrown his hat into the ring. The stage was set for another civil war. Severus was an arch manipulator. First he bought Albinus' cooperation by offering him the post of heir apparent. Next, he set out first to secure Rome and then to destroy Niger. Severus was confident that in the meantime Julianus would be deposed; he could then turn against Albinus, destroy him and emerge, as Vespasian had in 69, as the supreme power in the Roman world.[24]

For the moment Julianus depended almost entirely on the fragile loyalty of the praetorians, men to whom he had promised a vast sum of money that he was unable to pay. His first move was inevitable, but futile. He ordered the senate to declare Severus a public enemy. His second was to have a defensible stronghold constructed and prepare the whole city for war, which included fortifying his own palace so that he could hold it to the end. Rome filled up with soldiers and equipment, but the preparations turned into a farce. Dio mocked what the praetorians and other available forces had become. Years of easy living, cultivated in the indulgent days of Commodus' reign, had left the soldiers without much idea of what they were supposed to do. The fleet troops from Misenum had forgotten how to drill. According to Herodian, the praetorians had to be told to arm themselves, get back into training and dig trenches; this implies that they were accustomed to being unarmed and were completely out of condition.[25] This depiction of the Praetorian Guard, however, suited the purpose of Dio and Herodian. A stereotyped derelict and incompetent Guard amplified the impression of the decadence of Commodus' reign and the incompetence of Didius Julianus, as well as creating a gratifying image of grossly overpaid and indolent public servants getting their comeuppance. Nevertheless, the indolence probably had a basis in truth and might also have been linked to a conservative attitude to equipment. By the end of the second century AD praetorian infantrymen were still habitually equipping themselves with the *pilum*, while legionaries had spurned this in favour of various new forms of javelin.[26]

The praetorians became agitated. Not only were they completely overwhelmed by all the work they had had to do, but they were also extremely concerned at the prospect of confronting the Syrian army under Severus that was approaching through northern Italy. Julianus toyed with the idea of offering Severus a share in the Empire in an effort to save his own skin. The praetorian prefect Tullius Crispinus was sent north to take a suitable message to this effect to Severus. Severus suspected that Crispinus had really been sent on a mission to murder him, so he had Crispinus killed. In his place Julianus appointed a third prefect, Flavius Juvenalis, whose loyalty Severus secured by writing to him confirming that he would hold the post when he, Severus, took power.[27] There is some confusion here. The *Historia Augusta* calls the third prefect Veturius Macrinus, so conceivably two new prefects had been appointed, both of whom seem to have transferred to the Severan regime.[28] Severus sent letters ahead, perhaps via Juvenalis, promising the praetorians that they would be unharmed if they handed over Pertinax's killers. They obliged, and this meant that Julianus was finished. Severus also sent an advance force to infiltrate the city, disguised as citizens. The senate, realizing that the praetorians had abandoned Julianus, voted that Julianus be executed. This happened in short order on 2 June 193. Next they declared Severus to be the new emperor. Didius Julianus had reigned for a little over two months.[29] In the space of five months in 193 the Praetorian Guard had played their first truly significant role in imperial events for well over a century. They had toppled an emperor and installed another, only to abandon him with unseemly haste, contributing significantly now to the inception of a new dynasty whose members would rule the Roman world until 235. Not since 69 had the praetorians made so much difference, though, ironically, it seems that in 193 as troops they were no more than a shadow of their former selves. They were to pay a heavy price for their interference in imperial politics.

The transition of power was not as smooth as the praetorians hoped. Their tribunes, now working for Severus, ordered them to leave their barracks unarmed, dressed only in the *subarmilis* (under-armour garment) and head for Severus' camp. Severus stood up to address them but it was a trap. The praetorians were promptly surrounded by his armed troops, who had orders not to attack the praetorians but to contain them. Severus ordered that those who had killed Pertinax be executed. This act was to have consequences forty-five years later when another generation of praetorians believed they were about to be cashiered too.[30] Severus harangued the praetorians because they had not supported Julianus or protected him, despite his shortcomings, completely ignoring their own oath of loyalty. In Severus' view this ignoble conduct was tantamount to disqualifying themselves from entitlement to be praetorians; oddly, the so-called 'auction of the Empire' seems to have gone without mention.

Severus had a very good reason for adopting this strategy. It avoided creating any impression that he was buying the Empire as Didius Julianus had, even though previous emperors, including very respectable ones like Marcus Aurelius, had paid a donative. Firing the praetorians en masse also saved him a great deal of money, in the form of either a donative or a retirement gratuity. Given the cost of Severus' own war, and the appalling state of the imperial treasuries, this must have been a pressing consideration. The normal practice would have been for the emperor to pay a donative out of his own pocket.[31] Severus was prepared to spare the praetorians' lives but only on the condition that they were stripped of rank and equipment and cashiered on the spot. This meant literally being stripped. They were forcibly divested by Severus' legionaries of their uniforms, belts and any military insignia, and also made to part with their ceremonial daggers 'inlaid with gold and silver'. Just in case the humiliated praetorians took it into their heads that they might rush back to the Castra Praetoria and arm themselves, Severus had sent a squad ahead to secure the camp. The praetorians had to disperse into Rome, the mounted troops having also to abandon their horses, though one killed both his horse and then himself in despair at the ignominy.[32]

Only then did Severus enter Rome himself. Rome was filled with troops, just as it had been in 68–9. This agitated the crowd, which had acclaimed him as he arrived. Severus made promises that he did not keep, such as insisting he would not murder senators. Having disposed of the Praetorian Guard in its existing form, Severus obviously had to rebuild it. He appears to have done so with Juvenalis and Macrinus still at the helm as prefects in reward for their loyalty over the transition. Severus' new Praetorian Guard represented the first major change in the institution since its formation under Augustus and amounted to a new creation. Valerius Martinus, a Pannonian, lived only until he was twenty-five but by then he had already served for three years in the X praetorian cohort, following service in the XIII legion Gemina. XIIII Gemina had declared very early on for Severus so Martinus probably benefited from being transferred to the new Guard in 193 or soon afterwards. Lucius Domitius Valerianus from Jerusalem joined the new praetorians soon after 193. He had served originally in the VI legion Ferrata before being transferred to the X praetorian cohort where he stayed until his honourable discharge on 7 January 208. Valerianus cannot have been in the Guard before Severus reformed it in 193, so this means his eighteen years of military service, specified on the altar he dedicated, must have begun in the legions in 190 under Commodus.[33] Therefore it is probable most of his time, between 193 and 208, was in the Guard under Severus. One of the most significant appointments to the Guard at this time was a Thracian soldier of epic height who began his Roman military career in the auxiliary cavalry. In 235 this man would seize power as Maximinus, following the murder of Severus Alexander, the last of the Severan dynasty.[34]

As discussed much earlier in this book, Dio's reference to there being ten thousand men in ten cohorts in AD 5 is sometimes assumed to be a reference really to the organization of the Guard in his own time, the early third century. It is possible that ten praetorian cohorts had been in existence from Flavian times on. It is beyond doubt, however, unusually for this topic, that from Severus onwards, the Praetorian Guard consisted nominally of ten thousand men in ten milliary cohorts as Dio had described. Diplomas of the third century certainly confirm that thereafter there were ten cohorts.[35] A crucial change made by Severus was to abolish the rule that the praetorians were only recruited from Italy, Spain, Macedonia and Noricum. Instead any legionary was eligible for consideration if he had proved himself in war. This had the effect of making appointment to the Guard a realistic aspiration for any legionary. The idea was that by recruiting from experienced legionaries, the Severan praetorian would now have a far better idea of how to behave as a soldier. This was not always the case. By the time Selvinius Justinus died at the age of thirty-two in the early third century, he had already served seventeen years in the VII praetorian cohort.[36] Unfortunately, there was an unintended consequence, or so Dio claimed. Italians who might have found a job with the Guard now found themselves without anywhere to go and resorted to street fighting, hooliganism and generally abusive behaviour as a result. Rome also now found itself home to provincial soldiers whose customs were regarded as lowering the tone. The reports seem likely to be exaggerated. A Guard of around ten thousand men would hardly have absorbed all of Italy's disaffected young men. Nor would ten thousand provincial praetorians have changed the character of Rome, especially as many of the new praetorians clearly spent much of their time on campaign.[37] An interesting peripheral aspect to this story is that the *paenula* cloak, apparently part of the Praetorian Guard's everyday dress, seems to have dropped out of use by the military by this date; it had, perhaps, become discredited by association with the cashiered praetorians.[38]

Severus had more pressing concerns for the immediate future. He had to dispose first of Niger and then turn on Albinus. Niger was defeated at Issus in Cilicia in 194. He fled to Parthia but was caught by Severus' agents and killed. Severus was distracted by various rebellions in the east before he was able in 196 to turn his attention to Clodius Albinus in the west, still nursing ambitions of becoming emperor after Severus even though Severus had withdrawn the title of Caesar from him. The climax came at the Battle of Lugdunum (Lyon) in Gaul in a vast engagement in which the Praetorian Guard played an important part. The figure claimed by Dio for the battle of 150,000 men in each army is simply enormous and equivalent to around thirty legions each, an implausibly vast number. It is better interpreted as the figure for both armies together, but there cannot be any doubt that the engagement was of major significance.[39]

The battle began badly for Severus because Albinus had placed his right wing behind concealed trenches. Albinus ordered the wing to withdraw, luring the Severan forces after them. Severus fell into the trap. His forces raced forwards, with the front lines crashing into the trenches. The rest stopped in their tracks, leading to a retreat with a knock-on effect on the soldiers at the back, some of whom collapsed into a ravine. Meanwhile the Albinians fired missiles and arrows at those still standing. Severus, horrified by the impending catastrophe, ordered his praetorians forward to help. The praetorians came within danger of being wiped out too; when Severus lost his horse it began to look as though the game was up. Severus only won because he personally rallied those close to him, and because cavalry under the command of Julius Laetus, one of the legionary legates from the east who had supported Severus in 193, arrived in time to save the day. Laetus had been watching to see how the battle shifted before showing his hand, deciding that the Severan rally was enough to make him fight for Severus.[40] It is a shame we do not know more about how many praetorians were present, and exactly how they were deployed but, given the claimed numbers involved in the battle, it seems very likely that all, or at least most, of the praetorians were amongst them. If so, the reformed Praetorian Guard must have been very nearly destroyed within a very few years of being organized because it is certain the body count on the battle-field was enormous.

The Battle of Lugdunum marks a point in the history of the Praetorian Guard when it seems to have become normal for all or most of the Guard to be deployed away from Rome as part of the main army. Conversely, it also represented a return to the way praetorians had been deployed during the period 44–31 BC. The only praetorians likely to be left in Rome during a time when the Guard was needed for war were men approaching retirement.[41] The II legion Parthica, formed by Severus, was based at Albanum, just 12 miles (19 km) from Rome from around 197 onwards. The legion would clearly have helped compensate for the absence of the Guard so long as some of the legion was at home.[42] It also bolstered the number of soldiers immediately available to the emperor as a field army, without having to rely entirely on the Guard or troops pulled from frontier garrisons. Alternatively it could fulfil some of the Guard's duties if the emperor took praetorians on campaign with him. A praetorian in Severus' Guard could expect to see a great deal of action. Publius Aelius Maximinus was a soldier in the V praetorian cohort under Severus. On his tombstone he was said to have participated 'in all the campaigns', which suggests that going to war had become routine for praetorians, though it simply could have been a stock, rather than a literal, claim.[43] Since the tombstone was found in Rome, Aelius Maximinus had presumably lived to tell the tale, expiring at some point after his return, though he was only thirty-one years and eight months old when he died.

The soldiers who took part in Severus' wars and who earned the right to transfer to the new Praetorian Guard found that a further Severan change in terms and conditions was an increase in length of service to eighteen years. This could include the time spent as a legionary. Lucius Domitius Valerianus was discharged in 208 after serving eighteen years. He had been recruited into the VI legion Ferrata in around 190 under Commodus, from which he transferred to the X praetorian cohort at an unspecified later date, serving in the century of Flavius Caralitanus. The date of discharge is provided by the reference to the joint consulship of Severus' sons, Caracalla and Geta, which they held that year.[44] The VI legion Ferrata had been based in Syria since at least AD 150 and had formed part of the eastern army supporting Severus, being awarded with the title *Fidelis Constans* ('always faithful') for not siding with Niger. The funerary memorial of another praetorian of this era, Lucius Septimius Valerinus of the VIIII praetorian cohort and formerly of the I legion Adiutrix, shows him bareheaded in the traditional praetorian tunic with sword at his side and holding a spear (Plate 26).[45]

The Praetorian Guard as an institution survived to fight another day for Severus. It remained an important symbol of imperial power and Rome's military strength. A praetorian standard was featured on the so-called Arch of the Moneylenders, dedicated in Rome in 204 (Plates 24 and 25). With Albinus destroyed and his supporters executed, Severus returned to Rome before turning his attention to Parthia in 198. A cash handout to the Roman people was accompanied by a large payment to 'the soldiers', as well as a pay rise and other privileges, such as being able to cohabit with wives. These must have included praetorians, but quite to what extent is unknown as the reference is to the army in general. Herodian was acutely critical of how the new arrangements could undermine military discipline.[46]

Parthia took advantage of the Roman civil wars of 193–7 and invaded Mesopotamia. By 199 Severus was crossing Mesopotamia to fight back but an assault on Hatra went badly, leaving him with numerous casualties and a lot of siege equipment destroyed. This provoked Julius Crispus, a praetorian tribune, to quote from Virgil's *Aeneid*, where Aeneas bemoans the fact that so many lives were being lost just because his enemy Turnus wanted to secure the hand of Lavinia. The meaning was obvious: Severus was sending numerous Roman soldiers to their deaths for a futile cause. Another praetorian reported Crispus' comment and was rewarded by Severus with Crispus' job. Severus also killed Julius Laetus, whose success in the field here, as in Gaul at Lugdunum, was beginning to make him the focus of the soldiers' loyalty.[47]

It is not known whether Laetus really did have ideas above his station but one of the praetorian prefects, Caius Fulvius Plautianus, a fellow Libyan of Severus, very definitely did. In or around 200, while Severus was in Egypt, Plautianus killed his co-prefect Quintus Aemilius Saturninus. He next removed privileges from the tribunes in case any of them imagined they were likely to be promoted. The implication from Dio's account is that both were with Severus in Egypt, or at least in the region. Plautianus' ambition was to make himself sole permanent prefect; it appears that Severus was complicit in Plautianus' designs and facilitated his prefect's advance. Dio accused Plautianus of engaging in a campaign of grand larceny and plundering. By far the most eccentric allegation was that Plautianus had castrated a hundred Roman citizens of 'noble' (senatorial) birth so that his daughter Plautilla could be waited on by eunuchs. Plautianus was honoured with innumerable statues, and was the subject of oaths both by soldiers (praetorians?) and senators. Plautianus steadily moved upwards, being appointed a consul, and in 200 having Plautilla selected for marriage to Severus' eldest son, Caracalla.[48] The nuptials did not take place until late 202 or 203, which coincided with the tenth anniversary of Severus becoming emperor, even though it had taken five years to annihilate his rivals. Plautianus handed over as Plautilla's dowry a huge sum of money, said by Dio to be fifty times the appropriate sum even for a woman of royal status. Plautianus bankrolled animal fights at games to celebrate Severus' decennalia (tenth anniversary), while the Guards themselves received from the emperor ten gold coins each, equivalent to 1,000 sestertii, the same amount awarded in Augustus' will almost two centuries earlier.[49]

The description of Plautianus' behaviour has echoes of both Sejanus and Tigellinus. It is difficult to believe that this was not deliberate on Dio's part, for example, the depiction of Plautianus gorging himself at a banquet and engaging in promiscuous sexual activity.[50] Eventually, Plautianus went too far, even by the standards of the day. The account of the fall of Plautianus is confused and difficult to follow but, essentially, what seems to have happened is that his ambitions had earned him the hatred of both of Severus' sons, Caracalla and Geta. Caracalla disliked his wife Plautilla, and this fuelled his determination to get rid of Plautianus. In Herodian's version, Caracalla's loathing for Plautilla led Plautianus to fear for his own life and to sidestep the threat by trying to seize power for himself. In 205 Caracalla used his tutor Euodus to talk a praetorian centurion called Saturninus and two other centurions into claiming that they were three of ten centurions ordered by Plautianus to kill Severus and Caracalla.[51] Herodian's version has Saturninus as a praetorian tribune who was completely loyal to Plautianus; Plautianus in this account offered Saturninus the praetorian prefecture if he killed Severus and Caracalla. Saturninus persuaded Plautianus to put all this down in writing. Saturninus headed off to the palace but realized there was no chance of murdering Severus and Caracalla, and decided to tell Severus about Plautianus' scheming.

Severus initially disbelieved Saturninus. Deciding that Caracalla was really the culprit, Severus tackled his son. Eventually, Saturninus concluded that the only way to prove his innocence was to send a message to Plautianus that the deed was done to trick him into coming to the palace. Plautianus fell for the ruse and turned up, only to be confronted by Severus and Caracalla. Plautianus tried to talk his way out and nearly succeeded, but when it emerged that he was wearing a breastplate under his ordinary clothes it became obvious that Saturninus had been telling the truth. The ancestor festival being held that day made it completely implausible that Plautianus would have needed to go around wearing a breastplate unless he was up to no good. Caracalla pointed this out, and ordered Saturninus and others to kill the prefect.[52] Plautianus' body was thrown out into the street. There is some debate about how much of either version is believable. The details do not matter as much here as the fact that it appears, once more, that a praetorian prefect had been given the opportunity to take advantage of his position and had succeeded in doing so. The parallels with Sejanus are obvious, including this time the more successful manipulation of an imperial marriage, the excessive trust, the greed, the duplicity and the tricking of the guilty prefect.

In the aftermath, Severus, who had learned a valuable lesson, returned to the traditional two-prefect system. The new men were carefully chosen. Quintus Marcius Laetus came up the traditional route from the prefecture of Egypt. Aemilius Papinianus was a brilliant and famous jurist.[53] They were to remain in post throughout the rest of Severus' reign. During their time Severus embarked on his war of conquest in Britain, which was designed to give Caracalla and Geta a chance to prove themselves. Dio's account of the period also includes a reference to the policing duties to which the praetorians were liable to be allocated. Bulla was an Italian bandit leader who ranged over Italy with impunity for two years. Despite being pursued by soldiers, Bulla led a marauding gang that even included disaffected imperial freedmen. Severus, by then on campaign in Britain, was irritated to hear that while he was fighting a war his forces in Italy were incapable of stopping a robber. Severus ordered that a praetorian tribune at the head of a cavalry force be sent, under threat of severe punishment if he failed, to capture Bulla. Instead of using brute force, the tribune persuaded Bulla's mistress to give him up on a promise of immunity. He was taken to Papinianus, who must therefore have still been in Italy. Papinianus asked Bulla why he was a robber. Bulla tartly responded, 'Why are you a prefect?' However gratifying Bulla must have felt his witty riposte to be, the answer turned out to be that as praetorian prefect Papinianus had a good deal more power than Bulla. The robber chief was promptly killed by being thrown to wild beasts.[54]

By 210 Papinianus was in Britain with Severus. Some of the Guard was on campaign with Severus. Gaius Cesennius Senecio was a centurion of the II praetorian cohort, which held the Severan Pia Vindex ('faithful avenger') decoration. He was killed, or died, in Britain and his remains returned to Rome for burial, where his tombstone survives.[55] It is not known whether he was actually involved in fighting or was merely serving as part of an escort, but he had reached the heights of being an *exercitator* 'of praetorian cavalry'. Caracalla, desperate for sole power (he had been made joint emperor in 198, and since 209 with Geta as well), seems to have spontaneously toyed with the idea of killing his father, raising his sword as they rode out to fight the Caledonians of northern Britain. Caracalla hesitated (he was in plain sight) and gave up. Severus taunted Caracalla, telling him he should go ahead with the attack, and even made a sword available. Papinianus was present as one of the witnesses. Severus egged on Caracalla and told his son that he could order Papinianus to kill him.[56] In the meantime Laetus must have remained in charge of the praetorians left in Rome. Caracalla resisted the opportunity to kill his father. Severus died soon afterwards in York on 4 February 211 but not before he had advised his sons to work together, make the soldiers rich, and treat everyone else with scorn. Caracalla ignored the advice to live in harmony with Geta but followed the rest.[57] He moved quickly. According to Dio he immediately removed Papinianus from his post and killed a number of others, including his tutor Euodus and his wife Plautilla, though it is possible that Papinianus remained in post until he was murdered in 212 after Geta was killed.[58]

After abandoning Severus' campaign in Britain by negotiating peace, Caracalla and Geta returned to Rome in May 211. The two brothers' mutual loathing was exhibited by continual plots against each other and the way they surrounded themselves with armed guards. They even went to the extent of dividing up the palace into separate fortified establishments, an arrangement that would be comic had the consequences not been so drastic. They even concocted a plan to divide the Empire between them. Only when their mother, Julia Domna, pointed out that they could not divide her between them was the plan abandoned.[59] This solved nothing. Since Geta had an armed escort of soldiers, Caracalla resorted to asking Julia to summon the pair of them early in 212. In Dio's version Caracalla had centurions on hand who had been briefed to murder Geta, which they did while Geta clung to his mother. This was followed by the murder of all those who had attended Geta, including soldiers, amounting to 'twenty thousand'. In Herodian's account Caracalla was blamed for the killing.[60] The likelihood is that praetorian centurions were responsible, but only because they had been bribed by Caracalla.

According to Herodian, Caracalla fled from the palace to the Castra Praetoria, claiming he had only just escaped an attempt on his own life, and made his way to seek sanctuary in the *sacellum*. Here Caracalla told his story in which Geta had supposedly been plotting to murder him, but that he, Caracalla, had managed to kill his enemy and escape. The praetorians were encouraged to believe Caracalla with an instant payout of 2,500 denarii and a 50 per cent pay rise, the latter being extended to the whole army at a cost of 280 million sestertii in total (70 million denarii). To provide the instant payout the praetorians were told to collect the cash from temples and treasuries in Rome. By this time the truth had reached the praetorians, but since they had already been bought they acceded to Caracalla's sole rule.[61] The *Historia Augusta*'s version is slightly different: when the news reached the Castra Praetoria it was a shock to praetorians who had not been bribed or been in on the plot, and who also believed they had sworn allegiance to both brothers. The praetorians therefore locked the Castra Praetoria and refused to see Caracalla. Any sense that this outrage was founded on solid moral rectitude was soon exposed as humbug when Caracalla paid out the money to purchase the Guard's support.[62] The versions are not necessarily contradictory. It is plausible that some of the praetorians were disturbed by the news, but it was also historically clear that the praetorians, like other soldiers, had their price and if it had been paid then there was nothing more to be said (at least for the moment).

The substantial pay rise offered by Caracalla inevitably incurred a significant charge on the state, which added to the problems experienced by Severus when he found the imperial treasuries drained in 193. Severus had resorted to debasing the denarius, reducing its silver content to 50 per cent.[63] The solution, introduced in 215, was even more cynical. The denarius was joined by a new coin, known today as the *antoninianus* after Caracalla's official name of Marcus Aurelius Antoninus. Apparently tariffed as a double-denarius, the new coin in fact only contained half as much silver again as one denarius. Therefore, the melting of three denarii provided enough silver to be alloyed with copper to produce two new antoninianii, apparently tariffed as the equivalent of four denarii. Clearly designed to make state expenses easier to pay, such as the praetorians' pay rise, inflationary consequences were inevitable but these took generations to impact on the economy. The new coin was issued until around 222, after which it was discontinued until 238 when it started to replace the denarius permanently.[64]

The killing of Geta was the manifestation of a new and vicious era. Marcus Aurelius and Lucius Verus had been joint emperors but Verus' death in 169 was not suspicious and nor had the two been rivals. Therefore the question of divided loyalties had not arisen with the Praetorian Guard. The Severan family presented a completely new problem. It seems not to have been in doubt to anyone at the time that Caracalla was responsible, and that he had arranged for the murder, apparently with sidekicks chosen from the Guard's centurionate. In the aftermath of Geta's death, the praetorian prefect Maecius Laetus was forced to commit suicide, even though it appears he might have helped Caracalla plan the murder. Other killings followed, including the former praetorian prefect Papinianus who was murdered with an axe after the praetorians made allegations about him. Worse, Caracalla even told the praetorians that since he ruled for them and not for himself, they could be both accusers and judges.[65] He confined himself to being annoyed that Papinianus was executed with an axe instead of a sword.

To compound the increasing tension, a mutiny broke out amongst the urban cohorts. The murder of Papinianus seems to have been ordered simply because he had backed Geta. As Papinianus was dragged off to be killed, he commented that whoever took his place would be a fool if he did not avenge this attack on the office of the praetorian prefecture. This may well be a literary device, since the observation turned out to be exactly what happened. Another praetorian prefect, the little-known Valerius Patruinus, was killed too.[66] There is a tenuous possibility that some of the praetorians were now based in premises on imperial property on the Pincian Hill in Rome, if they had not been previously. An inscription from here names Julia Domna as 'mother of Augustus [Caracalla] and of the camps'.[67]

Caracalla's reign degenerated even further into a series of increasingly arbitrary killings. In 213 he set out on a tour of the provinces, ordering executions as he went, including that of the proconsul of Gallia Narbonensis. By the time he reached Thrace, he was accompanied by an unnamed praetorian prefect. One possibility is that the post was already held by Macrinus, known to have been in post when he murdered Caracalla in 217. Alternatively, Gnaeus Marcius Rustius Rufinus is a possibility.[68] Marcus Opellius Macrinus was prefect by the end of the reign, apparently alongside

Marcus Oclatinius Adventus, a man whose remarkable career had seen him move up from being a *speculator*, serving in a variety of jobs including *frumentarius* (imperial spy), and procurator of Britain under Severus between c. 205 and 208, eventually rising to city prefect under Macrinus as emperor.[69]

In 216 Caracalla started a war against the Parthians, then ruled by Artabanus V.[70] By 217 the campaign had gone from indifferently to worse, but a most peculiar incident was to lead to Caracalla's demise. An African prophet had put it about that the praetorian prefect Macrinus, who had already reached the heights of consular status, was destined to become emperor along with his son Diadumenian. The news reached the prefect of Rome, Flavius Maternianus, who promptly alerted Caracalla. This was not a trivial incident. At the time such prophecies, along with signs and portents, could carry enormous currency, especially with the notoriously superstitious members of the Severan dynasty. The letter was delayed en route to Caracalla because it was sent first to Julia Domna in Antioch in Syria, where she was administering his affairs. Meanwhile, Macrinus (who was with Caracalla) was alerted by the censor in Rome, Ulpius Julianus, and realized that if he did not act then it was inevitable that Caracalla would try to have him killed.[71] Macrinus organized three co-conspirators. Two of them, Aurelianus Nemesianus and Aurelianus Apollinaris, were brothers and praetorian tribunes. The third was a disaffected *evocatus* called Julius Martialis who was nursing a grudge against Caracalla for not promoting him to the praetorian centurionate. Clearly then, the conspiracy was largely a praetorian one, though others were involved such as Aelius Triccianus, prefect of the II legion Parthica and Marcius Agrippa, commander of the fleet.[72]

On 8 April 217, Caracalla dismounted from his horse, momentarily dropping his guard while he relieved himself. It was not the sort of lapse of concentration a despot like him could afford. Spotting his chance, Martialis began the attack but was killed by one of Caracalla's Scythian personal bodyguards. At that moment Nemesianus and Apollinaris pretended to come forward to help the emperor but seized the opportunity to kill him.[73] The Scythians formed part of an eclectic band of freedmen and enslaved bodyguards whom Caracalla had employed in preference to the praetorians, something that had no doubt caused further grievance; though, as it had turned out, Caracalla's suspicions were well founded. Two days of chaos followed as the disorientated soldiers fumbled about wondering what to do. They were agitated at the prospect of Artabanus, who was approaching with a large force in an attempt to take advantage of a peace treaty. The soldiers decided to ask Oclatinius Adventus if he would be emperor. He declined on the grounds that he was too old, though it must also have been apparent that his origins were humbler even than those of Macrinus. The soldiers turned to Macrinus and offered him the position of emperor, largely because there was no one else suitable to hand and time was running out. Macrinus accepted and rallied the troops to face Artabanus, who still believed he was fighting Caracalla against whom he wanted revenge for the war.[74] As a result the fighting went on relentlessly for two days until Macrinus realized that Artabanus was fighting under a misapprehension and sent him a letter, offering a negotiated peace. Artabanus accepted and the war ended.

Meanwhile, the news of Caracalla's death reached Julia Domna in Antioch, who was mostly annoyed that his demise would mean a return to private life for her. Macrinus, however, allowed her to continue to enjoy the protection of a detachment of praetorians, the privilege that Nero had withdrawn from Agrippina over 150 years previously. For a while, some of the praetorians considered mutinying and supporting her bid to become sole ruler in her own right, which would have made her the first autonomous empress in Roman history. The scheme came to nothing because Macrinus forced her to leave Antioch. She died not long afterwards, either from suicide or breast cancer. The fate of her praetorian detachment is not known. Julia Domna left a grieving sister, Julia Maesa. Maesa had so enjoyed life at the imperial court during Julia Domna's reign that she was determined not to let an upstart praetorian prefect bring about the end of the Severan dynasty.[75]

The new emperor Macrinus was from Caesarea (Cherchell) in Mauretania Caesariensis (Algeria). The senate welcomed him on the basis that anyone was better than Caracalla.[76] He was an enthusiastic, if not always well-informed, supporter of the law, serving as Plautianus' assistant as a result but escaping execution by association. From that position he acted as *curator* of the Via Flaminia under Severus, then as a procurator under Caracalla, before finally being made praetorian prefect.[77] His ascent was a product of a curiously egalitarian aspect of the Roman world. It really was possible to rise from total obscurity to the most important posts in the Empire out of a combination of luck and ability, though this did not necessarily lead to acceptance, as Macrinus was to discover. He is the first of the praetorian prefects whose appearance is well and reliably known to us thanks to his coinage struck at Rome and mints across the Eastern Empire. Despite the brevity of the reign, his coins are still relatively common. They depict a mature and hardened man with a full beard, but without any of the studied brutality so characteristic of Caracalla's late coin portraiture. This is in spite of the *Historia Augusta*'s judgement of Macrinus as 'arrogant and bloodthirsty', and description of a litany of the vicious punishments he meted out such as burning adulterers alive. Herodian's description of life in Rome under Macrinus as a time of security and freedom, despite Macrinus' other shortcomings, is a considerable contrast and more balanced.[78]

Macrinus had achieved something that no other praetorian prefect, or indeed equestrian, had ever achieved. He declared himself emperor and took the name Marcus Opellius Severus Macrinus Augustus without waiting for the senate to vote him any titles. This was a crucial breach of protocol. His son, Diadumenian, was declared Caesar and thus his successor. Macrinus, who decided to continue with the Parthian war, was initially welcomed by the army. He fixed praetorian pay at a rate set by Severus. Nevertheless, Macrinus had problems from the outset and they were linked to his rank. His elevation of Oclatinius Adventus to the position of senator, consul and prefect of the city, incurred particular censure; it looked as if Macrinus was attempting to divert attention from his own lowly origins while promoting someone even less suitable to the status of senator. Macrinus' judgement was also called into question with his appointment of Ulpius Julianus and Julianus Nestor to the praetorian prefecture. Neither of these two had the right military or administrative skills. Their main credentials were principally their assistance of Caracalla in his decadent pursuits.[79]

In spite of Caracalla's expenditure on the war, no one in Rome immediately dared declare him to have been a public enemy out of fear of how
the praetorians might react. This did not stop other denunciations of his
deeds, destruction of his statues or punishment of his associates. Macrinus
benefited because most people were consequently prepared to overlook his
modest origins, at least for the moment. This did not last: before the year
was out Macrinus and Diadumenian were regarded as no longer having
any meaningful existence. After settling the Parthian war, Macrinus found
he had made an enemy of the army. They were resentful at having had to
go to war, at a pay cut and withdrawal of exemption from duties. Macrinus
also ordered that while existing soldiers would continue to enjoy privileges
granted by Caracalla, new recruits would serve on terms established by
Severus. Naturally enough, that simply alienated any new recruits. The
peace negotiated with Artabanus V had included handing back property
and paying 200 million sestertii as an indemnity.[80] This hardly constituted
a glorious triumph over Rome's enemies.

Julia Maesa could see that the window of opportunity had opened,
and she passed immediately through it. When Julia Domna died she had
been ordered by Macrinus to return home (the women came from Syria).
Maesa had two daughters, Julia Soaemias and Julia Mamaea, by a former
consul, Julius Avitus. These younger women each had a son, Varius
Avitus Bassianus (Elagabalus) and Gessius Bassianus Alexianus (Severus
Alexander) respectively.[81] Both boys were brought up in the worship of the
sun god, Heliogabalus, the central cult object of which was a huge conical
black stone.[82] The elder boy acted as a priest, being known by the derived
name of Elagabalus as a result. He was extremely popular with the military
garrison at nearby Emesa, and a rumour had started to circulate amongst
the troops that he was really the son of Caracalla. This was compounded
by the belief that Maesa was extremely wealthy (which she was) and that if
the soldiers made Elagabalus emperor then they would benefit from handouts. Maesa was delighted at the prospect of being able to return to court
life and agreed, though she seems to have either been assisted or led by
someone called Publius Valerius Comazon (also known as Eutychianus),
said to have been a dancer who had performed in Rome. The women and

their sons were taken to Raphaneae in Phoenicia where Elagabalus was declared emperor on 16 May 218. Macrinus' praetorian prefect Ulpius Julianus was nearby and, despite his shortcomings, rallied to the moment, initially killing a daughter of Mamaea and the daughter's husband before organizing a scratch force, presumably of praetorians, and attacking the fortress at Raphaneae.[83]

Unfortunately, Julianus' scratch squad was inconveniently beguiled into transferring their support to Elagabalus, whom the soldiers were displaying on the fortress walls. Julianus was either killed at the scene or made his escape and was killed later. When the news reached Macrinus he removed his court to Apamea, tried to appoint his ten-year-old son Diadumenian emperor and offer 20,000 sestertii (5,000 denarii) to every soldier, as well as reversing all the previous pay and ration cuts he had imposed on them. The cash offer was the same as the discharge grant for praetorians set originally by Augustus. Macrinus laid on an extravagant dinner to show that he was celebrating his son's elevation, only for one of the rebel soldiers to turn up with the wrapped-up decapitated head of Julianus disguised as the head of Elagabalus. The head was unwrapped, revealing the horrible truth, and Macrinus realized he would have to flee. As events spiralled out of control for Macrinus he promoted Julius Basilianus, prefect of Egypt, to the praetorian prefecture in place of the unfortunate Julianus.[84] Macrinus was defeated on 8 June 218 by a force under Gannys, the eunuch of Maesa's other grandson, Varius Avitus, and Comazon. Macrinus had his praetorians with him, whom he had ordered to abandon their scale armour and grooved shields so that they would be more lightly equipped and could move faster in battle. This single reference is one of the few detailed clues that exist about praetorian equipment. According to Herodian, the praetorians, notable for their height and for being hand picked, fought exceptionally well, even though Macrinus had already fled the scene.[85]

Macrinus tried to make his escape by heading north, but was caught and killed by a centurion called Marcianus Taurus at Calchedon in Bithynia. Diadumenian, who had been sent by his father to Artabanus V, was also caught and killed en route.[86] Macrinus, sometime prefect of the Praetorian Guard, had reigned as an emperor of Rome for three days shy of fourteen months. Dio's acerbic conclusion was that if Macrinus had been content with his station and supported the elevation of a senator (Dio's bias is obvious here) then Macrinus might have enjoyed considerable esteem; however, there must be some truth in the idea that in the context of the era a man such as Macrinus simply lacked the status necessary to advance beyond the prefecture and expect to survive.[87]

Elagabalus paid out 2,000 sestertii (500 denarii) each to the soldiers in Antioch and prepared for the journey to Rome. He styled himself Marcus Aurelius Antoninus in a further manifestation of the Severan policy of fabricating dynastic continuity from the Antonines, though he is invariably known to history as Elagabalus. He and his court began their slow progress to Rome, wintering between 218 and 219 at Nicomedia. Elagabalus, still only fourteen or fifteen, was already a fanatical follower of his cult, dressing in extravagant costumes and going about accompanied by flute and drums. Maesa was alarmed by this, comprehending immediately how it would alienate the Roman people. Elagabalus refused to tone himself down and resorted to the bizarre solution of sending ahead to Rome a huge painting of himself 'in action' as a priest. When he arrived he demanded that his god take precedence over all others, and forced the entire senatorial and equestrian orders to participate in his ceremonies, with military prefects amongst those obliged to carry the entrails of sacrificial victims.[88]

Comazon had now been appointed praetorian prefect, a promotion that turned out to be one in a series of unprecedented stages in his meteoric rise, much to Dio's disgust. Comazon, who had no professional experience and was considered something of a clown, as well as having been a stage dancer, went on to be consul three times, and then prefect of Rome. Comazon exploited his influence to pursue personal feuds. He had been punished by Claudius Attalus, governor of Thrace, for some earlier misdemeanour committed while he was serving there. Comazon, now in his exalted position, secured the execution of Attalus, though this was only one of a number of killings ordered by Elagabalus.[89]

In or around 219 Elagabalus married Cornelia Paula. He celebrated the occasion with a payout to the senate and the equestrians, a dinner costing

600 sestertii per head for the people, and a gift of 400 sestertii to the soldiers, presumably his praetorians. It was clearly an attempt to present Elagabalus as normal and counteract the mounting scurrilous stories about the emperor's promiscuous homosexuality, conducted in the passive role. Elagabalus divorced the unfortunate Cornelia Paula soon afterwards and moved on to Aquilia Severa, one of the Vestal Virgins, which caused even more offence than his previous activities. Elagabalus' behaviour unsettled the praetorians, something that the peculiar young emperor was himself well aware of. Under pressure from his grandmother and mother to placate them, he adopted his cousin, Bassianus Alexianus, who was renamed Severus Alexander, as his heir. Elagabalus was praised by the senate but observed that although the senate, the people and the legions loved him, the Praetorian Guard did not, regardless of how much he gave them. It seems that even the praetorians had their limits.[90]

Severus Alexander, who appears to have been a far gentler and more conventional boy, enjoyed the protection of his mother and grandmother, as well as that of the praetorians. Elagabalus bitterly resented the fact that Alexander's mother was clearly preparing him for succession as an educated and more appropriate emperor. It was also obvious that the praetorians preferred Alexander and, given that their prefect was allegedly a dancer, this is hardly surprising. Elagabalus turned against his cousin and tried to have him killed. Mamaea took the precaution of paying a secret donative to the praetorians to smooth her son's path to power; it was an astute investment. Elagabalus pulled his cousin out of public appearances and put it about that Alexander was dying in order to test the water. He also appears to have ordered the praetorians to deny Alexander the title 'Caesar', which denoted his status as heir, and to plaster mud over any inscriptions naming Alexander that were displayed in the Castra Praetoria.[91] The mud smearing was done but the praetorians were furious and upset.

The angry praetorians then set out to find Alexander, Mamaea and Maesa, and took them back to the camp for their own protection. Next, a band of praetorians went off looking for the emperor in the Gardens of Spes Vetus, where he was getting ready for a chariot race. Elagabalus heard them coming and sent one of his praetorian prefects (whose name is not known) to calm down the Castra Praetoria where most of the Guard still was under the command of a tribune called Aristomachus. The other, an otherwise unknown individual called Antiochianus, was told to calm down the praetorians in the Gardens. The praetorians in the camp told the anonymous prefect that their price for backing down was Elagabalus handing over his hangers-on and starting to live in a suitable manner for an emperor. They also demanded that the prefects guard Alexander. This must be the occasion to which Herodian was referring when he described how the praetorians refused to turn up to guard the emperor, locking themselves into the Castra Praetoria. Elagabalus had to go to the Castra Praetoria with Alexander to prove that all was well, suffering the soldiers' far more preferential greeting of Alexander, and also hand over some of his more nefarious associates.[92]

Elagabalus ignored the danger he was in. He demanded back his lover, the former Carian slave and charioteer Hierocles, to whom he regarded himself married, and refused to appear in public with Alexander. Maesa and Soaemias told him that his life was in danger from the praetorians but he ordered the senate to leave the city. In Dio's account this was followed by an irate Elagabalus haranguing the praetorians in the camp *sacellum*, followed by a second visit to the camp to reassure the praetorians all was well. This episode was accompanied by the unseemly sight of his mother Julia Soaemias and her sister Julia Mamaea competing to win over the praetorians to their respective sons. Soaemias lost. According to the *Historia Augusta*, the praetorians had had enough after Elagabalus told the senate to leave. They killed Elagabalus' associates, then found the emperor in a latrine where they murdered him before throwing his body in the river. In Dio's version, on 11 March 222 Soaemias and Elagabalus were murdered by praetorians in the Castra Praetoria, along with all their attendants. Their decapitated and stripped bodies were dragged around Rome. The victims also involved members of the court, including the praetorian prefects Comazon and Antiochianus.[93]

The transfer of power was immediate. Severus Alexander was acclaimed emperor there and then by the praetorians. Alexander also appointed two praetorian prefects, Flavianus and Geminius Chrestus, explicitly because they were soldiers who had experience in both military affairs and civilian administration. But, apparently at the behest of his mother Mamaea he also appointed Gnaeus Domitius Annius Ulpianus, a celebrated jurist (now usually known as Ulpian), to be a praetorian prefect and to oversee them, which infuriated Flavianus and Chrestus. Ulpian's legal knowledge and other skills made him ideal to take care of everyday government and also plan for the future. Ulpian had previously been exiled by Elagabalus.[94] He did not last long this time round. In 223 or 224 a dispute broke out between the Praetorian Guard and the people of Rome. It led to a three-day running street battle in the city. The Guard was outnumbered and resorted to setting fire to buildings to force the people to back down and agree to peace. Somewhere along the line Ulpian or Mamaea had Flavianus and Chrestus killed, apparently either because they were conspiring against him or simply to remove them. The whole story is confused and difficult to unravel but it is clear there was enormous tension between Ulpian and the praetorians. It is apparent that Ulpian had been made prefect as soon as Alexander became emperor and was also held in enormous trust, being the only person permitted to see Alexander on his own.[95] Ulpian was later killed by some of the Guard, who had been put up to the job by a freedman of Caracalla called Epagathus. They had already complained to Ulpian because they had heard that Cassius Dio (the historian), governor of Pannonia, had imposed a strict regime on the garrison there and were worried that something similar might happen to them. However, it must also be the case that Ulpian had no relevant experience of commanding troops. His death may have occurred as soon as 223, not 228 when his replacement is known to have been installed.[96] By 229 Dio, who was consul that year, was under threat from the praetorians and he moved on health grounds to his home in Bithynia for his own safety. With Dio's death at some point during the reign of Severus Alexander, the principal source for the period is lost. Alexander subsequently appointed another jurist, Julius Paulus, to the praetorian prefecture in 228.[97] During this time some praetorians decided to make a dedication to Asclepius in his conflated form with a local Thracian god called Sindrinus (or Zimidrenus). They all came from Philoppolis in Thrace and proclaimed this fact at the beginning of the dedication, which named each man, his cohort and rank.[98] The text invokes an image of a Guard made up of various subgroups of soldiers who clearly maintained their provincial ethnic identities and affiliations. It was a far cry from the early days of the Guard and its largely Italian nature.

Severus Alexander was the last of the Severan dynasty. He had become emperor at around the age of fourteen but it was inevitably the case that he would seek to become more independent, especially once his grandmother died around 224. Alexander is depicted by Herodian as a benign and merciful ruler, but one who grew increasingly frustrated by his mother's behaviour. She took opportunities to confiscate other people's property, ostensibly so that she could bankroll a payout to the army on her son's behalf, but in reality so that she could add to her private fortune.[99] Given the instability of the previous eleven years, it was remarkable that Alexander survived until 235. From the outset, much of the real power was in the hands of his mother Mamaea and his grandmother Maesa.

Mamaea and Maesa organized the creation of a council of sixteen senior senators to guide Alexander. It was an initiative that anticipated arrangements adopted for medieval monarchs who acceded while still minors. Herodian even observed that the new structure represented a significant change in the form of the principate.[100] This meant that senior appointments, such as the prefects of the Guard, were made only with senatorial approval, even though Alexander made the initial choice. This on one occasion included a candidate who had declined, Alexander arguing that it was better to give the job to a man who was not interested in office for its own sake.[101] Holding the prefecture under Alexander became an automatic qualification for senatorial status, unless the incumbent was already a senator (the prefecture had been opened up to senators as well by now), but Alexander had a serious purpose in mind. He objected to the way in which promotion had become merely the established method of removing a praetorian prefect from his post; he wanted his praetorian prefects to be senators so that they held an appropriate rank for passing a judgement on a senator.[102]

Alexander was married to a woman called Sallustia Barbia Orbiana but Mamaea, unwilling to share the position of empress, had her daughter-in-law removed from the palace. This so disgusted the girl's father that he took her to the Castra Praetoria for protection and accused Mamaea of insulting his daughter. This was a miscalculation. Mamaea, disregarding her son's feelings and exhibiting all the ruthlessness for which the Severan women were celebrated, had the father executed and Orbiana exiled to Libya.[103]

The latter part of Alexander's reign was overtaken by the return of the Persian threat, this time under Artaxerxes, who had killed Artabanus and taken Parthia. Attempts to negotiate a peace came to nothing, leaving Alexander with no choice by 230 but to introduce a form of conscription so that an army of sufficient size with legions at full strength could be sent against Artaxerxes. By 231 Alexander had left for Antioch where the necessary training could be organized. It must be assumed that he had taken at least a large part of the Guard with him. His first campaign involved dividing his forces into three separate armies, each of which would approach the Persians by a different route. The northerly army made its way through Armenia to attack the Persians, the central army under Alexander's personal command simply never invaded (a fact blamed by Herodian on Mamaea's reluctance to allow her son to go into danger), and the southerly third force was practically wiped out when Artaxerxes threw his whole army at it on the Euphrates.[104]

Nonetheless, Mesopotamia was recovered. Alexander was able to return to Rome and celebrate a triumph in 233, only to face instability on the Rhine and Danube frontiers, in particular in the form of a threat from the German Alamanni. This led to a serious split in the army. Units transferred from Illyricum to the Persian War had suffered serious losses and now believed their absence from the Danube and Rhine had contributed to the problems there. The German tribes presented a far greater threat to Italy than the Persians, so Alexander led an army north from Italy. Rather than throw himself into fighting, he opted to offer to negotiate a peace with the Germans, adding for good measure that he had enough money to provide a payment.[105] Alexander had placed his army's training under the management of a giant Thracian soldier called Maximinus, who proved extremely popular with the army and provided a considerable contrast to an emperor who was generally depicted as a mother's boy and lacking in any military guile, panache, skill or motivation. Maximinus had earned an early reputation for his physical strength and astonishing height, coming to Septimius Severus' attention as a wrestler. So impressed was Septimius Severus that Maximinus had been automatically offered a position in the Praetorian Guard.[106] He had subsequently retired under Macrinus, only returning to military service as an *evocatus* under Alexander.

Herodian added the observation that the soldiers had now experienced a relatively (by the standards of the time) long reign, meaning that it had been a considerable while since the last major donative. This made the prospect of promoting Maximinus attractive. Conversely, the *Historia Augusta* states that during Alexander's reign at least three cash gifts were made to the soldiers. Moreover, the same source says that Alexander always personally heard complaints made by soldiers against their tribunes and would punish the tribune appropriately if he were found guilty.[107] Under Alexander, the antoninianus, the new debased double-denarius introduced by Caracalla, was temporarily discontinued. Alexander produced only the traditional silver denarius, perhaps as part of his policy of restoring the coinage.[108] Since the troops would have been the first to notice that the antoninianus contained less silver than two denarii, this return to the old denomination ought to have helped restore their confidence. If so, the gesture failed.

The soldiers proclaimed Maximinus emperor, forcing him to accept.[109] Having acquiesced to their wishes, Maximinus told them they would have to take Alexander's bodyguard by surprise. To help them steel their nerves, he offered doubled pay, a donative and cancellation of punishments. Alexander got wind of what had happened, panicked and floundered around, begging his troops to stand with him. They abandoned him, one by one, demanding the execution of the praetorian(?) prefect and Alexander's household. When Maximinus arrived he sent a tribune and centurions into Alexander's tent where they killed the sometime favourite of the praetorians, his mother Mamaea and many of their associates.[110]

CHAPTER 10

DECLINE AND DISSOLUTION
(235–312)

By the fourth decade of the third century the Roman Empire was beset by endless threats to its frontiers. The emperor was increasingly forced to become a field commander, coordinating one defensive campaign after another. The problems were grossly exacerbated by what started to become an almost routine process whereby the praetorian prefect either led or formed part of a conspiracy to topple the emperor and seize power for himself. This reflected a world in which the Praetorian Guard was clearly either all, or mostly, in the field with the prefect(s) and the emperor. Diocletian's efforts in the 280s to stabilize the Empire and arrest the process of decline were only partly successful. By the early fourth century a new era of civil war had been initiated. In the middle of the conflict the Praetorian Guard backed the wrong side and was permanently disbanded, ending more than three centuries of existence.

FROM THE DEATH OF Severus Alexander in 235 the history of the Roman Empire, and more specifically that of the Praetorian Guard, enters the realm of unprecedented obscurity in Roman imperial history. For three more years we have the last part of Herodian and then there is nothing more than the increasingly bizarre, fabricated and fanciful biographies of the rest of the *Historia Augusta*, and other scattered references. In this context it is hardly surprising that the Praetorian Guard, already little better than an intermittent feature of the sources, disappears almost from sight. Instead, the praetorian prefects dominate the story, such as it is.

The accession of Maximinus in 235 marked a new phase in the deterioration of the principate. For more than half a century a succession of soldier emperors, usurpers and rebels tore the Empire apart. Maximinus' successful pursuit of the German war left his bravery beyond doubt. He had far less, if any, interest in civilian administration. He was accused by Herodian of being simply greedy for money, raising it from any possible source on the pretext that he needed it to pay the army. In reality, Maximinus must have been acutely aware that paying the army had become ever more vital if he was to retain his position, though all his rapacity achieved was to turn the general public more widely against the army. It appears that at least some of the Praetorian Guard was with Maximinus, because praetorians participated in desecrating his portraits in his tent when he fell. Others were certainly left in Rome because they were on hand during the short reign of Balbinus and Pupienus in 238.[1]

The first place to rebel against Maximinus was Libya, where the procurator had been particularly efficient in his harvesting of the province for wealth.[2] Maximinus must have been fairly successful in keeping the army happy, including the Praetorian Guard, if it took a civilian insurrection to start the process of unravelling his rule. The Libyan mob declared the proconsular governor of Libya, Marcus Antonius Gordianus (Gordian I), emperor. He gave in to the crowd's demands after first declining the offer. Gordian went from Thysdrus (El Djem in modern Tunisia), where he was at the time he was declared emperor, and travelled to Carthage, one of the largest cities in the Roman world after Rome. He was accompanied by the urban cohort based in Carthage, and 'the tallest young men in the city acting like the Guard in Rome'. These men were subsequently formed into a new Praetorian Guard, briefly led by Gordian's son as praetorian prefect. Gordian sent a letter ahead to Rome to inform the senate that he was in power.

Gordian also planned the elimination of Vitalianus, referred to by Herodian as the commander of the forces in Rome, and specified Vitalianus in the *Historia Augusta* as praetorian prefect.[3] Some praetorians were certainly with Maximinus, but part of the Guard must have been in Rome while others could have been deployed almost anywhere in the Empire. The only known candidate for Vitalianus is Publius Aelius Vitalianus. He is attested as procuratorial governor of Mauretania Caesariensis in 236 under his friend Maximinus, who had probably promoted him to the praetorian prefecture.[4] Gordian sent his provincial quaestor ahead with an advance squad of centurions and soldiers. The plan was that they would tell Vitalianus they had an urgent message from Maximinus; while he was reading it they would pull out their swords and dispatch him.[5] Remarkably, on 22 March 238, the plan worked and the squad proclaimed the accession of Gordian and the death of Maximinus which was, of course, not true. The senate declared Gordian and his son, also Gordian, to be joint emperors (known to history respectively as Gordian I and II) and a pogrom was launched against any supporters or associates of Maximinus. In an impressively efficient move, the Roman mint immediately started turning out coins for both the Gordiani.

Maximinus, when he heard the news, made for Rome with his entire army, which included such praetorians as he had with him. He sent ahead the Pannonian legions to seize and hold key positions in Italy. Meanwhile, Capellianus, senatorial governor of Numidia, used his garrison to march against Gordian. Gordian's largely civilian supporters in Carthage were no match for Capellianus' trained soldiers. The outcome was a rout in which Gordian's son, Gordian II, was killed. Gordian then committed suicide. The date was 12 April 238; the reign of Gordian I and II had lasted precisely twenty-one days.[6] The news occasioned panic when it reached Rome, for it was fairly obvious that Maximinus would not take kindly to the way the senate and Roman people had so rapidly gone over to the Gordiani. Two senators, Balbinus and Pupienus, were chosen to serve as joint emperors. They were not particularly popular, Pupienus being resented for his severe treatment of the mob during his tenure as prefect of Rome. They gave the praetorian prefecture to Pinarius Valens, one of Balbinus' relatives, and the prefecture of Rome to Vettius Sabinus.[7]

Supporters of the deceased Gordiani began to gather around Gordian I's grandson by his daughter. The boy, who was in Rome and aged about fourteen, was also called Gordian.[8] To appease them, the senate voted the young Gordian Caesar and thus heir apparent. About that time people gathered around the senate house simply to find out what was going on, so confused was the general state of affairs. This attracted some praetorians – older men who had been left behind in Rome because of their advanced age and proximity to retirement. As seems to have been customary for praetorians under normal circumstances in Rome, they were unarmed and wore only a cloak over a 'simple uniform'. The image of the political process under way created by the sight of the senate meeting, with the doors of the senate house open, generated a false sense of civilized normality. In reality, the situation was so tense that many of the senators had equipped themselves with daggers hidden in their togas. As a few of the praetorians stepped forward to see what was going on in the chamber, two of the senators, Gallicanus and Maecenas, pulled their weapons out and killed two praetorians. Gallicanus is described as a Carthaginian and may have been a supporter of the Gordiani.[9]

The other praetorians, appreciating the size of the crowd gathered and the inconvenient fact of their having no weapons, quickly made themselves scarce. Gallicanus accused them of being Maximinus' supporters, successfully whipping up the mob. Meanwhile, the praetorians sealed themselves in the Castra Praetoria and prepared for a fight. Gallicanus now equipped the mob from public armouries with weapons intended for ceremonies, collecting them from the gladiatorial barracks and indeed anywhere else. They headed off to assault the Castra Praetoria. The praetorians fired arrows at the mob and used spears to hold the crowd back, taking advantage of the protection of the walls and towers. Eventually the crowd gave up and began to drift away. Exploiting this opportunity, the praetorians burst out through the gates to attack, killing a number of gladiators and others, and chasing the rest off before going back into the camp and locking the gates.[10]

The volatile situation started to get out of control. Balbinus and Pupienus recruited a new army from across Italy, rounding up any associations of young men to bolster the numbers. Pupienus then set out with this army to fight Maximinus, but left behind some to hold Rome. The

Historia Augusta states that the Praetorian Guard stayed, but this must mean only those who had already been left by Maximinus, perhaps because their loyalty was in question. However, not including them was no less dangerous. The Roman mob continued to occupy themselves in a series of futile assaults on the Castra Praetoria.[11] Balbinus tried to pacify the situation by promising the praetorians an amnesty. They for their part were disgusted at being attacked by a mob, and the mob was disgusted that they had failed to defeat the praetorians. Eventually the crowd came up with a solution, cutting the water supply into the Castra Praetoria during an attack. The pipes affected were probably those installed under Caracalla and Macrinus, replacing or repairing earlier installations.[12]

The praetorians had no choice but to break out of the camp and chase the mob away. Unfortunately, the people simply climbed to the upper storeys of houses and apartment blocks in order to throw stones and other ammunition down on the praetorians in the streets below.[13] The praetorians retaliated by setting fire to buildings, causing a huge part of the city to burn down. This was in spite of the building regulations, brought in after the Great Fire of 64, designed to prevent fire spreading easily in the congested city.

None of this chaos dealt with the pressing problem of Maximinus' steady march into Italy in the summer of 238. The Thracian emperor's legionary infantry were laid out in a standard wide rectangular formation, *agmen quadratum*, with cavalry on either side. Behind them came the equipment and baggage, and then Maximinus with his praetorians. Once they had crossed the Alps they came down into the Italian plain and approached Aquileia, which had locked its gates when the advance column of Pannonian legions arrived, and prepared for a siege. This had involved a very rapid repair of the city walls, which had fallen into ruin during the long era of peace in Italy. Maximinus tried to negotiate his way in, using an Aquileian tribune on his staff to intercede. This failed because of Rutilius Pudens Crispinus, one of the two consular generals sent by the senate to hold the city. Crispinus persuaded the Aquileians to stand fast and Maximinus proceeded on towards Aquileia, only to discover his way was barred by the river Sontius (Isonzo), following destruction of the bridge by the Aquileians. A makeshift bridge was constructed, the army crossed and the siege began. Maximinus soon found the Aquileians were more than a match for even his battle-hardened army. Not only did the entire population participate in the defence, but the Aquileians also poured a volatile mix of bitumen and sulphur onto the attackers, as well as shooting torches at the siege equipment to set it on fire.[14] The result was that as the siege wore on confidence in Maximinus began to decline and the consequences of ravaging the surrounding countryside began to bite as the army's supplies ran out.

Additionally, Maximinus was operating in an information vacuum. Road and sea routes had been blockaded on the senate's orders. Effectively, Maximinus' army was now trapped in its own siege. The end came for Maximinus when the II legion Parthica mutinied, sick of the wasted time and the destruction of Italy.[15] Maximinus' fickle praetorians soon joined them and Maximinus was killed along with his son Maximus and all his advisers, including someone described by Herodian as the 'military prefect'. The *Historia Augusta* specifies that the 'praetorian prefect' and Maximinus' son were killed first before Maximinus. For good measure, Maximinus' portraits were torn off the standards. The siege ended immediately. Maximinus' severed head was carried to Pupienus in Ravenna and then on to Rome. In the reorganization that followed, Balbinus ordered the legions and auxiliary units to disperse back to their normal respective headquarters in the provinces, but took the praetorians, and probably also the II legion Parthica and the *equites singulares*, back to Rome where they had to rejoin those who had been holding out against the Roman crowd. The Castra Praetoria had to be reprovisioned, supplies apparently being brought from Aquileia, followed by an assembly of the praetorians to swear allegiance to Balbinus and Pupienus and to declare Gordian I's deification.[16]

These soldiers did not go happily. They were bitterly resentful at having to be under the command of emperors appointed by the senate, and equally annoyed that Pupienus had employed German auxiliary troops as his personal bodyguard.[17] The praetorians' belief, based on how in 193 Severus had dealt with the Guard responsible for killing Pertinax, was that Balbinus and Pupienus planned to use the Germans to replace them. They waited for their moment when the quinquennial Capitoline games started sometime in July 238. While the city was distracted, the praetorians went to the palace to kill the emperors. Pupienus wanted to call the German auxiliary bodyguards, but Balbinus believed Pupienus was planning to get rid of him. This wasted valuable time, allowing the praetorians to burst in, seize both emperors and take them to the Castra Praetoria. The German auxiliaries were alerted and rushed after them, but the praetorians killed both of the emperors before they were apprehended and proclaimed the young Gordian emperor. Gordian III was taken to the Castra Praetoria and locked in with the Guard. The Germans gave up the fight, given that neither Balbinus nor Pupienus was left to protect.[18]

At this point Herodian's text ends. For the remainder of the period we are left with the *Historia Augusta* and a diminishing number of other scattered references. Even the epigraphic record begins to dwindle. In Britain some *evocati* found new roles after their time as praetorians. The Guard was a very useful source of soldiers who had not had enough of military life by the time they retired, some as early as their mid-thirties. Trained and experienced, they could find work commanding auxiliary troops in remote provinces. The northern frontier in Britain remained a heavily garrisoned network of outpost forts occupied by dozens of auxiliary cavalry and infantry units. By some indeterminate point in the third century, Aurunceius Felicessemus had served as a praetorian to full term and then re-enlisted as an *evocatus*. In this capacity he was made a tribune and was based at the remote outpost fort of *Fanum Cocidii* ('The Shrine of Cocidius' at Bewcastle), beyond the north-west sector of Hadrian's Wall, where he must have commanded the First Cohort of Nervian Germans. The fort was named after the eponymous local warrior god Cocidius, and Felicessemus made the dedication there that preserved his name. He was not the only link to the Guard in this distant setting around that time. Quintus Peltrasius Maximus made a rather more elaborate dedication on an altar that also recorded his promotion to tribune from *cornicularius* on the staff of the praetorian prefects. To the east at Birdoswald, along the Wall, Flavius Maximianus commanded the First Cohort of Aelian Dacians during the reign of Maximinus. Before that he, too, had been a praetorian, serving in the I praetorian cohort, presumably under Severus Alexander.[19]

Meanwhile, Gordian III became emperor in 238, sponsored by the Praetorian Guard. As someone barely in his teens, Gordian was dangerously exposed and caught in the middle of a power struggle between the senate and the army. A turning point came in 241 when Gordian appointed as his praetorian prefect Gaius Furius Sabinius Aquila Timesitheus, who subsequently became his father-in-law when Gordian married his daughter Tranquillina.[20] Timesitheus was Gordian III's Burrus and Seneca rolled into one. Timesitheus effectively governed the Empire for Gordian, and his tenure of the praetorian prefecture showed how the office could still function as one of the highest offices of state, with little sense that it remained in theory only the military command of the imperial bodyguard in Rome. The Empire under Gordian III faced substantial external threats, mainly in the form of Shapur I of Persia who was in sole power by 242. By 243 a Roman army headed out to the east to confront Shapur. Ostensibly commanded by Gordian, it was really Timesitheus who organized a highly successful campaign that pushed Shapur back, something Gordian gratefully acknowledged.[21] A triumph for the pair was planned but before long Timesitheus had died, probably in late 243. He was succeeded as praetorian prefect by Marcus Julius Philippus (Philip), who may have been responsible for Timesitheus' death, though it is equally likely that the latter's demise was due entirely to natural causes. The version of events that blamed Timesitheus' death on Philip said it was occasioned by diarrhoea, the medication administered being changed on Philip's orders, making the condition worse and causing him to expire.[22]

Either way, Philip became prefect by the end of 243 and in that capacity, with remorseless inevitability, started to engineer a plot against Gordian. He did this by manufacturing a food shortage. Grain ships were turned away and soldiers stationed in places remote from food storage. This provoked a gradual rise in dissatisfaction with Gordian's leadership. There seems to have been a brief phase when the two men ruled together. Gordian appointed his own praetorian prefect, an otherwise unknown relative called Maecius Gordianus. Frustrated by Philip's arrogance, Gordian asked the soldiers to choose between them. He lost. Gordian offered to take a subordinate position, but it was clear that his time was up. In a location called Circesium (Zaitha) on the Euphrates, Gordian III was killed on 25 February 244.[23] He was around twenty years old.

Born in Arabia, Philip 'the Arab' was the second praetorian prefect to become emperor, though, unlike Macrinus, he had some authentic pretensions to high rank. He was the son of a chieftain who had been awarded equestrian status. The only biographies of him that have survived are by Zosimus and Aurelius Victor, neither being particularly satisfactory. Philip's brother, Gaius Julius Priscus, seems to have been co-praetorian prefect with Timesitheus under Gordian III, and apparently continued in post under Philip. The confusing array of fragmentary evidence indicates that by 248 Priscus had been made 'praetorian prefect and ruler of the east' in an effort to give him the necessary power to hold the eastern provinces.[24]

Priscus was made governor of Mesopotamia, or appointed commander of the army in Syria, unless he held both posts simultaneously. Philip negotiated a rapid peace with the Persians and then hurried to consolidate his position at Rome, sending ahead the sad news that Gordian 'had died of disease'. By 246, despite trying to focus his attention on establishing a new dynasty, Philip was having to fight on the Danube in Dacia but was able to celebrate Rome's thousandth birthday in 248. The regime started to collapse later that year in the face of a rebellion led by Pacatian with the support of the Danube legions, and Jotapian in the east, who appears to have objected to the authoritarian rule of Crispus, 'a man of intolerably evil disposition'. Jotapian was killed by his own troops and so was Pacatian, but in Pacatian's case, his troops simply transferred their allegiance to the prefect of Rome, Trajan Decius, who had been sent against them by Philip. In the war that followed between Trajan Decius and Philip, Philip and his son lost and were killed in the autumn of 249, being taken back to their camp by the praetorians for the purpose.[25]

Although very little is known about the comings and goings of the praetorian cohorts themselves in this era, the evidence of diplomas (discharge certificates) does provide some background. A diploma from Lugdunum (Lyon), dated to 7 January 244 under Gordian III, refers to soldiers being honourably discharged from the 'ten praetorian cohorts', a useful confirmation of the minimum number of cohorts in operation at that date; it also confirms the presence of Italian recruits in the Guard.[26] A novel feature, which had become increasingly common amongst legions and auxiliary units of the period, was the addition of a loyalist epithet, appropriate in this instance to the way Gordian was made emperor in 238. The veteran in this case, Gaius Julius Decoratus, belonged to the II Gordinian praetorian cohort, or in full: *coh[ors] II pr[aetoria] Gordin[i?]ana P[ia] V[index]*. This was a statement of loyalty, of affiliation to, and identification with, the regime. Such titles were tenuous at best, being swiftly dropped and replaced as emperors came and went in increasingly rapid succession. Two diplomas record similar honorific names under Philip I (244–9). One records the veteran Nebus Tullius Ma. . . of the *coh(ors) V pr[aetoria] Philippian[a] P[ia] V[index]* on 7 January 246, the date of his discharge. Another, exactly a year later to the day, records Marcus Braetius Justinus from Mantua of the similarly named VIII praetorian cohort.[27] Just as the Gordinian title was dropped in 244, so the Philippian one would be too (Plates 27 and 28).

The next few decades featured an increasingly chaotic sequence of short-lived soldier emperors and usurpers. Little or nothing is known about the praetorian prefects and even less about the praetorians themselves. Apart from the occasional tombstone and diploma, the fleeting glimpse of praetorians murdering Philip is about as good as it gets. Aurelius Vincentius, a Thracian, was forty when he died. He had served for five years in the XI legion Claudia, based since Trajan's time in Durostorum in Moesia Inferior (modern Silistra, Bulgaria), before transferring to the Praetorian Guard where he served in the III cohort for eleven years.[28] He can only be approximately dated to this period, but provides one example of the sort of career path possible for a praetorian in the third century. He appears to have died while still in service but, oddly, his tombstone was found in Caesarea in Mauretania in north-west Africa where he had probably been deployed on some service for the state.[29]

The coinage of the period shows increasing degeneration. Under Gordian III the double-denarius, the antoninianus, which first appeared under Caracalla, was reintroduced and gradually supplanted the denarius completely. The new coin was preferred by the state because of its reduced bullion content. By the time Trajan Decius ruled (249–51), the silver coinage was becoming visibly less pure, with the copper content now dominating. This was bound to frustrate the soldiers, especially praetorians accustomed to higher rates of pay and donatives. Loyalty was now so easily transferred that Decius lasted only two years before being supplanted by Trebonianus Gallus (251–3), who was killed by his own troops. He was succeeded by the governor of Moesia, Aemilian, in 253, who was declared emperor by his garrison. Valerian, who had been asked by Gallus to bring him help, was proclaimed emperor by his troops. Aemilian went to attack him but his men turned against him after only a few months and Valerian was left to rule, at least for the time being. Valerian (253–60) appointed otherwise unknown praetorian prefects called Baebius Macer and Mulvius Gallicanus, and his son Gallienus as co-emperor (253–68) within the year.[30]

The continual frontier warfare must have taken up most of the Guard's time, yet those older praetorians due to retire must likewise have been left in Rome to keep order there, just as they had been under Maximinus, unless they moved on to provincial auxiliary commands. A proclamation to Rome made by Aurelian (270–5) included an exhortation to show goodwill to the Praetorian Guard.[31] This was obviously a reference to the catastrophic feud between the Guard and the Roman people under Balbinus and Pupienus, but surely also implies that the Guard's presence in Rome had remained a normal feature of life in the intervening decades.

In the meantime, imperial government plumbed humiliating new depths when Valerian was captured by Shapur I in 260 and taken into Persia, from where he never returned. The coinage of Gallienus, Valerian's son and co-emperor, is the first since that of Claudius over two hundred years earlier to refer specifically to the Praetorian Guard. An antoninianus, apparently struck in Milan c. 260–1, bears a reverse legend honouring the Guard surrounding a lion wearing a radiate crown. The legend reads COHH PRAET VI (or VII). It is not clear in this case whether the numeral indicates a reference to specific cohorts or to victories. Other coins of the same series honour one or other of seventeen legions that, together with

254

the Praetorian Guard, formed Gallienus' field army under the command of Aureolus. Another type had the reverse legend FIDEI PRAET, honouring the 'Faithfulness of the Praetorians', which turned out to be a triumph of misplaced hope.[32]

The coins were probably intended to be used to pay the soldiers directly. There is no historical reference to the praetorians' involvement. All that is known is that Gallienus, to add to all his other problems, faced a rebellion by Aureolus, and another by Domitianus, one of Aureolus' generals. Aureolus was defeated by Gallienus, who then faced a conspiracy involving his praetorian prefect, Marcus Aurelius Heraclianus, as well as other commanders, including the future emperors Claudius II and Aurelian. The plot was successful. Gallienus was murdered when he raced off, having been given false information that Aureolus was approaching with his army. He was succeeded by Claudius II. Aureolus spotted his chance to save his own skin and tried to secure a peace with Claudius. He was immediately murdered by praetorians, who bitterly resented his treachery.[33]

In the remote province of Numidia, at a place called Rusicade (now Skikda), Aelius Dubitatus made a dedication to Jupiter during the reign of Claudius II (268–70). He was then serving in the VIIII praetorian cohort but, far from having a front-row seat to history by participating in the endemic warfare of the third century, Dubitatus belonged to a detachment of praetorians sent out to guard the grain route. He was based at a staging post (*statio*) at Veneria Rusicade on the road and had been there for nine years.[34] Such records are extremely rare but they show that references to praetorians on campaign with the various emperors of the era can be misleading. Evidently, members of the Guard were also dispersed on a number of different and innocuous duties, just as they had been for years. This inevitably meant that praetorians became ever more distanced from their original purpose – that of guarding the emperor's person – even though that very job had probably become more vital than it ever had been.

New ways had to be found to protect the emperor, whoever he was at that particular moment. In 267 at Aquincum (Budapest) in Pannonia Inferior a dedication to the Genius of Gallienus was made by Clementius Silvius, currently serving as a stand-in governor, and Valerius Marcellinus, a prefect commanding a legion and serving as a *protector* (defender) of the emperor.[35] The *protectores* seem to have started by this date, if not earlier, to do the job praetorians had once done. At this date this was perhaps no more than an ad hoc post, but in time the *protectores* would replace the praetorians completely. One of the most remarkable praetorian careers from this time was that of Trajanus Mucianus. This Thracian soldier was promoted steadily from being an auxiliary infantryman through the II legion Parthica to being a cavalryman with the VII praetorian cohort. He reached the heights of *evocatus* and then served in several centurionates as a *protector* under Gallienus, including being the *centurio protector* of the V praetorian cohort. He became eventually the commander of the *protectores*, the *princeps protectorum* ('first amongst the protectors'), before proceeding to further prestigious posts, including equestrian commands of legions. His career and those of others show the post of *protector* appearing within the existing hierarchy, with individual soldiers from different units acquiring the title, rather than as a distinct organization in the manner of the *cohors praetoria*.[36] The confusing terminology also includes the word *palatinus*, which appears to have become part of the titles of praetorian cohorts by this time. Paternius Maternus, tribune of an auxiliary cohort on the northern frontier in Britain in the mid- to late third century, made a dedication to a local native god called Cocidius. Maternus stated that he had previously been an *evocatus Palatinus*. This term is not fully understood. It may simply be a reference to palace duties or a more formal title for the Guard.[37]

Gallienus had also been directly challenged since 260 by Marcus Cassianus Latinius Postumus. This flamboyant pretender was governor of Germania Superior and Inferior when he was declared emperor by the Rhine garrisons. The western provinces had been placed under the rule of Gallienus' teenage son Saloninus and it was not entirely surprising that the north-west Rhine garrisons preferred the option of an experienced leader. Postumus ended up creating and ruling a breakaway empire from Cologne that in every formal respect emulated the legitimate Empire; this probably included creating his own praetorians but there is no evidence to substantiate this. Postumus controlled Britain, Gaul and the German provinces in a regime now known as the Gallic Empire. Postumus, murdered in 268, produced a vast amount of coinage but, unlike that of Gallienus, none of it honoured specific military units, and the same applies to his short-lived successors who finally capitulated in early 274. Unusually for emperors of the era, Claudius II had died in 270 from the plague and not as a result of violence.[38] He was briefly succeeded by his brother Quintillus, who was proclaimed emperor by the soldiers at Aquileia, but the declaration of Claudius' cavalry commander Aurelian as emperor by the army in the Balkans proved a more enticing prospect. Quintillus committed suicide and Aurelian proceeded unchallenged, initiating a highly successful reign cut short by yet another conspiracy.

Aurelian's praetorian prefect was Julius Placidianus, attested in the post on an inscription from the Augustan colony of Dea Augusta Vocontiorum (Drôme) in Gallia Narbonensis; he had previously served as prefect of the *vigiles* under Claudius II.[39] The presence of Placidianus in Gaul reflected the very dangerous situation on Rome's northerly borders, caused initially by the German Juthungi tribe, the Vandals, and next by the Alamanni. The absence of the praetorian prefect from Rome was certainly not new, and had become a necessary part of the increasing need to confront threats in various parts of the Roman world, especially in the third century. The idea of the Guard as an elite body of experienced and privileged troops with a permanent base in Rome was changing. The Guard now more resembled the ad hoc units of praetorians organized by the protagonists of the civil wars up to 31 BC.

The frontier threats faced by Aurelian were successfully fought off to begin with, but only at the price of rebellions breaking out in Rome. These seem to have included one by the mint-workers, led by the *rationalis* (official in charge) of financial affairs, Felicissimus. Aurelian returned to crush the rebels, which involved having to execute a number of senators and confiscate their property.[40] Aurelian also devised a scheme in which estates were to be bought up along the Via Aurelia at state expense and then operated by slaves captured on campaign so that a perpetual free dole of wine, oil, bread and pork could be made to the Roman people. This peculiar brand of slave-serviced socialism never came off, either because of Aurelian's premature death in 275 or because Julius Placidianus dissuaded him on the grounds that if the Roman people had been given wine then there would be nothing more to give them apart from chicken and geese.[41]

During Aurelian's reign the Castra Praetoria underwent its most significant change since its construction 250 years earlier. Aurelian ordered a vast new circuit of walls to be built round Rome. These would reflect the huge expansion of the settled area since Republican times, and also protect the city from the very real threat it faced from barbarian incursions across the frontiers. It may also have helped to contain a potentially volatile population.[42] Building began in 271 and continued for the next decade. The walls survive in large part today and bear witness to the colossal effort and resources involved. The Castra Praetoria's north and east walls formed part of this new circuit, the south and west stretches now facing inwards. The work was more complicated than simply joining the new walls up to the camp and bonding them in. The camp's walls were raised again, adding to previous periods of elevation, and a new type of tower added which served as a buttress to help support the heightened walls.[43]

Aurelian also faced a breakaway state in the east based around the great city of Palmyra under the queen, Zenobia. In 272 the regime's city of Emesa fell to Aurelian in an engagement that included a hand-picked selection of praetorians as well as a huge array of legions and auxiliary forces.[44] Palmyra fell too but Aurelian spared the city until a rebellion in 273 led him to destroy it.[45] Aurelian could now turn his attention to the crumbling Gallic Empire. The last of Postumus' successors, Tetricus I, capitulated to Aurelian in early 274 and participated in a triumph in Rome with Zenobia. In 275 Aurelian had to head east once more, this time to recover Mesopotamia from the Persians. En route in Thrace he became suspicious about his secretary Eros and evidently made an allegation to which Eros took exception. Eros decided to get his revenge by circulating a fictitious list of people whom he claimed Aurelian was planning to punish, encouraging them therefore to do what was necessary to save themselves. The outcome was almost inevitable: some of the accused, including a number of praetorian officers, watched Aurelian leave the city one day. They followed the emperor and killed him.[46] The conspiracy and assassination were the consequence of an unfortunate misunderstanding but the incident proves that the Praetorian Guard was a routine part of the emperor's field army.

Aurelian was succeeded by Marcus Claudius Tacitus, a senator of mature years. The *Historia Augusta* refers to an otherwise unknown praetorian prefect called Moesius Gallicanus, perhaps appointed under Aurelian, recommending Tacitus to the army on the grounds that the senate had made emperor the man the army wanted. Tacitus either replaced Gallicanus with, or appointed alongside Gallicanus, his brother Marcus Annius Florianus as praetorian prefect.[47] Since Florianus was sent east by Tacitus to fight the Goths, we can legitimately assume that the Praetorian Guard went with him. Tacitus, however, died and Florianus seized the chance to declare himself emperor. This was not the intention of the army in Syria and Egypt, who preferred to sponsor their commander, Marcus Aurelius Equitius Probus instead. The two sides came to a potential battlefield at Tarsus but Probus avoided fighting and in the ensuing stand-off Florianus was killed by his own troops.

Prior to his accession in 276, Probus allegedly wrote to his praetorian prefect, Capito, reluctantly accepting the post of emperor.[48] Unfortunately, Capito is otherwise unknown and the *Historia Augusta* for this period so unreliable in many ways that there is every possibility that 'Capito' and the letter to him were simply invented, unless Carus was meant. Even the hope expressed in the 'letter' that 'Capito' will stand alongside the emperor appears to have its origins in one of Cicero's orations.[49] However, there is perhaps a plausible basis in the context of Probus' time where the praetorian prefect had become the emperor's right-hand man. The reign was characterized by yet more endless frontier warfare. At Sirmium (Sremska Mitrovica) in Pannonia (Serbia), Probus was killed in a rebellion led by Marcus Aurelius Numerius Carus who had been appointed by Probus as praetorian prefect early in the reign.[50] Carus' presence and involvement in the death of the incumbent emperor replicated a scenario that was becoming all too familiar. Carus did not last long. He was found dead in his tent in July 283 on campaign in Persia. This time the culprit seems not to have been an accidental lightning strike, as reported in the *Historia*

Augusta, but his praetorian prefect and his son Numerian's father-in-law, Lucius Flavius Aper, who allegedly believed his own chances of power were likely to be better served if Carus was extinguished and replaced by his sons.[51] Carus' adult sons, Carinus and Numerian, succeeded their father seamlessly, Carinus taking the western half of the Empire, Numerian the east. It was an arrangement that was to be used extensively in the century to come. By 284 Numerian had been killed. The *Historia Augusta* blamed Aper, which, if true, made him the first praetorian prefect to kill two emperors in succession. Aper was apprehended by the soldiers of the eastern army who nominated the commander of the *domestici*, 'household troops', Diocles, who immediately killed Aper.[52] By 285 Carinus was in a position to challenge Diocles but was killed by one of his own officers during the battle at Margum on the Danube.

Diocles assumed the name Gaius Aurelius Valerius Diocletianus. As Diocletian he embarked on a sophisticated and disciplined recovery of the Empire. To begin with, he carried over Carinus' praetorian prefect, Titus Claudius Aurelius Aristobulus.[53] The reorganization culminated in 293 in the creation of the Tetrarchy, a collegiate system of emperors. He and another officer divided the Empire, Diocletian taking the east and Maximian the west as the Augusti. Each was assisted by a junior emperor, Galerius and Constantius Chlorus, known respectively as the Caesars.[54] In time Diocletian and Maximian were to abdicate and hand over power to their Caesars who would then become the Augusti and appoint their own Caesars. The system was designed to avoid the appalling problems their immediate predecessors had experienced trying to govern a sprawling empire beset by endless frontier problems, internal rebellions and succession by force.

The logical inference is that each tetrarch had his personal Praetorian Guard, and this does appear to have been the case. The Guard, still referred to as the praetorian cohorts, was dispersed by Diocletian amongst each of the four tetrarchs, with only a skeleton garrison left behind in Rome to man the Castra Praetoria. In 303, during a period of Christian persecution, a church in Nicomedia was raided by the 'prefect' in a search for images of Christ. The attack was conducted while Diocletian and Galerius watched from the nearby palace, and was carried out by part of the Praetorian Guard in battle order suitably equipped with axes and iron weapons. They systematically destroyed the church. In the fourth century under the Tetrarchy and later the position of praetorian prefecture continued, even once the Guard itself had been disbanded.[55]

From soon after Diocletian's accession, Britain had been controlled by a rebellious former fleet commander called Marcus Aurelius Mauseaeus Carausius. Seizing power in 286, Carausius was a colourful usurper whose ideology of a renewed and revived Augustan Roman Empire in Britain was depicted on a highly unusual series of coins. Carausius' power seems to have extended partly into northern Gaul since he was able to strike some of his coins at Rotomagus (Rouen), but this did not in any sense entitle him to the audacity of the military issues he had minted in Britain. These included coins which honoured some legions not based in Britain, such as the VIII legion Augusta and the XXII Primigenia, as well as those that were, such as II Augusta. Unless the coins were designated as a form of propaganda designed to entice these other legions into siding with Carausius, the only other explanation would be that detachments were then based in Britain. However, there is no other evidence to substantiate that, and so many legions are involved that the idea is implausible. It is much more likely that Carausius was simply trying to ingratiate himself with as much of the Roman army as possible. The series also included one with the legend COHR PRAET for the Praetorian Guard around four standards. The issue closely resembles one produced at Philippi in the first half of the first century AD in honour of the Praetorian Guard and was probably based on it.[56] There are three possible explanations: Carausius had a detachment of Diocletian's praetorians in Britain, he had his own praetorians, or he was trying to seduce the Guard into supporting him. The latter is the most likely, but there is no means of verifying this. It was the last time the Praetorian Guard was honoured on any coin issue. Clearly Carausius, who posed as a restorer of everything traditional about Rome, perceived the Praetorian Guard as an integral part of his manifesto and image.

In 293 Carausius was murdered in a plot by his finance minister, Allectus, who took his place as emperor in Britain. In 296 the Tetrarchy, which had already tried unsuccessfully to dislodge the regime, finally mounted an expedition involving a two-pronged attack. Constantius Chlorus headed for the Thames Estuary and London while one of the then praetorian prefects, Julius Asclepiodotus, was sent ahead with part of the fleet and leading a legionary force. The other prefect, Afranius Hannibalianus, was not involved. Allectus was killed in a battle somewhere in southern Britain after Asclepiodotus was able to sail unnoticed past his fleet off the Isle of Wight before landing his forces.[57] Asclepiodotus and Hannibalianus had already been consuls in 292, reflecting the transfer of the post to men of senatorial status, which had become institutionalized under Severus Alexander. Hannibalianus went on to become prefect of Rome in 297. By this time the praetorian prefecture had moved yet another stage further away from being a military command. The use of the Guard and its prefects to operate as an imperial police force had already been established since at least the late second century. Under Diocletian, the prefecture had become a regional administrative command. In the meantime, the Guard may have had another outing, this time with Maximian's army in North Africa in 297, engaged in suppressing a rebellion by a Berber confederacy called the Quinquegentiani.[58]

The details of the tortuous machinations of the Tetrarchy in the early fourth century are beyond the scope of this book. By 305 Diocletian and Maximian had abdicated, as planned, and been replaced by their intended successors Galerius and Constantius. However, the Tetrarchy rapidly disintegrated as individual ambition overtook events. Constantius Chlorus died in York on campaign in 306. The army there declared his son, Constantine, emperor on the spot, much to the annoyance of Galerius. Maximian's son, Maxentius also took exception to Constantine's unauthorized promotion, being declared emperor the same year. He persuaded his father to become emperor again, though after the two quarrelled, Maximian abdicated once more, only to try again to become emperor in 310, after which Constantine defeated and killed him. During this period a number of other participants in thwarted attempts to revive the Tetrarchy complicated circumstances even more, as did the death of Galerius in 311. The centrepiece of the conflict was the rivalry between Constantine and Maxentius which came to a head at the Battle of the Milvian Bridge at Rome on 28 October 312. This was the occasion when the Praetorian Guard made their last known appearance on the battlefield and, indeed, in Roman history (Plate 29).

The Guard, or what had been left of it at Rome by Diocletian, fought for Maxentius at the Milvian Bridge. They did so bravely enough for Constantine to be impressed. Their support of Maxentius had come about because Galerius had reduced the praetorians in number, and pushed up taxation levels.[59] The praetorians remaining in Rome had therefore decided to execute some magistrates and then nominate Maxentius as emperor. Maxentius was considerably better off in terms of troop numbers than Constantine. Maxentius had already used the Guard against a mob in Rome on a flimsy pretext, killing a number of people; however, our authority for this, Eusebius, provides the anecdote in a collection of evidence for Maxentius' brutality.[60] It is no less possible that the Guard was simply being deployed in a policing capacity and was attempting to restore order.

Maxentius' preparations to defend Rome included adding a gallery to the Aurelian Walls, and also blocking up the gates in the walls of the Castra Praetoria. Constantine advanced south down the Via Flaminia, after defeating Maxentius' praetorian prefect Ruricius Pompeianus along the way. Maxentius' praetorians stood fast while his cavalry and infantry were pushed back towards the Tiber, where Maxentius' pontoon bridge lay beside the masonry Milvian Bridge.[61] Maxentius tried to escape back across the bridge with his *equites singulares*, but the bridge gave way under the weight of fleeing troops. Maxentius was drowned along with his *equites*. The praetorians were left behind on the north bank, now facing Constantine more or less on their own. The action of the Battle of the Milvian Bridge was commemorated by depicting the drowning guardsmen in their distinctive scale armour on a relief subsequently installed on the Arch of Constantine in Rome. It was an ignominious end for what had once been the most esteemed part of the Roman army. The sculpture is today one of the very few visual manifestations of the Guard visible in Rome (Plates 30 and 31).

In the aftermath Constantine made the decision to dissolve the Praetorian Guard permanently. Unlike Severus over a century earlier, Constantine did not re-form the Guard with his own loyalists.[62] The discharged praetorians were dispersed along the Rhine and Danube. There they fought bravely and were recognized for their efforts.[63] The south and west walls of the Castra Praetoria were demolished and the north and east walls became merely part of the Aurelian Walls. The remaining gates were blocked up. This was a highly symbolic gesture. The Castra Praetoria and the praetorians were synonymous. Destroying the fort was a deliberate act that made it clear the Praetorian Guard had gone for good (Plate 32).[64]

EPILOGUE

I F THE PRAETORIAN GUARD has a legacy it is to serve as a warning to any leader whose power is sought and won through force, however skilfully cloaked in the paraphernalia of legitimacy and popular consent. The retention of power in such circumstances is vested in the possession and control of latent force. Augustus understood that precisely. Some of his successors were less perceptive. An emperor infused with self and vain conceit was liable inadvertently to rouse that latent force and turn it against himself. The Guard's 'precarious faith', as Gibbon put it, was a purchasable commodity. Its most dangerous assets were the privileged conditions, its size and proximity to the emperor's person, which conferred on its members an arrogance and illusion of inviolability.

The Praetorian Guard remained the most potent symbol of the state's military identity, but it had contributed in no small measure to the Empire's decline. By the early fourth century the Roman world was as militarized as it had ever been. Indeed, the state was now explicitly, rather than implicitly, a military autocracy and had been for some time. The prolific coins of the era, which record the various personalities in the struggle for power of the late third and early fourth centuries, all share the same style of austere, stone-faced portraiture. Diocletian's palace at Split in Croatia was modelled on a military fortress. His division of the Roman world was pragmatic but also an admission that the Roman world would never be the same again. A

265

century of almost endless warfare had seen to that. The Roman world was beset by frontier wars and ravaged by its own internal fragmentation. The breakaway regimes of Postumus and Carausius would have been impossible in earlier times. They also would have held no attractions when the Roman world's remarkable stability made for an unprecedented era of relative security and prosperity. By the reign of Constantine that world was a very distant memory, though that did not stop him or his successors from trying to fabricate an aura of continuity, albeit one in which the Praetorian Guard was to have no part.

Gibbon regarded the 'licentious fury' of the Praetorian Guard as the 'first symptom and cause' of the Roman Empire's decline.[1] There is some truth in that claim, but, as this book has tried to show, while the Guard was an essential component of imperial power, the responsibility often lay with deficient emperors for the Guard's more reckless episodes. In any case, for the majority of the time the praetorians (as opposed to some of their officers and prefects) were loyal to their emperors; inevitably, by far and away the greatest amount of attention has always been paid to the most notorious incidents that punctuated an otherwise comparatively stable existence. That did not mean, however, that the danger had gone away during the more peaceful periods. Like a dormant volcano, the Praetorian Guard was always liable to erupt whenever the circumstances permitted.

Constantine's decision, and ability, to bring the Praetorian Guard to an end in 312 was an unequivocal assertion of his own power. In destroying the Guard he showed that his power was pre-eminent. It was an essential decision to make. The perilous balance Gibbon identified was now skewed massively in the emperor's favour. It was also a pragmatic move because Constantine needed to remove a body of troops whose allegiance to his rival had threatened his ambitions. The Guard's shifting loyalty, particularly in the preceding century, had been a destabilizing force with serious consequences for the Empire. The end of the Guard in no sense amounted to a policy of concealing the militarized nature of the late Roman state. Constantine appeared on his coins in military dress, celebrated the army with slogans such as GLORIA EXERCITUS ('the Glorious Army') and

CONCORD(IA) MILIT(UM) ('the Harmony of the Soldiers'), and trumpeted his success with UBIQUE VICTORES ('conquerors everywhere').

The demolition of the Castra Praetoria permanently destroyed the Guard's power base and also any opportunity for it to be used by them or anyone else as a stronghold against Constantine's regime. The end of the Guard did not mean that the emperor had suddenly no need for a bodyguard, but the Praetorian Guard had become an anachronism.[2] In an era when the emperor needed to be able to move with exceptional rapidity around his fragmenting empire and deal with remote rebellions or frontier incursions, an armed bodyguard with a fortified base in Rome was a colossal liability. The Guard might have gone, but the Castra Praetoria's north and east walls remained an important component of the Aurelian Walls of Rome, and still stand. What survived of the camp featured in a wider programme of restoration and rebuilding work under Theodoric, the Ostrogothic ruler of Italy from 493 to 526, attested by bricks stamped with his name.[3]

Either during Constantine's reign, or possibly under Diocletian, a mounted palace bodyguard unit of *scholae palatinae* units was created. Along with the *protectores*, they guarded the emperor's person.[4] Much the most likely time for their inception is after 312 under Constantine, since this was when the need would have been most apparent.[5] However, with a strength of only five hundred mounted troops, the *scholae palatinae* served much more as a substitute for the *equites singulares Augusti*. In an age of fast-moving mobile field armies, a cumbersome infantry bodyguard was obsolete. The *scholae palatinae* came under the direct control of the emperor himself, as did the *protectores*, who since at least 267 had been supplanting the traditional role of the praetorians as the emperor's bodyguard. The position of *protector* seems to have been an award made to deserving veterans who, in a law of 328, were explicitly protected from 'unseemly abuse'.[6] The risks inherent in having an armed bodyguard had not gone away but they had been drastically restricted by keeping them close and fewer in number.

The praetorian prefecture continued in existence but was now permanently detached from the bodyguard with the dissolution of the Praetorian

Guard. Since the ambitions of the praetorian prefects had been so routinely destabilizing a feature of imperial politics in the third century it is perhaps surprising that this had not happened earlier, or that some other restraining administrative mechanism had not been devised. The prefecture remained as a very senior position in the late Roman Empire. For some time the prefects had served increasingly as the emperor's deputy in certain situations, used in either an administrative or a military capacity as the situation required. Rather than being renamed or reinvented, the prefecture simply continued independently of the organization it had originally been devised to lead. It developed into a system of regional administrative prefectures, with five known from inscriptions found in Carthage and Antioch, dating to around 335. Four seem to have been attached to individual emperors, and a fifth placed in charge of provinces in Africa.[7] This system then evolved into one of regional prefectures, with a prefect placed in charge of a defined geographical area.

The *Notitia Dignitatum* is a late Roman administrative document that lists the various great offices of state in existence by the late fourth or early fifth century. These included the Praetorian Prefect of Italy, the Praetorian Prefect of the Gauls in the west, the Praetorian Prefect of the east, and the Praetorian Prefect of Illyricum. Each is described as a *vir illustris*, 'illustrious man', indicating that the incumbents now belonged to the highest and most esteemed echelons of the senatorial class. Alongside these men were ranked the Prefect of Rome and the Prefect of Constantinople. The *Notitia* also lists the provinces under the control of each praetorian prefect, and provides a breakdown of his staff, such as record keepers, tax collectors, curator of correspondence, registrar and secretaries.[8] The absence of any military officials is conspicuous. The praetorian prefecture had ceased to bear any formal resemblance to the job as originally conceived by Augustus. The evolution of the prefecture into this new form had been long and gradual.

The tradition of a military bodyguard of some sort endured long afterwards, whether serving as active troops or as a symbol of status and power, though no such organization has ever quite matched the durability or political influence of the Praetorian Guard. The Byzantine Varangian Guard, formally instituted in 988 under Basil II, was made up of German and Scandinavian tribesmen, and subsequently Anglo-Saxons after the Norman invasion of England, all placed under an *akolouthos*.[9] They were perceived as being more reliable than Byzantine troops due to their tradition of service based on oaths. Their 'barbarian' origins made them useful in battle. In the first half of the eleventh century Anglo-Saxon kings of England employed three thousand Scandinavian warriors in a unit called the Thingmen. Like Varangians, though, these soldiers had more in common with Augustus' German ('Batavian') bodyguard than the Praetorian Guard. Genghis Khan and other Mongol rulers enjoyed the protection of the Kheshig bodyguard, divided into those who protected by night and those who protected by day; unlike the praetorians, they never fought in battle. In 1506, Julius II, pope from 1503 to 1513, created the Swiss Guard out of an initial recruitment of 150 soldiers, and of course their successors remain today in the pope's service. They helped consolidate papal power when he formed the Holy League with Venice, Spain and later Henry VIII's England. In 1509 Henry VIII formed the Troop of Gentlemen to serve as his personal mounted bodyguard; in 1526 they ceased to be mounted but continued to defend the monarch right up to and including the English Civil War of the 1640s.

In 1652 the Council of State for the Commonwealth of England ordered that the tenpence paid daily to ordinary soldiers be increased by twopence to a shilling for those allocated to guarding Parliament and the City of London.[10] The idea of a guard with special privileges and conditions had not gone away. On 21 November 1658, John Evelyn watched as Cromwell's funeral cortege passed by with 'a knight of honour armed *cap à pè* and after all his guards, soldiers and innumerable mourners'.

Napoleon, who had himself depicted on his coinage as a Roman emperor, employed an Imperial Guard that bore a number of similarities to the Praetorian Guard, and had been created out of the Directory's Consular Guard. It consisted of separate cavalry, infantry and artillery regiments as well as horizontal divisions based on age and experience. Like the praetorians, Napoleon's guards enjoyed better pay, conditions and privileges than other soldiers. When founded in 1804, its size at eight thousand was comparable to the Praetorian Guard. By 1812 it had grown by twelve times or more. Its use in battle, sometimes constituting almost the entire army, was potentially vital and even decisive. Lack of experience was no obstacle to the prestige of fighting under the banner of his Guard. This was not only unsuccessful but also resulted in the Guard being largely wiped out at Waterloo in 1815 and being disbanded soon afterwards. This, however, did not stop ageing veterans parading in what was left of their uniforms when Napoleon's body was returned to France in 1840.

The Fascist dictators of the 1930s used military units that superficially resembled the Praetorian Guard, but in reality the functions were quite different. Mussolini's *Fasci di Combattimento* consisted of gangs of Fascist thugs who were used to intimidate, attack and murder political opponents. They lacked centralized organization and a formal identity, unlike his Fascist Militia for National Security, formed in 1923. This, however, was a voluntary force, even though it absorbed the Fascist gangs. Hitler's SA, the *Sturmabteilung*, had no formal military training as a body and in that sense cannot be compared to the praetorians, but Hitler fully recognized precisely the dangers of armed force that had helped him get into power. He moved promptly to neutralize the leadership of his SA in the Night of the Long Knives on 30 June 1934 to destroy potential rivals and their brownshirt powerbase.

Elsewhere in the world today numerous honour guards attend heads of state. In Colombia the 37th Infantry Presidential Guard battalion is stationed at the Casa de Nariño in Bogota where it can protect the president. The US 3rd Infantry Regiment serves as the president's honour guard, while the US Secret Service functions as the *cohortes speculatores* and *frumentarii* once did. However, in this more general context, the Praetorian Guard is perhaps too easily confused with organizations to which it bears only the most superficial resemblance. The term is, for example, sometimes applied to any military coup.[11]

In its 340-odd years of existence, the Praetorian Guard remained one of the most enduring organizations in the whole Roman army, even if it never did acquire a single unifying name. The praetorian cohorts grew out of the Roman Republic and began a permanent and institutionalized existence under the principate. Its soldiers were a ubiquitous presence in Rome and elsewhere in Italy. The Castra Praetoria was a reminder that the emperor's power was ultimately determined by his capacity to command and control the military force that made the regime possible. The Praetorian Guard functioned both as a bodyguard in Rome and increasingly as the emperor's personal troops in the field. Praetorians were present at, and active participants in, some of the most decisive occasions and episodes in Roman history. They could also be detailed, individually or in units, to take care of the state's business in a number of different ways and places.

Becoming a praetorian guardsman could be the crowning moment in a Roman soldier's military career. Men of equestrian rank who were appointed as praetorian prefect could enjoy unparalleled influence over the emperor and, in exceptional cases, the opportunity to seize absolute power itself. Whether the praetorians found themselves hurling lances at an unfortunate whale in the harbour at Ostia to entertain a crowd on the emperor's orders, or marching with the emperor on campaign, the Praetorian Guard was at the emperor's side, or represented his power while exploring the upper reaches of the Nile or even in a remote roadside station in Numidia. These formidable servants of the emperor could make or break him. That tension, which Gibbon described with such lucidity, was the essence of their power and could only be held in check by an emperor whose guile was greater than their greed. In all too many cases it was not, leaving the Praetorian Guard as one of the most powerful and capricious forces in Roman history. No wonder there has been nothing quite like it since.

APPENDIX 1
KEY DATES

62 BC	Marcus Petreius uses praetorians at Pistoria
58 BC	Caesar creates a temporary cavalry bodyguard from X Gemina
50 BC	Praetorian cohort serving as garrison at Epiphanea
49 BC	Marcus Petreius creates a *caetrati* bodyguard
44 BC	Caesar dismisses his Spanish bodyguard shortly before his assassination
	Antony raises a praetorian force of six thousand
	Octavian raises a praetorian force of ten thousand
43 BC	Rival praetorians fight at Battle of Forum Gallorum
	Battle of Mutina: Antony defeated
	Formation of the Triumvirate: Antony, Octavian and Lepidus – praetorians enter Rome
42 BC	Battle of Philippi: defeat of the tyrannicides
39 BC	Marriage of Octavian and Livia
36 BC	Antony confronts Phraates IV with an army that includes three praetorian cohorts
32 BC	Antony's 'legionary' issue of denarii, including a praetorian type
31 BC	Battle of Actium: Antony defeated, commits suicide
29 BC	Octavian's triumph in Rome
27 BC	Octavian assumes the name of Augustus
	Praetorian Guard organized now (or later) at nine cohorts
	Augustus authorizes praetorian pay to be double a legionary's
23 BC	Death of Marcellus, Augustus' intended heir
22 BC	Conspiracy against Augustus led by Murena and Caepio
13 BC	Praetorian service fixed at twelve years
12 BC	Death of Agrippa
2 BC	First praetorian prefects appointed
5	Praetorian service adjusted to sixteen years. Praetorian Guard said by Dio to consist of ten thousand men in ten cohorts
6	Seven cohorts of the night watch, *vigiles*, formed
9	Varian disaster: three legions lost
	German *corporis custodes* sent away from Rome temporarily
14	Death of Augustus, accession of Tiberius
	Praetorians paid at a rate of 750(?) denarii per annum (3 x 250)

272

	Praetorians receive 250 denarii in Augustus' will
	Sejanus made praetorian prefect
23	Tacitus states the army has twenty-five legions, nine praetorian cohorts and three urban cohorts in this year
	Castra Praetoria built around now in Rome; all praetorian cohorts now based there rather than two-thirds being dispersed in Italy
31	Fall of Sejanus
37	Murder(?) of Tiberius, accession of Gaius (Caligula)
	XI praetorian cohort possibly attested
41	Murder of Caligula, praetorians make Claudius emperor
47	By this date, Guard possibly organized into twelve cohorts
51	Burrus made praetorian prefect
54	Murder of Claudius, accession of Nero
59	Murder of Agrippina the Younger
62	Death of Burrus, praetorian prefect
	Tigellinus made praetorian prefect
65	Twelve praetorian cohorts attested by this date
68	Praetorians abandon Nero, his suicide, accession of Galba
	Galba disbands German *corporis custodes* and forms no praetorian unit
69	(2 January) Declaration of Vitellius as emperor
	(15 February) Death of Galba, accession of Otho
	(April) Accession of Vitellius, disbandment of Otho's praetorians
	(17 April) Suicide of Otho
	Vitellius forms sixteen milliary (1,000) praetorian cohorts
	(1 July) Declaration of Vespasian
	(December) Vitellius deposed and murdered, accession of Vespasian
	Titus made commander of the Praetorian Guard
	Guard reorganized
76	Diploma notes nine praetorian cohorts
79	Death of Vespasian, accession of Titus
81	Death of Titus, accession of Domitian
	Permanent organization of praetorian cohorts as milliary, if not already
	Pay raised to 999(?) denarii (3 x 333)
96	Murder of Domitian, accession of Nerva
98	Death of Nerva, accession of Trajan
100	Diploma notes ten praetorian cohorts
117	Death of Trajan, accession of Hadrian
138	Death of Hadrian, accession of Antoninus Pius
161	Death of Antoninus Pius, accession of Marcus Aurelius and Lucius Verus
169	Death of Lucius Verus
177	Appointment of Commodus as co-emperor
180	Death of Marcus Aurelius, start of Commodus' sole reign
192	Death of Commodus
193	Accession of Pertinax
	Murder of Pertinax, accession of Didius Julianus
	Murder of Didius Julianus, accession of Septimius Severus
	Praetorian Guard cashiered and reformed
	Guard now in ten milliary cohorts, if not already
198	Joint rule with Caracalla
209	Joint rule with Caracalla and Geta
211	Death of Septimius Severus; Caracalla and Geta rule
212	Murder of Geta, sole rule of Caracalla

217	Murder of Caracalla, accession of Macrinus, former praetorian prefect
218	Murder of Macrinus, accession of Elagabalus
222	Murder of Elagabalus, accession of Severus Alexander
235	Murder of Severus Alexander, accession of Maximinus
238	(22 March) Declaration of Gordian I as emperor
	(12 April) Suicide of Gordian I
	Joint rule of Balbinus and Pupienus
	(24 June) Murder of Maximinus I
	(29 July) Murder of Balbinus and Pupienus, accession of Gordian III
244	Murder of Gordian III, accession of Philip I, former praetorian prefect
	Diploma confirms ten praetorian cohorts
249	Murder of Philip I, accession of Trajan Decius
251	Murder of Trajan Decius, accession of Trebonianus Gallus and Hostilian
	Death of Hostilian
253	Murder of Trebonianus Gallus, accession of Valerian I and Gallienus
260	Capture of Valerian I by Persia
268	Murder of Gallienus, accession of Claudius II
270	Death of Claudius, accession of Quintillus
	Suicide of Quintillus, accession of Aurelian
275	Murder of Aurelian, accession of Tacitus
276	Death of Tacitus, accession of Florianus
	Murder of Florianus, accession of Probus
282	Murder of Probus, accession of Carus
283	Death of Carus, accession of Numerian
	Joint rule of Numerian and Carinus
285	Murder of Carinus, accession of Diocletian
305	Abdication of Diocletian
306	Declaration of Constantine I as emperor
312	Battle of Milvian Bridge
	Praetorian Guard disbanded, Castra Praetoria largely demolished

APPENDIX 2
PRAETORIAN PAY AND ORGANIZATION

Praetorian Pay

Table 1: Praetorian pay in denarii (numbers in italics are speculative)

	Annual	Instalment (14–c. 90)	Notional day rate (denarii)	Actual day rate	Discharge grant	Augustus' will	Annual under Domitian	Instalment (c. 90 and later)
Praetorian	*750*	*250*	2 (32 asses)	*2.05*	5,000	250	*999**	*333*
Legionary	225	75	0.625 (10 asses)	*0.616*	3,000	75	300	100
Ratio (P to L)	3.33:1	3.33:1	3.2:1	3.33:1	1.67:1	3.33:1	3.33:1	3.33:1
Urban	*375*	*125*	*1*	*1.03*	*3750*	125	*498*	*166*
Ratio (P to U)	2:1	2:1	2:1	2:1	1.33:1	2:1	2:1	2:1
Ratio (U to L)	1:67:1	1.67:1	1.6:1	1.67:1	1.25:1	1.67:1	1.65:1	1.65:1

* If this figure is correct (and this is not certain), then it would probably have been rated formally as 1,000 denarii with one of the thrice-annual payments adjusted, and similarly for the Urban Cohorts (500?).

* * *

This table is based on the figures supplied by Tacitus for the state of affairs in AD 14 (*Annals* 1.17.6), the discharge amounts supplied by Dio 54.25.6 and 55.23.1, Augustus' legacy at Dio 56.32.2 and Tacitus, *Annals* 1.8.2, and the pay rise under Domitian given by Dio (67.3.5) and Suetonius (*Domitian* 7). All of these have been converted to the denarius equivalent. Italicized numbers are theoretical. Other figures for rates of pay are specifically attested in the sources. It is apparent that the key ratio for rates of pay between praetorians and legionaries is 3.33:1, which makes it possible to provide a rounded annual rate of pay divisible by three and corresponds to the amounts allocated in Augustus' will. The discharge grant ratio at 1.67:1 is almost exactly half of that and made it possible to set these at round figures. The notional day rates come from Tacitus for AD 14 and are simply explained as rounded equivalents of the actual day rate derived from the annual rate, hence the 3.2:1 ratio for the figures he gives rather than 3.33:1. The same principle has been applied to theoretical rates for the urban cohorts, though far less is known about these. It should also be pointed out that we know nothing at all about when or how pay was distributed, or the reliability of the pay system. It is also very likely that rates of pay varied much more over the period than we have evidence for.

Praetorian Organization

Table 2a: Under Augustus (nine cohorts)

Structure if based on quingenary cohorts (480)

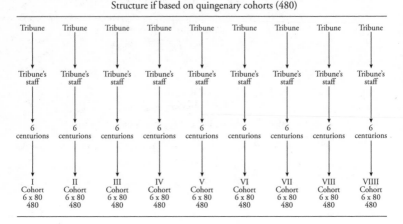

Structure if based on milliary cohorts (960)

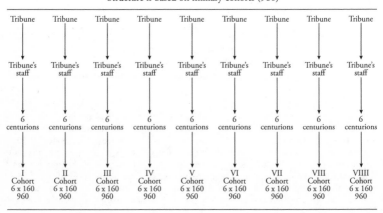

Table 2b: By 47–65 (twelve cohorts)

Structure if based on quingenary cohorts (480)

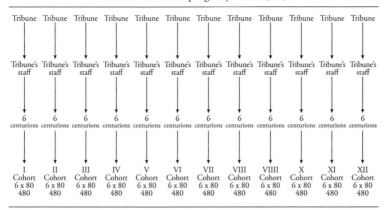

Structure if based on milliary cohorts (960)

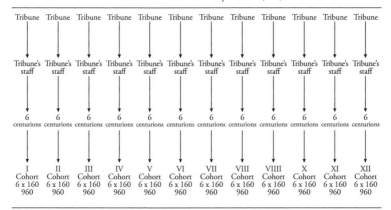

Table 2c: Under Vitellius (sixteen milliary cohorts)

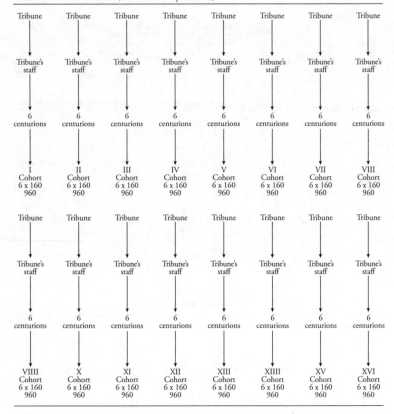

Tribune	Tribune	Tribune	Tribune	Tribune	Tribune	Tribune	Tribune
↓	↓	↓	↓	↓	↓	↓	↓
Tribune's staff	Tribune's staff	Tribune's staff	Tribune's staff	Tribune's staff	Tribune's staff	Tribune's staff	Tribune's staff
↓	↓	↓	↓	↓	↓	↓	↓
6 centurions	6 centurions	6 centurions	6 centurions	6 centurions	6 centurions	6 centurions	6 centurions
↓	↓	↓	↓	↓	↓	↓	↓
I Cohort 6 x 160 960	II Cohort 6 x 160 960	III Cohort 6 x 160 960	IV Cohort 6 x 160 960	V Cohort 6 x 160 960	VI Cohort 6 x 160 960	VII Cohort 6 x 160 960	VIII Cohort 6 x 160 960
Tribune	Tribune	Tribune	Tribune	Tribune	Tribune	Tribune	Tribune
↓	↓	↓	↓	↓	↓	↓	↓
Tribune's staff	Tribune's staff	Tribune's staff	Tribune's staff	Tribune's staff	Tribune's staff	Tribune's staff	Tribune's staff
↓	↓	↓	↓	↓	↓	↓	↓
6 centurions	6 centurions	6 centurions	6 centurions	6 centurions	6 centurions	6 centurions	6 centurions
↓	↓	↓	↓	↓	↓	↓	↓
VIIII Cohort 6 x 160 960	X Cohort 6 x 160 960	XI Cohort 6 x 160 960	XII Cohort 6 x 160 960	XIII Cohort 6 x 160 960	XIIII Cohort 6 x 160 960	XV Cohort 6 x 160 960	XVI Cohort 6 x 160 960

Table 2d: By AD 76 (nine cohorts)

Structure if based on milliary cohorts (960), maintaining Vitellian size

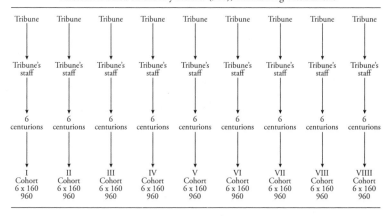

Table 2e: Under Domitian (?)/By Septimius Severus (ten milliary cohorts)

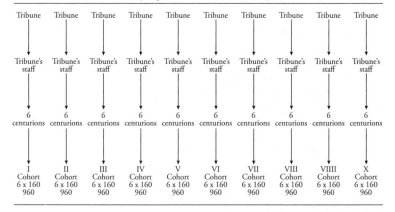

APPENDIX 3
PRAETORIAN PREFECTS

This appendix is only a list of prefects' names with dates for the period when the Guard was in existence. The reader is also referred to Menéndez Argüín (2006), 219–36, where a similar list of praetorian prefects complete with invaluable list of all the sources for each prefect will be found, though their names are given in Spanish form. It goes almost without saying that some of these names, and many of the dates, are very uncertain. It is impossible to compile a definitive or conclusive list. Inevitably readers may notice some discrepancies with details of prefects given in other works.

2 BC	Quintus Ostorius Scapula (fate unknown)
	Publius Salvius Aper (fate unknown)
?	Publius Varius Ligur
?–15	Lucius Seius Strabo (with his son Sejanus 14–15)
14–31	Lucius Aelius Sejanus (denounced, executed)
31–8	Quintus Naevius Cordus Sutorius Macro (deposed, committed suicide)
38–41	Marcus Arrecinus Clemens (i) (fate unknown)
	Lucius Arruntius Stella (uncertain)
41–4	Rufrius Pollo
41–3	Catonius Justus
43/4–51	Rufrius Crispinus (promoted to senatorial status)
44?–51	Lucius Lusius Geta
51–62	Sextus Afranius Burrus (murdered or suicide)
62–5	Lucius Faenius Rufus (executed for treason)
62–8	Gaius Ofonius Tigellinus (committed suicide)
65–8	Gaius Nymphidius Sabinus (killed)
68–9	Cornelius Laco (under Galba)
69	Plotius Firmus (under Otho)
	Licinius Proculus (under Otho)
	Publilius Sabinus (under Vitellius)
	Julius Priscus (under Vitellius)
	Publius Alfenus Varus (under Vitellius, replacing Publilius Sabinus)
69–70	Arrius Varus (under Domitian, in advance of Vespasian's arrival)
70–1	Marcus Arrecinus Clemens (ii)
	Tiberius Julius Alexander?

71–9	Titus Flavius Vespasianus (son of Vespasian, and emperor 79–81)
79–81	Unknown (under Titus)
81–3	Lucius Julius Ursus
81–7	Cornelius Fuscus
83–4	Lucius Laberius Maximus
84–94	Casperius Aelianus (or possibly under Nerva 96–8)
94–6	Titus Flavius Norbanus
94–7	Titus Petronius Secundus
98–101	Sextius Attius Suburanus Aemilianus
101–17?	Tiberius Claudius Livianus
117–20	Publius Acilianus Attianus
121–3	Servius Sulpicius Similis
120–3	Gaius Septicius Clarus
120–37	Quintus Marcius Turbo
138–43	Marcus Petronius Mamertinus
138–58	Marcus Gavius Maximus (the longest serving praetorian prefect)
158–60	Gaius Tattius Maximus
159–66/7	Sextus Cornelius Repentinus
159–68	Titus Furius Victorinus
168–77	Marcus Bassaeus Rufus
168–72	Marcus Macrinius Vindex
	Titus Flavius Constans
179–82	Publius Tarrutenius Paternus
180–5	Sextus Tigidius Perennis
185	Pescennius Niger
185	Marcius Quartius
185–7	Titus Longaeus Rufus
185–7	Pubius Aetilius Aebutanius
187–9	Marcus Aurelius Cleander
188–9	Lucius Julius Vehilius Gratus Julianus
189	Regillus
190	Motilenus
192	Quintus Aemilius Laetus
193	Titus Flavius Genialis (under Didius Julianus)
193	Tullius Crispinus (under Didius Julianus)
193–7?	Decimus Veturius Macrinus
193–7?	Flavius Juvenalis
197–205	Caius Fulvius Plautianus
198–9	Quintus Aemilius Saturninus
200–5	Marcus Aurelius Julianus
204	Marcus Flavius Drusianus
205–11	Aemilius Papinianus
205–15	Quintus Maecius Laetus
211–12	Valerius Patruinus
212–17	Gnaeus Marcius Rustius Rufinus
214–17	Marcus Opellius Macrinus (became emperor 217–18)
215–17	Marcus Oclatinius Adventus
217–18	Ulpius Julianus
217–18	Julianus Nestor
218	Julius Basilianus
218–21	Publius Valerius Comazon
221–2	Antiochianus

222–3/8	Domitius Ulpianus
	Flavianus
	Geminius Chrestus
223–?	Lucius Domitius Honoratus
223–?	Marcus Aedinius Julianus
230	Marcus Attius Cornelianus
228–35	Julius Paulus
238	Marcus Antonius Gordianus (son of Gordian I)
238	Vitalianus
238–49	Marcus Attius Cornelianus
241–4	Gaius Furius Sabinius Aquila Timesitheus
242–6	Gaius Julius Priscus
243/4	Marcus Julius Philippus (afterwards the emperor Philip I, 244–9)
249–51	Quintus Herennius Potens
253–6	Aelius Firmus
254–5/60	Successianus
	Mulvianus Gallicanus (under Valerian)
267–8	Marcus Aurelius Heraclianus
270–5	Julius Placidianus (under Aurelian)
275	Moesius Gallicanus (under Tacitus)
275–6	Marcus Annius Florianus
276	'Capito'?
276–82	Marcus Aurelius Numerius Carus (afterwards the emperor Carus, 282–3)
282–4	Lucius Flavius Aper
	Marcus Aurelius Sabinus Julianus
284–5	Titus Claudius Aurelius Aristobulus
285–97	Afranius Hannibalianus
285–97	Julius Asclepiodotus
306	Publius Cornelius Anullinus
310	Gaius Caeionius Rufus Volusianus
311	Manlius Rusticanus
311–12	Ruricius Pompeianus

APPENDIX 4
GLOSSARY OF TERMS

The Roman army, including the Praetorian Guard, had a number of technical terms that are associated with numerical values, such as the size of a century or a cohort. These values were 'nominal', literally just 'paper' figures. The reality, where we have the evidence, was that actual numbers varied considerably at any given time. Death, sickness and secondment all played their parts in this.

agmen quadratum

Literally, the 'square army in motion', a standard term denoting a block of troops on the move.

aureus

Standard Roman gold coin unit, nominally equivalent in value to 25 denarii, or 100 sestertii.

auxilia

Roman army units drawn from provincial recruits, usually identified by an ethnic component of the title, e.g. ala I Thracum, 'first cavalry wing of Thracians'. Paid less than legionaries but earned citizenship on honourable discharge.

caetratus/caetrati

Specialist light-armed Spanish infantry.

Castra Praetoria/Praetoriana

Literally 'the praetorian barracks', and also known as Castra Urbana, 'city barracks', where the singular noun castrum, 'camp', becomes plural to denote an encampment made up of individual tents or barrack blocks. Located in north-east Rome and founded by the prefect Sejanus in 23 under Tiberius in order to bring the whole Guard into Rome.

centuria (century)

The standard unit, nominally of eighty soldiers. Six centuries formed a quingenary cohort. Ten centuries formed a milliary cohort in a legion or auxiliary milliary cohort.

centurio

Commander of a century. Centurions could progress through a series of centurionates, each of increasing prestige. The most prestigious centurionate was the *trecenarius* (q.v.). See also *ordinarius* (q.v.).

cohors/cohortes

A military unit made up of centuries of eighty men each. Formed in quingenary (q.v.) and milliary (q.v.) sizes.

cohortes praetorianae (praetorian cohorts)

This was how the Praetorian Guard was known to the Romans. Formed by Augustus as a permanent institution, its original structure was either of nine or ten cohorts which may have been quingenary (five hundred) or milliary (one thousand) in size. No more than three were based in Rome until 23 when the Guard was installed in the Castra Praetoria. Nine cohorts are reported for 23, but three more may have been created by the mid-first century. By 100, ten cohorts existed and by the time of Severus these seem certainly to have been milliary in size. The singular was *cohors praetoria*, *cohors* being a feminine noun and thus the adjective *praetorius*, 'belonging to the praetor', adopts its feminine form, *praetoria*. Conversely, the plural noun *praetoriani* was used to refer to the praetorian soldiers themselves and was a masculine form.

cohortes urbanae (urban cohorts)

Rome's militarized police force, founded by Augustus and organized into three quingenary (five hundred) cohorts, each under the command of a tribune and the overall control of the *praefectus Urbanae*. Under the Flavians, a fourth cohort had been added and the cohorts increased to milliary (one thousand) size.

cohortes vigilum (night watch)

The night watch or fire brigade. Founded by Augustus and organized into seven cohorts to oversee fourteen administrative wards in Rome. These were probably each made up of 560 (3,920 in total) men, but by 205 had been increased to 1,120 each (7,840). Commanded by the *praefectus vigilum* and by Claudius' reign rotated between barracks in Rome, Ostia and Puteoli.

cornicularius

Senior clerk, assistant to the tribune.

denarius

The standard Roman silver coin, issued from Republican times regularly up until the mid-third century when it gave way to the double-denarius, the *antoninianus*. A denarius was equivalent to four *sestertii*. Twenty-five *denarii* were equivalent to one gold *aureus*. Purity declined during the period. Diameter typically 19 mm, weight c. 3.9 g.

diploma/diplomata

Usually incised on a bronze tablet, a diploma was a personal record of the honourable discharge of a soldier, the original of which was displayed in Rome. Diplomas, if complete, usually provide the emperor's name, the exact date when the discharge took place, details of the soldier concerned, a statement that the text is a faithful record of the original, and the location of the original, for example 'on the Capitoline [Hill] on the base of the statue of Jupiter of Africa', or 'on the wall behind the Temple of the divine Augustus at the statue of Minerva'.[1]

drachma

A drachma was the standard silver unit of currency in the Greek-speaking part of the Roman world. It weighed about 4.3 g. It was thus effectively interchangeable with a Roman silver denarius, even though its weight was about 10 per cent greater. Five hundred drachmae was a lot – rather more than twice the sum a legionary might have earned in a year. The praetorians in time would be paid at an even greater differential.

eques/equites

Generic term for cavalryman/cavalrymen. *Equites praetoriani/praetorianorum*, 'mounted praetorians', were an integral part of the Guard but it is not known how they were organized. They may have been distributed amongst the strength of the individual centuries or been additional to a century's strength.

equites singulares Augusti

Mounted imperial bodyguard, recruited first under the Flavians or by the beginning of the second century at the latest.

evocatus

A soldier recalled to service after retirement. *Evocatus* means literally 'a man summoned', and in a military context 'a man called to arms'. Such praetorians were soldiers whose exemplary service had already seen them rise to the privileged status of a *principalis*, enjoying double pay and serving under a centurion or on the prefect's staff.[2]

exercitator

Cavalry instructor, a position held by a senior centurion in the Guard.

extraordinarii

Selected cavalrymen from auxiliary cavalry wings.

frumentarius

Originally a collector of wheat, and normally attached to a legion. The *frumentarii* had exceptional local knowledge and this led incongruously to their being used by Hadrian as spies and informers for which the term became a synonym.

Germani custodes corporis

German bodyguards. Sometimes also known as Batavians. Formed by Augustus, disbanded by Galba.

immunis

A term applied to a soldier exempted from normal duties.

imperator

Original meaning was 'general', or 'commander-in-chief', but it evolved under the principate into being synonymous with ruling, leading to our word emperor.

imperium

The power of military command awarded usually to a consul by a vote of the senate. Such powers did not extend to commanding armies in Italy, but this was granted to Augustus as *imperium maius*.

manipulus

The maniple, a subdivision of a cohort, as used in battle and originally based on two centuries. A soldier of a maniple was a *manipularius*.

milliary

The Latin adjective *milliaria* (one thousand) applied to the names of certain military cohorts. This term indicates a nominal size of one thousand. In practice this varied, depending on the subdivisions of the unit concerned. A milliary cohort in a legion, for example, consisted of ten centuries of eighty men, equivalent to eight hundred men. Praetorian milliary cohorts seem to have been around a thousand men.

optio

Non-commissioned officer, second to a centurion and his deputy.

ordinarius

Literally 'one who keeps order', and an alternative word for a centurion, increasingly common at later dates, but the full range of potential meanings is not entirely clear. It seems also to have denoted military positions regarded as being of centurion rank. However, the word derives from *ordo*, meaning literally 'rank', in which case it may qualify the profession (such as a *plumbarius* – lead-worker, see Plate 19) of a man who served in that in a military unit.

ornamenta consularia

Often awarded to praetorian prefects. It entitled the holder to sit with senators of the most senior (consular) rank at public events and to wear the senatorial toga, but not to sit in the senate.

paenula

Military cloak, often hooded.

pia vindex

'Faithful Avenger'. Severan title awarded to praetorian cohorts, and useful for dating inscriptions of that date. Usually abbreviated to PV.

praefectus (prefect)

Equestrian position of command, ranging from, for example, commanding a cohort in the Praetorian Guard to the post of *praefectus urbi*, 'prefect of Rome', or *praefectus praetorio*, 'praetorian prefect'.

princeps iuventutis

Imperial heir apparent, literally 'first amongst the young'.

protector/protectores

A new form of imperial bodyguard, introduced under Gallienus in the third century. They eventually took over the role of the Praetorian Guard.

quingenary

This term indicates a military cohort of a nominal five hundred in size, based on six centuries of eighty men = 480 plus officers.

sacellum

'Small shrine'. Found in numerous contexts, but most relevantly here in the headquarters building (*principia*) of a fort.

scholae palatinae

500-strong late Roman mounted imperial bodyguard created under Diocletian or Constantine.

sestertius

The principal base-metal (brass) coin of the imperial era, produced from 23 BC in the reign of Augustus up till the mid-third century and briefly revived under the Gallic emperor Postumus. The name was an anachronism and meant 'two and a half asses', dating from the time when ten asses equalled one denarius. By the reign of Augustus it had been revalued at four asses but the name remained. The sestertius was also the standard unit of measure when sums of money were cited, even though in reality larger amounts were probably paid in silver denarii due to the weight and size of the sestertius. Four sestertii were equivalent to one silver denarius. Diameter c. 33 mm, weight c. 23 g.

signifer

Standard-bearer, one for each century.

speculatores

Mounted praetorian scouts/spies. Originally organized into their own unit, the *cohors speculatorum*, under Antony, they were gradually absorbed into the praetorian cohorts but seem to have enjoyed special status as a result of being chosen by height. There were three hundred and they were under the command of the most senior centurion of the Guard, the *trecenarius*.

statores

Military police, attested in both the Praetorian Guard and the legions.

tesserarius

Officer of the watchword, for example *tesserarius speculatorum*, 'officer of the watch of the mounted praetorian scouts'.

testudo

'Tortoise'. A military formation when soldiers raised their shields for protection, allowing them to move as one in the face of enemy fire or bombardment.

trecenarius

Most senior centurion in the Praetorian Guard, commanding the three hundred *speculatores*. See Southern (2006), 117. A legionary *trecenarius'* relative position is uncertain, as the most senior centurion in a legion was the *primus pilus*. Serving as a *trecenarius* could be a springboard to accelerated promotion in the legionary centurionate.[3]

tribunus

The commander of a praetorian cohort or a unit of the *equites singulares Augusti* (however, the term was also applied in a variety of other contexts). Praetorian tribunes were of equestrian rank and had usually had significant military careers as senior centurions, moving on first to command a cohort in the night watch, then the urban cohorts, and finally the Guard. Tacitus states that Sejanus 'selected centurions and tribunes personally', but this is probably a point being made in order to criticize the notorious praetorian prefect.[4] In general, tribunes only turn up in the sources where they are implicated in conspiracies or similar illegal acts. Everyday duties included keeping praetorians in the barracks, putting right any cheating of measures, controlling access through the gates, checking on the sentries now and then, and approving the corn.[5] The tribune also supervised his personal staff. These men were drawn from the praetorians themselves; the post of *beneficiarius*, for example, indicates literally a man who benefited from the privileges of relief from normal duty, and higher pay.

urbana militia

See *cohortes urbanae* (above).

vigiles

See *cohortes vigilum*.

NOTES

Introduction

1. Herodian 2.3.4, 2.4.4; Dio 74.1.2, 5.4, 8.4 (Loeb IX pp. 123, 133, 137); Herodian 2.5.1–9.
2. Herodian 2.6.4.
3. Dio 63.9.1., where Dio describes the loathing felt for Otho because he had shown the Empire was for sale, and that the praetorians could make or break an emperor.
4. *SHA* (Didius Julianus) 2.5–6.
5. Herodian 2.6.14.
6. Dio 74.11.3, 74.17.5 (Loeb IX pp. 143 and 159); *SHA* (Didius Julianus) 6.1.
7. Cowan (2007) discusses the advantageous conditions praetorians enjoyed.
8. Gibbon (1776), chapter 5, paragraph 3.
9. Zosimus 2.17.2. See below, p. 264. *Panegyrici Latini* 12 21.2–3, 'Now they fight for you, those whom he has stripped of impious weapons and rearmed against barbarian foes. Now forgetful of the delights of the Circus Maximus, the theatre of Pompey and famous baths, they are stationed, along the length of the Rhine and Danube they watch [and] suppress plundering; lastly, after having been vanquished in the civil war they vie with the victors to be matched with the enemy', in Nixon and Rodgers (1994), 326.
10. Roman military equipment is an enormous subject in its own right and the focus of continuous and ongoing analysis and publication. Lorusso (2011) is a just an example of a vast canon of material, in this instance the reliability and accuracy of sculptural representations of praetorians. Bingham (2013) has a very useful bibliography and discussion of the available literature.
11. For the less common latter form, see Tacitus, *Histories* 31.
12. *ILS* 2671; *CIL* 5.923.
13. Virgil, *Aeneid* 1.257–96.
14. See also Keppie (1996) in Keppie (2000), 100.
15. Alston (1999), 191.
16. By the time of the Empire these qualifications were one million sestertii and 400,000 sestertii respectively.
17. Alston (1995), 95 and 97, and below, p. 255.
18. Especially Juvenal, *Satires* 16.7–17. See also Taylor (2011) on this.
19. Busch (2007), 320.

1 Evolution (44–31 BC)

1. *Res Gestae* 1.1.
2. Plutarch, *Pompey* 6, who says three legions were raised. Appian at 1.80 says only one was involved at this stage, but that two were added later.
3. Festus 223M: *praetoria cohors est dicta, quod a praetore non discedebat. Scipio enim Africanus primus fortissimum quemque delegit, qui ab eo in bello non discederent et cetero munere militiae vacarent et sesquiplex stipendium acciperent.*
4. Polybius 6.26.6, 31.1–3.
5. Plutarch, *Sertorius* 14.4–5; Appian, *Civil War* 112.1.
6. Sallust, *Catiline* 60.5.
7. Caesar, *Gallic War* 1.40, 42, 7.13.1; Suetonius, *Julius Caesar* 86.1.
8. *AE* 1934.152; Caesar, *Civil War* 1.75.
9. Cicero, *Letters to Quintus* 1.1.4, *Letters to his Friends* 15.4.7, *Letters to Atticus* 7.2.3.
10. Plutarch, *Caesar* 57. In this context Plutarch's reference to a bodyguard for Caesar probably means a small group of 'heavies' on hand rather than a significant body of troops but the point is not affected.
11. Appian, *Civil War* 3.5.
12. Appian, *Civil War* 3.40.
13. Bingham (2013), 12, regards it as 'undoubtedly' an exaggeration but does not substantiate the judgement.
14. Appian, *Civil War* 3.41–2.
15. Appian, *Civil War* 3.45, 52.
16. Cicero, *Letters to his Friends* 10.30; Appian, *Civil War*, 3.67–9.
17. Appian, *Civil War*, 3.67–9, 72–4.
18. Appian, *Civil War* 4.2–3, 5.
19. *Res Gestae* 1.3–4.
20. Appian, *Civil War* 4.7.
21. Appian, *Civil War* 4.16.
22. Appian, *Civil War* 4.115. The incongruous allocation of two thousand men to a single cohort is another example of the irregular nature of military units in this period. The position scarcely improves for later dates where much yet remains unresolved, even when the Praetorian Guard had been made into a permanent institution.
23. Roman Provincial Coinage 1651. A very similar type was produced between 286 and 293 in Britain by the usurper Carausius. See p. 261.
24. Appian, *Civil War* 5.3. Lepidus took no portion because at this point he had been accused of betraying the triumvirate to Sextus Pompeius, son of Pompey the Great, who was prosecuting a naval war against the triumvirs.
25. Suetonius, *Augustus* 14; Appian, *Civil War* 5.24.
26. Plutarch, *Antony* 39.2.
27. Suetonius, *Augustus* 14.
28. Plutarch, *Antony* 53.1–2, 36.1.
29. Appian, *Civil War* 5.68. The problem with bringing in grain to Ostia was exacerbated by the Tiber silting up, and was not resolved until Claudius commissioned a new harbour. See below, p. 112.
30. Reece (2002), 14; *Natural History* 33.132. In fact such an alloy is impossible due to their different melting points.
31. See below p. 155 where *speculatores* in Otho's bodyguard are discussed (Tacitus, *Histories* 2.11). Also, Durry (1938), 108.
32. The information, *octo legiones classi superpositae, absque cohortibus quinque praetoriis*, is from Orosius 6.19.8, a fifth-century source and thus so long after the event it is debatable whether it can be relied on. Everitt (2006), 182, however, repeats this information without comment.

2 Foundation (31 BC–AD 14)

1. Dio 57.3.2, referring to 'the soldiers in Italy', which obviously included the praetorians.
2. *Res Gestae* 3.3; Dio 55.23.2, and 55.24.5; Webster (1996) 44, n.6. See also below, p. 29; Tacitus, *Annals* 4.5; Le Bohec (2000), 21; Campbell (1994), 42.
3. Dio 55.24.5; Tacitus *Annals* 4.5.3.
4. Scheidel (2005), 9–10; Durry (1938), 240; Keppie (1996), 117.
5. Durry (1938), 251–7, believed praetorians were less likely to come from better-off families, unlike Passerini (1939), 159–71.
6. For example, Durry (1938), 86, and Cowan (2014), 30, 'Dio . . . retrojecting the strength of the Severan cohorts onto the Augustan era'; Rankov (1994), 8, 'Dio anachronistically attributes 10,000 men in ten cohorts to Augustus' Guard'. Swan (2004) 171, n. 182, suggests that Dio had provided figures from his own day 'to smooth the path' for his readers. Menéndez Argüín (2006), 21, simply states quingenary cohorts to have been a fact, based on the idea that Augustus deliberately avoided 'for political reasons' the number ten so that the Guard could not be equated with a legion (which had ten cohorts). This is purely speculative – there is no evidence to substantiate this interpretation. Also, Cowan (2014), 29, says, 'from the time of Augustus to Otho, the cohorts had been quingenary – each 500 strong, the norm for the period', and that Tacitus 'emphasizes the milliary size' (*Histories* 2.93) and therefore must be distinguishing it from the 'norm'. The alternative is that Tacitus is simply being descriptive. There is no word or phrase in the Latin to suggest it is being specially emphasized.
7. It must be stressed that milliary cohorts are not specifically attested at this date, other than in Dio's reference; Keppie (2000), 105. The evidence for the X–XII cohorts in the Julio-Claudian era is discussed at pp. 91 and 92, with particular reference to the careers of Aulus Virgius Marsus and Gaius Gavius Silvanus; *ILS* 1993; *CIL* 16.21; Campbell (1994), 199–200, no. 327. This diploma is also discussed below (p. 178) with respect to the granting of legal marriage rights to veteran praetorians. For the Vitellian Guard, see Tacitus, *Histories* 2.93; see also below, p. 160.
8. Dio 55.8.7.
9. Birley (1966), 55. Under Vitellius (Tacitus, *Histories* 2.94) they were certainly milliary and the evidence of Pseudo-Hyginus, *On the Fortification of Camps* 6, by the early third century is that a praetorian cohort took up twice the space of a regular legionary cohort. Philo, *Embassy to Gaius (Caligula)*, 30–1, specifically refers to the centurion and tribune of 'a thousand' when clearly describing officers of the Guard in the year 40. Philo was personally in Rome on the embassy.
10. Bingham (2013), 75, discusses the vast accommodation provision that appears to have been feasible, based on the area of the camp and the availability of two-storied barracks.
11. For example, Passerini (1939), 44–53, and Keppie (2000), 105.
12. For example, the II legion Augusta commemorated its foundation under Augustus. Praetorian cohorts did sometimes adopt loyalist epithets in the third century. See p. 253.
13. Suetonius, *Augustus* 74; Tacitus, *Histories* 2.11, describing Otho's bodyguard; Caius Fabius Crispus, a Carthaginian praetorian buried in Rome, is described on his tombstone as having been a '*speculator* of the VI praetorian cohort', rather than having been a member of a specific *cohors speculatorum*, *CIL* 6.2607. Conversely, Bingham (2013), 89, suggests that this may be a later development and that to begin with there was a separate *cohors speculatorum*. Crispus' Carthaginian origin suggests he did not join the praetorians until after Severus' reform of 193.
14. Dio 53.11 for 27 BC; Tacitus, *Annals* 1.17.6: a denarius was equivalent to four sestertii and sixteen asses; Dio 67.3.5, and also Suetonius, *Domitian* 7 who cites the equivalent in gold. The rise was three gold *aurei*, equivalent to 75 denarii; Dio 56.32.2. The figure of 10 asses per day for a legionary in 14 comes from Tacitus' reference (Annals 1.17.4) to the mutinying Pannonian legions who were demanding a rise to 'a denarius (sixteen asses) a day' and therefore clearly the equivalent of half a praetorian's pay.

15. Dio 54.25.6 and 55.23.1; see below, p. 55 for AD 14; 'There is no consistency in the ratio given'. Bingham (2013), 67.

16. For the evidence from Egypt, see Christiansen (2004), 24–5. Tacitus says at *Annals* 1.17.5–6 that one of the demands of the mutinying Pannonian legions in 14 was that they be 'paid in their own camp', suggesting that they were not at the time receiving their wages. In Britain, on 7 November 83, one legionary loaned another 100 denarii. Evidently, while one was short of cash, the other had a store of bullion coin he was prepared to put out to interest (see *Britannia* XXIII, 1992, 147–9). As one might expect, individual circumstances could vary wildly. Didius Julianus (193) is one of the best examples of an emperor who fell soon after promising a vast accession donative to the praetorians that he was unable to pay.

17. Durry (1938), 133.

18. From *evocatio*, 'a calling forth'. For their carrying of a rod in the manner of centurions, see Dio 55.24.8. See, for example, Herodian 7.11.2 on the older praetorians left in Rome while the rest of the Guard was fighting with Maximinus in 238; Dio 53.25.

19. See Campbell (1994), 199–200, no. 327 (*ILS* 1993, dated to AD 76). No mention of praetorian prefects or tribunes is made on praetorian diplomas either; Asper's standard is illustrated in Rankov (1994), 25.

20. Tacitus, *Annals* 4.5.3. For the Severan reorganization, see p. 221. Dio, however, states that by AD 9 a number of Gauls and Germans ('Keltoi') were serving in the Praetorian Guard (56.23.4). Rankov (1994), 8, gives 15–32 as the age band for recruitment based on epigraphic evidence.

21. See Scheidel (2005), 5, table 2 (based on Phang (2001)). The reasons for this are discussed below at p. 205.

22. *ILS* 2028.

23. See below, p. 66.

24. Dio 55.24.7. See Speidel (1994), 31–5. Tacitus says that in 23 the urban cohorts were three in number (*Annals* 4.5.3); for Germans/Batavians see, for example, Tacitus, *Annals* 1.24.2, discussed below, p. 36. The tombstones of members of Nero's German bodyguard, *corporis custodes*, describe them as Batavian and German (see Plate 12 for an example, *AE* 1952, 148). Sherk (1988), no. 76; Suetonius, *Caligula* 55.2, 58.3. Swan (2004), 171, discusses in some detail these units and others, in particular how Galba disbanded the German guards and how Trajan reformed them.

25. Tacitus, *Annals* 15.58.3; for AD 9, see below, p. 36; Suetonius, *Galba* 12; Swan (2004), 171; and Dio 55.24.8. For the Trajanic *equites singulares Augusti*, see p. 190.

26. Suetonius, *Augustus* 49.1: 'he never allowed more than three cohorts to remain in the city and even those were without forts. The remainder he sent to winter and summer quarters in neighbouring towns around [Rome].' Suetonius does not use the word praetorian; he calls the Guard *custodia*, literally 'the watch' or 'the guard'.

27. Luttwak (1976), 17.

28. Suetonius, *Augustus* 7.

29. *Tamquam vetere re publica* (*Annals* 1.7.3.)

30. Gibbon (1776), chapter 5, paragraph 2.

31. *Annals* 3.56.

32. Dio 53.12 (and also Suetonius, *Augustus* 47.1). The other provinces, such as Africa and Greece, believed by Augustus to be less risky, were to be controlled by the senate and the people.

33. *Annals* 1–2.

34. Virgil, *Aeneid* 1.278.

35. Alston (1995), *passim*.

36. Keppie (2000), 113. For Ostia, see below and the case of the praetorian killed putting out a fire there. For Nuceria and evidence of a camp there in AD 56, see p. 126.

37. Pliny the Elder, *Natural History* 7.82. Vinnius Valens might also have been commemorated by Horace in Augustan times, who amused himself with the idea that 'Vinius [sic] Asina' might have to carry the 'heavy load of my paper' (i.e. his poetry) to the emperor (*Letters* 1.13). It is only an assumption that they were one and the same man, one made for example by Cowan (2014), 45. Horace uses a different form of the name and makes no reference to his being a praetorian or even being a soldier, as well as not making any specially obvious reference to exceptional strength.

38. Virgil, *Aeneid* 1.291; *Eclogues* 4.6–7.

39. Trajan's letters to Pliny the Younger during the latter's time as governor of Bithynia and Pontus show a certain amount of benign frustration at having to field endless queries about administrative affairs.

40. Estimated at approximately 500,000 by the time of Augustus, when there were 200,000 households in receipt of a monthly grain ration (Claridge 2010, 14).

41. Tacitus, *Annals* 1.7.5.

42. Cassius Dio 54.3–4. See also Suetonius, *Tiberius* 8.

43. Cassius Dio 54.15.1

44. *Annals* 1.2.1

45. *RIC* 251 (Octavian).

46. Suetonius, *Augustus* 49.1.

47. Durry (1938), 10; Passerini (1939), 210.

48. For example, see Tacitus, *Annals* 16.27.1 for an incident during the reign of Nero, the *Histories* 1.38 where Otho referred to Galba's praetorian escort in the palace dressed in *togata*, i.e. civilian dress. Also, Martial, *Epigrams* 6.76. See also p. 184 for a discussion of the evidence in the late first and early second centuries.

49. *Res Gestae* 8.5; *Aeneid* 1.282, cited by Suetonius, *Augustus* 40.5.

50. A number of these depictions are illustrated by Sumner (2004), 13, 46 and plate F3.

51. Bingham (2013), 19, suggests that a reluctance to create such a post earlier might have been connected with waiting until a point when the presence of the troops had become normal for the people of Rome. This is possible but it is surely the case that creating a commander of the Praetorian Guard was, to begin with, a very high-risk option and a far greater concern. Indeed, the career of Sejanus under Tiberius proves the point amply.

52. Cassius Dio 52.24–5.

53. A similar point is made by Suetonius when commenting on Augustus' policy of absorbing more men into the administration of the state. See *Augustus* 37.1. See also Durry (1938), 75.

54. Suetonius, *Augustus* 46.

55. 50.55.9–10.

56. Bingham (2013), 20, regards this as the primary explanation, echoing Dessau (1924) 1, 257.

57. Pers. comm., D. Kennedy (2015).

58. *ILS* 4902. See also Syme (1989), 301 and n. 10; ibid., n. 11; and *ILS* 171.

59. See chapter 3.

60. Durry (1938), 143.

61. Keppie (2000),111,113; Valens: *ILS* 2648; Larcianus *AE* 1962.312. See also, Spaul (1994), 247. Dobson and Breeze (1969) support the idea that Valens' career was atypical, unlike Durry (1938), 133, who thought the opposite.

62. For a discussion of how the urban cohorts were numbered, see below, p. 91 in connection with an inscription from Marruvium that might be evidence the urban cohorts were numbered in the same sequence as the praetorian cohorts; Keppie (2000), 108; Tacitus, *Annals* 4.5.3, *Histories* 2.93.

63. On Hitler's use of rivalry, see Rees (1997), 79; the ratio of urban cohort pay is implicit from the terms of Augustus' will (Suetonius, *Augustus* 101). See Table 1, Appendix 2. Keppie (2000), 108, conversely concludes that 'it seems probable' the praetorians and

urban cohorts were paid the same until somewhere between AD 6 and 14, when the former's pay was doubled.

64. The term *cohortes vigilum* means literally 'the cohorts of watchmen'; unlike the *cohors praetoria, vigilum* is the genitive plural form of the noun *vigil*, and not an adjective, and thus retains its masculine form; on the situation in 7 BC, see Dio 55.8.6; on the distribution of the *vigiles,* see Suetonius, *Augustus* 25.2; Strabo 5.3.7; Dio 26.4 (that freedmen were used); Suetonius, *Augustus* 30.1 (describing their distribution).
65. Rainbird (1976), 2.
66. See, for example, Sertorius Macro, below, p. 85.
67. *CIL* 6.1057; Rainbird (1976), 217.
68. These are the figures cited, without substantiation, by Campbell (1994), 38. The figures are simply: 7 × 80 = 560, 560 × 7 = 3,920.
69. The dead praetorian is recorded on *ILS* 9494; Campbell (1994), 39, no. 61; Suetonius, *Claudius* 25.2.
70. Dio 56.23.1–4.
71. Suetonius, *Augustus* 49.1. Tacitus, Annals 1.17.5, and at 1.24.1–2, refers to the praetorian cohorts, and the Germans being on hand soon after Augustus' death.
72. There is no reference that confirms if the Guard was involved in accompanying Augustus on any of these absences.
73. Frontinus, *Aqueducts of Rome* 1.10.
74. See Rossini (2009), 46ff.
75. 'He loved and esteemed her to the end without a rival.' Suetonius, *Augustus* 62.2.
76. Velleius Paterculus 2.93.
77. Augustus, *Res Gestae* 14; *RIC* 207 (and also on gold, *RIC* 206).
78. Tacitus, *Annals* 1.3.4, who suggested that Livia was behind the banishment in order to remove the threat he posed to her son Tiberius in succeeding Augustus.
79. For example, Tacitus, *Annals*, 1.3.3.
80. Levick (1999), 41. See also Pliny, *Natural History* 7.149.

3 Ambition (14–37)

1. Suetonius, *Tiberius* 22, suggests it was either a letter from Augustus or one written by Livia pretending to be Augustus and possibly with the full knowledge of Tiberius.
2. Tacitus, *Annals* 1.6.1–2.
3. Sextus Pompeius is not to be confused with the general who fought the triumvirs in the 30s BC. The consul of 14 appears to have been a descendant of Sextus Pompeius, uncle of Caesar's co-triumvir; Tacitus, *Annals* 1.7.
4. Dio provides the figures at 56.32.2, as does Tacitus, *Annals* 1.8.2. Discussed also by Goldsworthy (2003), 95; Swan (2004), 170; and Bingham (2013), 67.
5. Tacitus, *Annals* 1.17.1–6. His figures were rounded. See pp. 32 and 275.
6. Suetonius, *Tiberius* 24; Tacitus, *Annals* 1.7.5.
7. Suetonius, *Tiberius* 25. The rate of pay for the praetorians is recorded by Dio (53.11).
8. Suetonius, *Augustus* 99 (citing the number of praetorians involved, and that Augustus had had a premonition of this); Tacitus, *Annals* 1.8.7; Levick (1999), 64. See also below where this mutiny is discussed in more detail.
9. Tacitus, *Annals* 2.43.6.
10. Tacitus, *Annals* 1.24.2. It has been thought possible that an inscription, *ILS* 8996, refers to Seius Strabo and is evidence that the family was very wealthy; see, for example, Alston (1998), 39. Seager (2005), disputes this (p. 267, n. 10.); on Strabo's promotion Dio 57.19.6; on the number of prefects, the majority of known prefects appear to have ruled on their own; see Absil (1997), 87–95; Terentius' defence is at Tacitus, *Annals* 6.8.1–2; Dio on Plautianus and Sejanus is at 60.14.1.

11. Tacitus, *Annals* 4.2. The quotation is in the accusative, since Sejanus was the object of the sentence. The term thus would be *socius laborum*. The same term, in Greek, is also given by Dio at 58.4.3.
12. Tacitus, *Annals* 1.16.2, and 19.4-5.
13. On collecting the cohorts from Aquileia, see Keppie (2000), 113; for the praetorian cavalry and German troops see Tacitus, *Annals* 1.24.2, presumably what Dio (55.24) called the Batavian cavalry. See also p. 36; for the mutiny, Tacitus, *Annals* 1.27.1 and 1.30.1.
14. For the incident in 15 see Tacitus, *Annals* 1.77; on Gallus see Alston (1998), 37; Tacitus, *Annals* 1.77. His mother may have been a daughter of Agrippa, but his wife Domitia was a cousin of Germanicus.
15. Tacitus, *Annals* 2.30-1.
16. Tacitus, *Annals* on court rivalry, 2.44.1, 2.43.5; quashing of mutinies, 1.31ff; guardians, 2.41; mutiny collapse, 1.49.3. Caligula's nickname ('Little Boots') was awarded by soldiers who admired the way he was dressed in a miniature military uniform as a child (Suetonius, *Caligula* 9). Although he was never officially known as Caligula, it has been commonplace to call him this in modern times, so he is referred to by this name here too.
17. Tacitus, *Annals* 1.51.1, 1.61, 2.16.3.
18. Tacitus, *Annals* 2.26, 2.41.2.
19. Tacitus alleges that Piso, amongst other crimes, had appointed his own clients and other low life to the centurionate and tribuneships in the Syrian legions, *Annals* 2.55.5; 2.57.3-4; 2.69; 2.75; 3.9; 3.15. Tacitus also records an allegation that Piso had been murdered.
20. Tacitus, *Annals* 3.2.
21. Durry (1938), 277. In later years both Agrippina the Younger (Claudius, Nero) and Julia Domna (Septimius Severus, Caracalla) seemed to regard it as an automatic entitlement and badge of their status.
22. Tacitus 3.35 *passim*.
23. Tacitus, *Annals* 3.72.2-4. The Great Fire of Rome in 64 under Nero, forty-two years later, would show how vulnerable the city remained.
24. Tacitus, *Annals* 4.2.1.
25. Tacitus, *Annals* 4.7.2.
26. Dio 57.19.6.
27. The standard of the III praetorian cohort, depicted on the late first-century tomb of Marcus Pompeius Asper, shows a prominent scorpion above the inscription COH.III.PR; Rankov (1994), 25-6.
28. Webster (1996), 157.
29. Tacitus, *Annals* 4.7.1; 4.3.2; Dio 58.3.8.
30. Tacitus, *Annals* 4.8.1, 4.10.2.
31. For Tiberius' trust, see Tacitus, *Annals* 4.10-11.
32. Alston (1998), 41, counsels against taking the murder allegations too easily at face value.
33. For the divorce of Apicata see *Annals* 4.3.5.
34. Tacitus, *Annals* 4.1.2.
35. Levick (1999), 53; Barrett (1989), 17; Tacitus, *Annals* 4.58.1; Alston (1998), 39.
36. *Annals* 4.27.1.
37. Tacitus, *Annals* 4.28. Bingham (2013), 87, says that Lupus was ineffectual. It is quite clear from Tacitus, however, that Lupus suppressed the revolt in its entirety and that Staius merely mopped up.
38. See especially Tacitus, *Annals* 1.69.4, where it is stated that her influence exceeded that of 'legates', which could mean either legionary commanders or provincial governors.
39. Tacitus, *Annals* 4.17.1-3.
40. Tacitus, *Annals* 4.18.1-19.1.

NOTES to pp. 77–87

41. Tacitus, *Annals* 4.26.1–2.
42. Dio 57.24.5.
43. Tacitus, *Annals* 4.34.1.
44. Seneca, *ad Marciam* 22.4. Marcia was Cremutius Cordus' daughter.
45. Tacitus, *Annals* 4.39 *passim*.
46. Tacitus, *Annals* 4.40.4.
47. Tacitus, *Annals* 4.53–4 *passim*.
48. Tacitus, *Annals* 4.58–60 *passim*.
49. Tacitus, *Annals* 4.68.2, 74.2; Juvenal, *Satires* 16.7–17.
50. For the praetorian peacock thief, see Suetonius, *Tiberius* 60; Tacitus, *Annals* 4.67.4, 5.3, 5.4.3.
51. Dio 58.2.7.
52. Dio 58.4.1–2.
53. Dio 58.4.3; Josephus, *Jewish Antiquities* 18.182. See also Durry (1938), 364, and Passerini (1939), 277, for Sejanus' status as consul and prefect.
54. *RPC* (Bilbilis) I.398. After Sejanus' fall his name was often defaced on this issue. It was common practice for the names of current consuls in Rome to be used as a method of denoting a date, especially in provincial contexts.
55. Dio 58.4.1–4. An *imago* meant a representation or likeness and in this context an honorific one used in cult rituals.
56. *ILS* 6044. The text is given in various locations, such as Braund (1985), 48, no. 102, and Ehrenburg and Jones (1976), no. 53.
57. Suetonius, *Tiberius* 54, and Dio 58.8.1 and 4.
58. On Macro's prefecture of the Guard by 33, see Tacitus, *Annals* 6.15.2; Macro's name survives on an inscription from the amphitheatre at Alba Fucens, *AE* (1957), 250. The inscription can only be dated to the latter part of the reign of Tiberius. It states that Macro was prefect of the *vigiles* and later prefect of the Praetorian Guard, but supplies no other supporting detail. Bingham (2013), 211 n. 239, discusses the complications of the epigraphic evidence.
59. For Laco, see Dio 58.9.3. The date of Sejanus' death is recorded as 18 October 31 on the Ostian Calendar. Braund (1985), 47, no. 98.
60. The Temple of Apollo Palatinus, dedicated in 28 BC. What is left of its ruinous podium lies immediately next to the so-called 'House of Augustus' on the Palatine Hill. See Claridge (2010), 130 fig. 51, and 142.
61. Dio 58.10 ff.
62. Dio 58.10.8.
63. The Temple of Concordia Augusta. Its remains lie immediately north-west of the much later Arch of Septimius Severus at the foot of the Capitoline Hill, close to where the Gemonian Stairs stood. Claridge (2010), 62 fig. 1, and 80 fig. 21.
64. For the Gemonian Stairs, see Claridge (2010), 261; Strabo the Younger was strangled. Recorded on the Ostian Calendar as having happened on 24 October, six days after Sejanus was killed. Braund (1985), 47, no. 98.
65. Levick (1999), 161, and Tacitus, *Annals* 4.3.5. Apicata's suicide is recorded on the Ostian Calendar as having occurred on 26 October. Braund (1985), 47, no. 98.
66. For Junilla see Tacitus, *Annals* 5.9.1–2. Her name is recorded on the Ostian Calendar, which adds that her body and that of her brother Capito Aelianus were dumped on the Gemonian Stairs. Braund (1985), 47, no. 98; for the rest of the family, the relevant section of Tacitus is not extant but a retrospective reference at 5.7.2 makes it clear that Blaesus had been a victim.
67. Dio reports both versions at 58.11.7.
68. *Classical Numismatic Group* Auction Triton XVIII (January 2015), Lot no. 869.
69. Dio 58.12.3, and 7.

296

70. Dio 58.12.2.
71. Dio 58.13 *passim.*
72. Dio 58.18.1 and 3. Suetonius, *Tiberius* 48.2 supplies the sum awarded to each praetorian 'for not taking sides with Sejanus'.
73. Tacitus, *Annals* 6.3.2. The word for commander used is *imperator*, technically 'general' or 'commanding officer'. Tiberius, notwithstanding the existence of the praetorian prefect, surely meant himself.
74. Tacitus, *Annals* 6.9.3. The tribune was called Celsus. We may assume with good reason then that tribunes, and perhaps centurions, of the Praetorian Guard also came forward with evidence against Sejanus' associates; for Marcus Terentius, see *Annals* 6.8, *passim*. So impressive was the honesty of his speech that his accusers were punished instead.
75. Suetonius, *Claudius* 6.
76. Tacitus, *Annals* 6.19.2–3, and 23.2.
77. *ILS* 157. Sherk (1988), no. 40 C.
78. Sherk (1988), no. 40 B.
79. Tacitus, *Annals* 6.15.2–3.
80. Tacitus, *Annals* 6.20.1; Suetonius, *Caligula* 12.2, 26.1. Ennia is also known as Ennia Naevia.
81. Tacitus, *Annals* 6.46.4.
82. Tacitus, *Annals* 6.47.2–3, for example Lucius Arruntius.
83. Tacitus, *Annals* 6.48.2.
84. Tacitus, *Annals* 6.50.5; Dio 58.28.3.
85. *AE* 1978.286, created during Tiberius' reign, was dedicated to Aulus Virgius Marsus who served with both the IIII and XI cohorts as military tribune of the guard. See also Keppie (2000), 109.
86. Swan (2004), 171 and Keppie (2000), 105. For the XVI urban cohort see the career of Marcus Vettius Valens in Campbell (1994), 51 no. 90. *ILS* 9200 (Baalbek, Syria) lists an equestrian's career under the Flavians, which included being a tribune in the XIII urban cohort. For there being four urban cohorts by 69, see Tacitus, *Histories* 2.93.
87. *AE* 1978.20 and Keppie (2000), 107. See also Campbell (1994), 54, no. 96.
88. Keppie (2000), 108, and n. 87, citing a number of instances of cohorts where the unit, praetorian or urban, is not specified, such as Lucius Cassius Pollia, 'soldier of the XII cohort' (*CIL* 5.905).
89. Discussed below, p. 113.
90. Echols (1968), 380.
91. Suetonius, *Augustus* 101; the evidence for this similar treatment is summarized by Keppie (2000), 108.

4 Making History (37–51)

1. Suetonius, *Claudius* 30, 5 and 7 respectively. Until he was elevated to the senate by Caligula in 37, Claudius was of equestrian status (Dio 59.6.6.).
2. Suetonius, *Caligula* 58.
3. Suetonius, *Claudius* 10.
4. Josephus, *Jewish Antiquities* 19.14–15.
5. The nocturnal arrival is recorded by Dio 59.3.7. The military escort is recorded on an inscription from Ostia, which says that Tiberius' body arrived on 29 March [37] (Smallwood (1967), no. 31). For how Macro was complicit in his wife's affair with Caligula, see the previous chapter.
6. Dio 59.1.2.
7. Dio 59.1.3. and 59.8.1.
8. Suetonius, *Caligula* 13, 14.

9. *RIC* 56. The coin is stylistically dated to the reign of Caligula and also by the coincidence of the legend to the reference in Suetonius.
10. For Caligula's payout, see Dio 59.2.1; the AD LOCVT coin is *RIC* 40.
11. A vast drum-shaped tomb in the Field of Mars which housed the remains of Augustus and some of his family, and extant today in Rome, though in a ruinous state. Agrippina's tombstone is *AE* (1994), 234; *CIL* 6.40372. The tombstone is on display in the Capitoline Museum. For Antonia, see Dio 59.3.4.
12. These types are most conveniently accessed in Sear (2000), 354–62.
13. Philo, *Embassy to Gaius (Caligula)* 30.
14. Dio 59.8.1; Suetonius, *Caligula* 23.3; Philo, *Embassy to Gaius (Caligula)* 30–1; Dio 59.11.2.
15. Suetonius, *Caligula* 24.1; Dio 59.3.6, and 59.22.5–7. See below for Caligula's expedition. Allegations of incest with sisters had precedent as a method for damaging someone's reputation, for example Publius Clodius Pulcher in the first century BC.
16. Josephus, *Jewish Antiquities* 19.204; Suetonius, *Caligula* 24; Dio 59.3.6. For the coin, see *RIC* (Caligula) 33.
17. Dio 59.9.5.
18. Dio 59.10.6; on Caligula's rationality see, for example, Bingham (2013), 29.
19. Suetonius, *Caligula* 19.2; for these chariots, *esseda*, in a theatrical context, see Horace, *Letters* 2.1.192; for praetorians as tax collectors, see Suetonius, *Caligula* 40.1.
20. On elections, see Suetonius, *Caligula* 16.2; for the attitude of senators, see Dio 59.14.6; on Incitatus, see Dio 59.14.7. Alston (1998), 66, has an interesting discussion about this memorable anecdote which is often referred to nowadays as if the horse had actually been made a consul, which is not the case; for arbitrary rule, see Dio 59.4.6; his relationship with the people, see Dio 59.13.3.
21. Suetonius, *Caligula* 56.1 refers to prefects in the plural when describing the final plot to kill Caligula, as does Dio at 59.25.7. Clemens is named by Tacitus (*Histories* 6.68.2) when describing how Arrecinus Clemens' son of the same name was appointed to the same post in 68; the suggestion that a Lucius Arruntius Stella was the other prefect is included in Barrett (2015), 253 and n. 39, in the second edition of his biography of Gaius (Caligula), but this is very uncertain; Josephus, *Jewish Antiquities,* 19.37.
22. Suetonius, *Caligula* 26.5, 27.4. It is not in any sense irrelevant here to note the behaviour of the youthful North Korean leader, Kim Jong-un, and his predilection for increasingly bizarre methods of execution as widely reported in 2015.
23. On his cult, see Dio 59.4.4; his childhood fame, Suetonius, *Caligula* 22.1.
24. Dio 59.26.5–10. It seems that this had occurred early enough to include the time when his sisters were available, since he would dress as a god to seduce them. See also ibid. 59.28.5 and Suetonius, *Caligula* 22.2.
25. Dio 59.28.5–6. Caesonia was pregnant when Caligula married her, divorcing his first wife Lollia Paulina who had failed to bear a child. For the fee paid by Claudius, see Suetonius, *Claudius* 9.
26. For example, at Didyma and Miletus in Asia Minor, recorded on an inscription from the Temple of Caligula at Didyma c. 40–1. Sherk (1988), no. 43.
27. For the Batavians, see Suetonius, *Caligula* 43.1. Augustus' Batavians had been disbanded after the disaster of AD 9; for Gaetulicus, see Dio 59.22.5; for Lepidus, see Seneca *Letters* 4.7 (sometimes given as 1.4.7).
28. Barrett (1989), 104, citing the Arval record of 27 October 39, which refers to Gaetulicus' *nefaria consilia*, 'wicked plots'. The conspiracy is also referred to by Suetonius at *Vespasian* 2.3. Barrett (1989), 107, argues that Lepidus was not in Germany. Bingham (2013), 95, assumes that he was.
29. Dio 59.21.2–3.
30. Suetonius, *Caligula* 43 and 45.

31. For the *speculatores*, see Suetonius, *Caligula* 43.2; and see 25.3 for Caligula parading his wife Caesonia to his military escort.
32. Dio 59.26.3.
33. *ILS* 2032; *CIL* 6.2767.
34. Keppie (2000), 109, n. 88, rejects Montanus as satisfactory evidence for a XII cohort under Caligula, made originally by Syme reviewing Durry (1938), in *JRS* 29 (1939), 243, and prefers the idea that an expansion occurred under Claudius. See below for the career of Gaius Gavius Silvanus and evidence of the XII cohort by 65. See also Durry (1938), 78 for a list of inscriptions referring to the XI and XII cohorts.
35. Dio 59.22.5.
36. The conspirators are named by Dio 59.29.1 (vol. VII, pp. 357–9) and Josephus, *Jewish Antiquities* 19.47ff and 19.64 (vol. XII, p. 239ff); for Chaerea's resentment and the wider spread of the conspiracy, see Dio 59.29.2; Caligula's assassination is at Josephus, *Jewish Antiquities* 19.84–114, Suetonius, *Caligula* 58.2–3 and Dio 59.29.6–7.
37. A Euarestus Arruntius is mentioned by Josephus, *Jewish Antiquities* 19.145 acting to calm the Germans down, but is described only as a highly successful professional auctioneer whose prestige and wealth had enabled him to do much as he pleased.
38. Dio 59.30.2–3 and 60.1.1; the three (presumably) urban cohorts are referred to by Josephus, *Jewish War* 2.11.1. Suetonius states that the 'senate and urban cohorts' had taken possession of the forum and Capitol (*Claudius* 10.30). Saturninus is named as prefect of the city by Pliny, *Natural History* 7.14.62. See also Levick (1990), 31.
39. Dio 60.1.3; Josephus, *Jewish Antiquities* 19.162, 186–8.
40. Josephus, *Jewish Antiquities* 19.214ff.
41. Josephus, *Jewish Antiquities* 19.223.
42. On the argument that praetorians could fight, see Josephus, *Jewish Antiquities* 19.241–5; on the vote for Claudius, see Dio 60.1.4. Other candidates were considered but rejected. See Levick (1990), 32; on bribery to secure the Guard, see Suetonius, *Claudius* 10.4. Or 20,000 according to Josephus, *Jewish Antiquities* 19.247 (giving 'five thousand drachmas', equivalent to 20,000 sestertii). The same amount appears to have been promised to the rest of the army.
43. Suetonius, *Claudius* 10.1.
44. Josephus, *Jewish Antiquities* 19.246 and *Jewish War* 2.11.2–3.
45. Josephus, *Jewish Antiquities* 19.37. See also Jung (1972), 384, and Levick (1990), 34,
46. Josephus, *Jewish Antiquities* 19.268–9.
47. Dio 60.18.4. A man of the same name was a high-ranking centurion in Pannonia in 14, Tacitus *Annals* 1.29.2. The Claudian Catonius Justus is just conceivably the same person.
48. Josephus, *Jewish Antiquities* 19.268–9, Dio 60.3.2, 4–5.
49. For example, Alston (1998), 78, cites Dio 60.3.2–3 as the authority for this claim. In fact Dio makes two points: firstly, that Claudius went to the senate after thirty days and, secondly, that in a general sense Claudius exercised caution, including having soldiers present at banquets; for bringing the prefect and tribunes in to the senate, see Suetonius, *Claudius* 12.1
50. *RIC* 25 and 11 respectively. Note also that Suetonius used the phrase *Receptus intra vallumi*, 'received within the rampart', when referring to Claudius going to the praetorian camp when he left the palace with the Guard. There is some debate about the exact expansion of the legends, but the essential meaning seems beyond doubt. See also Sutherland (1974), 154, and figs 284–5.
51. Hekster (2007), 351.
52. Suetonius, *Claudius* 21.3–4.
53. Some authorities consider this to be the most likely context. For example, Menéndez Argüín (2006), 22, and Keppie (2000), 109.
54. *RIC* 115, 95 and 97 respectively. For Saturninus, see above, p. 106.

55. Barrett (1989), 172.
56. Suetonius, *Claudius* 25.1.
57. On the incorporation of Gaulish senators, Tacitus, *Annals* 11.23–5; for the Alpine tribes, *CIL* 5.5050, *AE* 1983, 445; cited in Lewis and Reinhold (1955), 130–1.
58. Strabo, *Geography* 5.3.5; Suetonius, *Claudius* 18, 20; Pliny, *Natural History* 9.15.
59. Suetonius, *Claudius* 17; on Silvanus, *ILS* 2701 (Turin). *CIL* 5.7003, Sherk (1988), no. 49 A, specifying [TRI]BUNO COH XII PRAETOR(IAE). For Silvanus as an *evocatus* in Britain, see Maxfield and Dobson (2006), 30, no. 14. His death from suicide in 65 is recorded by Tacitus, *Annals* 15.71; Valens is at *ILS* 2648 (Rimini); the entry to Colchester is at Dio 60.21. Thorne (2007), 218, states that praetorians accompanied Claudius into Colchester. This is not mentioned by Dio, our only source for the occasion.
60. Dio 60.30.3 and Tacitus, *Annals* 12.27–30.
61. On Livia, see Dio 60.5.1–2; Caligula's sisters are at Dio 60.4.1, 8.5, and 61.10.1. Seneca was exiled too, and was not allowed to return until after Julia Livilla was dead; the coins are most easily explored in Sear (2000), 372–7.
62. Tacitus, *Annals* 11.1–2, and 4.3. Rufrius Crispinus was also at some time married to Nero's mistress and later wife, Poppaea Sabina. Tacitus, *Annals* 13.45.4.
63. Tacitus, *Annals* 11.26ff.
64. Tacitus, *Annals* 11.33, calling him Geta. A fuller version of his name is supplied at 11.31.1. Rufrius Crispinus, the other prefect, is named at 11.1.3.
65. Suetonius, *Claudius* 26.2.
66. Tacitus, *Annals* 11.35.1–3, 38.1.
67. The barracks of the *vigiles* at Ostia are extant and may still be visited. For an Augustan praetorian engaged in putting out a fire at Ostia, see p. 57.
68. Tacitus, *Annals* 12.1–2.
69. Tacitus, *Annals* 12.6–7. Lucius Vitellius was the father of the future emperor Vitellius.
70. Tacitus, *Annals* 12.4.1–3, 8.1.
71. Tacitus, *Annals* 12.36–7.
72. For Nero's new title, see Tacitus, *Annals* 12.25–6. Coins of Nero struck under Claudius record these titles, for example *RIC* (Claudius), 76; for the handout, see Suetonius, *Nero* 7.2.
73. Dio 61.32.6; Tacitus, *Annals* 12.42.1
74. On the removal of Sosibius, see Dio 61.35.2–6 (Loeb VIII p. 21), for Nero, see 61.33.10–11 (p. 27).

5 A Tale of Two Prefects (51–68)

1. Nero 31; http://usatoday30.usatoday.com/tech/science/discoveries/2009–09–29–nero_N.htm.
2. *ILS* 1321. Sherk (1988), no. 57. Burrus presumably also served as a procurator under Caligula but this was omitted from the Vasio monument dedicated to him that records his career.
3. Tacitus, *Annals* 12.56.1–4.
4. Tacitus, *Annals* 12.42.1–2. Claudius was in the habit of awarding consular regalia to trusted equestrian procurators. See Suetonius, *Claudius* 24; Dio 60.34.1.
5. *RIC* 80 and 81.
6. Sear (1982), nos 502–8; the parallel bust design is known as 'jugate busts' and denoted equality of status. This should not be confused with the practice, common from the second century onwards, of striking separate coin issues in the name of the current empress.
7. Suetonius, *Claudius* 44.2, and Dio 60.34.3.
8. Tacitus, Annals 12.69.1–2; Suetonius, *Nero* 8.1; Dio 613.1 (Loeb VIII p. 37).
9. Suetonius, *Nero* 9 and 10.

10. Suetonius, *Nero* 9; *RIC* 1, 6.
11. Tacitus, *Annals* 13.2; Dio 61.3.3 (Loeb VIII p. 39).
12. Dio 62.13.2 (Loeb VIII p. 105), 61.4.1ff (Loeb VIII p. 39).
13. Tacitus, *Annals* 13.14.
14. It is not known whether Agrippina, like any other member of the imperial family, had an official entitlement to a praetorian escort or whether it was simply something she had decided for herself. Nero's withdrawal of the privilege might either have been a whim or enforcement of the 'normal rules', whatever those were. See also Durry (1938), 277.
15. See above, p. 123, and Dio 61.8.4 and 6 (Loeb VIII p. 53). This instance shows how the Guard's use was clearly at the emperor's discretion. Macrinus permitted Julia Domna, mother of the murdered Caracalla, to continue to have a praetorian escort in 218.
16. Sherk (1988), no. 76, Smallwood (1967), no. 293 (and *AE* 1952, 148). They are regarded as synonymous by Rankov (1994), 12; for the gardens, see Suetonius, *Galba* 12.2.
17. The consular date on the tablet appears to be Titus Cutius Ciltus and Lucius Iunius Gallio Annaeanus. *CIL* 4.3340.45 (Cooley and Cooley H79 – this reference not supplying Ciltus' name). The word for a camp or fort is not employed on the tablet, despite Cooley and Cooley's translation, so it is only an inference, though not an unreasonable one. See http://db.edcs.eu/epigr/epi_en.php for the full text.
18. Tacitus, *Annals* 13.48; for the evidence of individual praetorian soldiers in Pompeii in the lead up to 79, see p. 176.
19. Virgil, *Aeneid* 4.569–70.
20. Tacitus, *Annals* 13.5, and 13.32.
21. Suetonius, *Nero* 33.2; Tacitus, *Annals* 13.15.3.
22. Dio 61.7.5 (Loeb VIII p. 49).
23. The future emperor.
24. Dio 62.11.4 (Loeb VIII p. 61). That Nero was behind the murder is cited by Suetonius, *Nero* 34; Tacitus, *Annals* 14.3ff.; and Dio 61.13.
25. Dio 62.14.3 (Loeb VIII p. 67).
26. Tacitus, *Annals* 14.1ff.
27. Tacitus, *Annals* 14.15; Dio 62.20.3 (Loeb VIII p. 79).
28. Suetonius, *Nero* 32.2.
29. Tacitus, *Annals* 14.42–5, giving 'soldiers', though in the context it is certain they were praetorians.
30. Plautus was descended from Tiberius' granddaughter Julia Livia, and thus also from Agrippa, Antony and Octavia, but not Augustus as Tacitus says at *Annals* 13.19.3; on Nero's suspicions, see 13.19.3–20.1; for the comet, 14.22.1; for Plautus' killing, 14.58–9. The death of Plautus followed soon after the killing of Faustus Cornelius Sulla Felix, who was also murdered on Tigellinus' orders (14.57).
31. Dio 62.13.1–2 (Loeb VIII pp. 63–5).
32. Burrus' views on emperors, Dio 61.5.2 (Loeb VIII p. 43); on the allegation Burrus was poisoned, Dio 62.13.3 (Loeb VIII p. 105); on Tigellinus' evil, Tacitus, *Histories* 1.72; on enemies of the state, specifically the teacher and miracle worker Apollonius of Tyana, as recounted by Philostratus in his *Life of Apollonius* 4.43; on Nero's desire for a partner in crime, Tacitus, *Annals* 14.51.
33. On the choice of Naples, Tacitus, *Annals* 15.33.1ff; on the games of 64, Suetonius, *Nero* 12.3 and 21; on the use of praetorian spies, Tacitus, *Annals* 16.5.2; see also the reference to praetorian spies in a similar context under Domitian by Epictetus, p. 184.
34. On the equestrian and other supporters, Suetonius, *Nero* 20.3; on the deaths at the banquet, Tacitus 15.37 and Dio 62.15 (Loeb VIII p. 109); for the *decursio* coin, see *RIC* 108. The soldiers are not specifically identified as praetorians but it is hard to see who else they might have been.
35. Tacitus, *Annals* 16.6.1. Suetonius, *Nero* 35.3.

NOTES to pp. 134-44

36. On the conspirators, see Tacitus, *Annals* 15.49.1 and 50.1–3; for Silvanus see above p. 113 for his participation in the invasion of Britain under Claudius in 43. The inscription is *ILS* 2701, Sherk (1988), no. 49 A.

37. Tacitus, *Annals* 15.50.4–53.4.

38. On the discovery of a conspiracy, Tacitus, *Annals* 15.51.1–4; for the lack of a guard, see *Annals* 15.52.1. The term employed is *omissis excubiis*, 'with guards omitted'. The word *excubia* literally means 'a lying outdoors on guard'; on attacking innocent passers-by, see *Annals* 13.25.1–2.

39. On Milichus' concerns, Tacitus, *Annals* 15.55.1; for Statius Proximus, *Annals* 15.58.3–60.1.

40. Tacitus, *Annals* 15.60.4–61.4.

41. On Subrius Flavus, see Tacitus, *Annals* 15.67.2. His name is given as Flavius by Dio; see 62.24.1ff (Loeb VIII p. 129); for Faenius Rufus, see Tacitus, *Annals* 15.68.1.

42. On the payout, see Dio 62.27.4 (Loeb VIII p. 135); Tacitus, *Annals* 15.72.1. Sabinus is not mentioned by Tacitus in the *Annals* but is attested as prefect of the Praetorian Guard at this point by Plutarch, *Life of Galba* 2.1.

43. Thrasea Patus: Tacitus, *Annals* 14.12.1; Cassius Longinus: 16.7.2–9.1; Tigellinus and bribes, Dio 62.28.4 (Loeb VIII p. 137).

44. Dio 62.1–6 (Loeb VIII pp. 139–47). Corbulo had been the principal force behind settling the troubled Armenian question, and bringing Tiridates to a peaceful accommodation with Rome.

45. Suetonius, *Nero* 13.1; Tacitus, *Annals* 16.27.1; see also how praetorians could wear togas so they could act as spies, probably during the reign of Domitian. Epictetus 4.13.5, and see p. 184.

46. Suetonius, *Nero* 19.2.

47. Dio 62.17.2 (Loeb VIII p. 163).

48. Pliny, *Natural History* 6.181.

49. Dio 62.11.2 (Loeb VIII p. 157); Pliny, *Natural History* 18.7.35.

50. Dio 62.12.1, 62.20–1 (Loeb VIII pp. 157 and 169ff.).

51. Plutarch, *Life of Galba* 4.2–3; Suetonius, *Galba* 9.2, *Nero* 42

52. Dio 63.27.2 (Loeb VIII p. 185); Tacitus, *Histories* 1.72.

53. Virgil, *Aeneid* 12.646; the episode is recounted by Suetonius, *Nero* 47.2. The location of the Servilian Gardens is unknown, but since Nero was heading to Ostia they probably lay close to the Via Ostiensis, which led south from central Rome towards the east bank of the Tiber and down to the port; Dio 63.7.2 (Loeb VIII p. 207).

54. On Nero overhearing the praetorians, Suetonius, *Nero* 48.2; for Nymphidius Sabinus' role, see Plutarch, *Life of Galba* 8.1; Tacitus, *Histories* 1.5.1. Tacitus does not name him but it is clear from his comments that he believed the Guard had been manipulated into abandoning Nero, in spite of their traditional allegiance to the Julio-Claudians; for the offer of a payment by Sabinus, see Plutarch, *Life of Galba* 2. This presumably means that each praetorian not currently serving in Rome. Plutarch uses the drachma, equivalent to the denarius; Nero's suicide, Suetonius, *Nero* 48, 49.4.

55. Plutarch, *Life of Galba* 8.1, and see below, p. 144.

56. Tacitus, *Histories* 1.4, noting the latter revelation.

6 Civil War (69)

1. Tacitus. *Histories* 1.7.

2. Suetonius, *Nero* 57.

3. Tacitus, *Histories* 2.8.

4. Plutarch, *Life of Galba* 8.1–2. See also Ottley (2009), 242.

5. Tacitus, *Histories* 1.6.

6. Tacitus, *Histories* 1.6 and 1.72. Suetonius (*Galba* 14.2) says that Galba ignored popular calls for Tigellinus' punishment and even issued an edict castigating the people 'for their cruelty'.
7. Plutarch, *Life of Galba* 9.3. Ottley (2009), 254, speculates that Nymphidius was acting on behalf of another senatorial candidate. There is, however, no evidence to substantiate this.
8. Plutarch, *Life of Galba* 9.1–2.
9. Plutarch, *Life of Galba* 13.1–2, Tacitus, *Histories* 1.6; for the death of Nymphidius, see Plutarch, *Life of Galba* 14 and, more briefly, Suetonius, *Galba* 11.1.
10. On Galba's principles, see Tacitus, *Histories* 1.5 and Dio 64.3.3; for the disbandment of the Germans, see Suetonius, *Galba* 12.2.
11. Tacitus, *Histories* 1.14–15ff. Piso was descended from Marcus Licinius Crassus and Gnaeus Pompey ('the Great'). For his adoption at the camp, see Suetonius, *Galba* 17; for Otho's annoyance at being sidelined, see Suetonius, *Otho* 5.
12. Tacitus, *Histories* 1.23.
13. Suetonius, *Galba* 4.1 and 5.2. Tiberius saw to it that Galba never received the money. For the relationship with Claudius, see 7.1.
14. Tacitus, *Histories* 1.25, and Suetonius, *Galba* 16.1.
15. Tacitus, *Histories* 1.46.
16. Tacitus, *Histories* 1.26.
17. Tacitus, *Histories* 1.27.
18. Tacitus, *Histories* 1.28–9.
19. Tacitus, *Histories* 1.38 (Otho's speech includes this reference to the apparel worn by Galba's duty cohort).
20. Tacitus, *Histories* 1.30–1. Suetonius, *Galba* 12.2, reports that naval troops who had been made into regular soldiers by Nero were demoted to rowing duties by Galba.
21. Tacitus, *Histories* 1.34, and Suetonius, *Galba* 19, give different versions of this.
22. Tacitus, *Histories* 1.37–41, Suetonius, *Galba* 20.2.
23. Tacitus, *Histories* 1.43.
24. Tacitus, *Histories* 1.46.
25. Tacitus, *Histories* 1.46, 50, 52 and 55.
26. Tacitus, *Histories* 1.71–2.
27. Tacitus, *Histories* 1.74.
28. Tacitus, *Histories* 1.80. Suetonius, *Otho* 8.1–2, has a slightly different account in which naval troops rather than urban cohorts were involved.
29. Tacitus, *Histories* 1.81–2.
30. Tacitus, *Histories* 1.83–4.
31. Tacitus, *Histories* 1.85.
32. *RIC* (Otho) 14.
33. On the make-up of the force, see Tacitus, *Histories* 2.11; on Proculus' manipulating his position, and the presence of urban cohorts, see 1.87.
34. *RIC* (Galba) 284; *RIC* (Otho) 3, 4.
35. Tacitus, *Histories* 2.11. The legions were the VII, XI, XIII, XIIII, and the I Adiutrix from Rome.
36. Tacitus, *Histories* 2.14.
37. Tacitus, *Histories* 2.18.
38. Tacitus, *Annals* 13.35.
39. Tacitus, *Histories* 2.21–2.
40. Tacitus, *Histories* 2.23.
41. Tacitus, *Histories* 2.24.
42. Tacitus, *Histories* 2.25–6.
43. The XIIII legion, one of Britain's four legions, had already crossed the Channel to fight for Otho. Vitellius was counting on the remaining three: II, IX and XX; Tacitus, *Histories* 2.32.

44. Tacitus, *Histories* 2.31, 38.
45. Tacitus, *Histories* 2.42, 44. The I Italica was famous for having been raised by Nero exclusively from six-foot-tall Italians. Suetonius, *Nero* 19.2.
46. Tacitus, *Histories* 2.47–8.
47. Tacitus, *Histories* 2.49; Suetonius, *Otho* 8.1, refers to the very considerable level of affection and loyalty the praetorians had for Otho.
48. Tacitus, *Histories* 2.57, and 56.
49. Tacitus, *Histories* 2.60, 62, 63
50. Tacitus, *Histories* 2.66.
51. Suetonius, *Vitellius* 10.1.
52. Tacitus, *Histories* 2.67; for the original terms of discharge, see Dio 55.23: sixteen years and 20,000 sestertii (5,000 denarii).
53. Father and son bore the same name. The father is always referred to as Vespasian, the son as Titus. Collectively, together with Titus' brother Domitian, they are referred to as the Flavians; Tacitus, *Histories* 2.74.
54. Tacitus, *Histories* 2.76–7, 79, 80, 81.
55. Tacitus, *Histories* 2.82, 3.8.
56. Tacitus, *Histories* 2.82; the term Tacitus uses is *praetorianos Vitellio infensos*, 'the praetorians hostile to Vitellius'.
57. Tacitus, *Histories* 2.87–9.
58. Tacitus, *Histories* 2.91–2.
59. Tacitus, *Histories* 2.94, 'sixteen praetorian and four urban cohorts were formed, each a thousand strong'.
60. Tacitus, *Histories* 2.96.
61. Antonius Primus was commander of the VII legion Galbiana in Pannonia.
62. Tacitus, *Histories* 3.12, 14.
63. Tacitus, *Histories* 3.21.
64. Tacitus, *Histories* 3.23, 24.
65. Alfenus Varus was a former legionary camp prefect who had played an important role in suppressing a mutiny in Valens' forces. See Tacitus, *Histories* 2.29, 3.40.
66. Tacitus, *Histories* 3.42, 62.
67. Tacitus, *Annals* 6.22.
68. Tacitus, *Histories* 3.44; Dio 64.16.5 (Loeb VIII p. 247).
69. Tacitus, *Histories* 3.51 and 55. The Loeb translation for 3.51 states that 'six praetorian cohorts' were involved but this seems to be a translator's error. There is no number supplied in the Latin.
70. Tacitus, *Histories* 3.58–9. Wellesley (1975, 163) says that these were 'six of the nine praetorian cohorts then available in Rome'. This does not square with the statement by Tacitus that Vitellius had formed sixteen praetorian cohorts.
71. Tacitus, *Histories* 3.61. The Flavian force was led by 'Varus', presumably Quintilius Varus.
72. Tacitus, *Histories* 3.63–5.
73. Tacitus, *Histories* 3.68, 74, 78, 79.
74. Tacitus, *Histories* 3.84. Suetonius, *Vitellius* 18 states that it was Antonius Primus who killed Vitellius.

7 To the Victor, the Spoils (69–98)

1. Tacitus, *Histories* 4.1, 3.86, 4.2.
2. Tacitus, *Histories* 4.11.
3. Tacitus, *Histories* 4.46.
4. Tacitus, *Histories* 4.46.

5. *AE* 1995, 227; *ILS* 1993; *CIL* 16.21; and Campbell (1994), 199–200, no. 327, '*in cohortibus novem praetoriis et quattuor urbanis*'. See below p. 178 for discussion of this diploma in the context of marriage rights for retired praetorians.

6. These are recounted by Bingham (2013), 54, but inconclusively. Cowan (2014) states that 'the Flavian cohorts were most likely 1,000 strong', for example.

7. Goldsworthy (2003), 54. This is also borne out by archaeological evidence; Pseudo-Hyginus, *On the Fortification of Camps (De Munitionibus Castrorum)* 1–2, and 6.

8. For the addition of the tenth cohort, see below for the graffito from Pompeii (not after August 79), and diploma of AD 100 from Vindonissa. Dio (55.24.6) refers to ten cohorts of one thousand each, which he states was the case in Augustus' time; the issues involved in reconciling this with other evidence are discussed on p. 30.

9. Tacitus identifies five legions with Titus, as well as auxiliary units. *Histories* 5.1.

10. Suetonius, *Domitian* 1.3.

11. For the Arrecina sisters, see Suetonius, *Titus* 4.2. Levick (1999) (ii), 23. Clemens' father had been an equestrian, and see also Levick (1999) (ii), family trees on unnumbered pages following xxi; see also Tacitus, *Histories* 4.68.

12. Suetonius, *Vespasian* 6.3; Josephus, *Jewish War* 2.309; for an attested instance of a prefect of Egypt being promoted to the prefecture of the Guard, see Lucius Laberius Maximus under Domitian (below); Turner (1954).

13. Dio 64.22.2. 'The soldiers' are not specified and may or may not have been praetorians; Plutarch, *Galba* 2. Levick (1999) (ii), 95, gives sestertii but Plutarch supplies drachmae (=denarii).

14. Tacitus, *Histories* 4.86.

15. Suetonius, *Vespasian* 8–9.

16. Levick (1999) (ii), 155.

17. Dio 66.12, Suetonius, *Titus* 6.

18. Pliny, *Natural History*, preface 3.

19. Tacitus, *Annals* 4.2.1.

20. Bishop (2013) is a useful survey of legionary fortresses.

21. Busch (2007), 320.

22. Martial 10.48.1–2. That the cohort was praetorian is not specified, but this is the most likely.

23. See p. 199.

24. Pliny, *Natural History* 3.67.

25. Busch (2007), 323.

26. Dimensions cited by Menéndez Argüín (2006), 58, who supplies the comparisons with legionary fortresses, and also Bingham (2013), 179–80, n. 162.

27. Richmond (1927), 13, and fig. 1. These had mosaics and plastered walls and ceilings.

28. Cowan (2014), 47, points out that the need for fresh horses would have meant that many more horses were required than men who rode them. However, another way of looking at it is that praetorians in Rome simply would not have needed all their horses in the city. Moreover, identifying stables from archaeological remains is far from straightforward.

29. *CIL* 3.2887; *ILS* 9067; Campbell (1994), 41, no. 67 records the career of Aulus Saufeius Emax, a soldier of the VIIII praetorian cohort who progressed through a number of these posts; for Titius Alexander, see *CIL* 6.20; *ILS* 2092; Campbell (1994) 104, no. 167. For Harmodius, see *AE* 1952, 143.

30. Rankov (1994), 6, suggests twelve thousand or more; Josephus, *Jewish Antiquities* 19.253.

31. *RIC* 25; Herodian 4.4.5. The occasion was when Caracalla fled to the camp after the death of Geta in 212. See below, p. 229.

32. *CIL* 6.2256.

33. Josephus, *Jewish Antiquities* 18.228ff, referring to Herod being escorted to the baths from the Castra Praetoria at the time of Tiberius' death in 37.

34. For the 3.35 metres see Richmond (1927), 13; for the 5 metres, see Bingham (2013), 72. The towers proved vital for defence in 238 when the Castra Praetoria was attacked by an armed mob during the reigns of Balbinus and Pupienus. See below, p. 248.

35. Busch (2007), 328, and below, p. 200.

36. As happened in 238 during the reigns of Balbinus and Pupienus. The pipes had been renewed on several occasions in the camp's history. See p. 248.

37. Cooley and Cooley (2004), p. 156, G66–9 (English only). Latin texts at De Caro (1979) and images on the www.pompeiiinpictures.com website.

38. See above, p. 126.

39. Tacitus, *Annals* 14.17.1–2; Cooley and Cooley (2004), H59 and *CIL* 4.8405. The house is Regio I, insula X, building 11, known as the 'House of the Lovers' in the Insula of the Menander.

40. But see the discussion at the end of chapter 3 about the irregular numbering systems endemic in the Roman army.

41. *CIL* 4.4311, 1711, 1994 and 2145.

42. Gore (1984), 572–3.

43. Tomlin (2016), 56, and 98 no. WT20. Other examples of (named) praetorian veterans serving in Britain in a number of different capacities are attested in the third century, see p. 250.

44. See below, p. 186.

45. Blesius Taurinus, see p. 203.

46. *CIL* 10.1018; *ILS* 5924; Sherk (1988), no. 81. The inscription, which is extant in the Nucerian Gate cemetery at Pompeii, is only datable to Vespasian's reign (69–79), not a specific year.

47. *CIL* 16.21; *ILS* 1993. See also Campbell (1994), 199–200, no. 327. Diplomas are often found in incongruous locations, one explanation for which might have been either an interest in them in antiquity as collectible militaria, or simply for the scrap value; there are instances of diplomas that have clearly been reused for their metal.

48. Discussed by Campbell (2004), 201.

49. Smallwood (1967), no. GN297; Campbell (1994), 206, no. 337. See also Westermann (1941).

50. *CIL* 16.25; *ILS* 1994; see also Johnson et al. (2003), 152, no. 189.

51. Dio 66.26.2–3; Suetonius, *Titus* 9.3.

52. Dio 67.2ff.

53. Levick, 'Vespasian' in Barrett (2008), 151; Dio 67.3.1; Ursus' promotion did not confer the right to sit with the senate, but it entitled the holder to sit with senators of the most senior (consular) rank at public events and to wear the senatorial toga.

54. The office is denoted on the coinage from this date. Dio 67.4.3, and Suetonius, *Domitian* 8.3.

55. Sherk (1988), no. 98.

56. Suetonius, *Domitian* 6.1; Martial 6.76. Bingham (2013), 148–9, n. 181, appears to be under the impression that the deceased soldier was someone other than Fuscus. Fuscus is also mentioned by Juvenal, *Satires* 4.110–12, but apart from stating that he was killed in Dacia, no useful information about the Guard is supplied.

57. Dio 67.3.5. Suetonius, *Domitian*. Three hundred sestertii were equivalent to 75 silver denarii, or 3 gold *aurei*; Dio 53.11 notes that praetorians received double the pay of a legionary.

58. *RIC* 288. The coin has also been identified as representing the return of the governor Agricola from Britain. It is not possible to be certain either way; Dio 67.6.6.

59. *AE* 1972, 572; Rogers (2014), 18.

60. Roxan and Eck (1993). See next chapter for the diploma from Vindonissa dated to 100 and listing ten praetorian cohorts, perhaps organized in that number under Domitian.

61. Suetonius, *Domitian* 7.3.

62. Suetonius, *Domitian* 13.2; Dio 67.11.1–2, 68.2.

63. Dio 67.14.4, 68.3.3. See below for the mutiny he led against Nerva.
64. Rankov (1994), 46–7, shows this relief, now in the Vatican Museum, in excellent detail. This and other reliefs are named for the Palazzo della Cancellaria in Rome, on the site of which they were found. See also Sumner (2004), 13, 46 and plate F3.
65. Epictetus, *Discourses* 4.13.5; Tacitus, *Annals* 16.5.2.
66. Suetonius, *Domitian* 14.1.
67. Dio 67.15.1ff.
68. Tacitus, *Histories* 2.94.
69. *CIL* 6.2725. The tombstone is displayed in the Vatican Museum in Rome. The bottom part is missing and may have clarified exactly when his service finally came to an end. That Domitian's name has escaped erasure is interesting as it might suggest Moderatus had died during his reign, but the arithmetic of Moderatus' service makes that very unlikely.
70. *AE* 1979, 89. The stone is displayed in the gardens of the Museo delle Terme di Diocleziano in Rome.
71. Friggeri et al. (2012), 462, no. VII, 17.

8 Concordia Exercituum (98–180)

1. Suetonius, *Domitian* 23.1
2. *RIC* 80.
3. Dio 68.3.2–3 (and see the note Loeb VIII p. 365).
4. Pliny the Younger, *Panegyricus* 6.1; Berriman and Todd (2001), 328.
5. ἐποδῶν, literally 'put away from the feet', Dio 68.5.4 (Loeb VIII p. 369).
6. Dio 68.16.1 and 68.9.2.
7. Pliny the Younger, *Panegyricus* 23.3 and 25.2. The word used by Pliny is *milites*, 'soldiers'. Speidel (1994), 42 regards these troops as *equites singulares Augusti*.
8. During a food riot in Rome under Commodus in 189 or 190 the praetorians sided with the mob against the *equites singulares* who had been sent to quash the disturbance. See p. 215.
9. Campbell (1994), 42; Rankov (1994), 14.7; *RMD* IV, 231 in Roxan and Holder (2003).
10. The former argument is mainly that of Speidel (1994), 43.
11. *CIL* 6.3308; *ILS* 2210; Campbell (1994), 43, no. 74.
12. Note that the graffito from Pompeii that refers to the X cohort cannot postdate 79, though this may be a Vitellian cohort. *CIL* 4.8405; Cooley and Cooley (2004) 177, H59.
13. *CIL* 16.81. Note that Cowan (2014), 30, for reasons that are unclear, attributes the diploma to the year 89. Although the diploma is incomplete, the published restored text states that the emperor concerned is currently holding the tribunician power for the fifth time and his third consulship. This only corresponds to Trajan between 18 September 100 and the end of that year. Phang (2001) 67, n. 50, attributes the diploma to the early second century. See also Campbell (1994), 38, stating Domitian to have 'settled' the Guard's strength at ten milliary cohorts; see also below in the note at the beginning of the Bibliography.
14. See Cowan (2014), 38–9, for a reconstruction of the praetorian scorpion shield design. The scorpion was associated with Tiberius and probably dates from when the Guard was moved into the Castra Praetoria
15. Lepper and Frere (1988), 71 (and plate XVII), 81 (and plate XXV), 100 (and plate XXXVII).
16. *CIL* 2.4461; *ILS* 2661; *CIL* 11.5646; Campbell (1994) no. 91; *ILS* 2081. Clemens rose to be curator of the community of Matilica in Umbria after his military career was over.
17. Dio 68.9.2. Cornelius Fuscus, prefect under Domitian, had been killed in the war against Decebalus in 87. See above, p. 181.

18. Gilliver (2007), 196.
19. *CIL* 6.32709a; *ILS* 9180. For the Trajanic transfer possibility, see Summerly (1992), 107–8.
20. See below, p. 220.
21. *SHA* (Hadrian) 3–4 *passim*, 6.1–2.
22. Syme (1980), 67; *SHA* (Hadrian) 1.4, 5.10, 8.7; Dio 69.19.1, 22.2.
23. *SHA* (Hadrian) 5.5, 6.10; Birley (1997), 78.
24. *SHA* (Hadrian) 7.2–3, 4 and 6. The date of his arrival is recorded on *CIL* 6.32374.
25. *SHA* (Hadrian) 9.3–4; Dio 22.2.
26. *CIL* 3.14349. He was aged 38 and had served 14 years. The surviving text reads '(centuria) M(arcii) Turbonis'.
27. Dio 52.24–5; see above, p. 50.
28. Turbo's remarkable career is discussed by Syme (1962), 87–91.
29. Dio 69.18.1ff, 3–4.
30. Gaius Erucius Clarus. Syme (1962), 91; Pliny, *Letters* 1.1. Pliny died c. 112 while governor of Bithynia and Pontus. For the now lost dedication to Clarus by Suetonius, see Morgan (1986); Birley (1997), 96; *SHA* (Hadrian) 11.3; Dio 69.9.1; and Birley (1997), 113ff.
31. *SHA* (Hadrian) 11.3–4; Aurelius Victor, *Caesars* 14.8; for the *frumentarii*, see *SHA* (Hadrian) 11.6. The *frumentarii*, incongruously, had their origins in military supplies but had become involved in carrying imperial dispatches by the reign of Trajan, then evolving into imperial spies; for Hadrian's 'enemies', see *SHA* (Hadrian) 15.1. These included Aulus Platorius Nepos who had accompanied Hadrian to Britain, been made governor, and initiated the building of the Wall.
32. *SHA* (Hadrian) 5.2.
33. *ILS* 2726.
34. *ILS* 7741; *CIL* 6.8991; Campbell (1994), 122, no. 196.
35. Birley (1997) frequently assumes Turbo was in Rome. For example, see p. 173, 'At Rome itself . . . Marcius Turbo was there, commanding the Guard'. On Martialis, see Birley (ibid.), 143, who speculates in more detail about his accessibility; *SHA* (Hadrian) 13.4.
36. Dio 69.18.1; *SHA* (Hadrian) 15.7; Birley (1997), 280.
37. *SHA* (Hadrian) 13.6, 14.1ff.
38. Birley (1997), 173, and 183.
39. Pliny the Younger, *Letters* 10.27, 28.
40. Widely reported in the press in May 2016 when the discovery was made public. The location is the site of the Amba Aradam metro station on the new Linea C.
41. 'The majority [of auxiliary forts] ranged from 1 to 2.5 hectares'. Johnson (1983), 31; Marsden (1980), 85.
42. *RIB* 11.
43. Herodian 7.6.2 refers to the urban cohort stationed in Carthage. See also 7.4.5 and *SHA* (Maximinus) 14.1.
44. Syme (1980), 75.
45. *SHA* (Aelius) 3.3. and 6.1; *SHA* (Aurelius) 8.1 and 5.1 respectively.
46. *SHA* (Antoninus) 8.7; *ILS* 2182; *CIL* 6.31147; Campbell (1994), 130, no. 208. Gavius Maximus is also recorded as prefect on the tombstone of one of his freedmen; see Plate 21 and *CIL* 6.38411/*AE* 1904, 209.
47. Menéndez Argüín (2006), 65. The mosaic was found in 1889.
48. See van den Hout (1999), 414–15. Promotion to honorary consular status became the means by which a praetorian prefect was most conveniently removed from office. See *SHA* (Alexander) 21.4; for his character, see *SHA* (Antoninus) 8.7; for the Ostia forum baths, see Meiggs (1960), 415.
49. *SHA* (Antoninus) 5.3 and 8.6ff; Birley (1993), 112; for Lysistrata, see Levick (2014), 61. She is named as Antoninus Pius' mistress (*concubina*) on *CIL* 6.8972.

50. Campbell (1994), 126, no. 206. The ancient and modern names of the town are the same.
51. *SHA* (Aurelius) 7.3.
52. Dio 72.1–3 (Loeb IX p. 11).
53. *SHA* (Aurelius) 7.9; Bingham (2013), 42.
54. *ILS* 8846, and 9002; see also Grant (1996), 35, and Austin and Rankov (1998), 206; *ILS* 9002; *AE* 1907, 152. The text confirms that he had previously served as prefect of Egypt and before that as prefect of the night watch. *ILS* 8846, probably originally found in Egypt, commemorates his departure from the prefecture of Egypt, see Rossignol (2007), 146, n. 50.
55. For example, Bingham (2013), 41. See Whately's review in *Bryn Mawr Classical Review* 2013.09.66 where he notes that only *ILS* 8846 and 9002 serve as evidence for this assertion.
56. *Fragmenta Vaticana* no. 195. Accessed at: http://ancientrome.ru/ius/library/vatican/FragVat. htm#195. It is generally known that grandsons by a daughter do not count towards release from *tutela* or towards a claim for intestate property, unless you offer me [? trans. uncertain] a father-in-law who has become a grandfather by having a praetorian veteran as his son-in-law; for according to a speech of the deified Marcus, which he recited in the Praetorian Camp on 6 January 168, the grandfather will have (the same rights) as he has in the case of grandsons born of a son. These are the words of the speech: 'and so that our veterans may more easily find fathers-in-law, we will tempt the latter with a new privilege, that a grandfather of grandsons born by a praetorian veteran (son-in-law) shall enjoy the same advantages in their name as he would enjoy if he had them by a son.' (trans. R.S.O. Tomlin (2016))
57. Pliny, *Letters* 10.147, shows Trajan granting Roman citizenship to the daughter of a cavalryman; Campbell (1994), 154, no. 257.
58. Phang (2001), 152 and 160ff. See also Scheidel (2005), 5.
59. *CIL* 6.2164 (Rome). See also Phang (2001), 162.
60. Scheidel (2005), 11. This article also appears in Erdkamp (ed.) (2007). By the third century, 45 per cent were discharged within thirteen years.
61. *CIL* 3.3114, 5.5269, 9.4682; *AE* 1997.373.
62. *ILS* 2081; Campbell (1994), 51, no. 91. He was a quinquennalian *duumvir*, a position held every five years, that entitled him with his fellow quinquennalian *duumvir* to operate the civic census and determine eligibility to vote.
63. Phang (2001), 163.
64. *SHA* (Verus) 9.7.
65. Rossignol (2007), 142. See also Dio 72.5.3 (Loeb IX p. 19) for Bassaeus Rufus' modest origins.
66. Suetonius, *Augustus* 32; *CIL* 3.6085; *ILS* 2051.
67. *CIL* 9.2438, from Saepinum (Sepino), cited in Lewis and Reinhold (1955), 186.
68. Dio 72.3.1 (Loeb IX p. 17), and 12.3 (ibid. p. 23). The earlier reference has Vindex leading a cavalry charge so it is possibly in this context he was later killed.
69. *SHA* (Pertinax) 2.9. The later emperor, who succeeded Commodus in January to March 193.
70. Philostratus, *Life of the Sophists* 2.1.2; Rossignol (2007), 143–4.
71. Dio 72.3.5 (Loeb IX p. 17); *SHA* (Commodus) 4.1. Rossignol (2007), 143, states that his name follows that of Bassaeus Rufus on *CIL* 6.1599 but it has not been possible to confirm this.
72. Rankov (1994), 59; Dio 79.37.4 (Loeb IX p. 425); Cowan (2014), 59.
73. In Egypt in c. 175 a rebellion broke out amongst the Bucolici, a herdsman people. A general called Cassius Avidius Heliodorus (sometimes known as Avidius Cassius) was sent to quash the insurrection and given wide-ranging powers across the eastern provinces to help him carry out his instructions. He proceeded to declare himself emperor. It was a very dangerous development but the insurrection was quickly crushed on Marcus Aurelius'

orders, and Cassius killed. The point here, however, is that he had already created his own prefect of the guard and therefore presumably a unit of his own praetorians as well. *SHA* (Marcus Aurelius) 24.5–25.5; *SHA* Avidius Cassius *passim*.

9 The Age of Iron and Rust (180–235)

1. Dio referred to his accession as the onset of an 'age of iron and rust'. 72.36.4 (Loeb IX p. 69).
2. Herodian 1.4.3–4; Dio 72.34; Herodian 1.5.3.
3. For Commodus' accession, see Herodian 1.5.3–8; Dio on Commodus at 73.1.1–2 (Loeb IX p. 73).
4. Herodian 1.7.1; Dio 73.4.3 (Loeb IX p. 77); Herodian 1.7.6; the main plot was that of Claudius Pompeianus; Paternus and Perennis definitely served as colleagues for a period. Dio 73.10.1 (Loeb IX p. 91); Lucilla was the widow of Lucius Verus. Herodian 1.8.3.
5. *SHA* (Commodus) 4.7 claims that Paternus was the prime mover behind the plot; Herodian 1.8.4; Dio 73.4.4 (Loeb IX p. 77).
6. *SHA* (Commodus) 4.1–7; Dio 73.5.1 (Loeb IX p. 79). Perennis seems also to have played a part in Paternus' downfall: Dio 73.10.1 (Loeb IX p. 91).
7. Dio 73.9.1–2 (Loeb IX p. 89); *SHA* (Commodus) 5.1ff.; Herodian 1.8.1ff.; see also Adams (2013), 159–60.
8. Herodian 1.8.2, 9.1.
9. Herodian 1.9.4; Dio 73.9.2 (Loeb IX pp. 89–91); *SHA* (Commodus) 6.1ff.
10. Dio 73.10.1 (Loeb IX p. 91); Herodian 1.9.8–10.
11. On Cleander's rise, see *SHA* (Commodus) 6.6–10, 6.13; Dio 73.10.2 (Loeb IX p. 91); on Cleander's fall, *SHA* (Commodus) 7.1; Dio 73.13.1–6 (Loeb IX pp. 97–9); and Herodian 1.12.6.
12. For Motilenus, see *SHA* (Commodus) 7.4, 9.2. On Commodus' descent, see *SHA* (Commodus) 8.5–6; Dio 73.15.2 (Loeb IX pp. 101–3). Dio's judgement is at 72.18.3–4 (Loeb IX p. 109). Commodus 'was not as consistently malicious as he was often portrayed', Adams (2013), 15. Commodus also inevitably proved an acute contrast with Marcus Aurelius, exacerbating the perception of his deficiencies both then and since.
13. The plotters: *SHA* (Commodus) 17.1; Dio 73.19.4 (Loeb IX p. 111). On the end, Dio 73.22.1–6 (Loeb IX pp. 115–17).
14. *SHA* (Pertinax) 3.5–6, 6.4.
15. *SHA* (Pertinax) 15.7; Dio 74.1.2 (Loeb IX p. 123), though the sources differ over whether he paid all of it. The former claims only 50 per cent were ever produced. Dio 74.8.3 (Loeb IX p. 137) compares the amounts of the donative in 161 and 193.
16. Herodian 2.2.5.
17. Dio 74.1.3 (Loeb IX p. 123); *SHA* (Pertinax) 6.6 states that Pertinax confirmed all these concessionary practices.
18. Dio 74.5.4, 8.1–9 (Loeb IX pp. 133, 137).
19. Dio 74.9.1–10.3 (Loeb IX pp. 139–41).
20. Herodian 2.6.14.
21. Dio 74.12.1–4 (Loeb IX p. 145).
22. *SHA* (Didius Julianus) 3.1. This source also states that Julianus upped his promise to 30,000 sestertii but this conflicts with Herodian's more convincing claim that he failed to pay anything due to a lack of resources; for the coinage, *RIC* (Didius Julianus) 1 and 14; Herodian 2.7.1–2; Dio 74.13.1 (Loeb IX p. 147). *SHA* (Didius Julianus) 7.1–2.
23. *SHA* (Didius Julianus) 3.7; Dio 74.13.4–5 (Loeb IX p. 149). For Severus' appointment as consul, see Dio 73.12.4 (Loeb IX p. 97).
24. Dio 74.14.3 (Loeb IX p. 151); Dio 74.15.1–2 (Loeb IX p. 153).

25. Dio 74.16.2 (Loeb IX p. 155); Herodian 2.2.9. The problem was the same as in the civil war of 68–9; see Tacitus, *Histories* 2.18.
26. Cowan (2011).
27. *SHA* (Didius Julianus) 7.4 and 8.1; *SHA* (Severus) 6.5; *ILS* 2428 (*CIL* 8.2725) confirms Juvenalis' name in the office of praetorian prefect.
28. *SHA* (Didius Julianus) 7.5.
29. Dio 74.17.1–5 (Loeb IX p. 159); Herodian 2.12.4.
30. *SHA* (Severus) 6.11; Herodian 2.13.2–4; Dio 75.1.1 (Loeb IX p. 161); Herodian 8.8.2; see below, p. 249.
31. Herz (2007), 318
32. Herodian 2.13.5–12; Dio 75.1.2 (Loeb IX p. 161).
33. *CIL* 6.2578 and 210; Campbell (1994), 40–1, nos 65–6.
34. *SHA* (Maximinus) 3.5.
35. Dio 55.24.6. See above, p. 30 for a discussion of whether it is really necessary to make this assumption about Dio being in error for AD 5. See also p. 167 for the evidence for ten cohorts in Flavian times; a diploma of 228 (Campbell (1994), no. 328), for example, refers to the 'ten Severan praetorian cohorts'.
36. Southern and Dixon (2000), 8, call Severus' reforms 'democratization' of the Guard; *AE* 2004.319. The Severan title Pia Vindex ('faithful avenger') dates the inscription.
37. Dio 75.2.4–6 (Loeb IX p. 165). See also Herodian 2.14.5, who makes no mention of any troublesome or disaffected would-be praetorians. See below for evidence of Severan praetorians on campaign.
38. Sumner (2003), 10.
39. Dio 75.8.3, 76.4.1, 6.1 (Loeb IX pp. 181, 203, 207). See also Graham (1978), 625ff., who shows that the correct meaning is 150,000 altogether.
40. Dio 76.6.3–8 (Loeb IX p. 207ff.).
41. As specifically referred to by Herodian 7.11.2 under Maximinus (235–8). See below, p. 247.
42. Herodian 3.13.4 refers to a 'great army' camped near Rome at this time. Other evidence indicates a close relationship between II Parthica and the Praetorian Guard. See p. 224.
43. *CIL* 6.2553. The stone is dated by the Severan title Pia Vindex ('faithful avenger').
44. *ILS* 2103; *CIL* 6.210. There are other examples from this time and the next few decades, some of which indicate that eighteen years had become the minimum and some soldiers may have served longer. See Cowan (2014), 21.
45. Friggeri et al. (2012), 466, no. VII, 20.
46. Herodian 3.8.4–5.
47. Dio 76.10.1–3 (Loeb IX pp. 219–21); Virgil, *Aeneid* 11.371–3. It had been foretold that Lavinia would marry a foreigner (Aeneas) but she was already betrothed to Turnus who, after some divine prodding, took exception to this.
48. Dio 76.14 *passim*, 76.15.2 (Loeb IX pp. 227, 231).
49. Dio 56.32.2 and 77.1.1–5 (Loeb IX p. 239). On Severus' obsession with money, see Herodian 3.8.7.
50. Dio 76.15.7 (Loeb IX p. 233).
51. Herodian 3.10.8–11.1; Dio 77.3.1–3 (Loeb IX p. 243). Caracalla's legal name was Marcus Aurelius Antoninus, the name by which he is known in the sources. Today he is normally known by his nickname.
52. Herodian 3.11.6–12; Dio 77.4.1–5 (Loeb IX pp. 245–7).
53. Howe (1966), 21–2.
54. The *equites singulares Augusti* force sent to apprehend Bulla must have been with Severus in Britain; Dio 77.10.1–7 (Loeb IX pp. 257–61).
55. *ILS* 2089; *CIL* 6.2464. His name is sometimes given as Caesernius Senecio.
56. Dio 77.14.5–6 (Loeb IX p. 269).
57. Dio 77.15.2 (Loeb IX pp. 273–5).

58. Dio 78.1.1, 4.1 (Loeb IX pp. 279, 285). *SHA* (Caracalla) 3.2, 4.1 implies that Papinianus remained in post until he was killed too.
59. Herodian 3.15.6. The peace was a hasty one, Caracalla and Geta settling for meaningless guarantees from the Caledonian tribes. On their mutual loathing, see Herodian 4.1.5, 4.3.4, 4.3.8.
60. Dio 78.2.1–4 (Loeb IX pp. 281–3); Herodian 4.4.2–3.
61. Herodian 4.4.6–8; Develin (1971).
62. *SHA* (Geta) 6.1–3.
63. Burnett (1987), 48.
64. Sear (2002), 503.
65. For Laetus' suicide, *SHA* (Caracalla) 3.4; for Papinianus' execution Dio 78.4 (Loeb IX p. 287).
66. *SHA* (Geta) 6.4–5, (Caracalla) 8.8, 4.2.
67. Lanciani (1988), 148.
68. *SHA* (Caracalla) 6.6, 8.8; Howe (1942), 72–3; see also Levick (1997), 207, n. 82. Rufinus had previously been prefect of the night watch, *CIL* 14.4386 from Ostia and dedicated to Julia Domna for 205–7, and 14.4387 (Caracalla, 207).
69. Rankov (1987), 245; Pflaum (1960), no. 247; *RIB* 1234.
70. Dio 79.1.1 (Loeb IX p. 341).
71. Dio 79.4.1–5 (Loeb IX p. 347).
72. *SHA* (Caracalla) 6.6.
73. Dio 79.4.4–5 (Loeb IX p. 347).
74. Herodian 4.14.2–3, 15.6.
75. Dio 79.23.1 (Loeb IX pp. 391–3); Herodian 5.3.1.
76. Dio 79.11.1, 18 (Loeb IX pp. 361, 381); *SHA* (Macrinus) 2.4.
77. Dio 79.11.2–3 (Loeb IX p. 361).
78. Macrinus' beard seems to have been something he made a particular point of cultivating. Herodian 5.2.3; *SHA* (Macrinus) 12.1–11.
79. Dio 79.12.7, 14.4, 16.2 (Loeb IX pp. 367, 371, 375); the names of the prefects appointed by Macrinus are at 79.15.1 (Loeb IX p. 373).
80. Dio 79.17.4, 18.4, 20.3, 27.1, 28.2–3 (Loeb IX pp. 379, 381, 385, 405); *SHA* (Macrinus) 2.1; Herodian 4.15.8.
81. For convenience the boys' names as emperors are given here. At the time they were known as Bassianus and Alexianus.
82. Herodian 5.3.5. It was possibly a meteorite. The god's name is also given as Elagabal, but to avoid confusion with the emperor who was known by the same name Heliogabalus is used here.
83. Herodian 5.3.10, 4.2; Dio 79.31.1–4 (the numbering is confused here, see Loeb IX p. 411); *SHA* (Elagabalus) 12.1.
84. Herodian 5.4.4; Dio 79.32.3, 34.4–5, 35.1 (Loeb IX pp. 413, 417–19).
85. Dio 79.37.4 (Loeb IX p. 425); Herodian 5.4.8.
86. Herodian 5.4.11; Dio 79.40.2, 5 (Loeb IX pp. 431–3); and *SHA* (Macrinus) 10.3 and 15.1.
87. Dio 79.41.1–4 (Loeb IX p. 435).
88. Dio 80.1.1 (Loeb IX p. 437); Herodian 5.3.3–6, 5.10.
89. Dio 80.4.1–3 (Loeb IX pp. 445–7).
90. Dio 80.9.2, 17.2, 18.4 (Loeb IX pp. 459, 473–5); Herodian 5.7.1.
91. Herodian 5.7.5, 8.3; *SHA* (Elagabalus) 13.8.
92. Dio 80.19.2; Herodian 5.8.4ff.
93. Dio 80.20.1–21.1 (Loeb IX pp. 477–9); *SHA* (Elagabalus) 16.5–17.2.
94. *SHA* (Elagabalus) 16.4; Aurelius Victor 24.6; Zosimus 1.11.2.
95. Dio 80.1.1, 2.2 (Loeb IX pp. 479–81); *SHA* (Alexander) 31.3, 67.2.

96. *SHA* (Alexander) 51.4; Dio 80.4.2 (Loeb IX p. 485); Modrzejewski and Zawadski (1967), 565–611 argue that the assassination took place as soon as summer 223.
97. *SHA* (Alexander) 26.5. Paulus had been exiled by Elagabalus.
98. *CIL* 6.02799 (and also 32543).
99. Herodian 6.1.8.
100. Herodian 6.1.1–2. The arrangements resembled those, for example, created for Henry VI of England who acceded at less than one year of age exactly twelve centuries later to the year.
101. *SHA* (Alexander) 19.1.
102. *SHA* (Alexander) 21.4.
103. Herodian 6.1.9.
104. Herodian 6.3.1, 4.3, 5.5ff.
105. Herodian 6.7.2, 9.
106. Maximinus was reputed to be 8½ feet tall; presumably this is something of an exaggeration. *SHA* (Maximinus) 3.5 and 6.8.
107. *SHA* (Alexander) 26.2, 23.1 and 32.4.This source is, however, notoriously given to fanciful claims.
108. *SHA* (Alexander) 39.9–10.
109. Herodian 6.8.4–6.
110. Herodian 6.9.7.

10 Decline and Dissolution (235–312)

1. Herodian 7.29, 3.3, 3.5, 11.2, 8.5.9.
2. Herodian 7.4.1–3.
3. Herodian 7.5.2, 6.2; Aurelius Victor 27.1; *SHA* (Maximinus) 14.4, (Gordian) 10.5.
4. *AE* (1957), 278; on Vitalianus' promotion, Howe (1942), no. 40, expressed doubts.
5. Herodian 7.6.5–9.
6. Herodian 7.8.9, 9.5–10.
7. Herodian 7.10.4. The latter's full name was Marcus Clodius Pupienus Maximus, and he is rcferred to as Maximus by Herodian. He had earlier been prefect of Rome; *SHA* (Balbinus and Pupienus) 5.10 describes Pupienus as *severissimus*, 'uncompromising', in the post. On their choice of prefects, *SHA*, 4.4, 5.5.
8. The young Gordian's age is uncertain. The relationship, in Herodian, 7.10.7, is confirmed on inscriptions, e.g. *ILS* 498, *CIL* 8.848.
9. Herodian 7.11.1–5. *SHA* (Maximinus) 20.6 repeats some of the story, and specifies the number of murdered praetorians, but blames the crowd for the killing at the instigation of Gallicanus and Maecenas.
10. Herodian 7.11.6–9. The gladiatorial barracks lie immediately adjacent to the Colosseum on the south-east side, and are partially visible today.
11. *SHA* (Balbinus and Pupienus) 8.4 and 9.1 states that the Guard was left in Rome; Herodian 7.12.1–2.
12. Richmond (1927), 22; *CIL* 15.7237, 7238 are stamped pipes naming Caracalla and Macrinus' son Diadumenian respectively and also specifying the Castra Praetoria in the first instance.
13. Herodian 7.12.5.
14. Herodian 8.1.2–3, 2.2, 2.5, 3.7, 4.1, 4.9–11.
15. The evidence for the II legion Parthica comes from the tombstone of a soldier, whose name is lost, of the legion from Aquileia: *ILS* 2361. The legion is specified as having been based at Albanum (Alba), known to have been II Parthica. See *SHA* (Severus) 6.11, (Caracalla) 2.7 and (Maximinus) 23.6. There is some evidence for a close association between II Parthica and the Praetorian Guard: for example, *ILS* 2103, *CIL* 6.210 which associated a praetorian and a veteran of II Parthica on the same discharge occasion.

16. *SHA* (Maximinus) 32.4, 24.3; Herodian 8.5.8, 7.7.
17. Herodian 8.7.8 and 8.8.2.
18. Herodian 8.8.5, 8 and *SHA* (Balbinus and Pupienus) 14.3.
19. *RIB* 988, 989, 1896 (the latter dating to 235–8).
20. *SHA* (Gordian) 23.6.
21. *SHA* (Gordian) 26.3–6.
22. Zosimus 1.18.
23. *SHA* (Gordian) 29–30 *passim*.
24. On Priscus, see Scott (2008), 173. For Priscus' position by 248, see Grant (1985), 154, citing no authority for this information.
25. Zosimus 1.18–20 for Gordian's death and Pacatian and Jotapian's rise; ibid. 1.22 and Aurelius Victor 28.11 for the death of Philip and his son, the latter stating that the praetorians killed them.
26. *CIL* 16.147 (Lyon).
27. *CIL* 16.151 (Piedmont), 153 (Mantua).
28. *ILS* 2038; *CIL* 8.21021.
29. See below for the case of Aelius Dubitatus under Claudius II.
30. *SHA* (Aurelian) 13.1 is the sole source for Baebius Macer. *SHA* (Probus) 4.3 is the only source for Mulvius Gallicanus.
31. *SHA* (Aurelian) 5.5.
32. Zosimus 1.40, calling Aureolus commander of the field army's cavalry. The coins are *RIC* 370, 372, 568 (praetorians), the legionary series starts with *RIC* 315 for the I legion Adiutrix. See Sear (2005), 288 no. 10186. The legend COHH is probably a bungled COHR. *RIC* 568.
33. Zosimus 1.40. It is hard quite to understand why the praetorians would have regarded Claudius II as any less treacherous.
34. *ILS* 9073; Campbell (1994), 118, no. 187.
35. *CIL* 3.3424; *ILS* 545; Campbell (1994), 235, no. 378.
36. *ILS* 9479; *AE* 1908.259 (in Greek). See Southern (2001), 129–30, for a discussion of the development of the *protectores* at this date. For another holder of the post, see Lucius Petronius Taurus Vousianus, who served, amongst other posts, as tribune of the I praetorian cohort and 'protector of the emperors' (Valerian and Gallienus), dying in 268: *ILS* 1332; *CIL* 11.1886.
37. *RIB* 966. Cowan (2014), 61, speculates that this may be the origin of the *scholae palatinae* units of the fourth century.
38. Zosimus 1.46. *SHA* (Claudius) 12.2.
39. *CIL* 12.1551, 2228.
40. *SHA* (Aurelian) 21.6, and 38.2.
41. *SHA* (Aurelian) 48.1–3. The Via Aurelia ran north from Rome up the Italian west coast towards Genoa.
42. *SHA* (Aurelian) 21.9, 39.2; Zosimus 1.42.
43. Richmond (1927), 17–19.
44. Zosimus 1.52.
45. *SHA* (Aurelian) 30–31.
46. *SHA* (Aurelian) 36.4–6; Zosimus 1.62. Mnetheus (in *SHA*) is an error for Eros, the chief conspirator, see Loeb *SHA* (Aurelian) p. 266, note.
47. *SHA* (Tacitus) 8.3. Perhaps a relative of Mulvius Gallicanus, prefect under Valerian. *SHA* (Valerian) 4.3. Zosimus 1.62 calls Florianus 'prefect of the court'.
48. *SHA* (Probus) 10.6.
49. Cicero, *Catiline Orations*, 4.11: 'For so may I be allowed to enjoy the republic in safety in your company.'
50. Aurelius Victor 38.1.

51. Aurelius Victor 38.6; *SHA* (Carus etc.) 8.6–7.
52. *SHA* (Carus etc.) 12.1–2, 13.3.
53. Aurelius Victor 39.14. Verconnius Herennianus, given as praetorian prefect under Diocletian *SHA* (Aurelian) 44.2, is probably fictional.
54. Aurelius Victor 39.24.
55. Aurelius Victor 39.47; Lactantius, *de Mortibus* 12; Barnes (1992), 249 ff.
56. *RIC* 12; Sear (2011), no. 13556. For the Gallienus issues, see above, p. 254.
57. Aurelius Victor 39.39; *SHA* (Probus) 22.3; Eutropius 9.14. *Panegyricus Constantio Caesari Dictus* 15. These sources are most conveniently accessed in Casey (1994).
58. The participation of the Guard in this episode is cited by Rankov (1994), 16, without substantiation. Maximian's activities in Africa are discussed by Nixon et al. (1994), 175, with respect to the contents of *Panegyrici Latini* (*recte*) 5.5.2 (to Constantius – Nixon et al. give 8.5.2 in error), but without reference to praetorians whose presence seems to be speculative on the part of Rankov. Also, Eutropius 9.23 (no mention of praetorians), Orosius 7.25.4 and 8 (no mention of praetorians), refer to the episode.
59. Adams and Brennan (1990), 185, discuss the evidence for recruitment to the praetorians by Maxentius; Lactantius, *de Mortibus* 26.2.
60. Eusebius, *Church History* 8.14.3.
61. Richmond (1927), 21; 'Ruricius Pompeianus' is a name created from two references in the *Panegyrici Latini* (4.25.4, 25.7 and 12.8.1). The pontoon bridge appears to have been designed either to solve problems of limited access across the original masonry bridge or because it was damaged.
62. Zosimus 2.17.2: '[Constantine] abolished the praetorian troops and destroyed the fortresses in which they used to reside.' Aurelius Victor 40.25.
63. *Panegyrici Latini* 12 21.2–3, 'Now they fight for you, those whom he has stripped of impious weapons and rearmed against barbarian foes. Now forgetful of the delights of the Circus Maximus, the theatre of Pompey and famous baths, they are stationed, along the length of the Rhine and Danube they watch [and] suppress plundering; lastly, after having been vanquished in the civil war they vie with the victors to be matched with the enemy', in Nixon and Rodgers (1994), 326.
64. Busch (2007), 328, likens the act of destruction to a *damnatio memoriae*, drawing attention to how the representation of the camp on the coins of Claudius had emphasized its close identification with the institution of the Guard. See Menéndez Argüín (2006), 62, for a reproduction of Richmond's drawing of modifications to the east gate of the Castra Praetoria.

Epilogue

1. Gibbon (1776), chapter 5, paragraph 2.
2. Southern and Dixon (2000), 18–19.
3. *CIL* 15.1665; Claridge (2010), 31.
4. Campbell (1994), 233. Perhaps with origins in a third-century title apparently adopted by praetorians. See p. 256.
5. Hoffman (1969), 281.
6. '*incongruis iniuriis*', in the *Codex of Theodosius* 7.20.5
7. Barnes (1992), 249ff.
8. At the time of writing, the text of the *Notitia Dignitatum* is readily accessed online.
9. 'Attendant'. The term thus carried none of the connotations of a praetorian prefect.
10. Order Book of the Council of State, Tuesday, 6 January 1652, cited in Bisset (1867), 414–15.
11. Powell (1968).

Appendices

1. See Campbell (1994), 200–1, nos 327–8.
2. Rankov (1994), 9.
3. Durry (1938), 137.
4. Tacitus, *Annals* 4.2.2.
5. These are itemized by Justinian, *Digest* 49.16.12.2: *Officium tribunorum est vel eorum, qui exercitui praesunt, milites in castris continere, ad exercitationem producere, claves portarum suscipere, vigilias interdum circumire, frumentationibus commilitonum interesse, frumentum probare, mensorum fraudem coercere, delicta secundum suae auctoritatis modum castigare, principiis frequenter interesse, querellas commilitonum audire, valetudinarios inspicere.*

Bibliography and References

1. Shelton (1998), 230, and footnote 181.
2. One might note also Evans (1986) but this book is generally considered to be both seriously flawed and lacking in referencing.
3. Dio 55.24.6.
4. Tacitus, *Annals* 4.5.3.
5. See, for example, Campbell (1994), 38, where it is stated as a fact that 'Domitian settled the Guard's strength at ten cohorts, each with 1,000 men'. This is a legitimate theory but it is not an attested fact.

BIBLIOGRAPHY AND REFERENCES

Further Reading and Sources

The Praetorian Guard is mentioned in most books on Roman history but in the majority of cases only in passing, despite its enormously important role. Jo-Ann Shelton's excellent anthology (1998) of extracts from Roman sources makes one reference only to the Praetorian Guard and then only concerning the prefecture.[1] The most recent over-view of the Guard in English is Sandra Bingham's *The Praetorian Guard* (2013). Although subtitled *A History of Rome's Elite Special Forces*, the history of the Guard is covered in one chapter, with several other thematic chapters following, for example concerning 'Duties' and 'Organization'. The book is an essential trawl through the evidence, with almost half being made up of detailed footnotes. This makes it an invaluable reference work but one which also quite deliberately largely avoids the topic of praetorian prefects.

Also to be recommended is Adolfo Menéndez Argüín's *Pretorianos* (2006), which covers, in Spanish, both Guard and prefects in a mixture of historical and thematic chapters. He also supplies a useful section on the Castra Praetoria. This book's most invaluable feature is the sixty-one pages of appendices that itemize the literary and epigraphic evidence for the Guard, though inevitably each of these needs to be looked up elsewhere. Unlike Bingham, the references are in the text rather than in foot- or endnotes. Durry (1938) and Passerini (1939), although essential works, are virtually unobtainable now outside specialist libraries.[2]

Rankov (1994) and Cowan (2014) have both produced books on the Guard for Osprey. These volumes are primarily useful for students of military equipment. Their extensive illustrations and discussions of equipment and organization make them essential reference works too. Cowan's work is particularly useful for the large number of individual praetorian careers he cites. For relevant source material, Campbell's *Roman Army* sourcebook (1994) is indispensable, though, as with so many references to the Guard, the accompanying editorial material sometimes makes statements that are presented implicitly as factual rather than the suppositions they actually are. This is a point worth bearing in mind when reading any book on the Guard.

It is also worth reminding any readers not familiar with Latin and the Roman world's facility with abbreviating inscriptions that the translated texts in books like Campbell's sometimes have to make assumptions about intended meanings that are often in reality ambiguous or at least frustratingly imprecise. Readers are urged always to consult the original texts wherever possible. The availability of online resources to do this for many epigraphic sources at http://db.edcs.eu/epigr/epi_en.php makes this a realistic proposition in a way it has never been before.

A note about the ancient sources

The quality of ancient sources varies so wildly across the period concerned that the treatment in this book has had to make the most of what there is. The reader will therefore find that while, for example, the activities of the soldiers themselves can be tracked in some detail during the civil war of 68–9, for the period 98–180 the story is much more about the prefecture because that is very largely the only evidence we have. In that respect the story is different in focus, depending on the date concerned. A book of this type is dependent on the work of a great many other people without whose original research it would have been impossible to step into the subject. The result of course is that the book has a very large number of notes that it is hoped the reader will find helpful rather than overwhelming. Wherever possible these have been combined in order to keep them under control.

Our information about the Guard comes from references in ancient sources but to a very large extent these were written down some time after the events to which they refer. One of the curiosities of Roman history is the way in which ancient historians are treated as if they were primary sources when in reality they were, almost without exception, secondary or even tertiary sources. Moreover, such ancient sources are very unevenly distributed. The dramatic events of the late Republic, the rise of Octavian and his rule as Augustus attracted attention and are relatively well covered, even though the sources concerned are often not contemporary. Appian, for example, whose account of the civil war is crucial for understanding what happened during the rise of Octavian, wrote in the second century AD. Cassius Dio, whose history of the first two centuries of the imperial era is of great importance, wrote in the early third century AD. Tacitus, who wrote at the beginning of the second century AD, began his *Annals* with the accession of Tiberius and only includes some retrospective comments on Augustus' reign. His *Annals* would have included an invaluable description of the praetorians' role in the accession of Claudius in 41, but that is one of the lost sections, along with his account of the whole reign of Caligula. Instead, we rely on Cassius Dio and also the biography written by Suetonius to make good the gaps. Only the first part of Tacitus' *Histories* survives, covering little more than the civil war of 68–9. All of these authors had access to original sources about which we know little or nothing, making it impossible usually for us to verify much of what they say.

From the second century on, apart from Cassius Dio and the brief period covered by Herodian, we have very little source material that matches what is available for the first century AD. Cassius Dio's work finished in c. 229 and Herodian by c. 238, leaving us with nothing equivalent for the rest of the Guard's history. Worse, much of Dio's work survives only in the form of a later epitome by an eleventh-century monk called Xiphilinus. This affects mainly the sections from Book 61 on (which equates to everything after the year 54). These Roman historians for the most part were senators, members of Rome's senior tier of aristocrats who had access to state and imperial archives. Even Suetonius, an equestrian, was secretary to the emperor Hadrian and therefore also enjoyed access to records which are now completely lost. Despite this, references to the Guard are usually incidental and inconsistent. A scattered collection of imperial biographies, known as the *Scriptores Historiae Augustae*, is one of our few sources for the second and third centuries but is notoriously unreliable, especially for the later biographies. Fortunately, a number of other Roman sources such as Epictetus, Zosimus, Aurelius Victor and Eusebius provide us with occasional glimpses of supplementary information. Their incidental references to the praetorians are often all we have to go on for some episodes, and usually amount to no more than fleeting comments that may or may not be accurate. Their attention is usually far more closely focused on the comings and goings of emperors, and the part praetorian prefects played in toppling them is usually the only reason praetorians are mentioned at all.

It is typically the case that ancient written sources have to be scrutinized for any reference to the topic under study, however oblique. In the case of the Praetorian Guard this includes everything from an explicit and specific mention to fleeting references and oblique inferences. Using these references is not only complicated but also involves assessing each one for its likely reliability and even basic veracity. For most of the time no references are available at all. The student of ancient history is thus constantly challenged by gaps in the source material and, frustratingly, outright contradictions or obviously erroneous references.

Every effort has been made in this book to back up a statement with a reference to the source of the information. This gives the appearance of substantiating the text with reliable evidence but in reality we have almost no way of verifying the majority of what an ancient source supplies. Tacitus, for example, recounts both the fall of Galba and Otho's coup in 69 in considerable detail. Even so it is not always possible to be sure exactly whom he is talking about when he refers to soldiers. Sometimes he specifies, and sometimes he does not. When he wrote, he was recounting the events of a chaotic and fluid situation that erupted literally overnight around thirty years earlier; it is unlikely anyone recorded the occasion in detail as it happened or, if they did, that they would have been able to piece together a lot of simultaneous developments in the middle of the turmoil. The extant accounts of the dramatic overnight events of the October Revolution of 1917 in Russia and all the spin that followed are a salutary reminder of the impossibility of trying to recreate a reliable version of events. Tacitus' account is convincing to read and has the aura of credibility, but sometimes his points are contradicted by other sources. This does not mean that they were right and he was wrong, but merely that it is clear that we cannot be certain what the truth was.

Another excellent example is the differing accounts of the murder of Elagabalus in 222. The substantive point, that he was killed, is not in question, but the detail of how this happened is different in Dio and Herodian. Clearly, they cannot both be true and this raises the obvious question of whether we can accept detail when only one account is extant for other episodes. The inevitable consequence is that, with the best will in the world, a modern narrative of the period from whatever perspective is something of a pastiche.

Another useful example of the problems we face is Dio's reference to the size of the Praetorian Guard. He says that under Augustus in AD 5 the Guard was 'ten thousand in number and organized in ten cohorts'.[3] This phrase is the single most specific reference to the size and organization of the Guard that we possess. Dio did not, however, write until around two centuries later and because what he wrote does not tie up with other information about the Guard after the reign of Augustus, it has been assumed by some that he was transposing the arrangements in his own time back to the situation under Augustus. This does not mean that Dio's information was wrong because it is entirely possible, indeed even likely, that he had access to official records in Severan Rome. Tacitus, when describing the disposition of the Roman armed forces in 23, describes the existence of nine praetorian cohorts and three urban cohorts.[4] Just to complicate the problem further, we have no specific information about the size of the praetorian cohorts in 23. Epigraphic evidence suggests that a further three praetorian cohorts were created by the mid-first century. Vitellius organized sixteen milliary-sized cohorts for his Guard in 69, and this might have become permanent by Domitian's reign (81–96) unless they were simply carried over from Vitellius by Vespasian. Diplomas and other evidence suggest ten cohorts were in existence by the end of Domitian's reign, and certainly by Dio's time. Even the idea that, for example, evidence of a twelfth praetorian cohort proves that there were twelve sequential active cohorts may be quite wrong. In other instances we know that continuous numbering systems were not necessarily in operation (see chapter 3).

Such other information as we possess shows that the size of the centuries within the cohorts could vary considerably, and it is also well known that the terms 'quingenary' and 'milliary' were nominal and not absolute. What we have instead are the theories of scholars, based on this information, which have a habit of turning into 'facts'.[5] Underlying so many of these assumptions is the idea that these scattered pieces of evidence are all somehow linked to a detectable process of linear development based on precise numbers which, if scrutinized closely enough, will be revealed. The evidence, such as Dio's observations, is reinterpreted or rejected to make them fit. In reality though this inchoate evidence may very well be because the Guard's organization fluctuated considerably throughout its history, often in ways about which we know nothing but which manifest themselves in the contradictory and incomplete information that we do possess. If so, we will never resolve the detail. The solution is to accept that the precision we seek does not, and probably never did, exist. The Roman world simply did not operate like that.

A related problem concerns praetorian and legionary pay. This is discussed in the main text and in Appendix 2, Table 1. It becomes apparent, on closer scrutiny, that the Roman reliance on rounding and approximation makes it very easy to see a simple relationship of ratios between what we know about pay, imperial bequests and discharge grants. This makes sense of the discrepant evidence which turns out not to be discrepant at all because it was not based on precision. Annual pay had to be divisible by three because it was (in theory) paid every four months. This required rounded figures that did not equate to simple totals for day rates, but which could be expressed in another, very close, rounded sum or vice-versa. Bequests and retirement gratuities were computed in similar ratios but were rounded as well. Just as with the structure of the Praetorian Guard, the information is only irreconcilable if what is being sought is a non-existent rigid and precise solution.

For all their faults, the sources we have supply remarkable detail that, if treated with care, provides a basis for what is probably a moderately reliable narrative. However, the texts are replete with all sorts of problems ranging from contradictions to gaps, and outright errors combined with extreme bias.

To these we can add various pieces of epigraphic evidence in the form, almost invariably, of the records of individuals from tombstones, religious dedications or diplomas (discharge certificates). These itemize the careers of praetorians but tombstones and religious dedications rarely provide precise dates, if indeed they can be dated at all, and furthermore may not be complete. Diplomas were personally commissioned copies of discharge inscriptions posted in Rome. They turn up in often completely incongruous locations, attributable either to the fact their owners retired to different places from the ones in which they had served, reuse for their metal (which is attested), or to the possibility of an ancient trade in militaria. The latter is not specifically attested but it would be surprising in a world with such a widespread and long-lasting military community if there had not been such an interest. Being bronze, diplomas are also prone to corrosion and fragmentation, meaning many are incomplete.

Inscriptions erected by the Praetorian Guard as an institution, in the manner that legions created monumental building inscriptions, are not generally known so we cannot track the Guard's movements or activities that way. There are, however, a number of sculptural reliefs, such as those on the Columns of Trajan and Marcus Aurelius, that provide in visual form some record of the Guard 'in action' on campaign. These depictions tend to be stylized and idealized and do not really provide us with a reliable visual record of the Guard 'in real life'. Nevertheless, they do help create an impression of how the Guard was deployed when campaigning with the imperial army. More useful are the inscriptions from tombstones or religious dedications that provide so much invaluable information about individual praetorian careers, especially when they can be dated accurately (which is not usually the case). Tombstones also sometimes carry representations of individual praetorians with invaluable information about uniform and equipment.

A note about Cassius Dio

Cassius Dio is a crucial source for this book but confusion has resulted from the editing and typesetting of his account in the Loeb series volumes VIII and IX, the only realistically available printed source, and an essential one for any study of any aspect of Roman history. There is a bewildering discrepancy between the book numbers and the running heads, and the book number given at the start of each book. This was created by the editor and translator Professor Earnest Cary in an effort to produce an edition that was easy to use, thanks to corrupted sections of Dio's text and the survival only of the later parts of Dio in the form of an epitome. Cary therefore produced his own numbering system, but also included the older manuscript book numbering at the start of each book. The running heads and contents in the Loeb volumes are Cary's numbering, whereas the numbers at the start of each book are from the original system applied to the manuscript.

This has resulted in some modern authors using either system to refer to the same book in Dio. Cary's Book 79 (LXXIX), for example, can be referred to as Book 79 (LXXIX), or by the original numbering system as Book 78 (LXXVIII). Since the system being used in any one such instance is not always clear, a reference to Book 78 might mean the original Book 78 (Cary's Book 79), or is in fact Cary's Book 78 which would mean 77 in the original system. In some cases authors have inadvertently used both systems in their notes, an entirely understandable error given the confusion created. For the sake of simplicity I have observed the book numbers as given in the running heads of the Loeb volumes. Otherwise, anyone seeking to check a reference in these volumes constantly has to work out that running heads for Book 79 really mean Book 78 and so on. The enormous problems generated by this confusing mixture of numbers are graphically described by Bill Thayer at http://penelope.uchicago.edu/Thayer/E/Roman/Texts/Cassius_Dio/home.html

Thayer has also used the numbering from the running heads. His online Book 79 matches Cary's running heads and contents list. Therefore, in this book a reference to the books in volumes VIII and IX of the Loeb edition uses those running headers. For additional clarity the actual volume and page number has been added in the footnotes for certain references in volume VIII (especially for Books 61 and 62) and all of IX. The Loeb edition of Dio is the only one that is accessible to modern readers, either in printed or electronic form, so it seemed logical to make this decision. Thayer has also applied the page numbers of the Loeb edition in the margins of his web pages for clarification.

Select Bibliography

Abbreviations

AE = *L'Année épigraphique* (Paris, 1888–) (N.B. some of this material is now available on the Internet from the same source as *ILS* below)

CIL = *Corpus Inscriptionum Latinarum* (Berlin, 1863–) in sixteen volumes (N.B. some of this material is now available on the Internet from the same source as *ILS* below)

ILS = Dessau, H., 1892–1916 *Inscriptionum latinae selectae*, Berlin (three volumes) (now available on the Internet with full search facilities at http://db.edcs.eu/epigr/epi_en.php

JRS = *Journal of Roman Studies*, published by the Society for the Promotion of Roman Studies

RIB = *Roman Inscriptions of Britain:* see Collingwood and Wright (1965), revised edition Tomlin (1995), inscriptions reported 1995–2006, see Tomlin, Wright and Hassall, (2009). Available online at: http://romaninscriptionsofbritain.org/

RIC = *Roman Imperial Coinage:* Mattingly, H., Sydenham, E.A., Sutherland, C.H.V. and Carson, R.A.G. (1923), *The Roman Imperial Coinage*, London

RPC = Roman Provincial Coinage. Burnett, A., Amandry, M., Ripolles, P.P. (1992), *Roman Provincial Coinage*, vol. I (The Julio-Claudians), British Museum Press, London, and Bibliothèque nationale de France, Paris

SHA = *Scriptores Historiae Augustae*, available in the Loeb Classics Series, Harvard University Press, vols I and II (also in Penguin translation, *The Lives of the Later Caesars*, trans. by A. Birley, Penguin, 1976)

Publications

Absil, M. (1997), *Les Préfets du Prétoire d'Auguste à Commode*, Éditions De Boccard, Paris

Adams, G.A. (2013), *The Emperor Commodus: Gladiator, Hercules or Tyrant?* Brown Walker, Boca Raton

Adams, J.N., and Brennan, P.M. (1990), 'The Text at Lactantius, *De Mortibus Persecutorum* 44.2, and Some Epigraphic Evidence for Italian Recruits', *Zeitschrift für Papyrologie und Epigraphik* 84, 183–6

Alston, R. (1995), *Soldier and Society in Roman Egypt. A social history*, Routledge, London

Alston, R. (1998), *Aspects of Roman History AD 14–117*, Routledge, London

Alston, R. (1999), 'The ties that bind: soldiers and societies', in Goldsworthy and Haynes (eds)

Austin, N.J.E., and Rankov, N.B. (1998), *Exploratio: Military Intelligence in the Roman World from the Second Punic War to the Battle of Adrianople*, Routledge, London

Barnes, T.D. (1992), 'Praetorian Prefects', *Zeitschrift für Papyrologie und Epigraphik* 94, 249–60

Barrett, A.A. (1989), *Caligula. The Corruption of Power*, Guild, London

Barrett, A.A. (2015), *Caligula. The Abuse of Power*, Routledge, London

Barrett, A.A. (ed.) (2008), *Lives of the Caesars*, Blackwell, Oxford

Berriman, A., and Todd, M. (2001), 'A very Roman coup: The Hidden War of Imperial Succession, AD 96–8', *Historia. Zeitschrift für Alte Geschichte* 50.3, 312–31

Bingham, S. (2013), *The Praetorian Guard. A History of Rome's Elite Special Forces*, I.B. Tauris, London

Birley, A.R. (1993), *Marcus Aurelius: A Biography*, Routledge, London

Birley, A.R. (1997), *Hadrian. The Restless Emperor*, Routledge, London

Birley, E. (1966), 'Alae and Cohortes Milliariae', in *Corolla memoriae Erich Swoboda dedicata*, Röm. Forsch. In Niederösterr V, 54–67

Birley, E. (1969), 'Septimius Severus and the Roman Army', *Epigraphische Studien* 8, 63–82

Bishop, M.C. (2013), *Handbook to Roman Legionary Fortresses*, Pen and Sword, Barnsley

Bisset, A. (1867), *History of the Commonwealth of England*, Murray, London

Blois, L. de, and Lo Cascio, E. (eds) (2007), *The Impact of the Roman Army (200 BC–AD 476); Economic, Social, Political, Religious and Cultural Aspects*, Proceedings of the Sixth Workshop of the International Network Impact of Empire (Roman Empire, 200 BC–AD 476), Capri, Italy, 29 March–2 April, 2005, Leiden

Braund, D. (1985), *Augustus to Nero. A Sourcebook on Roman History 31 BC–AD 68*, Croom Helm, London

Burnett, A. (1987), *Coinage in the Roman World*, Seaby, London

Busch, A.W. (2007), '"Militia in urbe". The military presence in Rome', in de Blois and Lo Cascio (eds)

Campbell, B. (1994), *The Roman Army 31 BC–AD 337. A Sourcebook*, Routledge, London

Casey, P.J. (1994), *Carausius and Allectus: The British Usurpers*, Batsford, London

Christiansen, E. (2004), *Coinage in Roman Egypt. The Hoard Evidence*, Aarhus University Press, Aarhus

Claridge, A. (2010), *Rome. An Archaeological Guide*, Oxford University Press, Oxford

Cooley, A.E., and Cooley, M.G.L. (2004), *Pompeii. A Sourcebook*, Routledge, London

Cowan, R. (2007), 'Praetorian Guard: Easy Soldiering in Rome', *Ancient Warfare* I.2

Cowan, R. (2011), 'Peculiar Praetorian pila', *Ancient Warfare* V.2

Cowan, R. (2014), *Roman Guardsmen 62 BC–AD 324*, Osprey, Oxford

De Caro, S. (1979), 'Scavi nell'area fuori Porta Nola a Pompei', *Cronache pompeiane* 5, 179–87

Dessau, H. (1924), *Die Geschichte der römischen Kaizerzeit*, Berlin

Develin, R. (1971), 'The army pay rises under Severus and Caracalla and the question of the *annona militaris*', *Latomus* 30, 687ff

Dobson, B., and Breeze, D. (1969), 'The Rome cohorts and the legionary centurionate', *Epigraphische Studien* 8, 106–10

Durry, M. (1938), *Les Cohortes Prétoriennes*, Éditions De Boccard, Paris

Echols, E. (1968), 'The Rome city police: origin and development', *Classical Journal* 53, 377–85

Ehrenburg, V., and Jones, A.H.M. (1976), *Documents Illustrating the Reigns of Augustus and Tiberius*, Oxford University Press, Oxford

Erdkamp, P. (ed.) (2007), *A Companion to the Roman Army*, Blackwell, Oxford (reissued in 2011 by Wiley-Blackwell)

Evans, R. (1986), *Soldiers of Rome: Praetorians and Legionnaires*, Washington, DC

Everitt, A. (2006), *The Life of Rome's First Emperor, Augustus*, Random House, London

Friggeri, R., Cecere, M.G.G., and Gregori, G.L. (2012), *Terme di Diocleziani. La Collezione Epigrafica*, Electa, Milan

Gibbon, E. (1776), *Decline and Fall of the Roman Empire* (various editions)

Gilliver, K. (2007), 'The Augustan Reform and the Imperial Army', in Erdkamp (ed.)

Goldsworthy, A. (2003), *The Complete Roman Army*, Thames and Hudson, London

Goldsworthy, A. (2014), *Augustus. From Revolutionary to Emperor*, Weidenfeld & Nicolson, London

Goldsworthy, A., and Haynes, I. (eds) (1999), 'The Roman Army as a Community', *Journal of Roman Archaeology*, Supplementary Series no. 34, Portsmouth, Rhode Island

Goodman, M. (1997), *The Roman World 44 BC–AD 180*, Routledge, London

Gore, R. (1984), 'The Dead Do Tell Tales At Vesuvius', *National Geographic* vol. 165, no. 5, 557–613

Graham, A.J. (1978), 'The numbers at Lugdunum', *Historia* 27, 625ff

Grant, M. (1985), *The Roman Emperors*, Weidenfeld & Nicolson, London

Grant, M. (1996), *The Antonines: The Roman Empire in Transition*, Routledge, London

Hekster, O. (2007), 'The Roman Army and Propaganda', in Erdkamp (ed.)

Herz, P. (2007), 'Finances and Costs of the Roman Army', in Erdkamp (ed.)

Hoffman, D. (1969–70), *Die Spätrömische Bewegungsheer und die Notitia Dignitatum*, Epigraphische Studien 7, Rheinland Verlag, Düsseldorf

Howe, L.L. (1942 and 1966), *The Pretorian Prefects from Commodus to Diocletian*, L'Erma di Breitschneider, Rome

Johnson, A. (1983), *Roman Forts*, A & C Black, London

Johnson, A.C., Coleman-Norton, P.R., Bourne, F.C., and Pharr, C. (2003), *Ancient Roman Statutes: A Translation with Introduction, Commentary, Glossary and Index*, Lawbook Exchange Ltd, Clark, New Jersey

Jung, H. (1972), 'Die Thronerhebung des Claudius', *Chiron* 2, 367–86

Kennedy, D.L. (1978), 'Some Observations on the Praetorian Guard,' *Ancient Society* 9, 275–301

Keppie, L.J.F. (1994), *Riding for Caesar. The Roman Emperor's Horse Guards,* Harvard University Press, Cambridge, MA

Keppie, L.J.F. (1996), 'The Praetorian Guard before Sejanus,' *Athenaeum* 84, 101–24

Keppie, L.J.F. (2000), Legions and Veterans: Roman Army Papers 1971–2000, Steiner, Stuttgart

Kerr, J.L. (1992), 'The Role and Character of the Praetorian Guard and the Praetorian Prefecture until the accession of Vespasian,' Ph.D. diss., Glasgow University

Lanciani, R. (ed. A.L. Cubberley) (1988), *Notes from Rome*, British School at Rome

Le Bohec, Y. (2000), *The Roman Imperial Army*, Routledge, London

Lepper, F., and Frere, S. (1988), *Trajan's Column*, Alan Sutton, Gloucester

Levick, B. (1990), *Claudius*, Batsford, London

Levick, B. (1997), *Julia Domna: Syrian Empress*, Routledge, London

Levick, B. (1999) (i), *Tiberius the Politician*, Routledge, London

Levick, B. (1999) (ii), *Vespasian*, Routledge, London

Levick, B. (2014), *Faustina I and II: Imperial Women of the Golden Age*, Oxford University Press, Oxford

Lewis, N., and Reinhold, M. (1955), *Roman Civilization. Sourcebook II: the Empire*, Harper Torchbooks, New York

Lorusso, I. (2011), 'Portraying Praetorian Guardsmen', *Ancient Warfare* V.2

Luttwak, E.N. (1976), *The Grand Strategy of the Roman Empire. From the First Century A.D. to the Third*, Johns Hopkins University Press, Baltimore, MD

Marsden, P. (1980), *Roman London*, Thames and Hudson, London

Maxfield, V., and Dobson, B. (2006), *Lactor 4. Inscriptions of Roman Britain*, Association of Classical Teachers, London

Meiggs, R. (1960), *Roman Ostia*, Oxford University Press, Oxford

Menéndez Argüín, A.R. (2006), *Pretorianos*, Almena, Madrid

Modrzejewski, M., and Zawadski, T. (1967), 'La date de la mort d'Ulpien et la préfecture du prétoire au début du règne d'Alexandre Sévère', *Revue Historique du droit français et étranger*, 565–611

Morgan, J.D. (1986), 'Suetonius' Dedication to Septicius Clarus', *Classical Quarterly* 36, Issue 2, 544–5

Nixon, C.E.V., Saylor, B., and Rodgers, B.S. (1994), *In Praise of Later Roman Emperors: the Panegyrici Latini*, University of California Press, Berkeley, Los Angeles and Oxford

Ottley, S. (2009), 'The Role Played by the Praetorian Guard in the Events of AD 69, as Described by Tacitus, in his *Historiae*', PhD thesis, UWA (unpublished)

Passerini, A. (1939), *Le Coorti Pretorie*, Rome: Studi pubblicati dal R. Istituto italiano per La storia antica. fasc. 1

Pflaum, H.-G. (1960), *Les Carrières Procuratoriennes Équestres sous le Haut-Empire Romain*, Guethner, Paris

Phang, S. (2001), *The Marriage of Roman Soldiers (13 BC–AD 235): Law and Family in the Imperial Family*, Brill, Leiden

Powell, G. (1968), 'The Praetorian Guard', *History Today*, vol. 18, issue 12

Rainbird, J.S. (1976), 'The Vigiles of Rome', unpublished dissertation, University of Durham (accessed at: http://etheses.dur.ac.uk/7455/)

Rankov, B. (1987), 'M. Oclatinius Adventus in Britain', *Britannia* 18, 243–9

Rankov, B. (1994), *The Praetorian Guard*, Osprey, Oxford

Reece, R. (2002), *The Coinage of Roman Britain*, Tempus, Stroud

Rees, L. (1997), *The Nazis. A Warning from History*, BBC Books, London

Richmond, I.A. (1927), 'The relation of the praetorian camp to Aurelian's wall of Rome', *Proceedings of the British School at Rome* 10, 12–22

Rogers, G.M. (2014), *The Sacred Identity of Ephesos. Foundation Myths of a Roman City*, Routledge Revivals, Abingdon

Rogers, S.R. (1931), 'Lucius Arruntius', *Classical Philology* 26 (1)

Rossignol, B. (2007), 'Les Préfets du Prétoire de Marce Aurèle', *Cahiers du Centre Gustav Glotz* 18, 141–77

Rossini, O. (2009), *Ara Pacis*, Electa, Milan

Roxan, M.M., and Eck, W. (1993), 'A Military Diploma of AD 85 for the Rome Cohorts', *Zeitschrift für Papyrologie und Epigraphik* 96, 67–74

Roxan, M.M., and Holder, P.A. (2003), *Roman Military Diplomas IV*, Institute of Classical Studies, University of London

Scheidel, W. (2001), 'Marriage, Families, and Survival: Demographic Aspects', in Erdkamp (ed.) (2001)

Scheidel, W. (2005), *Marriage, families, and survival in the Roman army: demographic aspects*, Princeton/Stanford Working Papers in Classics, Stanford University [N.B. this article also appears in Erdkamp (ed.) (2007), pp. 417–34.

Scott, A.G. (2008), 'Change and Discontinuity within the Severan Dynasty: the Case of Macrinus', PhD thesis, Rutgers, State University of New Jersey

Seager, R. (2005), *Tiberius*, Blackwell, Oxford

Sear, D. (1982), *Greek Imperial Coins and their Values*, Seaby, London

Sear, D. (2000), *Roman Coins and their Values. Volume I. The Republic and Twelve Caesars 280 BC–AD 96*, Spink, London

Sear, D. (2002), *Roman Coins and their Values. Volume II. The Accession of Nero to the Overthrow of the Severan Dynasty AD 96–AD 235*, Spink, London

Sear, D. (2005), *Roman Coins and their Values. Volume III. The 3rd Century Crisis and Recovery AD 235–AD 285*, Spink, London

Sear, D. (2011), *Roman Coins and their Values. Volume IV. Diocletian to Constantine I, AD 284–337*, Spink, London

Shelton, J. (1998), *As The Romans Did*, Oxford University Press, Oxford

Sherk, R.K. (1988), *The Roman Empire; Augustus to Hadrian*, Translated Documents of Greece and Rome, vol. 6, Cambridge University Press, Cambridge

Smallwood, E.M. (1967), *Documents Illustrating the Principates of Gaius, Claudius and Nero*, Cambridge University Press, Cambridge

Southern, P. (2001), *The Roman Empire from Severus to Constantine*, Routledge, London

Southern, P. (2006), *The Roman Army: A Social and Institutional History*, ABC-Clio, Santa Barbara

Southern, P., and Dixon, K. (2000), *The Late Roman Army*, Routledge, London

Spaul, J.E.H. (1994), 'Governors of Tingitana', *Antiquités africaine* I. 30, 235–60

Speidel, M.P. (1994) (i), *Riding for Caesar: The Roman Emperors' Horse Guard*, Harvard University Press, Cambridge, MA

Summerly, J.R. (1992), 'Studies in the legionary centurionate', unpublished Ph.D thesis, Durham University

Sumner, G. (2003), *Roman Military Clothing (2) AD 200–400*, Osprey, Wellingborough

Sumner, G. (2004), *Roman Military Clothing (1) 100 BC–AD 200*, Osprey, Wellingborough

Sutherland, C.H.V. (1974), *Roman Coins*, Barrie and Jenkins, London

Swan, P.M. (2004), *The Augustan Succession: An Historical Commentary on Cassius Dio's Roman History Books 55–56 (9 BC–AD 14)*, Oxford University Press, Oxford

Syme, R. (1962), 'The Wrong Marcius Turbo', *Journal of Roman Studies* 52, 87–96

Syme, R. (1980), 'Guard Prefects of Trajan and Hadrian', *Journal of Roman Studies* 70, 64–80

Syme, R. (1989), *The Augustan Aristocracy*, Oxford University Press, Oxford

Taylor, M.J. (2011), 'Laughing at the Praetorian Guard: Juvenal's Sixteenth Satire', *Ancient Warfare* V.2

Thorne, J. (2007), 'Battle, Tactics, and the Emergence of the *Limites* in the West', in Erdkamp (ed.) (2007)

Tomlin, R.S.O. (2016), *Roman London's first voices: writing tablets from the Bloomberg excavations, 2010–2014*, MOLA Monograph 72, London

Turner, E.G. (1954), 'Tiberius Julius Alexander', *JRS* 44, 54–64

Van den Hout, M.P.J. (1999), *A Commentary on the Letters of M. Cornelius Fronto*, Brill, Leiden

Webster, G. (1996), *The Roman Imperial Army*, Constable, London

Wellesley, K. (1975), *The Long Year AD 69*, Elek, London

Westermann, W.L. (1941), 'Tuscus the Prefect and the Veterans in Egypt', *Classical Philology* 36, no. 1, 21–9

INDEX OF EMPERORS

GENERAL INDEX

Individuals are indexed here by the most familiar and/or individual part of the name; for example, Gaius Julius Caesar is indexed under Caesar. Individual soldiers and praetorian prefects mentioned in the book are not generally indexed unless their careers are especially noteworthy.

ILLUSTRATION CREDITS

Plates 6, 10 and 11 are open source images. All other photographs were taken by the author at the following locations:

Plates 9, 23, 32: Capitoline Museum, Rome

Plates 15, 16, 18, 19, 21, 26: National Museum of the Baths of Diocletian, Rome

Plate 17: Victoria and Albert Museum, London

Plate 27: British Museum, London

Plate 28: Neues Museum, Berlin

Plate 29: Ostiense Museum, Ostia